D1571627

The Films of Randolph Scott

ALSO BY ROBERT NOTT

Last of the Cowboy Heroes: The Westerns of Randolph Scott,
Joel McCrea, and Audie Murphy (McFarland, 2000)

The Films of Randolph Scott

ROBERT NOTT

foreword by Max Evans

McFarland & Company, Inc., Publishers
Jefferson, North Carolina, and London

LIBRARY OF CONGRESS CATALOGUING-IN-PUBLICATION DATA

Nott, Robert, 1960–
The films of Randolph Scott / Robert Nott ;
foreword by Max Evans.
p.   cm.
Includes bibliographical references and index.

ISBN 0-7864-1797-8 (illustrated case binding : 50# alkaline paper)

1. Scott, Randolph, 1898–1987.   2. Motion picture actors
and actresses—United States—Biography.   I. Title.
PN2287.S342N68   2004   791.4302'8'092—dc22   2004016409

British Library cataloguing data are available

On the cover: Randolph Scott in *Colt .45* (1950)

Manufactured in the United States of America

McFarland & Company, Inc., Publishers
Box 611, Jefferson, North Carolina 28640
www.mcfarlandpub.com

For Randy, Burt, Budd, and Harry Joe

Acknowledgments

As usual, when it comes to a book like this a lot of people end up helping an author, often with the understanding that if they're lucky the most they'll get out of it is a free book and a cold beer — preferably Randolph's Ride Red Ale.* So here we go:

Thanks to John Cocchi, who provided me with photos, publicity materials and historical information on Scott's films. He even offered to screen *Sky Bride* for me.

Boyd Magers should be called upon to help anyone who is contemplating writing about Western films. His *Western Clippings* newsletter is probably the best contemporary source for information on the genre. I hope he compiles them all into one book someday. Boyd also put me in touch with a few interview subjects and gave me access to the *Albuquerque* chapter of Thelma King's unpublished book on William C. Thomas and William Pine, *Hollywood's Famous Dollar Bills or How to Make Money Making Movies*.

Jon Tuska, celebrated Western film historian and author of *The Filming of the West,* among other books, was kind enough to exchange e-mails and letters with me between late July and late August 2002, providing me with background information on the relationship between Randolph Scott, Harry Joe Brown and Columbia Pictures. Likewise Jon sent me a copy of his book *Encounters with Filmmakers*, which includes a chapter on Bruce Humberstone, who directed two Scott films, and a chapter on Sam Peckinpah, director of *Ride the High Country*.

Tom Weaver, who seems to have a new book out every year (via McFarland), got me in touch with some interview subjects and helped me track down some obscure Randolph Scott films on video. James Robert Parish provided the same service. Thanks, guys!

I had the expected professional academic help from the University of Southern California's Doheny Library, which houses the Warner Bros. and Universal studio archives; the University of California's Film Library, which houses the 20th Century–Fox and RKO studio archives; and the Wisconsin Center for Film and Theater Research and New York City's Lincoln Center's Library for the Performing Arts, both of which have formidable clippings files on Scott. The University of California's Film and Television Archive also screened four of Scott's films for me and yes, they do have a copy of *Albuquerque*.

As for my interview subjects: thanks

---

*In his book *So You Wanna See Cowboy Stuff?*, Boyd Magers reports that the Rock Bottom Brewery and Restaurant in Charlotte, North Carolina, serves Randolph's Ride Red Ale, a medium-bodied ale that is named after Randolph Scott.

to them all. A few I had interviewed for my *Last of the Cowboy Heroes* allowed me to revisit them. A few, I'm sorry to say, have since passed on, including Budd Boetticher and Burt Kennedy. The interviewees include Richard L. Bare, Budd Boetticher, the late Rand Brooks, Harry Joe Brown, Jr., Polly Burson, William Campbell (who tried for years to get Scott to accept a Golden Boot Award), the late Anthony Caruso, Bill Catching, Roydon Clark, Jerome Courtland, the late Frances Dee, James Drury, Rhonda Fleming, Nancy Gates, Gary Gray, Karolyn Grimes, Earl Holliman, the late Roy Huggins, Myron Healey, L.Q. Jones, the late Burt Kennedy, Evelyn Keyes, Phyllis Kirk, Joan Leslie, A.C. Lyles, Donna Martell, Virginia Mayo, Steve Mitchell, Paul Picerni, the late Denver Pyle, Mala Powers, the late Walter Reed, Bill Reynolds, the late Craig Stevens, George Wallace, Jack Williams, Joan Weldon, Jacqueline White and Jane Wyatt.

In addition, Claude Jarman, Jr., Anne Jeffreys, Dick Moore, Michael Pate and Stuart Whitman provided me with anecdotes via letter. Conversations with New Mexico residents Max Evans, the late Edmund Hartmann and the late Vera Zorina were also helpful.

Contents

Foreword

by Max Evans

It would be very hard to imagine a more difficult man to record than Randolph Scott. He certainly was one of the most private stars of all time. He gave very few interviews. But the fact that everyone he worked with liked him, despite his aloofness, speaks well for "Randy" as a human being.

Scott was fondly observed by cast and crew members reading *The Wall Street Journal* far more often than he read his scripts, and many of his co-stars and fellow filmmakers stated that Scott loved the business of making money more than he did making films. However, after careful study of *The Films of Randolph Scott* one must question this.

Scott was uncomplaining in the unlimited hardships of making over 100 films—at least 50 of which were Westerns. This is a form of physical and emotional dedication that seems to speak for itself. Even when he knew he had a mediocre script or director, Scott somehow managed to give his part dignity and believability in a way that only a skilled and dedicated artist can.

Nott writes that Scott's World War I service is worth noting. That's almost an understatement, since Scott served with his close friend, Andrew H. Hariss, as forward observers in the 2nd French Mortar Battalion, 19th Field Artillery, in France. This position is exposed and is deadly to hold in any war. It draws the enemy's return fire almost immediately. Nott quotes Hariss' memories of the moment-to-moment uncertainty that comes with that vulnerable position and sagely notes that it was "an experience that must have imbued Scott's portrayals of frontier men with a sense of realism." No doubt.

During his Army tenure, Scott studied horsemanship, learning how to properly mount and dismount and ride at any speed from a trot to a dead run. He also had instruction in straight shooting (including the use of sidearms) and bayonet practice. All this experience put him ahead of the game in America's—and the world's—interest and addiction to our version of the Knights of the Round Table—the Western.

Scott was a very taciturn man. One story has him purchasing an expensive new automobile and inviting Gary Cooper, another strong silent type (to utilize a cliché prevalent at the time), for a drive to show it off. Scott drove for several hours around California's San Fernando Valley. Both men remained silent. Finally Cooper saw a bird fly across the street in front of them.

He raised his arms as if holding a rifle and said, "Bang!" That was the extent of their verbal exchange.

Since this book has biographical elements, be very glad for the mixture. It's a good seasoning indeed, for Nott has spiced every film listing with well-chosen quotes and actions. He uses his subtle humor to add a sweet and sour combination to the recipe. Like a well-plotted novel, this story moves forward, gaining momentum along the way until it reaches Scott's last — and best — film series made by the team of director Budd Boetticher, producer Harry Joe Brown and screenwriter Burt Kennedy. One could believe that no other team made finer Westerns than the Scott-Brown-Boetticher-Kennedy team. But then, of course, Scott wrapped up his career in 1962 with Sam Peckinpah's *Ride the High Country*, opposite Joel McCrea and with a cast of ac-

tors who would become regulars in Peckinpah's best films, including L.Q. Jones, Warren Oates, and R.G. Armstrong. This best of all Scott pictures launched Peckinpah into the stratosphere of immortal directors that included Fellini, Renoir, Huston and Welles.

Burt Kennedy, incidentally, would go on to greater film work than credited by critics with such comedy classics as *Support Your Local Sheriff* and *The Rounders*. One of the most grossly underrated Western character studies in film history is Kennedy's 1967 film *Welcome to Hard Times*, featuring Henry Fonda and Aldo Ray.

By that time, of course, Scott had retired, probably figuring that it would never get better than *Ride the High Country*. This book leads to one of the greatest cinematic endings any actor could ever hope for.

Texas-born Max Evans is the celebrated author of the Western novels *Bluefeather Fellini*, *My Pardner*, *The One-Eyed Sky*, *Southwest Wind*, *The Rounders* and *The Hi-Lo Country*. The latter two were made into motion pictures. Max was a working cowboy before World War II, an infantryman during World War II, and a rancher, painter and writer since then. His most recent books include *Madame Millie* (2002) and *Now and Forever* (2003). He currently lives in Albuquerque, New Mexico.

Introduction

To me, Randolph Scott was just about the best movie cowboy there ever was.

I grew up in the 1960s and 1970s in New York, about an hour north of New York City and God knows how many hours east of the Mississippi. I sure wasn't born to the saddle (unless it was on a Coney Island carousel) but come to think of it, neither was Randolph Scott. But unlike me, Scott had an imposing 6'2" frame, a genuine Southern accent to match his gentlemanly manners, and a seemingly natural ability to say or do the right thing at the right time, especially when he said it with lead.

We didn't get the "B" movie cowboys on TV up in New York in those days (except for a brief run of Tim Holt pictures that were trimmed down to under an hour for scheduling purposes), but we did get a lot of Randolph Scott films, as well as televised screenings of John Wayne, Gary Cooper, Jimmy Stewart, Joel McCrea and Audie Murphy pictures. The cowboy heroes of the 1960s and 1970s didn't interest me as much, although I did go to my local one-screen movie theater — the now-defunct Squire Cinema in New Windsor, New York — to see them: Wayne in his last, lackluster period; Lee Van Cleef in a myriad of spaghetti Westerns (not all good, not all bad, but most of them ugly); Charles Bronson in anything offered to him; and

Clint Eastwood in so-so shoot 'em ups like *Two Mules for Sister Sarah, Joe Kidd* and *High Plains Drifter* (although I still like 1976's *The Outlaw Josey Wales*). I even caught Audie Murphy's last starring Western, 1967's *Forty Guns to Apache Pass*, on a double-bill with a Jerry Lewis comedy, *The Big Mouth*. I liked *The Big Mouth* more then; I've since changed my opinion — though neither one is particularly good.

But on television, I could see all the classic cowboys. There was the Duke, and I liked almost anything he did up through the late 1960s. Gary Cooper was all right, but my respect for him was based on a half-dozen films that kept popping up on television over and over again, like *The Plainsman* and *The Westerner* and *Springfield Rifle* and *Man of the West* and *High Noon*. Jimmy Stewart was another favorite, but his Western film reputation has been built and maintained on the pictures he made with Anthony Mann: *Winchester '73, Bend of the River, The Naked Spur, The Far Country* and *The Man from Laramie*, all done within a five-year period when the actor wasn't working for Hitchcock or impersonating Glenn Miller or talking to invisible rabbits.

Scott seemed like the most genuine Westerner of the lot to me. He played one in his first starring film, 1932's *Heritage of the Desert*, and was still playing one when he rode into his last cinematic sunset in 1962's *Ride the High Country*. In between he made nearly 60 Westerns, as well as a lot of other genre films ranging from comedies to dramas to musicals to swashbucklers (1945's *Captain Kidd*; not a career high point for him or co-star Charles Laughton). He had a light touch when it came to the comedies, and he held his own in some war films, particularly the still underrated *Corvette K-225* (1943). Yet in many of his non–Westerns, he came off as an outsider visiting the wrong film set or as a guest who somehow didn't quite fit in at a social affair. He was so much at home in the Western genre that I can understand screenwriter Allan Scott's comment that Randolph Scott seemed lost without his horse. Scott (Randy, not Allan) must have realized this too after a while; from 1946 on, he stuck to playing men of the West, and he played them well. No wonder he made the Quigley Poll of Exhibitors' most popular box office attractions four years in a row, from 1950 through 1953, always nipping at John Wayne's heels. And am I the only one who wanted to see Scott beat John Wayne in that exhausting-to-watch fist fight that climaxes *The Spoilers*?

I'm not picking on Wayne, either, so holster your six-guns. I have to acknowledge he's a better actor than Scott. But Wayne also got bigger chances with better directors, which makes me wonder what Scott could have done under the direction of a Howard Hawks or a John Ford. Wayne, like Scott, went out on a great Western, *The Shootist*, but with the exception of 1969's *True Grit*, most of the stuff the Duke did in the late 1960s and early 1970s was pretty pedestrian. And compare Scott, physically, at age 63 in *Ride the High Country* to Wayne at the same age in 1971's *Big Jake*. Scott looked like a grandfather, to be sure, but the sort of grandfather who could still stare down a lynch mob if they were coming to get you. By the time Wayne hit

60, he was heavy and graying and wearing a toupee, and relying more and more on people like Christopher George and Rod Taylor to handle the rough stuff.

To this day, I get a bigger kick out of watching Randolph Scott than any other Western film star. He had humor, charm, grace and, one sensed, the ability to punch you in the nose if you got out of line with one of the saloon girls. Scott's career peaked when most actors' careers give out. In 1956, at the age of 58, Scott hooked up with director Budd Boetticher and screenwriter Burt Kennedy for a series of short, sharp Westerns in which Scott played men dead-set on achieving their goals— goals usually fueled by hate or revenge or love. Scott played a lot with a little, using his eyes and the slightest physical gestures to convey his inner emotion, always suggesting he was more torn up inside than he was ever going to admit. There's something about the final image of Scott in 1959's *Ride Lonesome* (scripted by Kennedy and directed by Boetticher) that says it all: His Ben Brigade watches the tree from which his wife was hanged go up in smoke. He's achieved his goal of killing the man responsible, set the outlaw's equally criminal brother on his way to justice, given a pair of less-violent offenders a shot at amnesty, and rescued a frontier woman. So what's next? To me, these Scott characters of the period don't really have a future. The hate left them when the last of their bullets found their mark; their sorrow will stay with them until the day they die. Nothing Brigade does next will have as much purpose, but he'll go about doing what he has to do to survive, like most of us, until his last breath. Scott played tragic heroes with such subtlety— look at his work in 1941's *Western Union*— that the audience hardly realized these characters *were* tragic until the final credits.

It was Scott's Westerns that set me on the trail of providing a more in-depth look at his entire body of film work than I did in my *Last of the Cowboy Heroes* (2000). I initially contemplated writing a biography of Scott, but decided against it for several reasons, including the fact that he was so discreet that digging up anything of interest would be difficult, and, frankly, because I suspect that off-screen he wasn't all that interesting. He liked golf, gardening, sports and investing money — hardly the stuff of high drama.

So this filmography is intended to be just that, hopefully peppered with enough background information, anecdotes, interviews and humor to satisfy Scott's fans. A caveat, however, before you proceed. I watched the vast majority of these films on video, not the best way to view them but one that allowed me to watch them re-peatedly and review particular sequences. (I did see about a dozen of his films on the big screen as well.) In revisiting some of Scott's films, including some that I covered in *Last of the Cowboy Heroes*, I found myself altering my opinion somewhat. For instance, I like *Return of the Bad Men* and *Thunder Over the Plains* quite a bit more, while I think a little less of *The Cariboo Trail*, *Sugarfoot* and *7th Cavalry*. But remember, this is all just my opinion, and we all know what opinions are analogous to, so feel free to disagree with me. I've kept the actual filmography information short in favor of more text on the films, and I've also gone off the trail now and then to illuminate some stories about Scott's costars, mostly because they struck me as interesting or funny.

The Early Years: 1898–1937

He was born George Randolph Scott on January 23, 1898, in Orange, Virginia (and not Orange, North Carolina, as erroneously listed in several sources, including my *Last of the Cowboy Heroes*). His mother, Lucille Crane Scott, was in her last stages of pregnancy when she decided to leave the family home in Charlotte, North Carolina, to visit relatives in Virginia. Scott himself would always claim North Carolina as his birth state. He was the only son of George and Lucy Scott, but he had five sisters. His father worked as an administrative engineer in a textile firm; his mother came from a monied family, and more than one associate of Randolph Scott's has commented on the actor's air of "Southern royalty."

Thanks to his family's monied situation, Scott was educated in private schools, including Woodberry Forest School (1914–1917), where he excelled in baseball, football ("He was good both on offense and defense," a 1917 school yearbook notes; "More speed would have made him a star"), singing, public speaking and math. He did less well in foreign languages, maintaining poor grades in German and Latin. His nicknames were Randy, Scotty and Blondey (!). Contrary to almost everything one hears about his personality during his Hollywood years, he was apparently quite the social butterfly in his teens, rarely missing a school dance. Sports remained a constant interest in his life; he was forever attending baseball games or horse races, and he also enjoyed swimming and sailing.

Thanks to a three-page article on Scott written by his former Woodberry Forest classmate Andrew H. Hariss in 1987 (the year of Scott's death), some insights into Scott's early personality can be gleaned. Hariss and Scott attended Woodberry Forest from 1914 to 1917, and they served together in World War I through 1918. "As close as we were," Hariss wrote, "we always reserved a sort of privacy between us. I always felt that Scotty was not comfortably designed to be an actor, which he most certainly became. My realistic evaluation of him based on the very hard and intimate conditions we jointly endured in the lines with infrequent rest periods from May to November 1918 enabled me to observe the patriotic Christian realist he was."

Scott's World War I service is worth noting. One of the only Hollywood fabrications about Scott deals with his age when he entered World War I. Once he signed a contract with Paramount in 1932, the studio did what most of studios did in regards to the age of their contract players: They set the clock back a few years. Scott, it was maintained in a 1932 Paramount publicity release, was born in 1903, making him a still relatively young 29. How Scott felt about going along with this ruse is not known; no doubt he saw it as a minor compromise to be made for film employment. This minor mistruth lead Scott to tell everyone he joined the Army in 1917 at age 14, when in fact he was 19. That said, most of the information one finds in Hollywood interview pieces with Scott seems to be based on fact, for he disliked perpetrating myths or exaggerating the facts as many stars and Hollywood journalists were wont to do.

According to Hariss' piece, he and Scott actually tried to join Gen. Pershing's border patrol in 1916 in an effort to track down Pancho Villa. After America entered World War I (April 1917), both men headed to Fort Caswell, North Carolina, to join the Army. Scott later told interviewer John Franchey that he served as an artillery observer in the 2nd Trench Mortar Battalion, 19th Field Artillery, in France. This fits in with Hariss' account, which gives an idea of what the two men went through during the war: "As artillery observers, we went into position and on duty as a team. If one of us purposely napped during our 24-hour stretch, the other would cover, in our forward observation bomb-proof shelter, where we observed artillery *overs* and *shorts*, *rights* and *lefts*, and signaled data to guns as estimated corrections calculated by trigonometry. We were senior-line sergeants and served without interruption until late afternoon of Armistice Day (November 11, 1918)."

Hariss wrote a few lines about the moment-to-moment uncertainty that came with their jobs, an experience that must have imbued Scott's film portrayals of frontier men with a sense of realism:

We were never plagued or tormented with the boredom and "too much of everything" that every foot soldier faces in the battle-zone. Each new noise coming out of the tense darkness of the long nights released our adrenalin and accelerated our blood circulation, resulting in the tightening of our trigger fingers. Very often, it was only some small animal, perhaps a large rat, whose ground space we were sharing. During our constant sojourn with death from snipers and the gory mess, we never spoke a harsh word toward each other. After every close call — and there were many — we ended with a labored and thankful smile, the reading of our personal pocket Testaments, and the blessing of our dog tags and the St. Christopher's crosses on our necklaces. After each experience, we awaited the "next time," hopefully and prayerfully wondering.

So Scott had real-life war experiences to fall back on in order to inject life into his cinematic characterizations of men of honor and violence. Scott also studied horsemanship in the Army, learning to mount, ride, gallop and take off in a dead run without a saddle in order to graduate equitation classes. Likewise he was schooled in bayonetry and marksmanship, including the use of sidearms — all talents that would serve him well in Hollywood.

After the war ended, Scott enrolled in Artillery Officer's School in Saumur, France. Hariss states that Scott was commissioned, and Scott would later tell interviewers that he was accepted but chose not to stay in the military as he was anxious to return to the States, which he did some time in 1919.

Back in America, Scott attended Georgia Tech on an athletic scholarship before transferring to the University of North Carolina to study textile engineering and manufacturing, which would keep him occupied into the mid–1920s. By his own account he did not finish college as he had no real interest in the family business. What he did during most of this decade, besides travel and essay the role of a playboy, is not entirely clear, though at least one later account of Scott's life, Gene Ringgold's "Randolph Scott Embodied Everyone's Idea of a Southern Gentleman" (*Films in Review*, 1972), states that Scott spent some time working for the textile firm with which his father was involved with in Charlotte, North Carolina. He listed his occupation as accountant when he joined the Masonic Scottish Rite in 1923 (he was a Mason for most of his adult life), and this may have kept him occupied from roughly 1923 (when he dropped out of college) until 1927, when he headed West.

Scott drove West with childhood friend Jack Heath (about whom little is known) in the autumn of 1927. It isn't clear whether the two men went simply to enjoy the experience, or because one or the other hoped to break into films. In a 1937 newspaper interview, Scott told journalist Inez Wallace, "I never intended to be an actor. But one day we were playing golf with Howard Hughes, and as a lark he got us both jobs as extras. Maybe it was the uniform I wore that first day, but I decided that, if one could become an officer merely by applying to the wardrobe department, I'd do the rest of my fighting in the movies."

Fifteen years later, in an interview with Sidney Skolsky, Scott modified the details of the story somewhat, saying he and Heath were playing one hole *behind* Hughes when they approached the millionaire–film producer about the possibility of visiting a movie set. Hughes replied by suggesting that the two play extras in a George O'Brien film at Fox, and that was that. (Most film historians write that Scott's father knew Hughes and arranged a meeting between the two.) The film in question was *Sharp Shooters*, and over the next two years Scott worked as an extra in at least five feature films, including Cecil B. DeMille's first talkie, *Dynamite*. Scott recounted that he auditioned for the role of Hagon Derk, the lead, but that DeMille re-

jected him, saying he didn't have enough experience. Scott would credit DeMille for advising the actor to get some stage experience at the Pasadena Playhouse. Scott spent much of 1929 and 1930 on stage in theaters in Los Angeles.

In 1942 Scott summed up his early Hollywood experience and relatively quick climb to the top to interviewer John R. Franchey in a perfunctory manner: "I had a perfectly wonderful time scrimmaging around on horseback (in *The Virginian*) when the director noticed me. I was offered tests, put in the usual trick at Pasadena Playhouse learning the fundamentals, and wound up on the Paramount contract list." This is a bare-bones description, to be sure, but it does tell the tale quickly. At the Playhouse, he played such roles as a minstrel in *Gentlemen Be Seated*, a butler in *Nellie, the Beautiful Model*, Bill Wrayburn, the laziest chap in Rocky Bottom, in *Atta Boy, Oscar* and, to give his stage experience some element of respectability, Metellus Cimber in *Julius Caesar* and Hector Malone in George Bernard Shaw's *Man and Superman* (Robert Young was in that one too). At the Vine Street Theatre, he played the juvenile lead in Kenneth Cole's *Under a Virginia Moon* and did a couple of other plays, including *The Broken Wing*, directed by Leo Carrillo, at the El Capitan Theatre. Scott was always appreciative of his theater training, suggesting that the experience imbued him with the talent to graduate from "B" Westerns at Paramount. "If it hadn't been for little theaters, I'd still be on a horse today," he told a *New York Post* journalist in August 1937. He'd be getting back on horses soon enough.

According to Carrillo, several Hollywood studio talent scouts, including a persistent chap from Warner Bros., approached Scott during the run of *The Broken Wing* to offer the actor film contracts. Although he accepted a small supporting role in the Warner Bros. George Arliss comedy *A Successful Calamity*, Scott chose not to sign with Warners and pretty much waited all the studios out, taking a lead part (his first) in the bargain basement production *Women Men Marry*, distributed by Headline Pictures, which went bankrupt shortly after the film's release in July 1931. Scott never mentioned this film in later interviews, perhaps figuring it would fade into obscurity (it did). Late in 1931, however, Scott accepted a seven-year contract from Paramount Pictures. Carrillo claimed that Scott had waited for Paramount to approach him because, according to what Scott had told him, the Southerner had tried to wrangle a contract with them back in 1929 while he was working as dialogue coach and extra on *The Virginian*, and they rejected him.

Paramount started Scott at $400 a week and gave him a small speaking role in the Jack Oakie–Richard Arlen comedy-drama *Sky Bride* before casting him as the lead in the Zane Grey "B" *Heritage of the Desert* (released a month before *Sky Bride*). Paramount then announced that Scott would be their new cowboy star in a series of "B" films based on Zane Grey's still popular novels. "At about that time both Gary Cooper and Richard Arlen were graduating from Westerns," Scott said in 1935. "A new series was to be made, and somebody suggested me for them. I was delighted to get the chance, and I enjoyed doing them, but I didn't have much chance to show versatility."

It wasn't easy work, as Scott discovered. "Most people have the mistaken notion that acting in the movies is a cinch," he explained in the mid–1930s. "My working day is frequently from 12 to 16 hours, particularly on Westerns, which have to be finished in about 12 days. I like making them, but they're hard work." Still, the training would come in handy, as Scott would discover when he turned to producing his own films in the 1940s and 1950s.

Paramount portrait of Randolph Scott, autographed, circa 1932. (JC Archives, Inc.)

Scott was good-looking, a fast study with lines, and easy to work with. But he wasn't exactly a great actor, or even a good one, in the early to mid–1930s. He had a light touch with a comic line and could convey charm easily enough, but film producers and directors quickly realized he wasn't capable of projecting deep emotion. Paramount was interested in getting as much out of their new contract player as they could, so they dropped him, like any human commodity, into all sorts of movie genres, from Westerns to comedies to horror films to musicals. They were not above loaning him out to other studios during this period, and at least one of those studios, RKO, valued Scott more than Paramount. RKO gave Scott some of his best acting opportunities during this period in *Roberta, She* and *Village Tale* (all 1935). Still, the Paramount experience proved invaluable, teaching Scott to adapt quickly, build confidence and develop his talent.

Early in 1932, Scott went to work on the Paramount drama *Hot Saturday*, playing in support of Nancy Carroll and Cary Grant. Scott and Grant remained friends into the 1940s, and their seemingly too-close relationship has since made fascinating fodder for scandal-seekers. The one controversial aspect of Scott's life to this day remains the nature of his relationship with Cary Grant.

Grant was born Archibald Alexander Leach, January 18, 1904, in Bristol, England. By his teen years he was working as an entertainer on the stage (he had a propensity for acrobatics) and came to the United States in the 1920s, appearing in stage dramas, musical comedies and operettas. Like Scott, Grant exuded charm, but he was no great shakes as an actor in the early 1930s. Unlike Scott, however, he had that indefinable star quality about him, and he got the chance to work with bigger and better co-stars, including Gary Cooper, Mae West, Marlene Dietrich and Katharine Hepburn. By 1935 Grant, though not yet a major star, was headlining "A" pictures while Scott remained ensconced in the Zane Grey "B" series at Paramount.

Scott and Grant were both known as shy, private men who nonetheless enjoyed a free-wheeling approach to life. Scott had an innate financial sense that Grant lacked; he advised Grant to invest in real estate, oil wells and the stock market. Grant would repay the favor, first by offering Scott acting advice and later by giving Scott suggestions on how to negotiate successful freelance deals in Hollywood in the late 1930s. They began rooming together early in 1932 in a rental property on West Live Oak Drive, below the famous Hollywood sign in the Hollywood Hills. They would live together, on and off, for about ten years, presumably because they liked each other's company and wanted to save on living expenses (they were both considered notorious tightwads). "Both boys are scared of saying something which might be misconstrued to their detriment," a *Silver Screen* article reported in November 1935 on Scott and Grant's relationship. "They are anxious to avoid the mistakes and tragedies they have seen preceding their own assault on Hollywood. Consequently, Randy, his opinions now in demand, has all the earmarks of a trained diplomat."

In fact, while the Scott-Grant friendship *did* come under some scrutiny from certain Hollywood quarters in the early 1930s, the rumors surrounding their assumed homosexual relationship did not start until the 1980s and 1990s, when a spate of books on Grant began suggesting or assuming that the British actor was gay or bisexual, hence making his close friendship with Scott suspect. Geoffrey Wansell, in his book *Cary Grant, Dark Angel*, is less sensationalistic than most celebrity bios when he writes that Scott and Grant were "a good deal less comfortable in the company of young women than young men, no matter how it may have appeared to the gossip columns." Most books on Grant from the 1980s and 1990s presume the British actor was bisexual without offering solid proof.

Still, the duo's living situation remains questionable, and they did pose for some silly publicity photos for *Modern Screen* magazine in 1933 that make them look like a couple of fey fellows: They're lounging by the pool, playing with a medicine ball, wearing aprons and washing dishes with sly smiles on their faces, clowning around in the shower (separately) and jogging down the beach in swim trunks. Keep in mind that neither actor was a major star at the time, and that they were likely following the publicity department's orders in an effort to draw attention to themselves. Then there's the issue of their living arrangements, which were unconventional, to say the least. When Virginia Cherrill married Grant in February 1934, she moved into the West Live Oak Street house with her husband. Scott didn't move out, much to the bride's surprise. At Cherrill's insistence, Grant and she moved to the La Ronda apartments in Los Angeles.

Shortly thereafter, Scott moved into the apartment next door, leading gossip columnist Edith Gwynn to write at the time, "The Grants and Randolph Scott have moved, all three, but not apart." This sort of living arrangement was a mainstay of the men's relationship throughout the 1930s, no matter who was married to who. "On and off for a decade, from 1932 to 1942, the two actors shared apartments and houses; a convenient arrangement that was interrupted when one or the other got married, then resumed when both were free," wrote Gerald Clarke, writing for a special 1996 *Architectural Digest* magazine issue on Hollywood homes. That still doesn't mean the duo were gay, although that's how writer David Ehrenstein interpreted the sentence when he utilized it to bolster his argument that Scott and Grant *were* gay for his 1998 book *Open Secret*.

And therein lies one of the problems of ferreting out the truth. Most historians just assume that Scott and Grant were gay or bisexual. Charles Higham and Roy Moseley, in their biography *Cary Grant: The Lonely Heart* (1989), write that gay costume designer George Orry-Kelly was both Scott and Grant's lover during this period. The book also notes that the two Hollywood heroes took starlets Sari Maritza and Vivian Gaye out on a number of "sexless" dates—additional proof, apparently, that the men were gay. Other books, including William J. Mann's *Wisecracker: The Life and Times of William Haines, Hollywood's First Openly Gay Star* (1998) also take it for granted that Scott and Grant were gay. So does Charles Higham's *Howard Hughes: The Secret Life*, in which the author offers up two paragraphs on Scott's sexuality, including this zinger: "Scott was coolly indifferent to most people, using

men and women to get ahead…. Hughes pushed him into a movie career." Higham does not cite sources to back this claim up, and the second part makes little sense, since the only movie work Hughes got Scott was a bit part in the film *Sharp Shooters*.

There is really no direct evidence that Scott or Grant were gay, and most of the material utilized in books on the subject is second-hand (including Orry-Kelly's claim—the costume designer died in 1964). Graham McCann's book *Cary Grant: A Class Apart* (1996) actually persuasively challenges every argument that Scott and Grant were romantically involved. It is true that after Grant divorced Cherrill, he and Scott moved into new digs at 1018 Ocean Front in Santa Monica. But of this period William Randolph Hearst, Jr., said, "There were girls running in and out of there like a subway station." Budd Boetticher has an amusing off-color story to tell of this period. One evening in the late 1950s, Boetticher maintained, Scott called him at home to say he was upset to have witnessed Rock Hudson and George Nader holding hands in a screening room at the Universal studio.* Boetticher, bemused, replied, "Well, what about all those rumors about you and Cary Grant?," to which Scott, chuckling, responded with the following story: Scott would bring a potential female conquest back to the beach house in Santa Monica and leave her downstairs while he ran upstairs to take a shower (Scott was a cleanliness freak) and dress to the nines. Upon returning downstairs to the lady in question, Scott would often find her on the couch, skirts up above her waist and panties down, and Grant ("Archibald," as Scott referred to him) having his way with her.

---

*Boetticher told this story to at least two other people I know, altering the details somewhat: in one case it was Hudson and Tony Curtis; in the other it was Hudson and Tab Hunter. My question is, what was Scott doing in a screening room on the Universal lot in the late 1950s, unless it was to see some footage of a Universal contract player such as James Best, who appeared in *Ride Lonesome* (1959)?

"He was not gay," protests Scott's son Chris in his 1994 biography *What Ever Happened to Randolph Scott?* "In my opinion it seems that some people just like to muddy the water about people who can no longer debate the issue." Actor Jerome Courtland, who appeared in two films with Scott and whose family knew Scott since the early 1940s, found the rumors implausible. "He was always the Southern gentleman," Courtland said. "I heard that stuff [about Scott and Grant]. I never believed it. Having known Randy for as many years as I knew him, I never saw anything in him remotely related to that. There were always stories at that time about this guy or that guy — and most of them were just that, stories." Producer A.C. Lyles, who began working for Paramount in the 1930s, agreed: "I don't know why those rumors sprung up. I've heard them about so many stars and I pay no attention to them." Edmund Hartmann, a screenwriter who worked at nearly every studio in Hollywood from 1934 through the 1950s, said he never heard the rumors about Scott and Grant until after both men were dead. "Scott was a second string star who made a lot of Westerns, and those Westerns made a lot of money," noted Hartmann, who would sometimes see Scott at one of the California race tracks. "But I never heard he was gay until years later."

Typical of the way people see the relationship between Scott and Grant is the view of stuntman-actor Jack Williams, who figures he worked on at least six Scott films beginning with 1940's *Virginia City*. Williams never heard Scott was gay or bisexual during all that time; he first heard about Scott and Grant when he read Kenneth Anger's 1983 book *Hollywood Babylon*, and immediately assumed that the duo were lovers. "The biggest mystery about Randy is his association with Cary Grant," Williams said. "I read somewhere that just before he died, that he and Grant met and were holding hands, but you never saw that [element] in him. He was always very virile and masculine. During all that time in Hollywood there were no rumors that he was gay. But nobody cared anyway. Gays were accepted as long as they stayed in the closet. I never spoke to anyone in Hollywood who thought Randy was bisexual or gay. He was always a reserved person; very polite and considerate."

You can make a point for either side of the argument, but bet your bottom dollar that if you had to take the issue of whether Randolph Scott was gay or bisexual to court, you wouldn't be able to prove it. Still, this doesn't mean that the rumors won't continue to haunt Scott, since there's also no way, some 70 years after the fact, to disprove it either. Budd Boetticher summed the whole issue up with one word: "Bullshit."

Scott was romantically tied to several women during this period, but some of these relationships were studio-manufactured (with Paramount starlets Lupe Velez and Sally Blane, for instance), some were totally non-existent (as with Columbia starlet Jinx Falkenberg), and some were genuine, such as his dates with Dorothy Lamour and Claire Trevor. On the record, Scott said he intended to stay a bachelor for as long as possible. "I've never believed much in marriage," Scott said in 1933. "I haven't since I was a kid and my sister's marriage turned out badly. I can count the happy couples I know on one hand. Given even the best set-up, it doesn't seem to work out, and I certainly wouldn't pick Hollywood as the ideal place for married people to live."

But he did get married, on March 23, 1936, to Marion duPont (1894–1983), a Virginia horse breeder and owner of Montpelier estate, once the home to President James Madison. She was heiress to nearly $100 million, thanks to her grandfather William, President and Chairman of the Board of the Delaware Trust Company. Marion had a hatchet face and manly demeanor, but she also had a reputation for loving both horses and men. She was married to trainer-jockey Tom Summerville for some time before marrying Scott. Seth Greer, former publisher of *The Orange Record,* is quoted as saying that duPont had an insatiable appetite for men, so much so that she was willing to pay for them. She may have paid high for Scott; it was rumored that she invested in Paramount stock in the mid–1930s in an effort to get the studio to give her husband better roles. Scott and duPont knew each other from his Woodberry Forest days; he often spoke of a young woman he loved before he joined the Army in World War I, and it may have been Marion. They reportedly toured Europe together in the mid–1920s before she wed Tom Summerville (who she divorced in the autumn of 1935).

Scott and DuPont wed in secret in Charlotte, North Carolina. Scott told no one in Hollywood of his marriage for six months. Why? Because he did not want Hollywood to destroy the union, a scenario he had already witnessed several times. That was Scott's explanation, anyway. "The whole setup was very unsatisfactory from the start," he later told Jerry Asher for the 1939 magazine piece "A Gentleman Tells," explaining why the marriage was falling apart. "I kept the marriage a secret for six months because my wife had to wind up her business of breeding, training and raising race horses." Of Marion, Scott said, "My wife comes from a world where human emotions are not a commodity on the market." Another challenge was that duPont refused to move to Hollywood, while Scott could not leave Hollywood until his Paramount contract ended in 1938. In any event, the two worlds did not merge, and the Scotts lived separately for most of their married life. "His very closest friends could only guess that this had

been one of those flames that once upon a time had flared high; but when the time came to make it real, it was obvious their interests were no longer the same," a friend of Scott's (perhaps Jack Heath) told the press when the marriage came to an end in 1944. "After that first year, it was just sort of generally understood that Randy and his wife were estranged."

Trying to pinpoint Scott's attitude about film acting at this point is also a challenge. In 1942, at the peak of his early fame, Scott gave a number of interviews to journalists, offering more honest self-evaluation than most celebrities of the time. "If anyone is in Hollywood on a pass, it is me," he said that year. A decade earlier, when first starting in pictures, he had told a fan magazine, "My outlook is purely mercenary." Just three years later, in 1935, he is quoted in the fan magazine *Screenland* as saying he wanted to climb out of the ranks of "B" players and into high-budget film productions. He did want to expand his range past Westerns in those days, and he was always grateful to RKO for giving him the chance to act in non–Western films. "*Roberta* ... graduated me out of Westerns," Scott said after that film's release in 1935.

And for about two years, Paramount did keep Scott out of Westerns while moving him up to "A" productions including *So Red the Rose, Go West, Young Man* and *High, Wide and Handsome.* Still, his lot at Paramount was succinctly and accurately summed up by Western film historian Don Miller in his book *Hollywood Corral:* "Fortunately for Scott, he was yanked from the Paramount (Zane) Grey rut and nurtured from a serviceable but somewhat anonymous cowboy lead into a serviceable but somewhat anonymous leading man." Scott was an efficient lead in "B" films and an agreeable second lead in "A" pictures, but the studio never really gave him solid opportunities until late in his contract period with them. He did miss out on a couple of winners in the late 1930s: Paramount announced he would play opposite Grant and Carole Lombard in Henry Hathaway's *Spawn of the North* (1938), but those roles went to Henry Fonda, George Raft and Dorothy Lamour. Scott seemed a natural for Frank Lloyd's Paramount epic *Wells Fargo* (1937), but the actor's Southern bearing lost him the lead in the latter film. "The climax of the story is a serious row between the boy, who is a Northerner, and the Southern girl he is in love with, over her devotion to Southern traditions and customs," Scott related to the *Brooklyn Daily Eagle* in 1937. "Mr. [Frank] Lloyd said he just couldn't hear me attacking the south." Joel McCrea got the part.

Scott's best picture during this period was 1936's *Last of the Mohicans*, a loan-out to United Artists. Unfortunately that year he was also in Paramount's "B" melo-drama *And Sudden Death*. That was the nature of Scott's film career for most of the 1930s: one step forward, one step back. He remained a lead in "B" films, a lead in "A" films for other studios, and a supporting actor for most of the "A" films he got at Paramount. The two exceptions to this rule are the last two films he did under his Paramount contract, *High, Wide and Handsome* and *The Texans*. The first offered Scott his first real chance to emote, and while it may not remain one of his best films, it still holds one of his more ambitious portrayals. The latter was a good-looking, competently made "A" Western that concluded his Paramount contract, and from that point on, Scott pretty much remained a freelance agent. Yet in 1938 there was little to suggest that Scott (then 40 years old) would go on to become a bigger star and better actor. But he would do just that—although it took some time.

BIT PARTS: 1928–1930

Scott reportedly appears as a bit player in several silent/early sound films from the 1928–30 period. I can't verify his participation in all of these films, and even repeated viewings won't mean you'll be able to pick him out.

Sharp Shooters (Fox, January 1928, 60 minutes)

CREDITS   Director: James Tinling; Producer: Howard Hughes; Story by Randall H. Faye, titles by Malcolm Stuart Boylan

CAST   George O'Brien (George), Lois Moran (Lorette), Noah Young (Tom), Tom Dugan (Jerry), William Demarest ("Hi Jack" Murdock), Gwen Lee (Flossy)

Synopsis: George, a sailor, falls for a French dancer in a Morrocan cafe.

Scott and his pal Jack Heath show up as Austrian officers in one bar sequence. Scott later recalled his first film bit as being in a Western, perhaps indicating that he either a) had no idea what was going on or b) was mixing the film up with *The Virginian*. In 1946 he recalled for Fox publicists that his first movie job was on Stage Three on the Fox lot for a George O'Brien film, but he couldn't remember the title. *Variety* (1/25/1928) liked the film, calling it "one of the best programmers turned out by Fox."

Sailor's Holiday (1929)

CREDITS   Director: Fred C. Newmeyer; Screenplay: Ray Harris and Joseph F. Pollard; story by Pollard

CAST   Alan Hale (Adam Pike), Sally Eilers (Molly Jones), George Cooper (Shorty), Paul Hurst (Jimmylegs), Mary Carr (Mrs. Pike)

Some Scott filmographies claim that he has an unbilled bit part in this film; others do not. I was unable to obtain a copy of the film. The American Film Institute believes it is lost. The film is a romantic comedy with Hale as a brawny sailor who falls for Eilers. Eilers would later marry producer Harry Joe Brown, who produced nearly 20 Randolph Scott Westerns.

The Far Call (Fox, 1929)

CREDITS   Director: Allan Dwan; Producer: William Fox; Screenplay: H.H. Caldwell (titles), Seton I. Miller and Edison Marshall (story)

CAST   Charles Morton (Pat Loring), Leila Hyams (Hilda Larson), Arthur Stone (Schmidt), Warren Hymer (Soup Brophy), Tiny Sanford (Capt. Storkerston), Charles Middleton (Kirs Larson). With Randolph Scott, Boris Karloff and Warner Baxter

I know nothing about this film aside from these credits; Allan Dwan did not mention it during his lengthy interview with Peter Bogdanovich for the book *Who the Devil Made It?* and it may be lost.

The Black Watch (Fox, June 1929, 92 minutes)

CREDITS   Director: John Ford; Producer: Winfield R. Sheehan; Story by John Stone, from the novel *King of the Khyber Rifles; A Romance of Adventure* by Talbot Mundy

CAST   Victor McLaglen (Captain Donald Gordon King), Myrna Loy (Yasmani), David Rollins (Lt. Malcom King), Lumsden Hare (Colonel, Black Watch; also dialogue director), Roy D'Arcy (Rewa Chunga), Mitchell Lewis (Mohammed Khan), Francis Ford (General), Walter Long (Harrim Bey)

Synopsis: During World War I, Scottish officer Gordon King pretends to be a coward in order to go undercover to rescue imprisoned British soldiers in India.

"Gentleman, this is war!" intones Scottish colonel Lumsden Hare early in *The Black Watch*, a talky, creaky, hammy and dull film with unconvincing action sequences and horrid dialogue. You would never know that John Ford directed it, although after Ford completed the film, actor Hare (credited with stage direction) added wordy scenes to the script and reshot some scenes, which made Ford furious. "They were really horrible — long, talky things. I wanted to vomit when I saw them," Ford later said. The title refers to Victor McLaglen's Scottish Regiment. If you're looking for Scott, there is a Scottish officer sitting at McLaglen's table in the first scene who looks just like him.

Columnist Richard Eder, commenting on the film in *The New York Times* (August 31, 1975), wrote: "When the directors didn't abide by the rules of the talkies; the results were such instructive disasters as Ford's *The Black Watch* in which Victor McLagen and Myrna Loy seemed to be trying to drown out their dialogue with their eyeballs."

Weary River (First National–Vitaphone, March 1929, 84 minutes)

CREDITS   Director: Frank Lloyd; Scenarist: Bradley King; Story: Courtney Riley Cooper

CAST   Richard Barthelmess (Jerry Larrabee), Betty Compson (Alice), George E. Stone (Blackie), William Holden (Warden), Louis Natheaux (Spadoni)

Synopsis: Gangster prisoner Jerry Larrabee's song *Weary River* is such a hit that he's paroled, but on the outside he is reduced to performing as the criminal crooner in vaudeville.

"Talking! Singing!" the ads proclaimed for this early talkie, which combines elements from both crime films and musicals. Star Richard Barthelmess, a major star of the silents and early talkie period, claimed he did his own singing in the film until his vocal double 'fessed up to the press, causing the star and his studio some embarrassment. The title song was nominated for an Academy Award. Scott can reportedly be seen as an audience member in one sequence. The only known public copy of this film is at the Smithsonian in Washington, D.C., and in all honesty I did not want to travel there just to see if I could spot Scott in a bit role.

Newark Ledger (3/25/1929): "The theme song … is the picture's biggest asset."

Dynamite (MGM, December 1929, 127 minutes)

CREDITS Producer/director: Cecil B. DeMille; Screenplay: Jeanie Macpherson, John Howard Lawson and Gladys Unger

CAST Conrad Nagel (Roger Towne), Kay Johnson (Cynthia Crothers), Charles Bickford (Hagon Derk), Julia Faye (Marcia Towne), Joel McCrea (Marco), Muriel McCormac (Katie Derk)

Synopsis: In this fascinating early talkie that plays better than most films of the era, Kay Johnson stars as a socialite who marries a death row convict (Bickford) in order to inherit a fortune under the ridiculous provisions stipulated in her grandfather's will. When the convict is reprieved at the last moment, complications ensue.

Scott said DeMille tested him for the role of Hagon Derk, rejecting him due to the actor's lack of experience. DeMille then urged Scott to get some stage experience at the Pasadena Playhouse, and gave the actor a few days' work as an extra in *Dynamite.* But even repeated rewindings of the video machine didn't help me to pinpoint Scott in this film. DeMille utilized his usual "cast of thousands" so Scott could be among the black-tuxed partygoers at Johnson's house, or among the throngs of extras in the early country club sequence, or even one of the miners in the cave-in scene (yes, there's a cave-in). Scott reportedly also auditioned for the role of the gigolo Marco, but Joel McCrea, another newcomer to film, got the part, which was, in McCrea's words, "a

glorified bit." DeMille fired a feisty Carole Lombard during production; she was, I suspect, probably playing Julia Faye's role (as the other woman).

Oddly enough Scott would not work for MGM again until his final film, *Ride the High Country* (1962) also with Joel McCrea. And while McCrea hoped *Dynamite* would lead to a long-term MGM contract, the actor was to be disappointed. "An executive called me into his office and told me that they had Johnny Mack Brown and James Murray under contract, and that they were concentrating on them among the younger actors," McCrea recalled of the day in 1929 when MGM fired him. "It was still an era of medium-sized heroes and at six-foot-three I looked like the community flagpole. He suggested that I retire from pictures, wait until I was a bit older, and then do character parts like Ernest Torrence. 'But how,' I asked him, 'am I going to eat until I'm as old as Ernest Torrence?' That stumped him too, and I left without the matter being resolved."

Whether you can spot Scott or not, *Dynamite* is fun viewing, and it contains a nightclub confession scene that is worth the price of admission.

The Virginian (Paramount, released January 1930; often listed as a 1929 film, 90 minutes)

CREDITS Director: Victor Fleming; Assistant Director: Henry Hathaway; Producer: Louis D. Lichton; Screenplay: Howard Eastbrook, based on Owen Wister's novel The Virginian

CAST Gary Cooper (The Virginian), Walter Huston (Trampas), Richard Arlen (Steve), Mary Brian (Molly Wood), Chester Conklin (Uncle Hughey), Charles Stevens (Pedro), Eugene Pallette (Honey Wiggin), Jack Pennick (Slim)

Synopsis: The Virginian settles a longstanding feud with his arch-rival Trampas, falling for schoolteacher Molly and taking part in the hanging of his friend Steve along the way.

Owen Wister's 1904 novel *The Virginian* may be a well-written book, but it has yet to make for a good film. This early talkie is notches above the 1946 remake starring Joel McCrea and the 2002 version with Bill Pullman. All three versions are short on action and long on dialogue, although at least this production has a sense of humor, as in the scene where Gary Cooper and Richard Arlen deliberately mix up a room full of sleeping babies to confuse their parents. Likewise, the bit where the schoolchildren warble an awful rendition of "Three Blind Mice," driving schoolmarm Molly out of the room, is worth a smile. And dramatically, the sequence wherein the Virginian must take part in the hanging of his friend Steve still grabs you.

Scott is credited with being Cooper's dialogue coach, but he does not receive screen credit and it is still difficult to confirm this report. (Cooper's Southern accent is pretty inconsistent.) Scott is also reportedly one of the extras on horseback, but I couldn't spot him in any of the riding scenes, and he's most certainly not a member of Trampas' rustling gang. Scott later listed both *Dynamite* and *The Virginian* as films in which he played bit roles, so although it's difficult to find him in either movie, I see no reason to question his claim.

Scott told gossip columnist Sheilah Graham a story about taking Gary Cooper out for a ride in his new car. "They drove around an hour without speaking a word," Graham later recalled. "On the way back a bird flew overhead. Coop put his arms and hands into the shape of a rifle, said 'bang'

and that was it." So much for giving either actor extensive dialogue.

Cinema (January 1930): "An audible but ordinary Western of the ancient order." *London Times* (2/1/1930): "Mr. Gary Cooper is everything he should be as the Virginian, strong, attractive and serious without being over-solemn."

In addition, film historian John Cocchi believes that Scott appeared as an extra in the films *Half-Marriage* (1929) and *Born Reckless* (1930) although I've never seen these films listed in any Scott filmography. One 1940s publicity piece on Scott claims the actor has a bit in Howard Hughes' 1930's aviation drama *Hell's Angels* as well. Good luck finding him in that one.

Finally, some sources claim Scott, as well as Alan Ladd and Buster Crabbe, are hidden underneath monster-man makeup in Paramount's 1933 horror classic *Island of Lost Souls*. The film is a creepy shocker that is worth watching, but I don't think you'll be able to tell whether Scott is one of the half-human denizens of Charles Laughton's island of horrors. There are a couple of tall, hirsute creeps who *could* be Scott, but I bet we'll never know for sure. Would Paramount put a new contract player who they were building up in such a demeaning, anonymous part? It doesn't make sense to me, but nearly 20 years later Warner Bros. did just that to starlet Joan Weldon. When she casually mentioned to a Warners executive that she had a day off in between shooting pictures, the studio ordered her to report to the wardrobe department. There, they dressed her up like a prostitute and put her in a long shot with a group of extras in a brothel scene for the 1954 film *The Boy from Oklahoma* just to get another day's work out of her.

FEATURE FILM ROLES: 1931–1937

Women Men Marry (Headline Pictures Corp., July 1931, 60 minutes)

CREDITS Director: Charles Hutchinson; Story: John Francis Natteford

CAST Natalie Moorhead (Dolly Moulton), Sally Blane (Rose Bradley), Randolph Scott (Steve Bradley), Kenneth Harlan (Fred Moulton), Craufurd Kent (John Graham), Jean Del Vey (Pierre Renault), James Aubrey (Jimmy)

Synopsis: A nice couple come to the big city, where they run afoul of a bad couple who lead them into a netherworld of gambling, goons and guns.

Not much is known about Scott's first starring film other than the fact that he has a relatively large role as a likable but simple-minded sap. Headline Pictures was one of the many *low*-low-budget film studios striving to make a name for themselves in the early sound era. Director Charles Hutchinson's credits read like a "C" movie buff's dream: *Night Cargo* (1938), *Desert Guns* (1936), *Found Alive* (1933) and *Killers of the Wild* (1940). Hutchinson worked as an actor up through the war years before dying in 1949 at age 70. The American Film Institute could not confirm whether *Women Men Marry* is a lost film, nor could they locate an available screening copy. If anyone knows of a copy in private hands somewhere, drop me a line.

Variety (7/10/1931): "With a fair cast eclipsed by an incredibly stupid story and dialogue, *Women Men Marry* is the type of production 15 cent audiences first laugh at and then become peeved. It's like a puppet

Scott and Sally Blane in a film now believed to be lost, ***Women Men Marry*** (1931). (JC Archives, Inc.)

show. The dead come to life and everyone's reformed." *The New York Times* (7/13/1931): "There is a general feeling that New York is a sinister sort of place, and *Women Men Marry* takes considerable pains to prove it."

Heritage of the Desert (Paramount, March 1932, 63 minutes)

CREDITS   Director: Henry Hathaway; Producer: Harold Hurley; Screenplay: Harold Shumate and Frank Partos, based on Zane Grey's novel *Heritage of the Desert*

CAST   Randolph Scott (Jack Hare), Sally Blane (Judy), J. Farrell MacDonald (Adam Nash), David Landau (Judson Holderness), Gordon Westcott (Snap Naab), Guinn "Big Boy" Williams (Left), Vincent Barnett (Windy)

Synopsis: Land surveyor Jack Hare runs afoul of an evil rancher and falls in love with the daughter of a good rancher. Gunfire ensues.

"Reach for it!" Scott drawls in that wonderful Southern accent of his late in the film *Heritage of the Desert*, and a saloonfull of badmen, realizing the jig is up, do just that. It is an extremely satisfying moment in an otherwise disappointing film that serves as Scott's full-fledged introduction to the Western film genre. This creaky oater doesn't give Scott much of a chance to be a hero—he unwisely trusts the villains repeatedly, stupidly allows himself to be led into the desert to die, loses one fistfight, gets his gun knocked out of his hand over and over again, and only wins the final fistfight because a comrade shoots the bad guy. Not an auspicious start for the man who would eventually stare down the likes of Richard Boone, Lee Marvin and the Hammond Gang.

Clocking in at just over an hour, *Heritage of the Desert* (later retitled *When the West Was Young*) is an okay time-filler with some good dialogue. While scenarists Harold Shumate and Frank Partos apparently did away with much of the original Zane Grey story, they fleshed out the main villain, Judson Holderness, giving him a sense of humor and introspection rarely seen in Westerns of the time. When Holderness threatens to blackmail his rival's son with incriminating evidence that would turn the boy's father against him, the young man stutters, "You wouldn't do a thing like that, would you?" Without missing a beat, the unrepentant villain replies, "I do things like that every ten minutes."

Hathaway makes the most of the romantic give and take between Scott and Blane (one of Loretta Young's sisters, and just as talented and *more* sensual, in my view), particularly in a brief, silent scene wherein the duo playfully drip water on each other while basking in the sun at the base of a tree.

Comic relief is plentiful and threatens to capsize the film. Holderness has a dumb ox sidekick in Guinn "Big Boy" Williams, while Blane has an idiot Indian-Latino ranch hand (Vincent Barnett) who keeps saying things like, "Come quick, Miss Judy in trouble," sounding like Chico Marx in *A Day at the Races*. The action scenes are fast but forgettable, with a bear attack coming off as embarrassingly inept. Terrible cross-cutting and some clumsy editing choices kill the scene: Blane is up in a canyon, the bear is obviously in a forested meadow, and the old "let's-put-a-stuntman-in-a-bear-costume" idea is a bad one.

Director Hathaway blamed editor Billy Shea for this shameful sequence. Shea, Hathaway maintained, wanted to direct the film himself, but Paramount wouldn't give him a shot at it, so the editor got even with Hathaway by ruining the scene. Hathaway told a lengthy story about the whole incident: "Number one, I can't find a canyon with a precipitous cliff where we were shooting in Arrowhead because there's just no such thing. It's just all rolly up there. So I said, 'I'll get the sheep and the meadow stuff in Arrowhead and do the reverse direction in the studio against rear projection. They wouldn't let me go out to shoot the canyon background. [Instead], on the stage they built a rock out of cloth and it sagged and wiggled. They put it on the back project, and instead of a little canyon, it was the Grand Canyon!

"They had the set with the fake rocks out of the canvas, and we had a trained bear, but as soon as the bear put one foot on the damn thing he wouldn't get up on the rocks. They brought Harold Hurley [the producer] in and he says, 'Get Billy Jones [the stuntman] and put him in a bear outfit and let him go up.' So we had the Grand Canyon in the background and Billy Jones as the phony bear, which always shows, and the set sort of wobbles. And when Billy Jones walked on the damned stuff, it sagged.

"I worked that night until 2:00 and I never saw the footage before they cut it in. It's obviously a fake bear, you could see, and Scott comes up to him and shoots him and it looks like a man getting shot and Randy comes to pick up Sally and his foot goes through the cloth rock. He finally carries her to the cabin, puts her down on the bed, and her father comes in and catches him putting her down on the bed. The audience [at the preview] starts to laugh when they see the Grand Canyon behind her. They kept laughing with the bear and then when he tried to pick her up and couldn't quite make it because there was no footing on the cloth rock, they laughed even more. Billy Shea had stayed on the long shot with all the fake stuff and Randy staggering with Sally. Then when we finally put her down on the bed and the father came in the door, they were screaming. And they never quit laughing." How did Hathaway exact his revenge on Shea? "In the lobby, I poked the son of a bitch right in the jaw." Paramount replaced Shea with editor Fred Allen (not the radio comic)

who, with Hathaway's help, improved the scene somewhat.

Hathaway on the Zane Grey series: "They were all cut for double bills. I know that when we finished one of them, we ended up with four reels of film and had to go back and shoot some more. Our scripts were so carefully worked out that it was almost impossible to get an excess of footage. And another thing, we always had footage taken from another picture that was cut in." Hathaway said the films were made for about $80,000; Paramount records indicate that they were more in the $100,000 to $125,000 range — still incredibly cheap. The film was remade several times.

The New York Sun (3/15/32): "It isn't a super Western … in fact it is a weaker than usual Western and, I'm afraid, a weaker than usual Zane Grey." One exhibitor complained in a letter to Paramount that the film "abounds in lawlessness, making it unsuitable for children."

Sky Bride (Paramount, April 1932, 80 minutes)

CREDITS   Director: Stephen Roberts; Screenplay: Joseph L. Mankiewicz, Grover Jones and Agnes Brand Leahy

CAST   Richard Arlen (Speed Condon), Jack Oakie (Alec Dugan), Virginia Bruce (Ruth Dunning), Robert Coogan (Willie), Charles Starrett (Jim Charmical), Tom Douglas (Eddie Smith), Louise Closser Hale (Mrs. Smith), Harold Goodwin (Bill), Randolph Scott (Capt. Frank Robertson)

Synopsis: Barnstorming flyer Speed Condon suffers remorse after inadvertently killing his pal Eddie Smith during some aerial antics. Redemption in the form of a good woman, a loyal pal and a precocious tyke, follows.

Sky Bride, shot before but released after *Heritage of the Desert,* is an okay pre-Code programmer that mixes action and comedy well. The cast is good, aside from little Robert Coogan (Jackie's younger brother) who is so annoying that you hope he gets run over by a steamroller before film's end. Scott makes what amounts to a one-minute cameo appearance about an hour into the film as a military officer who agrees to take part in a flight competition. Jack Oakie's character points out that Scott has done more for the aviation industry than anyone in the whole wide world, but the script doesn't specify just what that "more" is, and Scott only has about three lines before flying off into the wild blue yonder. It's a negligible part, and Scott fans shouldn't go too crazy trying to track the film down if they're planning on seeing it just for him.

As a whole, *Sky Bride* is watchable fare, and the aerial stunt work really is impressive. I, for one, certainly wouldn't climb out onto the tail section of a biplane without a parachute — or even with one. According to film historian John Cocchi, director Stephen Roberts was a World War I pilot who later performed stunt aerobatics at county fairs around the country. After an accident ended his flying career, Roberts became a stuntman in Hollywood and made about a dozen films before his death in 1936.

An apocryphal story has it that Pop Jones, a Paramount electrician who was screenwriter Grover Jones' father, was asked by his son what he thought of the script. "I could tie a pencil to a cow's tit and she could walk a better one," he replied.

New York Herald Tribune (5/2/1932): "A reasonably good program picture. In advance you should be warned that the picture has nothing to do with a girl aviator who gets married in an airplane. *Sky Bride*, you see, is merely the name of the hero's plane."

A Successful Calamity (Warner Bros., September 1932, 75 minutes)

CREDITS   Director: John Adolfi; Screenplay: Austin Parker, Maude Howell and Julien Josephson, based on the play by Clare Kummer

CAST   George Arliss (Henry Wilton), Mary Astor (Emmie), Evalyn Knapp (Peggy), Grant Mitchell (Connors), David Torrence (Partington), William Janney (Eddie), Hardie Albright (George), Hale Hamilton (Belden), Randolph Scott (Larry), Fortunio Bonanova (Pietro)

Synopsis: Wealthy financier Henry Wilton discovers that money has corrupted his family's values, so he decides to play "bankrupt" to test their loyalty.

An easy-to-take comedy that displays George Arliss' subtle humor quite well, *A Successful Calamity* is an early example of screwball comedy. It never quite shifts out of first or second gear to go full-throttle, but for what it is, it's entertaining enough. Arliss is a financier who returns home after a year abroad to discover that his wife, son and daughter have all become caught up in a social whirlwind of appointments, engagements and love affairs. After Arliss' butler Connors (well played by Grant Mitchell) tells him, "The poor don't get to go very often," Arliss pretends to be ruined to get his family to reconsider the important things in life. This successful calamity achieves the desired results, and all ends happily with the rich staying rich.

The appeal of Arliss may be difficult to understand today, particularly when he over-emotes in such films as *The Green Goddess* (1930) and *The Iron Duke* (1935). However, in the early 1930s he made several pleasant comedies, all following pretty much the same theme. Arliss would be a rich man who finds a way to connect to the poor, or to exact vengeance on his greedy family, or pose as a humble worker to worm his way into a rival's business, and so on. *A Successful Calamity* is about as good as any of these films, and Arliss plays with a light, dry touch that's appropriate for the scenario. "I should like you to see our house," one obnoxious house guest says to Arliss during a party scene. Without missing a beat, Arliss deadpans back, "Oh, have you brought it with you?"

Scott, on loan from Paramount, plays the polo-playing pal of Arliss' son Eddie, and he's also a suitor for Arliss' daughter Peggy. It's little more than a bit part, though he manages more screen time than he did in *Sky Bride*. Why Warner Bros. would bother to borrow him for such an insignificant role is beyond me, since they could have pulled any one of a number of nondescript performers from their own contract list to fulfill the role. Scott received a flat fee of $500 for his efforts, but he obviously hadn't yet made an impression on the critics, based on *The New York Times*' (9/25/1932) comment that "Randolph Scott is acceptable as the son." But it is William Janney who plays the son, and in such an annoyingly feeble manner that one wishes it had been Scott who essayed the role.

Hot Saturday (Paramount, November 1932, 73 minutes)

CREDITS   Director: William Seiter; Screenplay: Seton I. Miller, based on a story by Harvey Ferguson

CAST   Cary Grant (Romer Sheffield), Nancy Carroll (Ruth Brock), Randolph Scott (Bill Fadden), Edward Woods (Conny Billop), Lillian Bond (Eva Randolph), William Collier, Sr. (Harry Brock), Jane Darwell (Mrs. Brock), Rita Le Roy (Camille), Grady Sutton (Archie), Ruth Coghlin (Annie)

Synopsis: Virtuous Ruth Brock is the victim of malicious small-town gossip, so she decides to live up to her reputation.

"Everyone knew on Sunday what everyone else did on Saturday — and the rest of the week," the opening title card for *Hot Saturday* reads. This pre–Code programmer, designed by Paramount as a testing ground for two new contract players (Cary Grant and Scott) and fading star Nancy Carroll, doesn't date well. The act-

ing is melodramatic, the facial makeup is heavy on the pancake, and the clothing styles—particularly where the women are concerned — are unflattering. This is a film full of self-obsessed, mostly unlikable people who say and do stupid things.

And yet it's watchable. Some of the racy dialogue and physical shtick is fascinating: "She said to tell you to go to he … to the devil," one character says. A female singer caresses her breasts (twice!) while crooning, "I'm burning for you…" in a nightclub scene. And Carroll upends her younger sister Annie (Rose Coghlin) on the bed and divests her of her panties, exclaiming "Bottoms up!" as she does so.

The basic plot concerns good girl Carroll and her supposed affair with rich cad Grant. When Carroll spends just a few extra moments with Grant and then accepts a ride home from the latter's chauffeur, well, the whole town's talking. Carroll is fired from her job, forced to resign from the Women's Social Club, and slapped around by her mother, who pretty much calls her a whore. Since she's earned a dubious reputation, Carroll decides to live it up as a bad girl, and the film's denouement is rather surprising under the circumstances.

Scott plays a geologist who acts like a buffoon around the opposite sex. "I'm a clumsy ox around women," he acknowledges to Carroll after she's come to his cave in the midst of a raging tempest (which means he has to undress her so she doesn't catch cold). Scott doesn't appear until about the half way mark of the film, but he's adequate in a low-key, natural manner as the other man. He and Grant only share one brief scene together, exchanging a few lines of dialogue and a handshake. Though he's by no means effective here, Scott's easy going style makes him stand out among the ensemble of mugging thespians, none of whom are helped by the trite dialogue.

Carroll is one of those actresses of the

1401-99

Scott as a rock-headed mineralogist who comforts a nude-under-the-covers Nancy Carroll in 1932's *Hot Saturday.*

Golden Era who has been forgotten. From the late 1920s until the early 1930s she was a major star, nabbing an Oscar nomination for her work in *The Devil's Holiday* (1930). A Clara Bow for the talkie era, Carroll's career inexplicably stalled by the mid–1930s and she drifted out of films by the end of the decade. She died in 1965 at the age of 60.

An okay relic of its time, *Hot Saturday* still maintains novelty status due to its pairing of Grant and Scott, and what it says about small-town gossip still holds true.

Brooklyn Daily-Eagle (11/5/1932): "*Hot Saturday* falls into that class of second-rate entertainment … and seeing her newest vehicle at the Paramount, we can't help feeling a little sorry for Nancy Carroll."

New York World-Telegram (11/5/1932): "It is a generally feeble narrative, made even more feeble by lifeless dialogue and uninspired direction. Miss Carroll is charm-

ingly natural as the much-maligned little secretary, and both Mr. Grant and Mr. Scott squeeze the most they can out of their sketchily written parts."

Wild Horse Mesa (Paramount, November 1932, 65 minutes)

CREDITS   Director: Henry Hathaway; Screenplay: Harold Shumate and Frank Howard Clark, based on Zane Grey's novel *Wild Horse Mesa*

CAST   Randolph Scott (Chane Weymer), Sally Blane (Sandy Melberne), Lucille La Verne (Ma "The General" Melberne), Charley Grapewin (Sam Bass), Fred Kohler (Rand), James Bush (Bent Weymer), Jim Thorpe (Indian Chief), George F. Hayes (Slack), Buddy Roosevelt (Horn), E.H. Calvert (Sheriff)

Synopsis: Horse wrangler Chane Weymer tries to corral the infamous wild mustang Panquitch while contending with the nefarious plans of his rival Rand.

A sturdy enough entry in Scott's Zane Grey series (and a considerable step up from *Heritage of the Desert*), *Wild Horse Mesa* is an action fan's delight. It features a night-time desert chase, a horse stampede, a fistfight between Scott and villain Fred Kohler alongside a string of barbed wire fencing, and a sequence wherein Scott ropes the near-mythical mustang Panquitch and then gets taken for an unexpected drag over rock and sagebrush. The initial plot of Scott trying to lasso Panquitch falls by the wayside once the evil Kohler starts fomenting trouble with Scott's kid brother (ineffectively played by James Bush). Kohler is the sort of guy who needs a good punch in the nose, but don't worry, he gets it, and then some.

Zippy scripting and tight ensemble playing elevate this "B" oater. Sally Blane is particularly fetching here, and Charley Grapewin is a delight as a seafaring gob, inexplicably transplanted to the Old West, who has a pet monkey. (The simian is clad in a sailor suit, which seemed to be stock costuming for monkeys in 1930s Hollywood.) James Bush, however, is really bad as Scott's younger brother. His character is supposed to be a trouble maker with a past, but he's about as threatening as the monkey. His goofy smile, buffoonish gait and "aw shucks" smile may remind you of Henry Aldrich's clownish pal Dizzy, if anybody remembers those 1940s comedy films from Paramount.

Scott isn't called upon to emote much at all in this one, but he displays a confident sense of cowboy style. And as with many of the Zane Grey movies of this period, he proves to be a helluva horseman. The film was reportedly shot partially on location near Flagstaff, Arizona, using local Navajo Indians as extras.

Hello, Everybody! (Paramount, January 1933, 69 minutes)

CREDITS   Director: William A. Seiter; Story by Fannie Hurst (no screenplay credit given)
CAST   Kate Smith (Herself), Randolph Scott (Hunt Blake), Sally Blane (Lily Smith), Charley Grapewin (Jed), George Barbier (Mr. Marshall)

Synopsis: The power company wants to take over the farmland valley where Kate Smith lives, but they didn't figure on the power of radio!

Hello, Everybody! is a real oddity that will likely never air on television in this age of political correctness thanks to the inclusion of the song "Pickinninny Heaven," sung by Smith to a room of black orphans who smile with delight at the condescending lyrics involving watermelons and pork chops. "Even though the good Lord took your mammy, she'll be waiting for you in pickininny heaven," Smith happily warbles. Needless to say, if she tried to pull that one over on a listening audience today, they'd run her off the air. The film is Kate Smith's one full-fledged attempt at film stardom, though she played small roles in other films.

Scott plays a representative of the General Power and Water Company who is ordered to wrest control of Smith's land deed (this is pure melodrama). "There's only one way to tackle a woman," Scott's supervisor advises him; "Around the waist." But Scott wasn't counting on Kate's girth, so his supervisor's method doesn't work in this case. Scott does get a rare shot at physical comedy early in the film in an amusing sequence of events in which a stubborn gate, an oily tractor and a runaway calf come together to cause him endless confusion. Our tattered and torn hero ends up spiraling into a nearby river with the protesting calf. It's a brief but funny bit that shows Scott could have been a good light comedian in the nature of a Fred MacMurray or Ray Milland had Paramount given him the chance. Unfortunately, within a matter of minutes Scott woos and wins Smith's sister Lily (Sally

Blane), and once he's wed, our boy becomes nothing more than part of the scenery.

Smith repeatedly sings her theme song "When the Moon Comes Over the Mountain" as well as "Sweet Moon Song" (she must have had a thing for moons) and an array of other forgettable tunes that do not showcase her fine vocal talents. She ends up saving the day by singing on the radio (a quick montage of shots shows her rising stardom, culminating in a neon light advertising her appearance in *Hello, Everybody!*) and convincing the power company to reroute their water plans. A fascinating failure of a film, *Hello, Everybody!* remains corny, bizarre and sometimes unintentionally funny. A little more than a decade later, director Seiter would guide Scott through another musical misfire, *Belle of The Yukon*. I'm not sure which film is better, but neither of them are very good.

The New York Times (1/30/1933): "The picture is obviously designed for those special admirers who never tire of hearing Miss Smith describe the moon coming over the mountain." *New York World-Telegram* (1/30/1933): "*Hello Everybody!* should be regarded as a pretty bad picture." *New York Herald-Tribune*, (1/28/1933): "The large supporting cast gives competent performances ... Randolph Scott and Sally Blane, as the juvenile leads, are pleasant."

The Thundering Herd (Paramount, March 1933, 59 minutes)

CREDITS   Director: Henry Hathaway; Screenplay: Jack Cunningham and Mary Flannery, based on Zane Grey's novel *The Thundering Herd*

CAST   Randolph Scott (Tom Doan), Judith Allen (Millie Fayre), Harry Carey (Clark Sprague), Raymond Hatton (Jude Pilchuk), Noah Beery (Randall Jett), Blanche Frederici (Jane Jett), Barton MacLane (Pruit), Monte Blue (Smiley), Buster Crabbe (Bill Hatch)

Synopsis: Rival buffalo-hunting parties vie for bison and blood as a *Romeo and Juliet*–esque subplot develops around them.

Early talkie Westerns always seem a bit creaky to me, but everyone involved in the Zane Grey series at Paramount — Hathaway, Scott, the heroines, the horses and certainly the stuntmen — imbued the series with energy and innovation. *The Thundering Herd* ties with *To The Last Man* as the best of the Scott Zane Greys. Sporting a pencil-thin moustache and looking slick enough to be the bad guy, Scott gives a solid performance as a man torn between his loyalty to his own clan and his love for Millie (Judith Allen), daughter of his father's rival. More assured than in any previous film, Scott shows enough confidence to tackle a risky stunt in which he first jumps on some horses off of a moving stagecoach and later swings from one of the horses to a waiting tree branch. Still, he had a long way to go when it came to serious emoting.

A bizarre subplot, featuring an incestuous relationship between head villain Randall Jett (Noah Beery) and his daughter Millie, is more interesting than the buffalo hunting or family rivalry. Adding fuel to the fire is the presence of actress Blanche Frederici as Mrs. Jett, a woman wise enough to see what's what. Playing a Lady Macbeth of the prairie, Frederici sees to it that frontier justice is served out nicely, engaging in a murderous series of duels with knives and pistols to do in whoever gets in her way — including her own clan — before she kicks the bucket.

And just when you think the bad guys are out of the way and all is well, the Indians attack Harry Carey's wagon train. Hathaway captures the confusion of the battle well: smoke, snow and fire mix together to limit vision as the Indians clamber over the wagons and into the camp. Scott rides to a second wagon train party to enlist their help, and what follows is a once-in-a-lifetime wagon train attack in which the second wagon train makes a circle around the Indians, who are circling around the first wagon train, and you just know by watching the sequence that people and horses got hurt during the filming.

The Thundering Herd is an exciting little "B" that does justice to the genre. The Zane Grey movies were getting better, and so was Scott — as long as he stuck to Westerns.

Murders in the Zoo (Paramount, March 1933, 62 minutes)

CREDITS Director: Eddie Sutherland; Screenplay: Philip Wylie and Seton I. Miller

CAST Lionel Atwill (Eric Gorman), Kathleen Burke (Evelyn Gorman), Randolph Scott (Dr. Woodford), Gail Patrick (Jerry Evans), Charles Ruggles (Peter Yates), John Lodge (Roger Hewitt)

Synopsis: Insanely jealous zoologist Eric Gorman has an array of animal accomplices to help him get rid of any man who looks twice at his flirtatious wife Evelyn.

Though Paramount wasn't known for making horror films, when the studio got around to producing one, it was usually a doozy. *Island of Lost Souls* (1933), *Dr. Cyclops* (1940) and *The Uninvited* (1944) are three prime examples of superb shockers bearing the Paramount brand. *Murders in the Zoo* is just as good, and downright gruesome in places, containing enough lurid violence to terrify anyone with a vivid imagination.

Murders opens with a now-famous scene wherein Lionel Atwill sews up a bound man's lips in the Indo-Chinese jungles as punishment for the man's romantic pursuit of Atwill's wife (Kathleen Burke). Atwill leaves the unfortunate man there, but director Eddie Sutherland gives us a quick close-up of the man's tattered face as he gives feeble pursuit to Atwill (who boards an elephant to depart). This short shot of

the man's terrified eyes as he realizes his fate is horrifyingly memorable and likely to give the viewer a good nightmare. Afterwards we discover the man made a nice meal for the jungle cats.

On the surface, Atwill's character appears to be offering financial and moral support to the Municipal Zoo, which is run by Dr. Woodford (Scott). But the real plot revolves around Atwill's attempts to dispose of his wife Evelyn's many boyfriends. Why Evelyn is afraid of her husband is obvious, as he's the sort of guy who can scare you with the line, "I'd like to show you around the zoo."

Now would you invite an argument with a insanely jealous man like Atwill on the bridge over the alligator pond? Not me, brother. This animal-loving maniac uses the gators, the boa constrictors and the lions to eliminate anyone who gets in his way — including Scott, who ends up with a serious snake bite (the actor refused to handle the big snakes in close-up, and those are the hands of bit player Dennis O'Keefe in many of the Scott-snake scenes). Atwill gets his just deserts when he seeks refuge from his pursuers in the boa constrictor cage. The shock potential of this scene is dampened considerably by its absurd set-up: Surely Atwill knows the zoo well enough to avoid the snake cage, and in any event, when he does lock himself in, rather than casting a nervous eye about the joint to spot any approaching serpents, he keeps facing forward to look through the gates, sort of like the Three Stooges did in that one short where they lock themselves in the lion's den and then tell each other to stop roaring. Atwill ends up as a snake snack while Scott survives to embrace ingénue Gail Patrick.

Way too much footage is devoted to actor Charles Ruggles as a buffoonish press agent with a penchant for booze — the sort of role Bob Hope might have played had the film been made five years later. After

falling into a dead faint upon encountering a killer mamba, the first thing Ruggles
says after reviving is, "Is there a good laun-
dry in this town?"

The Los Angeles Times (3/10/1933):
"Roars, shrieks and cacklings of the wild
animals on the screen at the Paramount
yesterday were echoed to an amazing degree by the audience, at times driven to a
mild state of hysteria by scenes in *Murders
in the Zoo.*" The film was banned in Que-
bec, Australian, Germany and Sweden.

Supernatural (Paramount, April 1933, 65 minutes)

CREDITS   Director: Victor Halperin; Producer: Edward Halperin; Screenplay: Harvey
Thew and Brian Marlow

CAST   Carole Lombard (Roma Courtney),
Alan Dinehart (Paul Bavian), Vivienne Osborne (Ruth Rogen), H.B. Warner (Dr. Houston), Randolph Scott (Grant Wilson), William
Farnum (Mickey Hammond)

Synopsis: The spirit of death row victim
Ruth Rogen enters the body of Roma Courtney, causing considerable mayhem. Complicating matters is a blackmailing spiritualist, Paul Bavian.

Supernatural is the sort of cheesy film
you'd expect to find in a *Films of Peter Lorre*
book. But Scott was then one of Paramount's
all-around handymen and hence was
thrown into all sorts of studio projects in an
effort to give him experience and broaden
his range. His role in the supernatural
shenanigans in this film is subsidiary to the
main plot, but let it be said that he handles
his lines with conviction and doesn't em-
barrass himself. Neither does the rest of
the cast — an achievement in itself, given
Supernatural's absurd scenario, which is
well worth detailing.

Ruth Rogen is a death row inmate
who killed three men with her bare hands
("Ruth Rogen, Notorious Strangler, Doomed
to Die!" one newspaper headline reads,
while another headline informs us that the

"Women's Federation Bureau Refuses to
Aid Her"). She goes to the electric chair
vowing revenge on the man who betrayed
her, spiritualist Paul Bavian (Alan Dinehart). Her plan to get him from beyond the
grave is inadvertently given legs thanks
to the meddlesome antics of Dr. Houston
(H. B. Warner), who believes that Rogen's
spirit could get loose and inhabit another
person's body, thus leading to a slew of imitation killers. "That's an interesting the-
ory, doctor," the prison warden says, agreeing to turn Rogen's body over to Houston
for some vague experiment.

The doc sure has an odd way of con-
ducting science: He takes Rogan's corpse to
his penthouse, dresses her in a seductive
evening gown, hooks her up to some elec-
trical apparatus and starts shooting juice
into her body. "If no imitation crimes take
place, I'll have negative proof that my the-
ory is correct," the doctor says to no one
in particular, giving the audience the best
explanation that scenarists Harvey Thew
and Brian Marlow can offer for all this
nonsense. Unfortunately, beautiful blonde
babe Roma Courtney (Carole Lombard)
pops by the doc's home the same night that
the old guy's giving the corpse the current,
and before you can say "boo!," Rogen's
spirit electronically escapes and enters
Roma's body.

As if Roma doesn't have enough problems of her own. Her brother John died
under mysterious circumstances, and spiritualist Bavian claims to be in touch with
his ghost. Roma believes him, though her
fiancé Grant (Scott) tells her that the
medium is just trying to scam her. Bavian
gets more than he bargained for when
Rogen's ghost uses Roma to exact her revenge on him. The ridiculous finale sees
Grant leading a one-man rescue mission
upon Bavian's yacht after Roma, still pos-
sessed by Rogen, entices the deceitful spiritualist there in an effort to kill him. Bavian
catches on that something's amiss and

makes a run for a dinghy; Grant literally yanks Rogen out of Roma, and the vengeful spirit catches up to Bavian and hangs him (for some reason he's placed a noose around his own neck in an effort to board the dinghy). Rogen's spirit goes to her final resting place and, at the last moment, the ghost of Roma's brother swings by to suggest that Grant and Roma honeymoon in Bermuda. I'm not kidding.

Supernatural is only 65 minutes long, a blessing given that it's not very good. The promising opening credits sequence suggests we're in for a hair-raising scare film, as lightning, thunder and wailing voices combine with title cards that offer such questionable platitudes as Confusius' *"Treat all supernatural beings with respect, but keep aloof of them."* The Halperins did a first-rate job with their 1932 horror classic *White Zombie*, shot on a budget of next-to-nothing. Perhaps having a bigger budget at a mainstream studio sapped the brothers' creativity, for *Supernatural* never comes close to equaling *White Zombie*'s terror. The séance and spirit scenes in *Supernatural* are accomplished without decent special effects or suitable tension, and one can see why Scott's character thinks it's all baloney. It looks like baloney.

There are nonetheless enough unintentionally funny moments to make the film worth sitting through, and the cast gives it their all. Scott managed an easy rapport with Lombard, one of the sexiest actresses of the 1930s. She was just one year away from her breakthrough role opposite John Barrymore in *20th Century*, and hokey films like *Supernatural* would remain very much a part of her past from then on. George Raft, who co-starred with Lombard in two films, *Bolero* and *Rumba*, liked to tell a story about the day he entered her dressing room on the Paramount lot and found her standing nude in front of a pan of blonde hair dye, which she was applying to her pubic curls with cotton balls. "Relax, Georgie," Lombard playfully told Raft. "I'm just making my collar and cuffs match." History does not record whether Scott enjoyed a similar sight.

Lombard did not want to do *Supernatural*, according to Sidney Salkow, assistant director. When she first read the script, she was so incensed that she stormed the Paramount front office where she threatened to kill the studio brass, Victor Halperin and then herself. Lombard gave Halperin a difficult time throughout the shoot, firing off a steady stream of profanities at him and warning him that God would exact revenge for his directorial incompetence. Late on the afternoon of March 10, 1933, God seemed to do just that when a major earthquake hit Long Beach, knocking one of the sets of *Supernatural* to pieces. While the cast and crew ran away in panic, Lombard strode defiantly over to a cowering Halperin, pointed a finger at him and said, "Victor — *that* was only a warning!" The Long Beach earthquake, as the disaster was known, took over 50 lives.

New York Evening Post (4/22/1933): "[A] dull picture, largely because it doesn't make you believe in its supernaturalness. It is also rather difficult to follow, in spite of the fact that Vivienne Osborne, Carole Lombard, H.B. Warner, Alan Dinehart and Randolph Scott do their best to make it plausible." *New York American* (4/23/1933): "A silly lot of claptrap, neither exciting, shocking, nor amusing. Oddly enough, there can be nothing but praise for the players in this strange mélange."

Cocktail Hour (Columbia, May 1933, 73 minutes)

CREDITS   Director: Victor Schertzinger; Screenplay: James Kevin McGuinnes; story by Gertrude Purcell

CAST   Bebe Daniels (Cynthia Warren), Randolph Scott (Randolph Morgan), Sidney Blackmer (William Lawton), Muriel Kirkland (Olga), Barry Norton (Phillippe)

Bebe Daniels and Scott in the minor comedy *Cocktail Hour* (1933), his first film for Columbia. (JC Archives, Inc.)

Synopsis: Socialite Cynthia Warren can't choose between faithful but bland Randolph Morgan or exciting married lover William Lawton, so she goes off on a cruise to figure it all out.

Cocktail Hour's pre-credit shot shows a clock striking four—cocktail hour, apparently. Aside from this scene, there's nothing in the film to explain why the title is *Cocktail Hour*. This is one of those early 1930s drawing room comedies wherein people have nothing better to do but mix drinks and toss off flippant witticisms. Scott, described early on by heroine Bebe Daniels as "the nastiest man in town," appears in book-end sequences that suggest he's a dull old-fashioned suitor who would rather make money than love. However,

nothing in his performance indicates that he's nasty, so Daniels' comment remains a mystery. Scott is first seen practicing his golf game in his office, a bit that makes me wonder whether the golf nut–actor didn't suggest it himself to give the scene some nuance. Though second-billed, Scott is really the third male lead, and has less to do here than in any other 1930s film except *Sky Bride* and *A Successful Calamity*.

Cocktail Hour is a passably amusing imitation of better screwball comedies that contains a few funny scenes, including the old gag wherein Daniels makes a big show of leaving a room only to enter the closet. The film is full of people who pose as someone else or hide in closets or under beds, and the dialogue veers between camp, corn and comic, as in this exchange between Cynthia (Daniels) and her gal pal Olga (Muriel Kirkland):

> OLGA: Men are all alike — one day they kiss you, the next day they kick you.
>
> CYNTHIA: Well, you can see them every other day.

Hardly a good film, *Cocktail Hour* may provide harmless fun, though I bet you could leave the room for five minutes and not miss a thing. Randolph Scott fans will be disappointed by both the size and depth of his role, for the actor gives this cardboard characterization of a businessman no more than it deserves. This was Scott's first film for Columbia, a studio with which he became successfully associated in the 1940s and 1950s.

Sunset Pass (Paramount, May 1933, 61 minutes)

CREDITS   Director: Henry Hathaway; Screenplay: Jack Cunningham and Gerald Geraghty, based on Zane Grey's novel *Sunset Pass*

CAST   Randolph Scott (Ash Preston), Tom Keene (Jack Rock), Kathleen Burke (Jane Preston), Harry Carey (John Hesbitt), Kent Taylor (Clint Peeples), Noah Beery (Marshall Blake), Leila Bennett (Hetty Miller), Fuzzy Knight (Willie), George Barbier (Judge), Charles Middleton (Williams), Vince Barnett (Windy)

Synopsis: Government agent Jack Rock goes undercover to infiltrate a gang of rustlers hiding out at the Half Moon Ranch.

A weak entry in the Paramount Zane Grey series, *Sunset Pass* suffers from a number of cinematic wounds. It eschews ensemble characterizations in favor of focusing on Tom Keene's rather staid Jack Rock, who ends up working at the Half Moon Ranch where his newfound pal Ash Preston (Scott) schemes in cahoots with the rustling gang. Little development is given to the romance between Rock and Preston's sister Jane (Kathleen Burke), making his gallant actions on behalf of her crooked brother hard to take. Likewise, the film has a cheap feel to it and the fight scenes are clumsily choreographed. The stock footage from the 1929 movie version is badly edited in here; at certain points, the film veers from night to day and then back again in a single scene just to make use of this footage. In addition, there's literally no humor, and Keene plays one note throughout. The only real amusement the film offers is a brief scene wherein Scott plays a game of Montana Shuffle with an anonymous bad guy, but to reveal more would ruin what little fun this bit offers.

Of interest is the casting-against-type of both Scott and Harry Carey. The latter is the ruthless head of a cattle-rustling gang, while Scott is an out-and-out bad guy, though one with a winning smile and Southern charm. The part calls for more emoting than Scott could muster at this point, and he's far from convincing as a hard-drinking, woman-slapping wastrel. The actor suffers the first of his five screen deaths in this film, taking a bullet to the belly, courtesy of his pal Keene. Scott's screen death is rough going for the audience, as he basically makes a pained face and then does everything else as if he's about to tee up at the first hole of the nearest golf course. It doesn't help that he has an incredible amount of expository dialogue to deliver before he kicks off.

There is one line of dialogue worth noting when you consider how long Scott lived in real life. "I got a lucky spot," he tells Keene in one scene. "Fortune teller told me I'd live until 90." He actually made it to 89.

The Grey novel was used for source material once again when RKO remade the film in 1946 with James Warren in the Tom Keene role.

Man of the Forest (Paramount, August 1933, 62 minutes)

CREDITS   Director: Henry Hathaway; Screenplay: Jack Cunningham and Harold Shumate

CAST   Randolph Scott (Brett Dale), Verna Hillie (Alice Gayner), Harry Carey (Jim Gayner), Noah Beery (Clint Beasley), Barton MacLane (Mulvey), Buster Crabbe (Yegg), Vince Barnett (Little Casino), Guinn "Big Boy" Williams (Big Casino), Blanche Frederici (Mrs. Forney), Tom Kennedy (Sheriff Blake).

Synopsis: Woman-hating trapper Brett Dale is framed for the murder of his friend Jim Gayner. He sets out to clear himself, falling for Jim's daughter Alice in the process.

Scott, sporting a mustache that makes him look like the Douglas Fairbanks of the prairie, seems to be having fun in this enjoyable "B" Western. He has a friendly cougar pal and a horse that comes running when he whistles for it, and engages in a wonderfully playful relationship of conflict with the feisty Verna Hillie. At one point Scott kidnaps Hillie to prevent her from being kidnapped by the bad guys. "You'll be sorry for this," she yells, kicking and screaming. "I already am," he deadpans back.

She later pulls a gun on him in an effort to escape. He disarms her, turns her upside down and spanks her good. "I'll kill you for that," she vows. "If you do, I'll spank you again," Scott matter-of-factly responds.

Man of the Forest has several dark moments, including a near-rape, the shooting of the friendly cougar and kidnappings and shootings galore. There's some weak scripting in this one, with a lot of coincidental eavesdropping sequences that lead to plot points being neatly tied up for both the audience and the actors. Still, it's a good film. Guinn "Big Boy" Williams and Vince Barnett are a pair of buffoonish brothers who wage a losing battle against an ornery mule, while Barton MacLane and Buster Crabbe are a pair of gunmen in Noah Beery's pay. The film climaxes with a massive gun fight around a burning building with Beery and his gang assaulting Scott and his crew, followed by a bruising brawl between Beery and Scott.

Man of the Forest was a film beset by animal problems. Scott's cougar pal attacked him for real. The trainer told Scott the cougar was milk-fed and wouldn't hurt him, but at one point the cat dug his claws into Scott's back and sunk his teeth into the actor's shoulder. Scott went still until the cougar was pulled off. The actor asked the trainer why he hadn't stopped the cat from attacking. "It was a good take and I didn't want to spoil the scene," the trainer said. But later, as Scott walked by the cougar on the set, the big cat lunged at him again. Then the trainer admitted that the lion enjoyed horse meat on occasion, and Scott's clothes had the scent of horse on them. Film close ups do reveal that it is Scott, and not a stuntman, fending off the cat attack.

Buster Crabbe recalled that Williams had his own problems wrestling a mule: "He [Williams] tried to pick up the mule to turn it over, but the mule braced and Big Boy couldn't do anything with the damned thing. At one point Big Boy bent over and the mule kicked him right in the fanny — moved him real quick about three feet. We kept that in."

Verna Hillie on Scott: "He really set the tone as a gentleman. He was impressively handsome. Those closeups where I stared at him are for real." (*Western Clippings*, #24, July-August 1998.) However, film historian John Cocchi says Hillie once told him that she looked upon Scott with some disdain, especially after Scott complained about all the fan mail that arrived on location for him. "What am I going to do with all this?" he asked Hillie, who told him he had a responsibility to answer it all — a response the Southern gentleman

A mustached Scott with heroine Verna Hillie in a peaceful moment from a superior Zane Grey "B," *Man of the Forest* (1933). (JC Archives, Inc.)

reportedly didn't like hearing, as he didn't have a secretary at the time. The blonde Hillie wore a brunette wig in the film to match footage from an earlier (silent) version of the story that Hathaway spliced in throughout.

Hollywood Reporter (August 1933): "Better-than-average Western entertainment. Everybody in the cast shows Scott up as an actor, but he's good-looking, rides a horse well and acts the he-man without chewing scenery."

To the Last Man (Paramount, September 1933, 74 minutes)

CREDITS   Director: Henry Hathaway; Screenplay: Jack Cunningham

CAST   Randolph Scott (Lynn Hayden as an adult), Jay Ward (Lynn Hayden as a child), Noah Beery (Jed Colby), Esther Ralston (Ellen Colby), Jack LaRue (Jim Daggs), Egon Brecher (Mark Hayden), Buster Crabbe (Billy Hayden), Gail Patrick (Ann Hayden Stanley), Barton MacLane (Neil Stanley), Muriel Kirkland (Molly Hayden), James C. Eagles (Eli Bruce)

Synopsis: In post–Civil War Kentucky, the Colby-Hayden rivalry continues unabated. When the Haydens move to Nevada in an attempt to escape the feud, they discover the Colbys, intent on wiping them out, have moved in next door. Complications ensue when a Colby gal falls for a Hayden boy.

A little *Romeo and Juliet* mixed with a little Hatfield and McCoy, *To the Last Man* is a black, bleak and breathtaking Western that benefits from a lively, sensual performance from Esther Ralston as a spirited

Scott prepares to take a conk on the head from villain Jack LaRue in another top-notch Zane Grey "B," _To the Last Man_. That's James Mason (_not_ the British actor) on the ground. (JC Archives, Inc.)

backwoods gal full of spite, hate, lust and compassion. The actress, once known as "the American Eve," was talented and beautiful, and it's a shame she retired from cinema in the early 1940s to pursue various business careers. Voyeurs will get a kick out of watching her in a relatively tame nude swimming scene early in the film, though that's probably a double taking the plunge in the long shot. (In her memoirs, Ralston acknowledged that she did enjoy skinny-dipping.) Listen closely and you may hear the sound of an airplane flying overhead during this scene.

Henry Hathaway's focused direction, combined with tight acting on the part of almost everyone in the ensemble, lifts the material above the ordinary. Scott's natural charm helps offset his wooden delivery,

and he's convincing in a knock-'em-down fistfight with baddie Jack LaRue. Hathaway's constant close ups reveal that the actor wasn't using a stuntman this early in his career.

Scott almost becomes the first of the singing cowpokes in this film. "I could sing you a song," he innocently says to Ralston in an effort to impress her when she stops by his campfire at night (they don't realize they're from rival clans). "I think I'd like you better if you didn't," she says, which is worth a laugh. "You're a disturbing sort of gal," Scott replies by way of romancing her, and that's about as seductive as our guy gets.

The dialogue is sharp and to the point. "What does it matter if you're a Hayden or a Colby if a bullet gets you," says Muriel

Kirkland, playing Scott's sister Molly, who aspires to stop the feud. Grandma sees things differently when her son Mark wants to let the law handle matters: "It ain't honorable to take a family feud to court — they won't spill no blood for you."

LaRue is out of place as a dapper and dangerous dandy, a role George Raft probably would have played had this been an "A" production. Young Shirley Temple is adorable in her brief scenes as Barton Mac-Lane and Gail Patrick's daughter; she has a cute bit with a Shetland pony that provides the film with one of its few chuckles. John Carradine has a short, silent bit as Noah Beery's sidekick in an early scene.

Most of the Zane Greys are dark films. The killing goes on unabated until it becomes difficult to sympathize with either side, and you *can* see how a never-ending feud can never end. A particularly gruesome scene sees the Colbys shooting down Buster Crabbe's character and then fastening his prone, dead body to a horse so it appears as if he's riding into the ranch to join his family. A puppy is shot dead, Temple's doll gets its head blown off, the elder Haydens are callously blown to pieces; then almost everyone perishes in a climactic rock slide. Scott and LaRue survive, the former badly hurt. The finale sees Ralston fighting it out with LaRue in an effort to save the wounded Scott's life.

Hathaway on Temple: "A producer friend of mine recommended her. She came over and it was Shirley Temple. Four years old. And she was marvelous, a darling little thing, just as sweet as she could be, and I used her in the picture. I remember that there was something about the outlaws coming, and she was outside playing at a little table with a tea set on it, a little teapot and a sugar bowl, and she's got a little pony to play with. 'Would you have some tea?' And the pony came down and went over and started to smell the sugar and she slaps his nose and says, 'Get away,'

get away,' and he's still snuggling trying to get some sugar. So she stood up and pushed him and he did something and she kicked him, and he looked at her, turned around, went on two feet and with the two feet he kicked at her and missed her by about that far. Oh, Jeez, I was scared to death. And she stood there and she said, 'You ever do that to me again, I'll kick you.' I said, 'Didn't that scare you?' She said, 'Yes.' 'Well, you didn't stop.' She said, 'Oh, I wouldn't dare stop.'"

Ralston on Scott and the film (from her autobiography *Some Day We'll Laugh*): "What a lovely and charming man ... the only thing that bothered me was that no longer being a star, I had to walk by the beautiful dressing room I had once enjoyed, and was relegated to the 'also in the cast' dressing rooms."

Broken Dreams (Monogram, November 1933, 68 minutes)

CREDITS   Director: Robert Vignola; Producer: Ben Bershleiser; Story: Olga Pintzlau, adaptation by Maude Fulton

CAST   Randolph Scott (Dr. Robert Morley), Martha Sleeper (Martha Morley), Buster Phelps (Billy Morley), Joseph Cawthorn (Pop), Beryl Mercer (Mom), Adele St. Maur (Mademoiselle), Martin Burton (Paul)

Synopsis: Dr. Robert Morley turns his back on his newborn son after his wife dies during childbirth. Six years later the doc has a change of heart, causing grief for everyone.

Broken Dreams is not the sort of film that you'll want to shell out $14.99 for (on video, that is). It's a low-key, low-budget and often downbeat cheapie from Monogram, one of those studios that resided near the bottom of the studio food chain. The film eschews exposition in favor of economy, and to that end it takes only about four minutes in celluloid time for Scott's Dr. Morley to lose his wife, go on a

Beryl Mercer and Joseph Cawthorn try to reassure a bitter Scott in a Monogram "B" picture from 1933, *Broken Dreams*. (JC Archives, Inc.)

binge, serve four years as a doctor in Vienna, marry again and reunite with his long-lost son. The rest of this 68-minute long film deals with the ramifications of Scott's choice.

The film is melodramatic and cheap, but it's not dreadful. It manages to touch on compelling marital issues, like how children can first come between, and then later hold together, two people. I'm guessing Scott was either banished to Monogram by Paramount for some infraction or chose to slum at the studio in an effort to land a juicier role. Scott is not always up to the task of conveying grief or anger in the early scenes, but he tries to convey sincerity in a later scene where he tells his fiancée about his son. Nonetheless, it was a big mistake to let the actor play this important dramatic moment while sporting a goofy-looking child's party hat on his head. Nor can we feel much sympathy for Scott after he regains custody of the child and immediately tears him away from the surrogate parents. Worse, he dresses the confused kid up in a Little Lord Fauntleroy outfit, sticks him with a stern French tutor and forces a Chihuahua on him ("That's not a dog; that's a rat," the little boy sobs). At least the French tutor gets her comeuppance when a simian sidekick of the boy's jumps on her back.

The film could use more such comic relief. The child, Buster Phelps, is given a mischievous monkey and playful puppy as playmates, but these cuddly critters have little more than extended cameos. The dramatic subplots both thicken and sicken:

Scott's drunken pal makes a play for the doc's wife, little Billy suffers a concussion trying to save his mom from the would-be rapist, and the surrogate parents file a lawsuit to stop Scott from taking the boy away from them. There's enough plot here to feed *Days of Our Lives* with a year's worth of material.

Broken Dreams remains of interest to Scott fans who may enjoy seeing their hero take an acting risk so early in his career. Others should beware.

Variety (11/28/1933): "Scott hitherto has been used in Westerns. He's with Paramount but *Broken Dreams* gives a little better than a rough idea of what he can do outside of a saddle." *New York Mirror* (11/21/1933): "*Broken Dreams* is slightly feeble. The doctor is Randolph Scott, who has had a successful career in the movies riding herd on cattle and saving the ranch for the sheriff's daughter."

The Last Round-Up (Paramount, January 1934, 61 minutes)

CREDITS   Director: Henry Hathaway; Screenplay: Jack Cunningham, based on Zane Grey's novel *The Border Legion*
CAST   Randolph Scott (Jim Cleve), Barbara Fritchie (Joan Randall), Monte Blue (Jack Kells), Fuzzy Knight (Charles "Bunko" McGee), Fred Kohler (Sam Gulden), Richard Carle (Judge Savin), Barton MacLane (Charley Benson), Charles Middleton (Sheriff), Frank Rice (Shrimp), Dick Rush (Rush)

Synopsis: Cowpoke Jim Cleve is saved from a lynching by amiable outlaw Jack Kells. The innocent Westerner decides to join Kells' gang, falling for his pal's gal Joan in the process.

Any film that opens and closes with a passel of shootin' and ridin' gets my vote. *The Last Round-Up* is another solid Zane Grey effort from Paramount. Scott is the nominal hero here, ceding footage to Monte Blue's colorful outlaw character. The friendship between Scott's Jack Cleve and the criminal Jack Kells is at the cornerstone of this story, but there's room enough for considerable plot complications, such as Kells' antagonistic relationship with his second-in-command, played by Fred Kohler, and the love triangle between Scott, good-bad girl Barbara Fritchie and Blue.

The title actually comes from the then-popular cowboy song (words and music by Billy Hill), which is crooned early in the picture by a poker-faced cowboy in a smoky saloon. The facial reactions of the bar crowd are somberly memorable as they all take a moment to contemplate the lyrics and consider their own mortality — all except Scott, that is. Back to the camera and concentrating on the poker hand in front of him, he simply casts a glance towards the camera that suggests he's figuring to live forever!

The plot follows Scott as he loses his mining grubstake in a poker game before being accused of back-shooting an old miner. Blue saves Scott from a hanging and the latter eagerly joins Blue's gang of thieves. But when Kohler kidnaps Fritchie (whose Joan Randall character used to have a thing with Blue's Jack Kells), the sexual tension in camp rises to the boiling point.

Scott and Fuzzy Knight take part in a sexually tinged comic sequence wherein the luscious hostage Fritchie insists on taking a bath. Knight decides that one of the men has to stick around to watch her bathe just to make sure she doesn't run off, but the sexually savvy heroine doesn't cotton much to that. She doesn't make things easier on Knight when she snaps at him, "Hey, where's the soap?" before demanding more water for the tub. Knight fetches the *aqua* but then takes a delicious pratfall into the watery mix, apparently catching a glimpse of the bare bathing beauty along the way, which only makes matters worse.

The film advances the plot and builds characterization at the expense of action, but

A rather silly publicity photograph featuring Scott and Indian chieftain Monte Blue wrestling, from *Wagon Wheels* (1934). (JC Archives, Inc.)

it does end with a dandy scene when Blue and his men are ambushed in a mining camp. The smoky night-time duel that follows is a beauty. I won't give away anything else because there's still a lot of surprises between that gunfight and the final fade-out, but suffice to say *The Last Round-Up* is another gem of a "B," and Scott gives a winning low-key performance. It was the last Zane Grey "B" that Hathaway directed, although Scott would appear in three more and the studio kept grinding them out until at least 1940.

Hollywood Reporter (1/4/34): *"The Last Round-Up* is one of the best of the best Westerns. It packs a wallop that is high, wide and fancy."

Wagon Wheels (Paramount, September 1934, 56 minutes)

CREDITS   Director: Charles Barton; Screenplay: Jack Cunningham, Charles Logan and Carl A. Buss, based on Zane Grey's *Fighting Caravans*

CAST   Randolph Scott (Clint Belmet), Gail Patrick (Nancy Wellington), Billy Lee (Scott Wellington), Monte Blue (Murdock), Raymond Hatton (Jim Burch), Olin Howlin (Bill O'Meary), Jan Duggan (Abby Masters), Leila Bennett (Hetty Masters)

Synopsis: Clint Belmet and his comrades lead a wagon train to Oregon in 1844.

The first of some 75 films that Charles Barton would direct in a 30-year career, *Wagon Wheels* is an effective, action-filled programmer that moves quickly and jams a lot of plot and character into less than an hour's running time. The usual wagon train perils surface, but Scott also has to deal with a murderous half-breed, Murdock, who incites his Indian brothers (or half-brothers) to the warpath in an effort to stave off westward expansion. The final attack is solid enough, but obviously Barton wasn't as good as Henry Hathaway when it came to staging action scenes. He did, however, have an instinctive feel for comedy (he later directed several top-notch Abbott and Costello comedies) and imbued his actors with comic confidence. One particularly funny sequence has the mannish Abby Masters (Jan Duggan) singing a song about daisies to an exhausted and disinterested group of hardened pioneers. The deadpan looks that the men give one another as she continues to murder bar after bar of the song is priceless. Abby and her spinster sister Hetty later engage Scott's partners Burch and O'Meary in a conversation about the food supply.

> ABBY: What would happen if we ran out of food?
> BURCH: I knew a wagon train that ran out of food. They ate each other.
> HETTY: I don't believe it.
> O'MEARY: He oughta know — he's the sole survivor.

Gail Patrick was an engagingly beautiful but low-key actress whose career never quite took off. Billy Lee starts out so well in this film that he seems like an overlooked candidate for the *Our Gang* series, but he soon wears out his welcome with his over-the-top cuteness. And the business of his using a slingshot to hit rampaging redskins in the rear is a bit too much. (Margaret O'Brien would use a pea-shooter for similar purposes in a later Western, *Bad Bascomb*.)

New York Daily News (10/4/1934): "For the most part, the people are all out of stock, played in a pleasant conformist manner by Randolph Scott, Gail Patrick and small Billy Lee. It is a well-made, nicely photographed piece, written and directed with a lack of originality that will probably insure its success."

Home on the Range (Paramount, December 1934, 55 minutes)

CREDITS   Director: Arthur Jacobson; Producer: Harold Hurley; Screenplay: Ethel Doherty and Grant Garrett, based on Zane Grey's novel *Code of the West*

CAST   Randolph Scott (Tom Hatfield), Jackie Coogan (Jack Hatfield), Evelyn Brent (Georgie Haley), Dean Jagger (Boyd Thurman), Addison Richards (Beady Pierce), Fuzzy Knight ("Cracker" Williams), Ann Sheridan (Else Brownly), Allen Wood ("Flash" Roberts), Richard Carle (James Butts), Howard Wilson (Bill Morris), Philip Morris (Benson)

Synopsis: Ranching brothers Tom and Jack Hatfield work against all odds to overcome a treacherous trio who plan to take over their ranch and fix a race involving Jack and his horse Midnight.

In my book *Last of the Cowboy Heroes* I suggested that the 1948 Scott Western *Albuquerque* might be a "lost" film. I was wrong. So I'm a bit reluctant to state that *Home on the Range* is a lost film, but I couldn't find it, and it's one of only two Scott talking pictures that I couldn't track down (the other being *Women Men Marry*). *The American Film Institute Catalog* gives a fairly detailed synopsis of the film (noting that they didn't view a print), which sounds like a combination of race track melodrama and ranching intrigue. Jackie Coogan plays the jockey brother of Scott, who attempts to forestall the mortgage on the family ranch by winning the big race. Evelyn Brent and Ann Sheridan are a couple of bad dance hall girls tied in with a pair of murderous con men played by Dean Jagger and Addison Richards. Brent falls for Scott and turns on her double-dealing partners while Coogan wins the big race and saves the ranch. The film is the shortest, and reportedly the worst, of the Zane Grey Scott films.

In *The Overlook Film Encyclopedia: The Western*, Phil Hardy writes, "This is a typical racetrack melodrama unsurely transferred to the range. The movie is a lackluster semi–Western most notable for the early appearance of Sheridan as a nightclub entertainer and Scott's growing assurance as a leading man." Hardy credits Harold Shumate with the script; *The American Film Institute Catalog* says Ethel Doherty and Grant Garrett wrote it. Either way it's not supposed to be very good, which doesn't mean I don't want to see it. Incidentally, I contacted Phil Hardy to see if he knew how I could get a copy of the film, but he said he didn't know where a copy existed in the United States (he apparently saw his copy in Britain, so diehard Scott fans can travel there to track the film down if they want). I also wrote Diana Serra Cary, author of *Jackie Coogan, The World's Boy King: A Biography of Hollywood's Child Star*, to see if she had seen a print. No luck. If anyone out there has a print, let me know.

The film was ready for previews in October 1934 under the title *Code of the West*, but once Paramount got the rights to the song "Home on the Range," they pulled the film back for a few retakes and to change the title and incorporate the title song. Though released late in 1934, the film had a successful run into 1935, and many sources cite it as a 1935 release. Scott only had one Zane Grey "B" left to do— *Rocky Mountain Mystery*.

Hollywood Reporter (December 1934): "The story is so jerky, disconnected and freighted with clumsy wisecracks that a synopsis is beyond the prowess of this appraiser. Sympathy and congratulations should go to Scott. He makes the best of a bad deal and shows that he can take it."

Rocky Mountain Mystery, a.k.a. *The Fighting Westerner* (Paramount, March 1935, 63 minutes)

CREDITS Director: Charles Barton; Producer: Harold Hurley; Screenplay: Edward E. Patemore, Jr., based on Zane Grey's novel *Golden Dreams*

CAST Randolph Scott (Larry Sutton), Ann Sheridan (Rita Ballard), Charles "Chic" Sale (Tex Murdock), Mrs. Leslie Carter (Mrs. Borg), James C. Eagles (John Borg), George Marion, Sr. (James Ballard), Kathleen Burke (Flora Ballard), Howard Wilson (Fritz Ballard), Willie Fung (Ling Yat)

Synopsis: The Black Rat, a masked killer, terrorizes an isolated radium mine in Nevada.

An okay programmer, *Rocky Mountain Mystery* plays like an old dark house comedy, with a full quota of creaking doors, clutching hands and howling winds. Scott is a mining engineer who rides into an abandoned mountain town seeking his missing brother-in-law. What he finds are some ham and eggs on the grill and a corpse in bed. While this is a wonderfully filmed set-up scene, little else in the film lives up to this early promise of suspense, as the story relies on red herrings, conniving relatives and the unfrightening Black Rat to maintain viewer interest.

Fortunately, Scott has some comic relief in the form of deputy sheriff Tex Murdoch, the Barney Fife of the geriatric set. As played by Charles "Chic" Sale, Murdock is good for some laughs as he investigates the murders despite the fact that he's scared stiff. The sum total of his detecting skills is revealed in one sentence after reading a threatening note. "You can tell by the handwriting that the fellow who wrote this is a crook," he tells a dubious Scott.

Heroine Ann Sheridan is plump and pale, displaying little acting talent and none of the sensuous "oomph" that she would be associated with a few years later at Warner Bros. In 1966, shortly before her death, Sheridan told interviewer Ray Hagen that "Mr. Scott cast an eye on me. He was fond of me, and of course ended up kissing the horse, but at least it was the lead. I ran around in a pair of riding britches and a

Scott with a pre–"Oomph" Ann Sheridan in *Rocky Mountain Mystery* (1935), the actor's final Zane Grey Western for Paramount. (JC Archives, Inc.)

pair of boots and they'd say, 'Which way did they go?' and I'd say, 'That way!'" Actually, Sheridan's most memorable line is, "Gee, I hope nothing else happens"— right before something else happens.

The rest of the cast is made up of an odd mix of stage veterans, film newcomers and Paramount contract players. The climax is ridiculous but funny: The old coot of a deputy gives chase to an effete lad and an old lady, both of whom outrun him. Scott engages in a silly brawl with the sissy and an old, pudgy man (who flies backwards out of a window to his death in an unintentionally amusing bit). Scott and Sheridan catch the killer, marry and move to Hawaii to open up a pineapple ranch!

Maybe it's not such a good film after all, but *Rocky Mountain Mystery* is divert-

ing and certainly more humorous than any of the other Zane Greys of the period. It wasn't the best to go out on, but it wasn't the worst, and Scott later said he owed the whole series a debt for teaching him the business: "The work is hard, terribly hard," he told *The New York Post* in August 1937, when he was filming *High, Wide and Handsome*:

They usually make them in fourteen days; working all hands six days a week and on Sunday. You get up at 4 o'clock and work all day under a broiling sun … when the sun sets you have a brief recess for supper and then start making the interior scenes which keep you going until about midnight. So for fourteen days you get an average of about four hours sleep out of every 24. But I believe it is the finest training in the world. I worked in 15 [*sic*] of these films in two and a half years and I believe in that time I faced every obstacle that a film actor or production unit can find.

Roberta (RKO, March 1935, 106 minutes)

CREDITS   Director: William Seiter; Producer: Pandro S. Berman; Screenplay: Jane Murfin, Sam Mintz and Allan Scott, additional dialogue Glenn Tryon, based on the novel by Alice Duer Miller and the Broadway play *Roberta* by Otto Harbach and Jerome Kern

CAST   Irene Dunne (Stephanie), Fred Astaire (Huckleberry 'Huck' Haines), Ginger Rogers (Countess Scharwenka), Randolph Scott (John Kent), Helen Westley (Aunt Millie, 'Roberta'), Claire Dodd (Sophie), Victor Varconi (Laidslaw), Luis Alberni (Voyda)

Synopsis: John Kent, an American in Paris, inherits the swanky dress shop Roberta. Much song and dance then takes place.

Even those who don't like musicals will probably get a kick out of *Roberta*. It's an agreeable musical comedy bolstered by a lovely Jerome Kern score, including the songs "I Won't Dance" and "Smoke Gets in Your Eyes." While Scott has considerable footage as a dumb-ox American caught up in Paris society, he looks out of place in the world of cocktails, tuxedos and Jerome Kern. At one point, leaning against a chair in the salon and listening to the other players pontificate, Scott looks like he's anxious to strap on a six-gun and call them all out into the street. Scenarists Jane Murfin, Sam Mintz and Allan Scott either didn't pay enough attention to his character, or realized that since they had Astaire and Rogers they didn't *have* to pay enough attention, and therefore the actor is given inconsistent character traits: One moment he's a bumbling oaf; the next a stern puritan.

The story involves the usual musical comedy plot complications that occur when people pose as other people: Scott pretends to be the manager of Fred Astaire's band,

Ginger Rogers pretends to be a Polish countess, and a real Russian duke pretends to be a doorman. The film does have Astaire and Rogers to recommend it, and the dialogue, albeit quite corny, is sometimes amusing:

> GINGER: You can call me Tanka!
> FRED: Tanka!
> GINGER: You're welcome!

One amusing scene has Astaire and Scott taking French lessons from a oh-so-serious linguist, leading to considerable mayhem in his studio. I bet this scene was an inspiration for a similar musical number with Donald O'Connor and Gene Kelly in the classic musical *Singin' in the Rain* (1952). Likewise the two actors, who generate an easygoing straight man–comic chemistry, take part in a humorous scene wherein a local gossip columnist interviews them and then, judging by their improvised, far-fetched responses, declares them both insane!

In 1945 MGM bought the rights to the film with the plan of remaking it. They did so in 1952, calling it *Lovely to Look At* and casting Red Skelton in Scott's role. The RKO film was then dispatched to that never-never-land of cinema, where movies disappear for decades, before it resurfaced in the late 1970s. It's neither the best nor the worst of the Astaire-Rogers films, which means it's still pretty good. The film's budget was $750,000, and it earned a little more than twice that when released in March of 1935. Scott became both a friend and golfing partner to Astaire, which resulted in another teaming in *Follow the Fleet* (1936).

The New York Times (3/8/1935): "[A] bright and shimmering pleasure dome ... if there is a flaw in the photoplay, it is the unfortunate circumstance that Mr. Astaire and his excellent partner, Miss Rogers, cannot be dancing during every minute of it."

Village Tale (RKO, June 1935, 80 minutes)

CREDITS   Director: John Cromwell; Producer: David Hempstead; Screenplay by Allan Scott, from the novel by Phillip Strong

CAST   Randolph Scott (Slaughter Somerville), Kay Johnson (Janet Stevenson), Robert Barrat (Drury Stevenson), Arthur Hohl (Elmer Stevenson), Janet Beecher (Amy Somerville), Dorothy Burgess (Lulu Stevenson), Guinn Williams (Ben Roberts), Donald Meek (Charlie), Andy Clyde (Billy), Edward Ellis (Ike)

Synopsis: Mean-spirited backwoodsman Drury Stevenson prods his half-witted brother Elmer into action when he believes Elmer's wife Janet is having an affair with upper-class village resident Slaughter Somerville.

Shot in the early winter months of 1935, *Village Tale* is a touching, still-obscure melodrama about small-town gossip and hypocrisy. It comments on love, friendship and sacrifice, and does so without being too mawkish (most of the time). Kay Johnson plays a woman unhappily married to a slow-witted farmer, but she's really in love with Scott. Scott and Johnson give subdued performances while the rest of the ensemble deliver with more determined portrayals. Particularly good is Donald Meek's Charlie, a wisp of a man who has stores of inner courage and who pays a high price for his loyalty to Scott. Likewise, Guinn Williams, still playing a bit of a lunkhead (he manages to lose his girl to the train conductor who only comes through town for about a minute a day), nonetheless makes the station man a caring human being.

For Scott, the romantic lead in a loan-out film offered him an opportunity to step out of the "lead in B films, second lead in A films" rut he was in over at Paramount. Watching his performance under director John Cromwell, you can see how far he progressed from his juvenile lead days of 1933 (particularly *Broken Dreams*). He takes it

nice and easy and displays a sense of character and place throughout. He doesn't stint on the action scenes either, taking part in a one-on-one brawl with bad guy Robert Barrat, and working with Williams to break up a chivvy (an annoyingly persistent attack with harsh musical instruments) by knocking out the dozen or so townsmen who are harassing Johnson.

Cromwell, another studio director who has remained in the shadow of greater talents, had just delivered a commercial and critical hit for RKO with 1934's *Of Human Bondage*, so it wasn't hard for the studio to give him what he wanted when it came to casting *Village Tale*. What he wanted was his wife Kay Johnson and Randolph Scott. But RKO screenwriter Allan Scott wasn't overly impressed with the script, the source material or the casting, as he related some 30 years later in the book *Backstory 1: Interviews with Screenwriters of Hollywood's Golden Age*. According to Scott, RKO producer Pandro Berman gave him a screenplay already written by Marc Connelly based on the 1934 novel *Village Tale* by Phillip Strong. "It was second rate, but it was popular," Scott recalled. He went to work rewriting the piece. "Pandro liked it and suddenly, out of nowhere, John Cromwell, who was one of our star directors, liked it. Cromwell persuaded Kay Johnson (his wife) and Randolph Scott (a rising movie star who was probably the last of the period Arrow-Shirt type heroes) to be in it."

Scott — that is, Allan — didn't care for Scott — that is, Randolph: "I felt during this picture that Randolph was at a big loss without his horse. And can you imagine writing anything (except possibly for his horse) for Randolph Scott? In fact the end of the horse had more warmth and geniality than poor old Randy himself."

Allan Scott is being hard on Randolph Scott. Though some viewers found Scott to be stiff (he is), he is more relaxed and

An angry-looking Scott with Kay Johnson in *Village Tale* (1935), an overlooked soap opera from RKO.

confident than he'd been up to this point. Perhaps the actor, a shy man, was doubly reticent and hard to get to know on the set of a foreign studio. Likewise, the actor later acknowledged that he had a hard time playing romantic scenes opposite Johnson because her husband was on the set directing.

Reviews were positive. "*Village Tale* ... reveals again director John Cromwell's mastery of moods and is terrifying even when it is funny," wrote Philip K. Scheuer in *The Los Angeles Times* (6/28/1935). "Scott has never been better although there is a stiffness in his playing. *Village Tale*, although it stops this side of perfection, will make you grit your teeth more than once. It is strong stuff."

Some 40 years later, William K. Ever-son, writing a mini-review on the film, called it "powerful and honest; the unsympathetic characters are bitchy and narrow rather than evil and the good characters often act with weakness and stupidity. Melodrama may rather take over towards the end, but we seem to be finding increasingly that life *is* full of melodrama."

Allan Scott remained contrite about the film. "I got one fan letter," he said. "It read, 'This is the stuff to feed the troops.' It was signed by Eugene O'Neill."

The RKO studio files, housed at UCLA, reveal that the film was shot in 35 days at Sherwood Lake, about 400 miles from the RKO studio. There is no record of what Scott earned on this one, but Paramount must have profited from the loan-out.

She (RKO, July 1935, 94 minutes)

CREDITS   Directors: Irving Pichel and Lansing C. Holden; Producer: Merian C. Cooper; Screenplay by Ruth Rose; adaptation from the novel by H. Rider Haggard; Additional dialogue: Dudley Nichol

CAST   Helen Gahagan (She), Randolph Scott (Leo Vincey), Helen Mack (Tanya Dugmore), Nigel Bruce (Horace Holly), Samuel S. Hinds (John Vincey), Lumsden Hare (Dugmore), Jim Thorpe (Captain of the Guard), Noble Johnson (Amahaggar Chief), Ray Corrigan (Guard)

Synopsis: American adventurer Leo Vincey joins family friend Horace Holly on an Arctic expedition to find a legendary flame of life.

Outlandish fun, *She* is a minor classic of the 1930s. It takes some liberties with Sir Henry Rider Haggard's 1887 novel in that it transplants the actions to the Arctic, when in fact the novel is set in the steamy East African jungle. Perhaps producer Merian C. Cooper and RKO did this in an effort to avoid repetition of set pieces from their earlier jungle horror classics, *The Most Dangerous Game* (1932) and *King Kong* (1933). Nonetheless the great double-door that Kong crashed through in the latter film is put to good use in *She*, and other sequences—particularly a climactic chase over a mountain gorge—suggest a *King Kong* influence.

The film opens with implausible and extensive exposition regarding the history of the legendary flame of life. Scott is passed off as an Englishman from the part of the family "that went American," and he listens rather calmly as his dying uncle (Samuel S. Hinds) tells a far-fetched tale of the flame's history before the oldster acknowledges that his impending death is the result of years of efforts trying to recreate the flame of life in his own lab! (He didn't have the ingredients or nothing.) "It's all so mysterious it doesn't make sense," Scott accurately notes. The old guy kicks off quickly after telling Scott that one of his ancestors, explorer John Vincey, found the flame just before his death.

Scott and his companion Holly (Nigel Bruce) take off on an Arctic expedition to find the flame. A title card tells us that they've been at it for months when they happen upon Tanya, an orphan (Helen Mack), who was, according to her story, brought up in a Russian convent. So far all of this is rather absurdly presented, but the production values are top-notch and the Arctic scenes are mounted with conviction and superb miniature work. To their credit, Scott and Bruce throw themselves into their work like a couple of schoolboys playing "expedition" in their backyards. An impressive avalanche follows suit, opening a pass to a secret world.

Up to this point the film moves along briskly and offers several horrific scenes, including the discovery of a huge sabertooth tiger and its prey trapped in ice, and the death of Mack's no-good stepfather in an ice floe (his kicking, flailing and screaming body seems to fall forever into an Icelandic black hole). Things get more frightening and more amusing. Scott, Bruce and Mack happen upon a band of rather hungry-looking natives who sport perpetually demonic grins. "Don't judge them by their looks," the nonplussed Bruce says, "they're probably very friendly people." Friendly indeed—they can't wait to fit Bruce with a red-hot face mask. The native gang's interpretive dance towards the camera, with their mouths open in cannibalistic glee, is enough to send faint-hearted viewers scurrying for cover. "This doesn't look very good to me," Scott deadpans, and it *is* a funny line. Soon Scott and company are fighting a losing battle against the native horde. They are rescued by the palace guard, led by none other than Jim Thorpe, the Oklahoma Indian athlete who was disqualified from the Olympics when it was discovered that he had taken part in professional sports. Thorpe eked out a living

Scott looks like Helen Gahagan's manservant in this shot from *She* (1935). Fortunately, most of the film is much more exciting than this scene indicates. (JC Archives, Inc.)

in the 1930s in bit parts; here he has a meaty supporting role as She's right hand man, although he sounds suspiciously like Bela Lugosi.

Once inside the temple, our trio come across She (Helen Gahagan in her only film), who is about a thousand years old and believes Scott to be the reincarnated spirit of her former lover. After a too-long scene involving much romantic talk and problems resulting from a three-sided love triangle, the film races into a superb climax in which Scott rescues Mack from a sacrificial ritual and then flees from the pursuing guard through the palace and over a mountain pass. Gahagan heads them off at the pass, and offers Scott one last chance to join her in the flame of life. He is contemplating this option when Mack dares Ga-

hagan to test those flames herself. Gahagan bites at the bait, jumps into the flames and then does a Dorian Gray, aging rapidly to the shock of Scott and company. The sight of Gahagan's mummified remains shuffling towards Scott is enough to scare the pants off of any self-respecting 43-year old (I'm talking about myself) and I'm sure it terrified youngsters who saw the film back in 1935. True love prevails with Scott and Mack living happily ever after.

The acting is fairly good. Even when clad in goofy imperial attire, Gahagan, in a role intended for Greta Garbo, gives a credible performance as a woman torn by both her dependence on her flame and her love for a mortal man. This was Gahagan's only film appearance; in the 1940s she moved into politics and served two terms in the lower house of the U.S. Congress as a representative of California. In 1950 she made a bid for higher office and was defeated by none other than Richard Nixon. She died in 1980 at 80. As for Scott, given his propensity for remaining young, one can't help but wonder if the afterglow from that flame of life didn't shine on him just a little bit.

Haggard, who also penned *King Solomon's Mines* (1885) and *Allan Quatermain* (1887), moved to Africa at age 19 to work as the secretary to the governor of Natal. He ended up serving six years in government service in Africa, and based many of his works on his experiences there. A silent version of *She*, reportedly the most faithful, was made in Germany in 1925. Haggard wrote the title cards for that film; later that year he died at age 69. In 1965 Ursula Andress portrayed the title character in a Hammer Films remake with John Richardson playing Scott's part and Peter Cushing in Bruce's role. Incidentally, Haggard came up with the name for the title character from a rag doll he had as a child. My question is, what was Haggard doing playing with a girl's doll anyway?

"A gawdy, spectacular and generally fantastic photoplay," noted *The New York Times*, (7/26/1935). Robert Garland of *The New York World Telegram* (7/26/1935) wrote that the film garnered unintentional laughter at a New York screening, adding that it was "an out-and-out burlesque of H. Rider Haggard's best-seller … the acting, with Randolph Scott's exception, is none too desirable."

So Red the Rose (Paramount, December 1935, 82 minutes)

CREDITS   Director: King Vidor; Producer: Douglas MacLean; Screenplay: Lawrence Stallings, Maxwell Anderson and Edwin Justus Mayer, based on the novel by Stark Young
CAST   Margaret Sullavan (Valette Bedford), Walter Connolly (Malcolm Bedford), Randolph Scott (Duncan Bedford), Janet Beecher (Sally Bedford), Harry Ellerbe (Edward Bedford), Dickie Moore (Middleton Bedford), Elizabeth Patterson (Mary Cherry), Charles Starrett (George McGehee), Robert Cummings (Archie Pendleton), Daniel Haynes (William)

Synopsis: The decline of a noble Southern family, the Bedfords, in Mississippi during the Civil War.

A disappointing and ridiculously melodramatic failure of a film, *So Red the Rose* belongs to Sullavan, who was probably the strongest actress to play opposite Scott. Here she portrays a "flower of the Old South," who pushes Scott into the war and then regrets what the conflict does to his persona. The story really revolves around the women in the Bedford family, who are left behind on their Mississippi plantation (named Portabello, which made me wonder whether they raised mushrooms rather than cotton) after all their men folk go off to war. The women have to contend with Yankee raiders, a slave revolt, destruction and death. None of this is compelling, due to an erratic script that King Vidor's steady direction could not balance.

Scott has some effective sequences early in the film as a Southerner educated in the North who doesn't want to see the country divided by bloodshed. "I don't believe Americans should fight Americans," he tells hotblooded George McGehee (Charles Starrett in his pre–Durango Kid days). "I can't kill another American just because he's wearing a different uniform." A series of events, including the battlefield death of Sullavan's brother (played indifferently by Harry Ellerbe), leads Scott to change his mind, and he takes part in a brief but affecting film scene when he rushes into his first battle, letting out a war cry and a rifle shot despite his obvious fear. Otherwise the script eschews action, which is unfortunate. It could have used some thrilling battle scenes on the scale of Vidor's silent classic *The Big Parade* (1925).

It doesn't help that the script suggests that the entire war took place in the backyard of the Bedford plantation. After Bedford matriarch Sally (Janet Beecher) hears psychic calls for help from her son, she simply hops into a carriage and trots off to a nearby battlefield where she finds his dead body. There are a lot of scenes of Yankees coming in one door of the mansion and then out the other as Confederates chase them, and visa versa — the sort of thing that must have happened in real life but that nonetheless make the film look like a vaudeville turn at times. And *So Red the Rose* perpetrates the then-common racial stereotypes of blacks. With the exception of one noble, loyal servant (played by Daniel Haynes), the servants are seen as lusty, greedy, disloyal, savage or, at best, simpleminded, hymn-singing layabouts. Even when the black characters are treated with humor, it's insulting, as when Sullavan jokingly suggests to Scott that they shoot a young black boy who has a splinter in his foot because he's no longer any use to the plantation. These scenes would be hard to cut out or downplay while maintaining continuity for television showings, which is probably one reason the film has fallen into cinematic obscurity.

The film ends on a disappointingly absurd note: Sullavan, having not seen Scott in some time, hears his voice calling to her through the trees of a nearby forest. She rushes down to the creek to find him standing on the other side. As they rush to each other across a footbridge, he says, "I've been in military prison." Sullavan responds, "Oh, darling," and they embrace. Fade out and THE END.

Scott and Sullavan exude a pleasant warmth with each other but it's hardly romantic or sensual. The actress couldn't fathom why Scott didn't respond to her, onscreen or off, complaining to Vidor, "He's such a sexy-looking guy! What the hell's the matter with him?" Onscreen, the fault lies in the script, for the scenario barely gives the duo time to build a romance let along maintain one, and Sullavan is saddled with such clichéd lines as, "Come back to me alive — I'll be waiting for you." Offscreen, Vidor suggested Sullavan take Scott into her dressing room for one-on-one instruction, leading Sullavan's husband William Wyler to suspect the two were carrying on. Maybe they were, for Sullavan came away from it all liking Scott but hardly respecting him. "God, the man's an ignoramus!" she told Vidor, though one wonders what sort of conversation she was trying to engage him in, for Scott certainly knew his politics, world affairs and finances. (On the other hand, that does sound dull, doesn't it?) Scott tried to explain to a *Modern Screen* magazine writer that he was intimidated by Sullavan: "Maggie's so much more talented than I am that she gets me plain nervous." Vidor later said that Sullavan had the unfortunate tendency to tell other actors how to read their lines, which true novices like Robert Cummings (animated as a Texan fop) and Johnny Downs may have tolerated but which may have thrown Scott off-balance. During production Sullavan supposedly engaged in affairs with Cummings, Downs, Starrett *and* Scott. No wonder Wyler was suspicious!

Vidor liked Sullavan's unpretentious manners. "She rode her motorcycle to work every day," author Lawrence J. Quirk quotes Vidor as saying in the book *Child of Fate: Margaret Sullavan.* "Blue jeans were not the 'in' thing then, but that's what she usually wore. She was playing a Southern Belle and of course all the dresses of the period had full skirts and petticoats; so when she had close-ups, she'd come out on the set with her hair all done and her blue jeans on. It was hilarious."

Vidor later had little to say about Scott, but then again maybe nobody really asked him penetrating questions about the actor. When Nancy Dowd and David Shep-

A family portrait from Paramount's prestigious 1935 Civil War drama *So Red the Rose*, with Walter Connolly, Randolph Scott, Elizabeth Patterson, Margaret Sullavan and Janet Beecher. (JC Archives, Inc.)

ard interviewed Vidor for the book *King Vidor: A Directors Guild of America Oral History*, the only thing they could think to say to the director about the Southern gentleman was, "Randolph Scott is certainly good-looking in this film," to which Vidor responded, "Yes, he was. It was in the era in which most leading men were good-looking. Today, none of them are good-looking."

Shot in the spring of 1935 near Malibu Lake, *So Red the Rose*, based on Stark Young's novel, opened at the end of the year to good reviews but so-so box office returns. The film's unbalanced story line and lack of action probably worked to diminish its appeal, despite the star power of Sullavan and Scott. *The New York Eve-*

ning Journal (11/27/1935) found the film a "genuinely affecting story of the Civil War days; Vidor has handled the sequence of events with exceptional skill." *The New York American* (11/29/1935) liked Scott's work, stating that he was "splendid as the unwilling soldier," while *The Brooklyn Daily Eagle* (12/18/1935) went further, writing that "Scott contributes more than anyone else in the cast to giving the picture the punch of reality." He was finally beginning to garner some decent reviews for his acting, which remained natural and low-key if sometimes stilted. For his work in the film, Scott was awarded the Southern Cross of Honor by the United Daughters of the Confederacy. The South must have loved Scott's films; think of how often he portrayed the gallant Confederate soldier.

Young, incidentally, was the Mississippi-born son of a Civil War veteran who managed to transcend various creative fields with his writing: He was a playwright, novelist, drama critic and journalist, and in 1951 he published his autobiography, *The Pavilion*. His novel *So Red the Rose* focuses much more on the McGehee character played by Starrett than it did on the Duncan Bedford (Scott) character. In any event, while *So Red the Rose* remains necessary viewing for Scott fans, it's not a good film.

Four years after the making of *So Red the Rose*, *Gone with the Wind* was released. Reportedly Sullavan wanted the role of Scarlett O'Hara while Scott lobbied to be cast as Ashley Wilkes. Yet with the exception of *Variety*'s 1987 obituary of Scott, I could find little evidence that Scott was even considered for the role, either in biographies of author Margaret Mitchell or in any of the many *Gone with the Wind* history books. Only one of these books, William Pratt's *Scarlett Fever: The Ultimate Pictorial Treasury of "Gone with the Wind,"* mentions Scott at all: "It was generally agreed that *So Red the Rose* had put a permanent damper on ideas of using either Miss Sullavan or her co-star Randolph Scott." Maybe so, but Vidor, who stayed in touch with Scott for some time, later commented, "Randy Scott was sorry not to have landed the role of Ashley Wilkes. He would have been better than Leslie Howard was, I always felt. For one thing he was an authentic Southerner by birth, whereas Howard was English. And certainly he was a younger man and looked more like the matinee-idol type who would have won Scarlett's love. Of course, Howard could act circles around Randy, but Randy *looked* the part, and his chemistry was right."

Shortly after *So Red the Rose* was released, Scott appeared in the MGM Technicolor short *Pirate Party on Catalina Is-* land, along with his pal Cary Grant and colleagues Charles "Buddy" Rogers, Virginia Bruce, Marion Davies, Errol Flynn and his wife Lil Damita, Chester Morris and Mickey Rooney. The film is fun to watch just for its "spot the star" novelty, but it plays as little more than a home movie set on Catalina Island, spliced together in pseudo-narrative form by writer-director Gene Burdette.

Follow the Fleet (RKO, February 1936, 110 minutes)

CREDITS   Director: Mark Sandrich; Producer: Pandro S. Berman; Music & Lyrics by Irving Berlin; Screenplay by Dwight Taylor and Allan Scott; adapted from the stage play *Shore Leave* by Hubert Osborne; Dances by Hermes Pan

CAST   Fred Astaire (Bake Baker), Ginger Rogers (Sherry Martin), Randolph Scott (Bill Smith), Harriet Hilliard (Connie Martin), Astrid Allwin (Irene Manning), Lucille Ball (Kitty Collins)

Synopsis: Sailor Bake Baker (Astaire) attempts to get ex–dancing partner Sherry Martin (Ginger Rogers) back into his arms and on her feet while lone wolf Bill Smith (Scott) tries to resist falling in love with Sherry's virginal sister Connie (Harriet Hilliard).

Follow the Fleet is a good Astaire-Rogers musical that opens with "We Saw the Sea," an amusing song and dance number performed by Fred Astaire and company.

This was the work of song genius Irving Berlin, who had also written songs for the previous Astaire-Rogers film *Top Hat*. Berlin's tuneful score for this film includes the standards "Let Yourself Go," "Let's Face the Music and Dance" and "I'm Putting All My Eggs in One Basket." The film turned out to be the second most financially successful Astaire-Rogers film, following *Top Hat*.

Fans of classic musicals are bound to enjoy *Follow the Fleet*, which is lightweight

Hump and dump 'em sailor Randolph Scott romances virginal Harriet Hilliard (later Harriet Nelson) in the Astaire-Rogers musical *Follow the Fleet* (1936).

nonsense about two gobs and two girls. Randolph Scott fans have to accept the fact that their hero plays second fiddle to the Astaire-Rogers plotline. Playing a brawny brute of a man, Scott instills his character with ape-like physicality, playing a full-fledged wolf for the only time in his career. Basically he humps and dumps the women, which sets off a mini-crisis when he gets involved with the ever-pure Harriet Hilliard (later Harriet Nelson, mother of Ricky and spouse of Ozzie). Scott, who spouts such lines as "Full steam ahead" while trying to seduce women, gets to do a few double-takes and make Moe Howard–like grimaces at Astaire in one comic sequence, but otherwise it's a relatively straight forward portrayal of a girl-happy sailor. He's clearly not quite at home in the musical world of Astaire and Rogers. Most critics felt the secondary love story was bland, and they may have been right.

The film is fun to watch in terms of spotting up-and-coming talent, including Betty Grable, Tony Martin and Lucille Ball. Ball, as Ginger's gum-chewing blonde bimbo pal, garners a few laughs with some one-liners and double takes, and her potential did not go unnoticed by film-goers. One preview card read, "You might give the tall gum-chewing blonde more parts and see if she can't make the grade — a good gamble." But RKO wasn't about to listen to one starry-eyed patron, and Ball was wasted, more or less, at the studio for another five years before she switched over to MGM, who also wasted her for five years but paid her more money. In the late 1950s, Ball and husband Desi Arnaz would buy RKO and turn it into Desilu Studios. The joke was on somebody.

Other points of interest include an adorable capuchin monkey in a sailor suit who engages in antics, and the memorable introductory shot of Rogers' character, clad in tight glossy dance pants and bent over, back to camera, in an effort to find a pair of shoes in her closet. Director Sandrich allowed the cameraman to linger on Rogers' delectable rump for some time, and one can only imagine what racy thoughts Depression-era men had in their minds while enjoying this revealing pose.

Noteworthy dialogue:

ASTAIRE TO SCOTT (who is about to arrest his shipmate for desertion right before

the curtain goes up on Astaire's new show): The show must go on!
SCOTT: Why?

Eight years later the line would be appropriated for another Scott film, *Belle of the Yukon*, with Gypsy Rose Lee delivering the punch line.

Production Code representative Albert M. Persoff wrote the studio (in a memo dated 9/13/1934) that the script looked like it would pass the censors if RKO toned down the suggestive comedy sequences, including the one involving Scott, Astaire and Astrid Allwin set in a bedroom. Persoff suggested they move the scene into the living room, "with a couch used for the comedy prop" instead of a bed. What was wrong with those censorship people? Didn't they realize that a couch just isn't as funny as a bed?

Scott was paid $1,000 a week for his work in the film, which started production Halloween, 1935. He finished up at mid day on New Year's Eve; the daily production log shows that on some days he had worked from 9 A.M. until nearly midnight, while on other days he only put in a couple of hours at most. He got an incredible week-long break from filming in mid–December and probably went golfing a lot during that time.

In his autobiography *Steps in Time* (1959), Astaire recalled a stunt mishap on the set: "I had a scene with Randy Scott where I was supposed to hit him for some reason or other. I hadn't had much experience with fight scenes and it was explained to me how to hit at Randy, but of course just miss him, and it would come off on the screen as if I had nailed him.

"When the time came for me to swing, I got carried away and brought one way up from my shoe laces that really clipped Randy on the mouth, bringing blood and almost flooring him. The 'Sheriff' had every reason to be annoyed with me but if he was he never showed it. Always the Southern gentleman."

New York Evening Post (2/21/1936): "Not their [Astaire & Rogers] best picture but is far ahead of the average screen musical."

And Sudden Death (Paramount, July 1936, 67 minutes)

CREDITS   Director: Charles Barton; Producer: A.M. Botsford; Screenplay by Joseph Moncure March, from a story by Theodore Reeves and Madeleine Ruthvan

CAST   Randolph Scott (Lt. James Knox), Frances Drake (Betty Winslow), Tom Brown (Jackie Winslow), Billy Lee (Bobby Sanborn), Fuzzy Knight (Steve Bartlett), Terry Walker (Bango), Porter Hall (District Attorney), Charles Quigley (Mike Andrews), Joseph Sawyer (Sgt. Sanborn), Jimmy Conlin (Mr. Tweets)

Synopsis: Traffic officer James Knox tries to cut down on reckless driving but falls for socialite Betty Winslow, who has taken the rap for her brother when the latter kills a child in a drunk-driving accident.

A real stinker that should have put an end to the careers of everyone involved, *And Sudden Death* seems like ripe material for Ed Wood, Jr., and one almost wishes that Wood's pal Criswell were narrating the whole thing from his coffin. There's little good to say about the film — aside from the fact that it is well-meaning — but there's some fun to be had in touching upon the many absurdities that pop up in the script.

For example: To discourage reckless driving, Scott's Knox character orders his men to paint a skull and crossbones on the site of every car accident. Then, to get his miscreant driving students to realize that death drives a car too, he shows them a training film that opens with World War I battle footage. He tells them that car accidents affect 36,000 victims a year. "In every one of those accidents, at least one person was killed — and it might have been you!" he sternly admonishes his shell-shocked

class. The poor dupes are in for more horrors. Knox gives one wise guy student his revolver, then ties a blindfold around the fellow's eyes and spins him repeatedly in his swivel chair. Then he urges the blind guy to fire the gun into the class to prove that the man doesn't know where his classmates are sitting. The guinea pig declines, but Knox has more shocks in store for his hapless students. He takes the entire class to the local mortuary where they are forced to view corpses and grieving mourners. "It sort of gets you," one traffic violator says before rushing out to vomit. Betty Winslow (Drake), forced to take the class after a speeding violation, says, "It's awfully silly of me but I feel faint," before inviting Knox to a society barbecue. He accepts, and more unintentionally funny nonsense follows.

Knox has a fellow officer drive him to Miss Winslow's shindig (taxpayer money is footing *that* bill, I guess). En route, the duo come across Winslow, whose car has broken down. Scott offers to help restart her car just as a speeding car flies by. Knox orders his driver to take chase after the speeder while he remains behind with Winslow. The two begin casually walking along the road to God-knows-where. They come across a model home and enter it, and for a few moments the film veers into screwball territory (appropriately whimsical music plays on soundtrack). They rearrange the furniture in the house for laughs, and when the realtor, one Mr. Tweets, comes by, he surprises them by telling them the place never looked better.

The two return to Miss Winslow's car — now inexplicably working — and take off, only to be forestalled by a flat tire. They make it to the barbecue just in time to find the party gang, all liquored up, heading out to yet another party. Winslow gets into a car which her drunken brother Jack (Tom Brown) is driving. Jack plows into a passing school bus, killing a child. The boy happens to be the son of the police

Scott lighting up, with Frances Drake, in *And Sudden Death* (1936), a "B" stinker worthy of the talents of Ed Wood, Jr.

sergeant (Joe Sawyer) who first brought Betty in for speeding. She takes the rap for her brother and is sent to women's prison, and the only thing missing from this dark sequence is a good shower room scene. Knox, sensing something is amiss with her story, begins investigating. He comes across a police lab photo showing a cigarette with lipstick on it in the car's passenger seat ashtray, which is enough evidence for him to surmise that Betty wasn't driving. He confronts her brother, who runs away and leads Knox on a wild car chase through city streets which ends when Jack smashes into a post. As Jack lies dying in the hospital, Knox convinces a nurse — who has never been seen before this moment — to impersonate Jack's sister in an effort to exact a deathbed confession.

Jack 'fesses up and kicks off; Betty is freed and she and the heroic traffic officer marry. They buy Mr. Tweets' house, vowing never to rearrange the furniture again. Fade out.

And Sudden Death really is dreadful. In a year in which Paramount was giving Scott some good opportunities — including a loan-out for *Last of the Mohicans* — it's baffling as to why he got stuck in this turkey. Paramount saw it as a major contribution to society. The ads proclaimed it as "A Dramatic Expose of Today's Biggest Problem — Death on the Road!" and traffic judges around the country used the film as a training tool. In Brooklyn, New York, one Judge Sabbatino ordered traffic violator William Tenant, who made an illegal U-turn and nearly crushed a police officer, to see the film. "Have you ever been in a morgue?" the judge asked Tenant, who was, according to the *New York American* newspaper article on the incident, properly chastised. *To-Day's Cinema* reported in September 1936 that Judge Frank Yuse was offering to cut 30-day sentences for drunk driving in half if defendants agreed to see the film. "We ourselves would gladly see the Paramount epic without any such inducement," the magazine editorial went on — a boast to be regretted later, I'm sure.

The critics' response was mixed, with *Variety* (7/22/1936) panning the film but praising Scott: "Randolph Scott gives a creditable performance as the crusading traffic officer, doing one of the few life-like interpretations in the script." Irene Thirer of the *New York Evening Post* (7/18/1936) must have been paid off to write that the film "packs a terrific wallop." *The London Times* (8/10/1936) said, "American methods of educating motorists seem much more thorough than our own, and although the film, as a film, has little to recommend it, the film, as propaganda, has quite a lot. Its intentions are admirable."

On a personal note, Scott's father died during the filming of *And Sudden Death*.

Last of the Mohicans (United Artists, September 1936, 91 minutes)

CREDITS   Director: George B. Seitz; Producer: Edward Small; Screenplay: Phillip Dunne, based on the novel by James Fenimore Cooper

CAST   Randolph Scott (Hawkeye), Binnie Barnes (Alice), Heather Angel (Cora), Bruce Cabot (Magua), Henry Wilcoxon (Major Duncan Haywood), Hugh Buckler (Col. Munro), Phillip Reed (Uncas), Robert Barrat (Chingachgook), Willard Robertson (Capt. Winthrop)

Synopsis: During the French and Indian War (1757, to be exact), scout Hawkeye and his two Mohican companions find themselves protecting the two daughters of British commander Col. Munro from Huron enemies.

I suppose film historians would argue that *Last of the Mohicans* is not nearly as good a film as the two Astaire-Rogers musicals that Scott appeared in, but in my view this is the best thing Scott did in the 1930s. As an action hero, he's superb, and his enjoyment in playing the role shines through in every scene. It's as if producer Edward Small and director George B. Seitz gave the actor permission to play. Away from his home lot and with a script that had "Made for Randolph Scott" stamped on it, Scott went all out, displaying confidence and tight comic timing. If not his best all-around film, it certainly is one of his best acting roles, and makes up for a lot of the dreck he did during the decade.

The New Jersey–born James Fenimore Cooper wrote over 30 novels, the best of which is probably *Last of the Mohicans* (1826). The film takes considerable leeway with Cooper's book (which, frankly, I haven't read since I was a young teenager) in that it downplays the issues of racism (Cora's mother, in the book, has Negro blood in her) and pretty much eliminates the character of the folk singer Gamet (in the film, he is reduced to a cameo). It also alters the ending, which sees Cora killed by a Huron; Uncas killed by Magua; and Magua forced to jump off of a cliff to escape capture. In the film, Uncas is killed by Magua and his men, Cora jumps off the cliff to avoid being raped by Magua, and Magua is killed by Chingachgook. Likewise, there is no hint of a romance between Hawkeye and Alice in the novel, though the film flirts with this idea.

All that said, *Last of the Mohicans* remains loyal to Cooper's intent, and is a good action film in its own right. Scott's Hawkeye is the man of the hour *every* hour, constantly showing up at just the last moment to right things or shoot a rampaging Huron or throw caustic barbs at his rival, Major Heywood (Wilcoxon, who was married to actress Heather Angel at the time). Asked by the major why he hasn't enlisted in the British Army, Hawkeye smiles and replies, "I've got too much sense to wear a red coat in the woods." Later still, as Wilcoxon and Scott prepare to enter a Huron camp in an effort to free the female hostages, Wilcoxon asks Scott of the braves, "Any of them know you?" "Only at shootin' range," Scott answers.

Seitz did a great job with the action scenes, maintaining suspense with canoe chases, Huron attacks and the siege on Fort William Henry. Seitz's direction is so deft and effective here that it makes me wonder what he could have done with a film about the Alamo. Also memorable is a horrifying scene where the Hurons break ranks from the French to attack the unarmed British prisoners. In real life this event was even more terrifying, with the lusty blood-mad Indians chopping the British soldiers to pieces. Scott shows off his physical prowess in this scene by lifting up an extra playing a Huron and throwing him into a crowd.

Loud, bloody and violent, *Last of the Mohicans* is required viewing for any Scott fan. I like the 1992 remake with Daniel Day-Lewis well enough, but prefer this one for it's 'get-to-the-point' attitude. Even the studio-bound scenes are done with panache, and the film rarely gives viewers a chance to catch their breath.

Scenarist Phillip Dunne wasn't happy with what United Artists did to his original screenplay. "Eddie Small, the producer, had succeeded in turning our authentic 18th Century piece into a third-rate Western," Dunne recounted in his autobiography, *Take Two: A Life in Movies and Politics*. "The characters even spoke to each other in Twentieth-Century colloquiums, and each had been rendered banal beyond belief." Anxious to avoid further desecrating of his script, Dunne volunteered to go on the set to doctor the script as per Small's

wishes. "The best I could do was rescue our poor Mohicans from total illiteracy," Dunne wrote. "At least Colonel Munro didn't tell Hawkeye, 'I'll contact you next week,' nor did Randolph Scott as Hawkeye say to Magua, 'You thinkin' of startin' somepin'?'" I think Dunne was being hard on the finished product, but suspect he did write a much more literal (meaning, perhaps, a less exciting) screenplay.

The studio's study guide to the screen version is a hoot to read. The guide starts out praising Cooper and then turns on him, criticizing his writing: "Of all the early writers he [Cooper] was the most truly and consistently American. Cooper is a great story-teller; some of his tales may be dull in places, but the interesting adventures soon immerse us again in the story. His English is chronically bad; slovenly, confused, involved, the second part of his sentences sometimes seem to have forgotten the first part." (I think the writer of this phrase must have taken some lessons from Cooper.) Under the sub-title "The North American Indian," the study guide confidently states, "The Indian cannot be pigeonholed under one type, but is as full of contradictions as all humanity. He has hard and stern features stamped by Nature. Ambition, revenge, envy and jealousy are his ruling passions. A wild love of liberty and an utter intolerance of control lie at the basis of his character. Treacherous himself, he is always suspicious of treachery in others. He is trained to conceal passion, not subdue it." I hope this guide was never used for arts education purposes in the public school system.

Edward P. Lambert, research consultant for Small's Reliance Pictures, made a detailed study of the fine art of scalping and released his findings to the press. His three-part approach went like this: grasp your left hand on your adversary's hair, pass the knife in your right hand around the head, cut a swath through the skin as

A pen-and-ink portraiture of Scott, Binnie Barnes and Henry Wilcoxon used for a 1940s reissue of the 1936 action classic *Last of the Mohicans.*

large as a palm, and then give the hair a good yank away from the skull. Afterwards, hang and dry the scalp for use as an ornament. One can only imagine what sort of bloodshed Lambert's conclusions lead

to on the playgrounds of American elementary schools in the autumn of 1936.

Just as embarrassing to the Indian extras in the film was a story by the *New York World-Telegram*'s Paul Harrison, which reported that between them, a mixed band of Sioux, Comanche, Utes, Osages, Cherokees and Blackfeet couldn't make a campfire for the film. A Boy Scout was hired to come in and show them how to do the job. Apparently these Indians caused Small and company considerable headaches when they refused to shave their heads for the usual $7.50 per day extra fee — but for another two bucks, they were happy to go nude up top.

The film was a big box office hit for United Artists, and gave Scott his first unqualified "A" picture success as a lead. For the record, the role of Alice was intended for Merle Oberon, but Binnie Barnes is quite good. She would work with Scott again in *Frontier Marshal* (1939).

London Times (10/4/1936): "Mr. Scott almost succeeds in making something human out of Hawkeye." *The New York Times* (9/3/1936): "Randolph Scott, we must admit, is our Hawkeye to the life." *New York Evening Journal* (9/3/1936): "Young Mr. Randolph Scott is properly dashing as the heroic Hawkeye." *New York Sun* (9/3/1936): "Randolph Scott, never outstanding for his acting ability, fits in exactly as the independent colonial scout."

Go West, Young Man (Paramount, November 1936, 80 minutes)

CREDITS   Director: Henry Hathaway; Producer: Emanuel Cohen; Screenplay: Mae West, based upon Lawrence Riley's play *Personal Appearance*

CAST   Mae West (Mavis Arden), Warren William (Morgan), Randolph Scott (Bud Norton), Lyle Talbot (Harrigan), Alice Brady (Mrs. Struthers), Isabel Jewell (Gladys), Elizabeth Patterson (Aunt Kate), Margaret Perry (Joyce), Nicodemus (Nicodemus), Johnny Indrisano (Chauffeur), Jack LaRue (Rico in the film-within-the-film)

Synopsis: Temperamental movie star Mavis Arden's car breaks down and she finds herself stuck in a hick town — but she comes to appreciate country living.

An interesting look at stardom, fandom and the power of the paparazzi, *Go West, Young Man* is pleasant but hardly prime Mae West. Much of the film's humor evolves out of things like off-screen crashes, pratfalls, tepid one-liners, malapropisms and watered-down sexual innuendo. The film's biggest fault is its failure to play up its "fish out of water" scenario. The play had been a big hit on Broadway for actress Gladys George, and MGM tried to buy the property for their platinum blonde siren, Jean Harlow. West, at the urging of producer Emanuel Cohen, bought the rights instead, and set about rearranging the script to showcase her own special talents. Even the title, which is misleading in that the whole thing takes place in rural Pennsylvania, is a play on West's name and reputation.

Director Henry Hathaway later said he wasn't enthused about the film. "Look, none of her pictures are very good — unless you like Mae West," he told Cohen. But he agreed to direct it and had considerable say in casting it, which included bringing in Randolph Scott, his old cowhand from the Rio Grande, to play an over-age virgin named Bud. Scott doesn't appear until about 30 minutes into the picture, and he only has one line of dialogue before the film is half-over, but he is okay as a mechanically inclined mulehead who can't figure out that West is coming on to him. At 38, Scott still projected a youthful innocence, but he really was too old for the role. At one point a character in the film refers to him as a cigar store wooden Indian, an appropriate comment on both his role in the film and his standing as a matinee idol at the time.

"Your interior is just as picturesque as your ulterior," West intones at one point, sounding as if her dialogue coach was Leo Gorcey. That's about as amusing as the one-liners get. According to Hathaway, the actress pretty much wrung most of the humor out of the scenario to prevent anyone else from getting laughs. "She called the shots—all of them," Hathaway said. "In many ways she was one of the smartest women I ever met, but she used her intelligence only to protect herself, her creation of this fabulous character—Mae West. Any direction I might have given her she regarded as demeaning. That is the reason she always gave exactly the same performance." Asked how Scott reacted to West's antics, the director replied, "Randolph Scott was always courteous, but she was not his kind of woman." The director had to put Scott in a hole whenever the actor had a two-shot with West due to their height difference.

"She's an amusing person to work with," Scott later said of West. "Tells grand stories to anyone who's a good audience. They told me she'd be difficult to work with. But I found her peaches and cream." West was perhaps easy to deal with because two of her then-current lovers, Johnny Indrisano and Jack LaRue, had small parts in the film. An amusing enough romp, *Go West, Young Man* is hardly the best showcase of Scott's talents. The film made money, needless to say, but it was the last profitable West picture for Paramount. The actress left Paramount shortly thereafter and made only a few films afterwards—none of which were very successful.

New York World-Telegram (11/19/1936): "The humorless yokel is played to perfection by Randolph Scott." *New York American* (11/19/1936): "It's always sex o'clock at the Paramount, and the Paramount is crowded! A typical Mae West picture." *The New York Post* (11/19/1936): "Judging from the crowds that packed into the Paramount the opening day, the Mae West act has not yet run its course. A wagon hitched to a star of sex always seems to be in for a long run."

High, Wide and Handsome (Paramount, July 1937, 113 minutes)

CREDITS   Director: Rouben Mamoulian; Producer: Arthur Hornblow, Jr.; Book & Lyrics by Oscar Hammerstein II; Music by Jerome Kern

CAST   Irene Dunne (Sally Waterson), Randolph Scott (Peter Cortlandt), Dorothy Lamour (Molly Fuller), Raymond Walburn (Doc Watterson), Charles Bickford (Red Scanlon), Alan Hale (Walter Brennan), William Frawley (Mac), Akim Tamiroff (Joe Varesi), Elizabeth Patterson (Grandma), Irving Pichel (Stark), Ben Blue (Zeke)

Synopsis: Peter Cortlandt discovers oil in rural Pennsylvania, leading to the loss of his wife Sally and a violent battle with big business for drilling rights.

"As a work of art the film is negligible, but as a musical comedy it is delightfully refreshing," wrote the critic for *The London Times* of *High, Wide and Handsome* in August 1937. I feel just the opposite about it. As a musical comedy, it doesn't hold up as well today—only one of the film's six songs is memorable—but as a film, it remains vastly entertaining and contains Scott's most ambitious performance. He takes chances in *High, Wide and Handsome* that he never took before (and, sad to say, would rarely take again), playing an animated, determined hero who becomes a rather single-minded, dark representative of capitalism. His Peter Cortlandt is not an entirely sympathetic character, and Scott, under the guidance of director Rouben Mamoulian, gave the role everything he had, screaming, clawing and nearly crying his way through the scenes in an effort to hold onto what he believes is his—the rights to an oil line. In doing so, he forsakes his wife and friends and leads them on a near-impossible mission to beat big business (in the form of Alan Hale, playing a character named Walter Brennan!).

The genesis for this film came from a reporter who came across the story of one E.L. Drake, who built the first oil drill on the bank of Oil Creek in Titusville,

Scott gave one of his most ambitious portrayals in the 1937 musical-drama *High, Wide and Handsome* (1937). Here he and Irene Dunne celebrate their characters' wedding day.

Pennsylvania, in 1859. The railroad companies wanted that oil and engaged in a spirited battle with the local farmers who rightfully felt the oil was theirs. The reporter wrote Jerome Kern and Oscar Hammerstein a letter suggesting they turn the story into an operetta, and the duo began working on the project in the summer of 1936. Paramount cast actress Irene Dunne, fresh from her success in both the stage and screen versions of *Showboat*, as Sally, the daughter of a traveling medicine show hawker (Raymond Walburn, delightful even though he always gives the same performance no matter what character he's playing), who falls for Scott's prim and pure Peter.

Sally becomes disillusioned after Peter discovers oil and begins working full-time to ensure that the oil remains the property of his neighbors and friends, despite the nefarious efforts of the evil railroad magnate Brennan (Hale) and his henchman Red Scanlon (Bickford, nastier than ever). Sally loses Peter and watches as Brennan and Red team up to sabotage his oil wells and lines. His friends turn against him, choosing to sell out one by one to the bad guys. Peter is forced to conspire with the greasy saloon owner Varesi (Tamiroff), selling off some of his holdings to stay afloat. Lamour, playing a tart named Molly, works the saloon but is the proverbial whore with a heart of gold.

For the viewer, it may be difficult to watch Scott start out with the best of intentions in both marriage and money matters only to turn his back on everything he once valued as the building of the oil line obsesses him. Only late in the story, after Dunne has left him and he sits alone contemplating his life, does he have a moment of regret. "What was I trying to be?" he rhetorically asks, near tears. "Who did I think I was?" Still, he has enough gumption left in him to scream in pain and anger at his comrades when they decide to quit the oil line in defeat. It's an admirable display of unaffected, uninhibited performing on Scott's part, and I don't think he ever came close to revealing so many inner emotions again on-screen. (Well, maybe in *Decision at Sundown*, 20 years later.)

The nail-biting action finale is marvelously surreal. Bickford's whip-yielding bullies surround Scott's men at the river in an effort to stop the farmers from getting the oil line across. Scott's men, using wrenches, pipes and fists, fight a valiant but vain defense. But then Bickford and company are in turn surrounded by Dunne, who is leading a cavalry charge of circus animals and performers in a rescue ride. (She joined the circus. Don't ask for more details; watch the film.) Scott takes quite a beating from Bickford before the latter is upended by an elephant and thrown to the midgets and the strongman for his comeuppance!

With Oscar Hammerstein II having a hand in the proceedings, the film has an equal share of comedy, drama, tragedy and love. Mamoulian mixed them nicely, though I don't think any of the songs, except for "The Folks Who Live on the Hill," are any good. Dunne and Lamour team up for "Allegheny Al," while William Frawley, of all people, leads the ensemble in a spirited rendition of "Will You Marry Me Tomorrow, Maria?" Hammerstein somehow managed to rhyme *village green* with *bombazine* in this song, so perhaps it's not totally forgettable.

It had taken Paramount over five years to give Scott some big breaks. It wasn't too little, but it was too late. By the time *High, Wide and Handsome* went into general release, the actor was working on the last film under his Paramount contract, *The Texans*, while negotiating multi-picture freelance deals with RKO, Universal, 20th Century–Fox, Columbia and Warner Bros.

High, Wide and Handsome was not a commercial success. According to Hugh Fordin's book *Getting To Know Him: A Biography of Oscar Hammerstein II*, "Paramount spent so much money on salaries and elaborate location sets and later marketed the picture so poorly that it never recouped its investment. However, it was a fine motion picture ... ahead of its time in many ways." Paramount studio head Adolph Zukor had high hopes for the film's success and, after watching the positive reaction of a Hollywood sneak preview audience, he shook Hammerstein's hand and said, "That's the greatest picture we ever made." A few months later, when it became clear the film would not even break even, Zukor walked right by Hammerstein in a Hollywood restaurant without acknowledging his presence.

Wanda Hale of the *New York Daily News* (7/22/1937) wrote, "Randolph Scott's performance is outstanding because it fits the fine actor to a T." The film, she added, "was as purely a piece of Americana as the Declaration of Independence." Frank S. Nugent of *The New York Times* predicted a lengthy run for the film, calling it a "richly produced, spectacular and melodious show ... Mr. Scott's portrayal of Cortlandt is resolute and consistently natural. Akim Tamiroff steals so many scenes he should be arrested for kleptomania."

Dunne later recounted that it was not an easy or fun film to make; her mother died during the production. Scott's hair had to be curled and recurled every single day, which meant he had to get up a lot earlier than usual. During the final fight scene, Mamoulian praised Scott's realistic and desperate battle to hold the small river bridge against a force of several stuntmen playing hooligans. "You'd fight too if you had this gang trying to throw you off," Scott responded. It turned out that the stuntmen had placed bets to see if they could deviate from the script and throw the stalwart lead into the water. The stuntmen lost the bet.

Fan magazines speculated that Scott and Dorothy Lamour were an item at the time. Given that Scott was still married to Marion duPont, it shows how little credence Tinseltown was giving to the legitimacy of *that* relationship. Years later, Lamour discounted these rumors, writing in her autobiography, "Gossip columnists kept trying to build up a romance between us, but we were really just good friends ... critics never gave him [Scott] raves, but he did many films and saved his money."

The Freelance Years: 1938–1945

Scott was not an actor to talk at length about his Hollywood career or individual movies, though now and then you can find a quote from him regarding a film he was proud of, such as *High, Wide and Handsome* (1937) and *Corvette K-225* (1943). To many of his co-stars, he remained a reserved, polite, knowledgeable actor who gave off the air of caring about his work without investing that care with a lot of angst about his performances. In later years he would neither disparage or credit Paramount for giving him his break in Hollywood, but by the late 1930s it was obvious he was dissatisfied with his lot there. He departed Paramount by the end of 1937 after filming *The Texans* (released in the summer of 1938) with a desire to branch out and acquire better roles at other studios. According to A.C. Lyles, who was then working in the studio's publicity department, there were no hard feelings between the studio and Scott. "He left Paramount because he wanted to test his wings in other places," Lyles explained. "He was in demand and he thought he could do better as a freelancer at other studios. It wasn't that Paramount wanted him to leave—*he* wanted to leave. It was risky to leave unless you were established, but he

was established. And he went on to do very well." Scott would never return to Paramount, though he did make one Western, *Albuquerque*, for the studio's Pine-Thomas unit in 1948.

Scott began making lucrative freelance deals, an uncommon occurrence among film stars of that era. Over the next decade or so Scott would work for nearly every major studio in town except MGM: Columbia, Warner Bros., Universal, United Artists, RKO and 20th Century–Fox. This independence, which Scott forged mostly on his own ("I handle my business affairs myself," he told a reporter in the early 1940s), also gave him the opportunity to try other types of characters: as an aviator, a gigolo, a radio station manager, a Mountie (!), a pirate, a naval commander, a bad guy opposite John Wayne (*The Spoilers*), a good guy opposite John Wayne (*Pittsburgh*) and, when he felt like it, a cowboy.

Scott's friendship with Cary Grant cooled during this period, probably because both men left Paramount about the same time (Grant also freelanced from that point on). While Scott remained legally wed to Marion duPont, the two spent little time together, and the actor could be spotted on the town with other women. He remained a private man, rarely indulging in publicity interviews unless he trusted the journalist. "I consider myself a perfectly normal person, reared in the school of suppressing the emotions, from which fact people have drawn various conclusions," he said in 1942 (a banner year for Randolph Scott interviews, actually). "I happen to be an introvert—not extrovert—which may or may not explain me." He admitted he didn't like revealing his inner self to either friends or film audiences: "Breaking down reserve has been a painful process. At first I used to suffer tortures—I actually got ill. You can't change from introvert to extrovert overnight."

He did not make film friends easily and only a handful of actors, like Cary Grant and Donna Reed, became personal pals. "Randy didn't socialize much with people off the set," said Columbia contract player Jerome Courtland, who made two films with Scott. "He was extremely nice and well-mannered, but he kept very much to himself," recalled former child star Gary Gray, who worked with Scott in *Return of the Bad Men* (1948). Most of Scott's co-stars echoed these comments. "One thing about Randy—he was a quiet guy," recalled actor Myron Healey. "You'd start the day and he'd say, 'Hello, Myron, how's it going?' And that was about it." Actor Walter Reed, who made three films with Scott, felt privileged when the Southerner agreed to have an after-work drink with him—but just *one* after-work drink—while filming *Seven Men from Now* (1956): "Some days after a shoot he would say to me, 'Let's go in [to the bar] and have a dusk cutter.' And we'd have a drink—but he'd only have one before going back to his room."

Scott preferred the company of writers and directors more than fellow actors, and there are hints that he wanted to become a writer himself. What was one of his frustrated desires, he was asked in 1943? "Writing," Scott replied. "I've always envied successful writers and wished I could express myself as well on the written page." Given this comment, consider the number of times Scott worked with the following screenwriters: Kenneth Gamet, eight; Harold Shumate, six; Jack Cummingham, six; Burt Kennedy, four; and Allan Scott, three. In addition, Lamar Trotti, Tom Reed, Robert Carson, F. Hugh Herbert, Alan LeMay, Frank Gruber, John Twist, Charles Lang and Thomas Blackburn contributed at least two screenplays to Scott's filmography. The actor learned to develop a good sense of a tight screenplay in his post–Paramount years—which still didn't stop him from choosing some literary stinkers.

Then too, Scott got to know which directors he could trust, and he constantly re-employed them, or let them re-employ him: Edwin L. Marin made nine Scott films; Henry Hathaway made eight; Budd Boetticher and Ray Enright each made seven; Andre DeToth made six; William A. Seiter made five, Charles Barton three and several others, including Allan Dwan, Gordon Douglas and Joseph H. Lewis, made two. Still, Scott generally didn't land top directors. Unlike Joel McCrea, for instance, Scott didn't get the chance to work with Preston Sturges, William Wyler, Howard Hawks, George Stevens or Alfred Hitchcock. He did, however, work at least once with Michael Curtiz, Garson Kanin, King Vidor, Henry King, John Sturges, Fritz Lang and Sam Peckinpah. All of these directors, with the possible exception of King Vidor, got strong performances out of Scott. And all of them, except for Vidor and Peckinpah, worked with Scott during the actor's 1938–49 freelance period.

During this era, the actor did not deviate much from the traditional Randolph Scott performance. His best work is as a supporting actor in *Jesse James*, *Virginia City* and *Western Union*. In all three he is a man of dignity, but one cursed with an inner turmoil revolving around abortive love or failing friendships or something similar. He tried something a little different only once during this period, playing a charming but hardened criminal in *The Spoilers*, but it is hardly a long stretch of the actor's talents. Scott learned around this time to stop trying to act and decided to concentrate on polishing the screen image that both he and audiences felt comfortable with: the strong, silent man of action.

"It occurred to me a couple of seasons back that I was going about this thing the wrong way," he said in a rare commentary on acting in 1942. "For a man who was, as you might say, hell-bent on being himself, I was sacrificing naturalness in favor of what is called in my trade 'technique.' It took several years and numerous unfortunate experiences to make me realize that acting in the accepted sense, at least as far as George Randolph Scott is concerned, should be subordinated to the natural personality. Once I made the discovery, I stuck to it." He decided, like many other film actors of the time, to more or less play slight variations on his own personality, a personality that may not have been strong enough to warrant his being cast as a drunken wastrel, a psychotic killer, an emotionally torn war veteran or a determined private eye, but which still held enough wattage to make him appealing when playing straight-laced leaders, be they sheriffs or sergeants or seamen. (Of note is the fact that he turned down the lead in RKO's 1943 psychological *noir* thriller *The Fallen Sparrow*, suggesting he was unwilling to tackle the challenging part of an emotionally battered war veteran haunted by his past. John Garfield played the role.) Scott's acting was not always inspired, but from the late 1930s on, it was always truthful. He acknowledged that he wasn't always happy doing romantic scenes on film. "I wish I were a combination of Boyer and Gable," Scott said. "I'm not a great-lover type, and I'm not often called upon to burn the celluloid with impassioned kisses, for which I'm grateful."

Scott fans may be angered by this next statement, but the actor's range was limited. He learned, however, to turn this into a strength, particularly when he decided to stick with Western films from 1946 onward. Film critics and cinematic journalists were not likely to make Scott the focus of attention for an article on acting, but Malcolm Phillips, who wrote for *Picturegoer*, penned a fascinating piece on Scott's film career in July 1941, several months after the release of *Western Union* (a film that offered Scott the promise of a new career). The piece, entitled "Stay West, Young Man," urged Scott to accept his acting limitations and focus on making Western films. "He is, metaphorically speaking, strong, silent manhood forever giving his overcoat to maidens in distress," Phillips wrote. "Men not nearly so attractive trust him with their girl friends. Orphaned daughters of ranchers can always count on Randolph to protect their property and their virtue." Phillips also looked at Scott's career to date and rather honestly noted, "Scott's career has not prospered as some people think it should have. He has for years been galloping nowhere fast." In analyzing Scott's film history, Phillips noted, "One is forced to the conclusion that while he is dependable he lacks dash. He has too many overcoats and too little verve." Phillips blamed this liability on directors and writers for not utilizing Scott in the right capacity: in Westerns. "Alone of those who now ride the range he is capable of reviving the great tradition of the Western, built up by Hart and Holt, Mix and Dix, in the happy days before the cow-country was invaded by the crooners and large-scale outdoor melodramas degenerated into a mere medium for demonstrating that matinee idols have hair on their chests."

Barton MacLane (seated) tries to parlay with Scott in *Western Union* while Dick Rich keeps a gun on our hero just to make sure he gets the point. (JC Archives, Inc.)

It's a telling point. It's possible Scott wanted to segue into Western films sooner, but the war put a patriotic strain on film actors to play red-blooded heroes. Between 1942 and 1945 Scott made six war films (not including *Pittsburgh*, which is partially set during the war years). In short, Scott traded in his cowboy clothes for an officer's uniform, more or less, playing the same sort of tight-lipped, no-nonsense leader he had essayed in Westerns. And as with his film work of the 1930s, the body of Scott's movies made between 1938 to 1947 constitute a bad one for every good one. The potential for advancement after his work in *Jesse James* and *Frontier Marshal* is offset by the banalities of *Coast Guard* and *20,000 Men a Year*, for example, in 1939 alone. In 1941 Scott gave what must

be considered one of the best performances of his career in *Western Union*, as a good-bad man who can no longer distinguish right from wrong and who cannot give in to the course of love. The film was a major hit for 20th Century–Fox, but Scott offset the gains won by his portrayal with indifferent performances in that year's *Belle Starr* (not a good film) and a Universal "B" called *Paris Calling*. The actor just didn't pick good scripts on a regular basis. One can understand him being forced to do whatever claptrap a studio asked him to do when he was under contract to Paramount. But in the late 1930s and early '40s, Scott made a lot of routine pictures, films designed to make money from undiscriminating, entertainment-starved audiences. And as a freelance agent, the actor willfully chose them all. Scott's films made money, and he remained a big draw, but by 1945 it was evident that he was in danger of slipping into "B" movie perpetuity what with his contribution to such hackneyed projects as *Captain Kidd, China Sky* and *Belle of the Yukon.*

Some of these poor film choices have less to do with Scott's lack of literary perception and more to do with his desire to make money. By the early 1940s he was earning $50,000 a picture; by 1950 he'd be pulling in $100,000 per picture. "Acting is a glamour business, but to my father, it was a business," Chris Scott wrote in 1994. His father might not have disagreed. "Acting — if that's what I do — merely happens to be a means of making a good living," Scott said in a 1942 interview. "I haven't the so-called temperament of an actor. I haven't the disposition of an actor. Why lie about it?" The people who worked with Scott in Hollywood felt the same way. "Scott was a Virginian gentleman, a member of the Los Angeles Country Club, and his general attitude was that he could have just as well been a banker," recalled Harry Joe Brown, Jr., son of Scott's business partner. "He was an elegant kind of man. My father was very fond of the process, so he never wanted to stop making movies. Randy saw it as a job; my father saw it as a passion." Phyllis Kirk, who made one film with Scott in 1953, summed it up like this: "He [Scott] was much more interested in finances than films." Claude Akins told Jefferson Brim Crow III that on the set of *Comanche Station*, Scott "read the *Wall Street Journal*, not Shakespeare."

Which is not to say that his co-stars didn't like working with him, or thought less of him as an actor. His thespian colleagues are almost entirely in synch about Scott's talents and attitude regarding acting. "Obviously he never had a tremendous range of emotion in films," Mala Powers explained. "As an actor he was very

quiet. He seemed to have a lot of confidence." Kirk agrees: "He was very present for me; very generous as an actor." Rand Brooks, who knew Scott (and Scott's second wife Marie Pat Stillman) and appeared with the actor in *Comanche Station*, felt that "Randy was a good actor. I wouldn't use the word *great* by any stretch of the imagination. I don't think people thought less of him for that; I think they thought more of him for it, because for his versatility he was *very* good."

While Scott did talk candidly about his career, he was less open about his rather unconventional marriage to Marion duPont. "We are still friends," he told a reporter in 1943. "We correspond. I don't pretend that this necessarily means that we are going to pick up where we left off." (They didn't.) Scott continued to be a man who guarded his privacy, saying, "One aim I have always had in the back of my mind — and I realize I represent the minority — is to detach my private life from my public life." As a result, by the mid–1940s he began giving fewer interviews; likewise, he refused to make television appearances, arguing that the public shouldn't see him perform for free. He did, however, make personal appearances in cowboy regalia.

His hobbies included playing bridge, golf, gardening, reading and gambling at the track (not seriously, but he acknowledged he wasn't very good at it). He was never a heavy drinker but he was a steady smoker, with a penchant for pipes and filtered cigarettes (years later he would chide Mala Powers on the set of 1955's *Rage at Dawn* about her smoking habit, saying it was bad for her health). By his own account he offered to serve in World War II, trying to get an officer's commission in the Marines. He was turned down (he turned 44 in January 1942). Instead, he raised food for the government on his ranch some 130 miles outside of Hollywood. He joined comic Joe DeRita (later of the Three Stooges) to do a comedy routine *a la* Abbott and Costello for the Victory Committee showcases both Stateside and in the South Pacific. The duo suffered through ten bombing raids in 12 days while they were holed up on the isle of Bougainville in the Solomon Islands, and one of their performances was interrupted three times by Japanese bombers. "DeRita was the fox hole champ of the island," Scott would later quip. Frank Tremaine's January 1944 UP wire story "Actor and Comedian Cheer Wounded Men" stated that Scott made a point of stopping at every single hospital bed to talk to the wounded servicemen; he resented being pulled away to chat with officers who were impressed with his stardom. "The boys would rather risk their necks in action than suffer the monotony of being stuck in some outpost way out to hell and gone," Scott told reporters when he returned to the States early in 1944. His most disquieting moment during the tour was encountering the skipper of a PT boat who had just undergone a leg amputation. Scott visited the man's parents in San Francisco to pass on a message for the soldier. (Scott and DeRita also teamed for a March 1944 *Command Performance* radio show, hosted by Kate Smith.)

On the romantic front, sometime in 1942 Scott met socialite Patricia Stillman, who was 20 years his junior. Like Marion, Pat came from a wealthy banking family, but her father had died, leaving her a sizeable fortune.* She and Scott dated, on and off, for about 18 months; at one time they gave up on the romance because duPont refused to grant Scott a divorce. But finally, early in 1944, duPont agreed and, that March, Scott married Stillman (who gave her age as 25) in a civil ceremony in River-

side, California. Interestingly, duPont would keep Scott's name until her death in the 1980s, though she made no mention of her actor husband in her 1976 memoir, *Montpelier*.

So having first married a woman several years older, Scott now married a woman young enough to be his daughter. Newspaper accounts of the time reported that Stillman was from San Francisco, but Rand Brooks thought she was a Beverly Hills baby. "She was a real doll," said Brooks of Pat, whom he dated briefly. "She came from Beverly Hills, attended Beverly High School, and lived in an apartment near there. Somehow or other she and Randy were thrown together and I think she admired him. Maybe she had some terrible experiences with some of the local jerks in Hollywood. She was perky and vital and he was so proper." There were newspaper reports and rumors that Pat Stillman had once been a model, but Brooks doubts it was true, and it could be that the media was mixing Pat up with one Priscilla Stillman, another young woman Scott dated in the early 1940s. Mala Powers called Pat "a striking woman" and recalled that, on the set of *Rage at Dawn*, the Scotts seemed to be a perfect fit for each other. "My husband Monty went on locale with me in Sonora; it was Indian summer and Randy and Pat were just so charming," she said. "They were really nice to my husband and me."

The upswing in Scott's personal life was offset by a spate of weak film choices in the mid–1940s. However, during this period Scott hooked up with film producer Harry Joe Brown, who produced 1941's *Western Union* and the 1943 Columbia Western *The Desperadoes*. In 1941 Brown was a 46-year-old producer who had been in films in one capacity or another since

*I'm not suggesting Randolph Scott was a fortune-hunter, but the fact that he married two heiresses does indicate that he wanted women who were financially well-off and not after him for his money.

1918. Brown had actually been a law grad (Syracuse University) but segued into staging vaudeville revues before he broke into Hollywood. Brown, who was married to actress Sally Eilers, initiated a long-term relationship with Columbia in the early 1940s.

According to Harry Joe Brown, Jr., Brown and Scott met a decade earlier. "Part of the relationship between Randy and Harry Joe was that they knew each other in those early Hollywood days when Randy first came to town," Brown, Jr. recalled. "I still have this wonderful image of them all at the Hearst Castle at a San Simeon party and my father was dressed as a clown, and Randy and Cary Grant were there, as well as Hal Roach. Randy and Harry Joe had a social acquaintance that was important in Randy's mind because he trusted my father as a partner."

Brown was one of two film producers that Scott would befriend and partner with, the other being Nat Holt. But Scott's relationship with Brown lasted longer and yielded better results in a series of mostly superior "B+" Westerns made for Columbia in the late 1940s and 1950s. Why did Brown and Scott get along so well? "My father's moral sense of who people were carried over into these films," said Brown, Jr. "He believed in the image of integrity and strong character, and of making the right moral choices. I think that is what Randy was able to project. It was kind of a slant from his being a Virginian gentleman — a

certain code of behavior, which was the Code of the West but, in Randy's case, the Code of the South." Scott would carry that mix of Code of the West and Code of the South into his film work beginning in 1946.

But for the period of 1938–45, Randolph Scott was still a contract player of sorts, albeit one who jumped from studio to studio with a little more power and choice. Scott never quite made it into the ranks of superstar players, but this period shows, despite some poor material, an effort to segue into that sphere. It's unfortunate that it also marks a period of indefinition for the actor. He became a general handyman actor, able to adapt to this or that film genre without altering his acting approach much. While this time era marks some of Scott's best acting, especially in *Jesse James*, *Virginia City* and *Western Union*, it would be a few more years before Scott would be fully confident to start delivering consistently compelling portraitures of men of the West. In the interim, he continued to jump back and forth between "A" and "B" films, leads and supporting parts, cowboys and commanders. (Just consider this: his female co-stars in this era ranged from Shirley Temple to Marlene Dietrich to Gypsy Rose Lee.) If this is an erratic period of the actor's career, it remains a fascinatingly erratic period, and there are a few gems amidst all the rhinestones. And even some of the rhinestones are fun to watch.

FEATURE FILM ROLES: 1938–1945

Rebecca of Sunnybrook Farm (20th Century–Fox, March 1938, 80 minutes)

CREDITS   Director: Allan Dwan; Producer: Raymond Griffith; Screenplay: Karl Tunberg and Don Ettlinger, suggested by the Kate Douglas Wiggin story; Music and lyrics by Mack Gordon and Harry Revel, Lew Pollack and Sidney D. Mitchell, Sam Pokras and Jack Yellen and Raymond Scott

CAST   Shirley Temple (Rebecca Winstead), Randolph Scott (Anthony Kent), Jack Haley (Orville Smithers), Gloria Stuart (Gwen Warren),

Phyllis Brooks (Lola Lee), Helen Westley (Aunt Miranda Wilkins), Slim Summerville (Homer Busby), Bill Robinson (Aloysius), Alan Dinehart (Purvis), J. Edward Bromberg (Dr. Hill), William Demarest (Henry Kipper), Paul Hurst (Mug), Paul Harvey (Cyrus Bartlett), Franklin Panghorn (Hamilton Montmarcy)

Synopsis: Radio ad executive Anthony Kent signs up child singing sensation Rebecca Winstead against the wishes of the precocious girl's family and friends.

Here's a trivia question for Scott fans: Which film has our hero pursuing a poor piglet across a lawn before flying headfirst into a well with the li'l porker? Yes, *Rebecca of Sunnybrook Farm* is chock-full of such buffoonery, and it remains a pleasant-enough musical comedy replete with a cadre of superb comic supporting players including Franklin Panghorn, William Demarest, Jack Haley and J. Edward Bromberg.

Scott is a talent agent for station FBC. He's first seen adversely reacting to a slew of untalented child stars who are auditioning for the Little Miss America show. For some reason every one of the kids warbles the insipid song "You Gotta Eat Your Spinach, Baby" (which was not, to the best of my knowledge, one of those tunes that made it to *Your Hit Parade*). Haley is Scott's nervous right-hand man, a studio sap who tries his best to control the proceedings but only incurs Scott's rancor. "Okay, chief, you know me," Haley says confidentially after receiving some orders from Scott. "Yes, and I'm still regretting it," Scott snaps back, leading to a typical Haley double-take. Scott seems to be having much more fun than usual in this light-hearted piece of entertainment, acting as if freedom from the constraints of his Paramount contract had empowered him.

Shirley Temple is the title character, a talented orphan whose guardians don't want success to go to her head. Gloria Stuart is Scott's romantic interest and one of

Temple's guardians. At one point little Shirley, noticing that Scott looks tired, suggests that Stuart "puts you to bed." Scott casts a delicious glance over the shapely Stuart and replies, "That would be a pleasant experience," a double entendre that somehow made it past the censors.

The majority of the film is taken up with Scott's efforts to utilize Temple's talents over the protests of her guardians, which includes a ruse to broadcast directly from a farm (it's far-fetched, but at least it ties in Rebecca with a farm so the title makes some sense). Demarest takes a terrific pratfall, Panghorn does his usual fussy shtick, and Haley — sort of a second-string Eddie Cantor — raises his eyebrows repeatedly in response to almost every line of dialogue in the film. Bill "Bojangles" Robinson shows up as a handyman on the farm and engages in a brief tap routine with Temple.

But this is a Shirley Temple vehicle, and Scott and the rest are simply hitch-hikers. At one point Temple pays homage to her own career, engaging in a medley of her hit songs ranging from "Good Ship Lollipop" to "Animal Crackers" — suggesting that Rebecca of Sunnybrook Farm, and not Shirley Temple, enjoyed this string of tuneful successes, I guess. Scott disappears for about 20 minutes midway through the film, and the finale sees all the would-be couples coupling (Scott and Stuart, Haley and Phyllis Brooks, etc.) while Temple and Robinson go on the air to perform "The Chocolate Soldier Parade," a tap number with ornate costumes and lavish sets that was unlikely to be fully appreciated by a radio audience. I never read Kate Douglas Wiggin's novel *Rebecca of Sunnybrook Farm* but I do know it was written in 1903 and had nothing to do with a kid singer on the radio.

Gloria Stuart, (from her autobiography *I Just Keep Hoping*): "I was sick to my stomach at the thought of doing a Shirley

Temple movie — but I did it. I still hear from friends and fans, 'Saw you last night with Shirley Temple…'"

Allan Dwan: "The book [*Rebecca of Sunnybrook Farm*] was sort of a *Pollyanna* — pretty sticky. I said, 'This *could* be made into something interesting … let's go after this with an updated attitude — put some music in it, give Shirley something to sing, let's get radio in.' Radio was very popular then. And we injected all that. The original book is nothing like that. In fact, when we were through, all we had left was the title and the names of the characters."

Marion duPont's horse Battleship won the Grand National just as the film was released, giving the picture extra publicity. Cary Grant was then dating Scott's co-star Phyllis Brooks, but 20th Century–Fox chieftain Darryl Zanuck refused to let Grant on the set as his presence was distracting the pretty brunette.

Of Temple, *The New York Times'* Bosley Crowther wrote (3/26/1938), "Any actress who can dominate a Zanuck musical with Jack Haley, Gloria Stuart, Phyllis Brooks, Helen Westley, Slim Summerville, Bill Robinson, et cetera, can dominate the world."

The Texans (Paramount, July 1938, 93 minutes)

CREDITS   Director: James Hogan; Producer: Lucien Hubbard; Screenplay: Bertram Millhauser, Paul Sloane and William Wister Haines, based on a story by Emerson Hough

CAST   Joan Bennett (Ivy Preston), Randolph Scott (Kirk Jordan), May Robson (Granna), Walter Brennan (Chuckawalla), Robert Cummings (Alan Sanford), Raymond Hatton (Cal Tuttle), Robert Barrat (Isiah Middlebrack), Francis Ford (Uncle Dud)

Synopsis: Ivy Preston, a proud Southern woman, starts gun-running in a last ditch effort to reverse the fortunes of the Civil War — and this after Gen. Robert E. Lee has surrendered!

Looking a bit like Gary Cooper and having considerable fun in a tailor-fit role, Scott's work in *The Texans* shows that he was capable of handling a lead in an "A" Western, and makes one wonder why he wasn't in Paramount's 1936 Western *The Texas Rangers*. The Paramount Westerns of this period have good casts and epic production values but still suffer from uninspired writing and action scenes. *The Texans* is no exception to this rule, and remains a watchable but hardly memorable effort. It is better than both *Wells Fargo* and *The Plainsman* (two other 1930s Paramount Westerns), but for all its potential, it nonetheless begins to fall apart about half way through its rather convoluted plot.

Scott's character, Kirk Jordan, is interesting in that he wants to forget the war and work to reconcile with the North — a notion that both Joan Bennett's Ivy Preston and diehard Confederate Alan Sanford (Robert Cummings) find repulsive. Scott is hired to lead Bennett's cattle north to Abilene because, she tells him, she wants to avoid paying taxes on the animals. In reality, Bennet wants to run the cattle to Maximilian in Mexico in hopes that the emperor will, in turn, support her efforts to wage a second Civil War. This far-fetched plotline not only puts Scott and Bennett at odds, but damages the film's potential. Still, it was directed and written with a sense of humor; with reliable veterans like Walter Brennan and May Robson (who gets considerable comic mileage out of a drunk scene) on board, *The Texans* is often enjoyable fun. There's even a nod to the then-popular notion of singing cowboys when the trail hands stop long enough to warble a pleasant Frank Loesser tune, "Silver on the Sage."

Given Scott's 1930s screen persona as a slow second lead, here's a snatch of

Scott and Joan Bennett somehow find time for a quick clinch amidst an Indian attack in his final film for Paramount, *The Texans* (1938).

memorable dialogue: After Bennett tells Scott he's blind for not seeing the possibility that the South could rise again, Scott replies deadpan, "I'm just a dull, stupid fellow, I guess."

Much of the film was shot at the La Mota cattle ranch, 100 miles from San Antonio, in Texas, and Scott was falsely promoted as a "native of Texas" to help boost the film's prospects.

The New Yorker (7/6/1938): "*The Texans* is the only major production I have ever seen in which love as a motivating force was subordinated to tax evasion, but after all, that's the way my life is organized so I can't very well quarrel with it in a movie." *The New York Sun* (7/28/1938): "Never outstanding for its performances, *The Texans* still does what it sets out to do. It is carried along in a rush of excitement."

Road to Reno (Universal, October 1938, 69 minutes)

CREDITS   Director: S. Sylvan Simon; Producer: Edward Grainger; Screenplay: Roy Chanslor and Adele Comandini, additional dialogue by Brian Marlowe; Story: Charles Kenton and F. Hugh Herbert, based on the book by I.A.R. Wylie

CAST   Randolph Scott (Steve Fortness), Hope Hampton (Linda Halliday), Glenda Farrell (Sylvia Shane), Alan Marshal (Walter Crawford), Helen Broderick (Aunt Minerva), David Oliver (Salty), Ted Osborn (Linda's Attorney), Samuel S. Hinds (Sylvia's Attorney)

Synopsis: Opera star Linda Halliday angles for a divorce from cowboy spouse Steve Fortness, but he doesn't want to let her go.

A silly semi-screwball comedy, *The Road to Reno* is a minor entry in Scott's filmography. The first film under his new

Scott, his horse and Hope Hampton relaxing on the set of *Road to Reno* (1938), a semi-screwball comedy from Universal. (JC Archives, Inc.)

Universal contract which called for a picture a year, *The Road to Reno* makes little sense when you think about it — how, for example, a New York opera star and a Nevada cowpoke ever hooked up and got hitched in the first place is never explained. Scott and Hope Hampton engage in all sorts of absurd bits of business, setting traps for each other involving collapsing bunkbeds and poison oak ambushes, but

Scott and Hope Hampton consider a legal writ in *Road to Reno* (1938).

overall the film is humorous rather than hilarious. But it does have its moments, the actors perform with an infectious spirit of playfulness, and the film affords Scott a rare chance to play out-and-out comedy.

Scott is a cowpoke not given to unnecessary exposition who, for reasons not made clear until late in the film, refuses to grant his wife a divorce. He has fun in the role, but he's not given a lot of funny business, aside from the rare witty line. ("Friend of yours?" Salty the foreman asks Scott, gesturing to incendiary Hampton. "No, just my wife," Scott replies in deadpan fashion.) He also has a brief but uproarious scene in a runaway airplane. Hampton, a lower level star of the silents, had come out of retirement for this comeback film. To the best of my knowledge, *Road to Reno* is the extent of that come-

back, although she played herself in the 1961 rock film *Hey, Let's Twist!* She and Scott try their best, but they are upstaged by second leads Glenda Farrell as a man-chasing divorcee and urbane Alan Marshal as Scott's rival.

Director S. Sylvan Simon was more at home in out-and-out slapstick scenarios, such as the hilarious Red Skelton film *The Fuller Brush Man. Road to Reno* only comes to life in one brief but raucous scene wherein suave Marshal takes Hampton and Scott on a madcap plane ride. Scott's array of terrified double-takes and looks of impending stomach illness suggest he could have done all right in a full-fledged slapstick comedy.

Archer Winsten of *The New York Post* (10/30/1938) wasn't too far off the mark when he wrote, "Not bad, but not too good either." *The Brooklyn Daily Eagle*'s reviewer gave the film a slightly better critique when he suggested that the cast "is always agreeable but never brilliant. No spectacular epic, *Road to Reno* is nonetheless a pleasant experience." I'm not sure pleasant is the right adjective. I prefer innocuous.

The film was budgeted at $350,000 but delays in shooting upped the cost another $19,000, which must have driven money-conscious Universal crazy. "This picture continues to be about the worst headache we have to keep anywhere near the budget figure," one weekly status report from company manager M. P. Murphy states. A week later (mid–July 1938), Murphy wrote, "Over-shooting on the part of the director is extending the shooting period on this production longer than we anticipated." Apparently the studio was willing to make up the lost time in the post-production phase; by late August the film was ready for previewing purposes!

Jesse James (20th Century–Fox, January 1939, 105 minutes)

CREDITS   Director: Henry King; Producer: Darryl F. Zanuck; Screenplay: Nunnally Johnson (also Associate Producer); historical data provided by Rosalind Schaeffer and Jo Francis James

CAST   Tyrone Power (Jesse James), Henry Fonda (Frank James), Nancy Kelly (Zee), Randolph Scott (Will Wright), Henry Hull (Major Rufus Cobb), Slim Summerville (Jailer), J. Edward Bromberg (George Rynan), Brian Donlevy (Barshee), John Carradine (Bob Ford), Charles Tannen (Charlie Ford), Jane Darwell (Ma James), Donald Meek (McCoy)

Synopsis: The life, times and death of outlaw Jesse James.

Jesse James remains an outstanding sample of the Western genre; a colorful if whitewashed account of the Missouri outlaw. It was a film beset by mishaps: During the shooting of a dangerous horse stunt at the Lake of the Ozarks at Bagnall Dam, stuntman Cliff Lyons and a horse plummeted off a cliff and into the lake below. Lyons wasn't hurt but the horse died in the fall. Outrage over the incident resulted in the American Humane Society's institution of a code of regulation governing the use of animals during motion picture production. The incident earned 20th Century–Fox a lot of unfavorable publicity, but it didn't hurt the film's box office chances one iota, for *Jesse James* was the fourth highest-grossing film of 1939, behind *Gone with the Wind*, *The Wizard of Oz* and *The Hunchback of Notre Dame*. In addition to the horse's death, Henry Fonda shot himself in his right leg with a load of blank shot that caused powder burns, Nancy Kelly was thrown from her mount into a barbed wire fence, and Lon Chaney, Jr. (in an unbilled bit as one of the James Gang) was run down by a horse in a bank robbery sequence.

Scott had it easier — he didn't even have to draw his gun or mount a horse. He shows up about 20 minutes into the story playing Will Wright, an easy going but firm U.S. Marshal who is a friend of Zee, Jesse's wife. He's the sort of lawman who doesn't mind bending the rules a little but who, if pushed, probably wouldn't be a good opponent to go up against in a showdown. He and Tyrone Power enjoy one effective sequence wherein Power's Jesse James pretends to be someone else. Wright knows full well who he is, however, and casually mentions that he hopes Jesse James stays out of his territory so he doesn't have to go a-gunnin' for him. Jesse gets the message and avoids Wright, impressed by the lawman's honesty and courage: "You got a better grade of law around here than it used to be," the outlaw tells his wife Zee.

Scott is stable and solid, and while I'm not going to suggest that he steals the film, I do think he registers strongly by under

Scott (right), as Marshal Will Wright, rides alongside outlaw Jesse James (Tyrone Power) in 20th Century–Fox's superior outlaw biopic, *Jesse James* (1939). (JC Archives, Inc.)

playing. It's as if the knowledge that he didn't have to carry a picture freed him, creatively, to build his confidence and take chances, even if those chances were subtle ones. He has one wonderful silent bit of physical emoting where he listens as Kelly's Zee, her newborn baby in arms, rages on about her husband's reckless ways. Scott's eyes betray the truth — he's in love with Zee, though not one thing in the script overtly states this.

Scott has little to do in the last 30 minutes of the film, which deals with the James Gang's abortive raid on the Northfield bank and the repercussions that follow, including the Ford brothers' back-shooting murder of Jesse. The performers gel as an ensemble and give nuanced performances, except for Henry Hull, who goes over the top as a newspaper editor who is sympathetic to Jesse's situation. "It's the lawyers that's messin' up the world,"

he intones to a befuddled newspaper aide at one point, demanding an editorial on the subject. "If we're ever to have law and order in the West, the first thing we gotta do is take out all the lawyers and shoot 'em down like dogs!" As the film progresses, we see Hull rewriting the editorial, exchanging the word *lawyer* for governor, railroad president and other law-abiding positions of power!

The film's view of the railroad and what it represents is almost the total opposite of Cecil B. DeMille's *Union Pacific* (also 1939) in that the railroad here is seen as evil incarnate, exemplified by company man Barshee (Brian Donlevy), the sort of bad guy who you want to see get beat up but good. It's because of the likes of Barshee that the James boys start robbing trains (in the film, anyway), and King stages a humorous railroad robbery sequence where Fonda's Frank James pleasantly advises the passengers he's stealing from to "sue the railroad for everything you give 'cuz they're responsible."

The finale sees Hull, Scott and Kelly standing over Jesse's grave as mourners gather to pay tribute to their fallen comrade. "I don't think America's ashamed of Jesse James," Hull states, extolling the bad guy as if he were performing a eulogy for a military hero. Hull goes on to state that America cherishes such daring, risk-taking, foolhardy youths—neglecting to mention that Jesse killed quite a few people in his day.

James was killed on April 3, 1882, at age 34. John Carradine, who played Bob Ford, the man who shot Jesse, had his own physical challenges to face *after* the film was released: "I was out in front of a theater where *Jesse James* was showing. A little kid said, 'Did you shoot Jesse?' and I said, 'Yes.' And the son of a bitch kicked me in the shin!"

Location shooting was done in Pineville, Missouri, in the summer and autumn of 1938. The cast and crew were treated like royalty by the locals, and Scott was a favorite of the townsfolk, according to reporter Jessie Hodges, who visited Pineville during the shoot. "Although Randolph Scott is not the star of the picture, as far as the Ozark people are concerned he is mighty popular," Hodges wrote. "All the children know him for his fine riding. Their elders like him because he has the straightforward manner and the soft-spoken voice of a Virginian. And down here in the Ozark hills they never have wholeheartedly joined the Union since they seceded before the war."

The New York Sun (1/14/1939): "Randolph Scott, as an overly amiable U.S. Marshal, is a pleasant addition to the cast." *New York Daily News* (1/14/1939): "Randolph Scott turns in an excellent performance as the sheriff." *The New York Times*, (1/14/1939): "An authentic American panorama, enriched by dialogue, characterization, and incidents imported directly from the Missouri hills."

Susannah of the Mounties (20th Century–Fox, June 1939, 78 minutes)

CREDITS   Director: William A. Seiter; Producer: Darryl F. Zanuck; Screenplay: Robert Ellis and Helen Logan; story by Fidel La Barba and Walter Ferris; from the book, *Susannah, A Little Girl of the Mounties* by Muriel Denison

CAST   Shirley Temple (Susannah Sheldon), Randolph Scott (Inspector Angus), Margaret Lockwood (Vicky Standing), Martin Good Rider (Little Chief), J. Farrell MacDonald (Pat O'Hannegan), Maurice Moscovitch (Chief Big Eagle), Moroni Olsen (Andrew Standing), Victor Jory (Wolf Pelt), Lester Matthews (Harlan Chambers), Leyland Hodgson (Randall)

Synopsis: Precocious tyke Susannah Sheldon helps Northwest Mounted policeman Angus "Monty" Montague quell a Blackfeet uprising in 1880s Canada.

Rebecca of Sunnybrook Farm worked so well for the Shirley Temple-Randolph Scott team that 20th Century–Fox wasted no time in appropriating another literary vehicle for them. Unfortunately, *Susannah of the Mounties* isn't successful as either a Western or a musical, for in combining the two genres and trying to give Temple as much footage as possible, it leaves the viewer wanting either more music or more gunfire. This film doesn't have enough elements from either genre to satisfy.

Scott tried a mustache one last time for this epic, and since he's also clad in rather formal looking Canadian police attire, he comes off looking like a bellboy. And while I love Westerns, it gets harder and harder for me to view those that showcase the settlers (or, in this case, the railroad) fighting the Indians. The Blackfeet in this film are portrayed as child-like simpletons who utter phrases like "Ugh!," "Me go," and "Catchem fast!" (I'm not joking.) Victor Jory, made up to look like a zombie, plays the chief's hot-headed son, and his half-hearted efforts to join a line of real Blackfeet extras in a war dance are unintentionally hilarious. Nor does it help to have Maurice Moscovitch playing Big Eagle, leader of the tribe, as a Charlie Chan wannabe.

The plot has to do with Scott and company's efforts to protect the Canadian Pacific railroad from rampaging warriors. Margaret Lockwood plays the daughter of Scott's commanding officer, while Temple is the survivor of a Blackfeet massacre who comes to live on the post. Shirley teaches Randy how to waltz in one embarrassing scene; later, she gets high smoking a peace pipe and groggily notes that, "This isn't bad — anybody can make a treaty like this!" Scott chides Temple for not acting like an adult around the Indians. "We're supposed to be much more grown-up than they are," he explains, and with dialogue and an attitude like that, whatever possible fun there is to be had with the set-up quickly dissipates. Scott is more Patric Knowles than Errol Flynn when romancing Lockwood; the two just don't gel as a team. Director William A. Seiter does manage to stage a couple of fairly exciting action scenes, but they are too short and incorporate far too much comic shtick (a balding soldier repeatedly has his toupee shot off, for instance). As such, *Susannah of the Mounties* is hardly involving.

Muriel Dennison, author of the book *Susannah of the Mounties*, was the daughter of the Minister of Education of the Northwest Territory and lived for some time near an Indian reservation in Regina, Saskatchewan. The Northwest Mounted Police started in 1873; the Canadian Pacific railroad was built between 1879 and 1886 (Scott would return to this subject matter a decade later with the abysmal *Canadian Pacific*). The film was neither a flop nor a success, but Fox canceled plans for a sequel, *Susannah at Boarding School*. I wonder what role Scott would have played in *that* one.

Associated Press reporter Thomas Brady wrote a very amusing newspaper piece detailing the studio's efforts to impress a band of 12 Blackfeet Indians who were appearing in the film as extras. Apparently the 20th Century–Fox executives did not succeed in leaving a good impression on the dozen (the article was titled "Indians Heap Much Unimpressed"). As for Shirley Temple, after the Blackfeet visitors witnessed one of her musical numbers, the group, led by Big Beaver (called "The Beaver" by Brady), applauded impassively and then bestowed an honorary name upon the talented tyke: The Flying Woman. No one at Fox could figure that one out.

New York Journal-American (6/24/1939): "It wasn't so long ago that one of Shirley Temple's pictures showed her saving the Khyber Pass for England, so it seems perfect that, as Susannah of the Mounties, she should help the Royal Mounted Police keep peace with the Indians and permit the Canadian Pacific to be built."

Frontier Marshal (20th Century–Fox, July 1939, 71 minutes)

CREDITS   Director: Allan Dwan; Executive Producer: Sol M. Wurtzel; Screenplay: Sam Hellman, based on the novel by Stuart N. Lake

CAST   Randolph Scott (Wyatt Earp), Cesar Romero (Doc Halliday), Nancy Kelly (Sarah Allen), Binnie Barnes (Jerry), John Carradine (Ben Carter), Edward Norris (Dan Blackmore), Eddie Foy, Jr. (Eddie Foy), Ward Bond (Town Marshal), Lon Chaney, Jr. (Pringle), Tom Tyler (Buck Newton), Chris Pin-Martin (Pete), Joe Sawyer (Curly Bill), Charles Stevens (Indian Joe)

Synopsis: Wyatt Earp, with some help from his pal Doc Halliday, cleans up the Arizona town of Tombstone.

Frontier Marshal is an overlooked little jewel of a Western that compares favorably

Two-gun lawman Wyatt Earp (Scott) tames Tombstone in Allan Dwan's 1939 beauty of a "B" Western, *Frontier Marshal*, with Nancy Kelly. (JC Archives, Inc.)

with just about every other cinematic telling of the old Gunfight at the O.K. Corral story. I wouldn't say it's as good as John Ford's semi-remake, *My Darling Clementine* (1946), but I'd wager it's better than the over-produced, glossy 1957 Hal Wallis production *Gunfight at the O.K. Corral,* and most of the other Earp-based films.

Scott's Wyatt Earp, a peaceful guy hoping to open a stage line, decides to take on the job of town marshal after the town's lawman (Ward Bond in an extended cameo that does not justify his billing above Lon Chaney, Jr., Chris-Pin Martin or Joe Sawyer) refuses to go into the saloon to arrest a drunken, violent Indian Charlie. As Earp pins on the badge and sticks a six-gun in his belt, there's something about Scott's manner that tells the audience that he'll do the job justice. Earp does just that, en-

tering the saloon and calmly but firmly ordering Charlie to drop his guns, even while the wild Indian continues to fire at him! Earp brings him down with one shot (not mortally) and drags his limp body across the town square, impressing everyone in sight — including bad guys Ben Carter, Curly Bill and Buck (John Carradine, Joe Sawyer and Tom Tyler). The Mayor then offers Earp the job of town marshal, which he declines. But Earp changes his mind after Curly Bill and a couple of his thugs ride him out of town and give him a good beating. Earp staggers back to town, wakes the Mayor, takes the badge, the job and a pair of six-guns, and strides into the saloon to exact his revenge. He then rides Curly Bill out of town and beats him up!

Allan Dwan knew how to stage action

sequences; they're all well-done and suspense-filled — street fights, a stagecoach robbery and the final showdown at the O.K. Corral. A subplot involves Doc Halliday's (Cesar Romero) romantic involvement with the bar girl Jerry (Binnie Barnes, good as always) and the prim and proper nurse Sarah (Nancy Kelly, under-used by 20th throughout her brief stay there). For once, Scott is not involved in a love triangle. The film succeeds in capturing the bustling and sometimes dangerous feel of a frontier town. Scott and Romero work well together, with the former allowing the latter, in the showier role, to dominate the film.

In terms of historical accuracy, the film takes great liberties and gets away with them. Romero is Doc Halliday, not Doc Holliday. In this movie, the events, including Halliday's death, take place in 1880, even though the real gunfight at the O.K. Corral took place in October 1881. In this cinematic gunfight, it's Earp alone against Curly Bill and three cronies (including Indian Charlie, who has gotten out of jail without explanation). There's no mention here of the infamous Clanton gang, and in fact the real Doc Holliday died of tuberculosis in 1887. Stuart Lake's book, reportedly written with Earp's help before the lawman passed on in 1929, is supposedly a much fictionalized account of his life, so one can't blame screenwriter Sam Hellman for taking additional liberties with the story. *Frontier Marshal* remains a sprightly little "B+" Western that holds up today.

Allan Dwan: (to Peter Bogdanovich, *Who the Devil Made It*): "I liked Randolph Scott and practically everyone in the cast; I think it was well done. We never meant it to *be* Wyatt Earp — we were just making *Frontier Marshal*, and that could be any frontier marshal. When I made *Suez* (1938) out there at Fox, I put about a million tons of sand on the back lot to make a desert, and someone said to me, 'What are we going to do with this sand when you get through?' I said, 'Well, some sucker will have to move it out of here.' When *Frontier Marshal* came along, I induced Zanuck to let me build a Western street back there but in order to do that, the sand had to be moved. So I was the sucker!"

The New York Times (7/29/1939): "From Randolph Scott, who walks through the role of Wyatt Earp with his customary sang-froid, to Eddie Foy, Jr., in the role of his own famous father, the players fit their parts with such perfection that it is hard to know whether to credit the setting or the casting director. *Frontier Marshal* is a cracking good Western, and in the movies there's nothing much better than that."
The New York Post (7/29/1939): "A bang-bang thriller. Hopalong Billy Boyd never shot more unerringly than Randolph Scott. There are so many villains that the picture is unable to identify them as more than shadowy figures biting the dust at the urging of Mr. Scott's incessant cannons."

Coast Guard (Columbia, August 1939, 72 minutes)

CREDITS   Director: Edward Ludwig; Producer: Fred Kohlmar; Screenplay: Albert Duffy, Richard Maibaum and Harry Segall

CAST   Randolph Scott (Speed Bradshaw), Frances Dee (Nancy Bliss), Ralph Bellamy (Lt. Doner), Walter Connolly (Tobias Bliss), Warren Hymer (O'Hara), Robert Middlemass (Capt. Lyons)

Synopsis: "Speed" Bradshaw is only interested in flying and womanizing until he meets Nancy Bliss. The two get hitched, but Speed can't stop his fast-moving ways, and he's headed for divorce and disgrace until he redeems himself by rescuing his old pal (Ralph Bellamy) in a daring Arctic salvage mission.

Coast Guard looks like it might be a snappy little "B" film — for about 20 minutes. The dialogue is fast and sometimes funny, and Scott has a ball playing a pilot playboy who is first seen singing "In the merry, merry month of May," as he plans to go on a date with four beautiful women. "I'm in for a big night," he says, warmly rubbing his hands together at the prospect of a "ménage a cinco." Then he's called to help on a salvage mission at sea, which means he has to cancel the date. In an effort to pacify the lusty quartet of ladies, he tells them that they've got the wrong night and to meet him same time, same place the following evening to fulfill their destinies. The beauty of it is, the four sirens buy it!

The salvage mission involves rescuing tugboat captain Tobias Bliss (Walter Connolly) in a storm. The use of miniatures and dummies in this action scene wouldn't fool a six year old. But at least there's action as Scott and pal Ralph Bellamy tow the stranded seamen in. Toby is sent to the hospital where the Coast Guardsmen meet Tobias' granddaughter Nancy (Frances Dee). Bellamy falls for her but Scott tries to steer him away.

"Don't tell me you call marriage living?" Scott incredulously asks Bellamy. "What do you call it?" Bellamy shoots back. "Blind flying!" Scott replies.

Scott works behind-the-scenes to undercut Bellamy's chances of wedlock, but in the process the devil-may-care pilot falls for the sweet and innocent Dee. Bellamy, in the sort of hapless pal role Scott might have landed a few years earlier at Paramount, fades away as Scott and Dee wed. A funny sequence follows wherein Scott and Dee prepare to consummate their marriage, only to be interrupted by an endless string of visitors: moving men, neighborhood watch representatives and a landlady who offers to teach them how to use the electric stove. "We eat our meat raw!" an amorous and short-on-patience Scott screams, leading the old crone to rush out contemplating the notion: "Cannibals!"

The film goes downhill from here. Scott continues to play the field—I don't know why; Dee was a pretty hot dish—and she leaves him. He in turn begins drinking, smoking and pacing around the house. Angry, he decides to raze Dee's new home with his airplane, but he loses control and crashes into the sea, resulting in a loss of wings and permanent grounding. Then Bellamy gets called out to rescue some snow-bound schooner sailors. Through a series of silly circumstances, Bellamy gets lost and falls unconscious in the snow.

You can predict the rest: Nancy convinces Speed Bradshaw, who is on a drinking binge, to go rescue his pal Doner. Newspaper headlines tell the tale: "Bradshaw Hops North!," "Bradshaw Reaches Alaska!," "Bradshaw Finds Doner!" (Apparently his flight took several days, which makes you wonder how Bellamy could have survived in the snow for so long.) Scott crashes within striking distance of the still-prone Bellamy. He figures the only way out of this wasteland is to push his plane down a one-way slope into oblivion and hope that the motor will start once they hit the air. This enjoyably unbelievable comic-strip solution works, Bellamy and Scott renew their friendship, and Scott vows to be a good husband to Dee. THE END.

Coast Guard is a by-the-numbers melodrama that has more to do with the three-way love triangle of the principals than it does with the Coast Guard, which is a shame, because it might have been a good little action picture. As it is, this lightweight film is slight entertainment, though it is interesting to see Scott playing opposite Joel McCrea's wife Frances Dee. The film did fairly well at the box office, in part due to a real-life incident in July 1939 in which the Coast Guard *did* save the crew of a freighter lost at sea. Columbia couldn't have asked for better publicity. And Scott commits to the material fully, although he's not capable of making the emotional transition from heroic playboy to self-destructive lout.

New York Daily News (8/27/1939): "There is little here that you haven't seen in other pictures about the heroes of various services, yet this particular cast puts some life into the old plot, refreshing it enough to satisfy." *The New York Post* (8/28/1939): "Everyone knows that the Coast Guard is constantly performing heroic deeds. But that does not justify attributing to them the combined powers of Pop-Eye, Donald Duck and God Almighty."

20,000 Men a Year (20th Century–Fox, October 1939, 84 minutes)

CREDITS   Director: Alfred E. Green; Producer: Sol M. Wurtzel; Screenplay: Lou Breslow and Owen Francis, from a story by Frank Wead

CAST   Randolph Scott (Brad Reynolds), Preston Foster (Jim Howell), Margaret Lindsay (Ann Rogers), Mary Healy (Joan Marshall), Robert Shaw (Tommy Howell), George Ernest (Skip Rogers), Maxie Rosenbloom (Walt Dorgan), Jane Darwell (Mrs. Allen), Kane Richmond (Al Williams), Sen Yung (Harold Chon), Sidney Miller (Irving Glassman)

Synopsis: The Civil Aeronautics Authority plans to train 20,000 men a year — with the help of flying daredevil Brad Reynolds.

20,000 Men a Year is an okay programmer in which Scott gives the material no more than it deserves. Sitting through an entire reel of Scott giving flying lessons to teenagers, painting airplane wings and bartering with a gasoline merchant is enough to make you want to see our hero load up his Winchester and open fire on the rest of the cast. He handles some comic lines with aplomb and gives a sincere performance as a former daredevil pilot coerced into working for the CCA, but it can't be said this film is among his finest. But that was Scott's lot in his career at this point.

The dialogue is enjoyably corny. "Flying's in my blood," one flying student says. "What didja get, a transfusion from an eagle?" quips his companion in Dead End Kid–type talk.

Margaret Lindsay plays Ann, a sociology teacher who attempts to dissuade her wimpy brother Skip from pursuing the same career, while Preston Foster plays Scott's former boss, a man who works behind the scenes to help Scott even while acting the role of rival to his face. No pun intended, but *20,000 Men a Year* never really takes off, though it's intentions are good. The film boasts some unintentionally humorous moments, including a scene where Scott flies in the air while using a microphone to broadcast his lesson to his class on the landing field below — a scene that ends with Scott recklessly attempting to run down his mechanic (Maxie Rosenbloom) as a joke. It also has a stock Jewish comic figure, a student who tells Scott he wants to learn how to fly so he can work his territory faster (he mentally calculates how many customers he can visit in the span of a day in a plane — assuming, I reckon, that all these fabric stores have landing fields).

In real life the CAA did train about 20,000 men a year to contribute to the aviation industry, instruction that came in handy two years later when World War II broke out.

New York World Telegram (10/28/1939): "Randolph Scott turns in a performance that is sincere and convincing. The unfortunate part of *20,000 Men a Year* is that it never sticks to its chief purposes— when the going gets tough it flies off in all directions." *The Brooklyn Daily-Eagle* (10/28/1939): "*20,000 Men a Year* turns out to be spotty entertainment; dull, slow and unoriginal in its beginning and moderately bright but far from convincing towards the end."

Virginia City (Warner Bros., March 1940, 112 minutes)

CREDITS   Director: Michael Curtiz; Producer: Hal B. Wallis; Screenplay: Robert Buckner

CAST   Errol Flynn (Kerry Bradford), Miriam Hopkins (Julia Hayne), Randolph Scott (Vance Irby), Humphrey Bogart (John Murrel), Guinn "Big Boy" Williams (Marblehead), Alan Hale (Moose), Frank McHugh (Mr. Upjohn), John Litel (Marshall), Douglas Dumbrille (Major Drewery), Moroni Olson (Dr. Cameron), Russell Hicks (Armistead), Dickie Jones (Cobby), Russell Simpson (Gaylord), Victor Kilian (Abraham Lincoln), Charles Middleton (Jefferson Davis), Monte Montague (Stage Driver), Paul Fix (Henchman), George Regas (Henchman)

Synopsis: Confederate officer Vance Irby works with Southern spy Julia Hayne to transport $5,000,000 in gold from Virginia City, Nevada, to Richmond, Virginia, to finance the Confederate cause. Standing against the duo is Union officer Kerry Bradford and Mexican bandit John Murrel, each of whom have their own plans for the gold.

When Michael Curtiz's *Dodge City*, starring Errol Flynn as an Irish soldier-of-fortune who tames the title town, was released in the spring of 1939, it proved such a hit that Warner Bros. immediately set about creating a sequel. *Dodge City*'s finale even set up the sequel in sending Flynn and new bride Olivia de Havilland to Virginia City to bring law and order to that territory.

For better or worse (for better, I think), *that* potential plotline was dropped and an entirely new scenario was created for *Virginia City* reuniting Curtiz, Flynn, de Havilland and Flynn's sidekicks Alan Hale and Guinn "Big Boy" Williams. For reasons that remain unclear, Olivia de Havilland did not do the picture, so Miriam Hopkins was cast in *Virginia City* as a Southern spy posing as a dance hall girl. Screenwriter Robert Buckner also made

room for a Southern gentleman (who else but Randolph Scott?) and a leering Mexican bandido (Bogart in a role intended for John Carradine).

Mark Hellinger, a writer-producer at Warners in the 1930s and 1940s, took the first crack at the *Virginia City* script in the summer of 1939. Robert Lord, a producer at the studio, looked at Hellinger's outline and wrote a memo (July 18, 1939) in which he gave his opinion: "Your basic story line is about as good (perhaps a little better) than the basic story line of *Dodge City* and *Union Pacific*. That is to say, 'It stinks and they stank.'" Obviously Lord was no fan of Westerns, but he went on to make a somewhat valid comment: "To be quite realistic, the basic story line of most Westerns, including the successful ones, is prone to be somewhat feeble-minded. Why not — since they cater to the lowest common denominator of our mass audience?" The project then fell into screenwriter Robert Buckner's hands, and he worked on the script with some uncredited help from Howard Koch through the autumn of 1939. Producer Hal B. Wallis lined up a cast, including Scott, and shooting began in November 1939 and continued through January 1940 on Warners' Calabasas Ranch and on location in Arizona.

The shoot was not entirely pleasant. Flynn was tiring of working with the mercurial Curtiz, and the actor, no fan of Westerns (he once referred to himself as the "Rich man's Roy Rogers"), proved difficult to handle. Hopkins was none too happy with her lot either, constantly arguing with Curtiz about the script and wardrobe. She also refused to report to work earlier than 10 A.M. She gave the film some negative publicity shortly after filming completed when she told Michael Mok, a reporter for *The New York Post*, "If you want to see me look tragic, you must take a peek at my new picture. I just finished — whoof — and came to New York for a few days' breath. I worked on it for almost 12 weeks. Why I was cast in it I shall never know. I had to do all the things I can't do. I had to sing, and I can't carry a tune. I had to dance, and I hadn't taken a step except on a nightclub floor in ten years. Oh, it's a honey. It's got almost as much in it as *Gone with the Wind*. I start with Jefferson Davis and end with Abraham Lincoln!"

Hopkins had a point about the film's complex, multi-faceted plot. You can pick apart a lot of story points and ridicule them, starting with the fact that if Scott is such a valuable asset to the Confederate cause, then why has his character been reduced to running a prison? (Flynn and his buddies escape said prison in the film's opening sequence, and then we're off to Virginia City, where the two once again cross paths.) Bogart hated his part and complained repeatedly, though it is to his credit that he committed 100 percent to the role, and he actually looks fairly good on horseback. I'm not sure the role would have fit Carradine well either. It would have been great to see Gilbert Roland do it, but I wasn't in charge of casting at Warner Bros. in 1939.

To top things off, many of the actors suggested new dialogue during shooting, which angered Wallis, who fired off a memo to director Curtiz, "I see no reason why everybody on the set should take potshots at every scene and supply their own version." He told Curtiz to stop the practice of letting the actors rework some of the scenes on the set. One day Flynn, Alan Hale and Guinn "Big Boy" Williams came to screenwriter Robert Buckner and Curtiz with a musical number they wanted to do. Buckner called it "corny crap" and predicted that Wallis would never let it be filmed. He was right.

Scott managed to float on the water like a drifting leaf amidst all this storm,

earning Curtiz's respect. "Randy Scott is a complete anachronism," Curtiz later said. "He's a gentleman. And so far he's the only one I've met in this business full of self-promoting sons of bitches." It's a shame Curtiz never directed Scott again (and really a shame, in my view, that Curtiz did not do *Carson City* with Scott after Errol Flynn turned it down). The two must have hit it off creatively as well as personally, for Scott gives one of his top performances as a dedicated Southerner fighting against all odds to change the outcome of the Civil War. "He could lead a cavalry charge to Hades and back," one character says of him, and I for one believe it. Scott gives a grounded performance, displaying ever-growing confidence, and he is certainly more at home in this Western epic than any of the other players. If you watch *Virginia City* once, you may acknowledge his work but keep your eyes focused on the likes of Flynn, Hopkins and even Bogart (who, if nothing else, is certainly flamboyant). But in viewing the picture a second time, it's Scott who will invite your attention. He gives the best performance in *Virginia City*.

Scott's character gets hard-driving near the film's end. Despite a lack of water and a dying child (Dickie Jones), he pushes the gold train further into the desert in an attempt to avoid both Flynn and Bogart. He refuses to bend to peer pressure or to Bogart's slimy bandit, who has decided to cross Scott and appropriate the money for himself. Pretty soon Bogart has thrown a monkey wrench of gunfire into the works, and Flynn's Union loyalist joins Scott's rebel leader to fend off a massive bandit attack on the wagon train. The action scenes, ranging from a shoot-out at an isolated way station to a stirring horseback chase across the desert, are superb. The final confrontation in which Bogie and his men assault the wagon train is well choreographed, with the bandits literally cas-

Southern officer Randolph Scott (left) and Union officer Errol Flynn team up to combat Humphrey Bogart's gang of bandits in the exciting conclusion to Warner Bros. epic Western *Virginia City* (1940). (JC Archives, Inc.)

cading down the surrounding mountain sides like water currents engulfing the small wagon train below. Curtiz captures the close-quarters engagements in tight fashion, letting the bandits ride into the camp to run over the defenders. Scott takes a bullet to the chest at close range (sorry to reveal the bad news to those who haven't seen the film). Dying, he puts Flynn in command of the defense. Scott has a beautiful, understated death scene, muttering to himself (or to God) in his last moments as the battle rages around him. The near-silent muttering bit is not in the script, making me wonder whether Curtiz or Scott suggested it.

Controversy erupted in March 1940 when the film premiered in Virginia City and Reno, Nevada. Seems Flynn and Hopkins were scheduled to make personal appearances at the opening on March 16 at the Virginia City Theater. Ticket prices were a steep $1.10 (average cost at the time was 40 cents). The two stars didn't show, so the townspeople, displaying a true sense of Western vigilantism, made hostages out of five buses of Warner Bros. guests, including a crew of minor executives, bit players, cowboys and politicians (five governors and the mayor of Reno). "Makes me so damned mad!" declared the theater's owner, Joe Hart, who told the press he'd have to give every moviegoer 70 cents back to make up for the lack of celebrities and that he'd like to give Flynn a good beating. Flynn, Hopkins, Bogart and a cadre of lesser contract players were indeed on a cross-country train trip to publicize the film, but no one knows why Flynn didn't pop up in Virginia City (there were rumors he was waylaid by an appealing waif in a nearby town). Scott was not scheduled for the publicity tour; probably because he was a freelance player and not under contract to Warner Bros. I bet he would have showed up as scheduled and quelled that crowd but fast.

Scott worked on the film from late October through late December 1939, earning $4,375 per week. He got along with everyone and, near the end of filming, told Curtiz he'd gladly come back to do any pick-up work or vocal tracking if they needed him. In 1950, as Warners prepared to re-release the film, they discovered that contractual commitments on the part of all three stars derailed their plans to highlight Scott's name. They had to maintain the original billing, with Flynn and Hopkins' names appearing above Scott's, and Bogart taking fourth billing. But by that time, Scott and Bogart were bigger stars than Flynn and Hopkins.

Stuntman Jack Williams (to author): "At the time Randy was doing *Virginia City*, he had what you would call a 'presence.' His stature at that time was almost equal to Flynn's, and Flynn was the number one guy at Warner Bros. Michael Curtiz was the director. He was the funniest guy who was ever in Hollywood. His use of the English language — or lack of use — was legend. He's the guy who said, 'The next time I send a dumb son of a bitch to do something, I go myself!'

Randy was a good actor, but not too many people wanted to pay to see him do it in films that weren't Westerns. So he fell back into that Western genre, and did all those pictures with Harry Joe Brown at Columbia."

Most critics felt *Virginia City* was not up to the standards of *Dodge City*. I think it's the superior film and at least one critic of the time agrees with me. "A lusty, lively and generally satisfying Western," the *Boston Globe*'s reviewer wrote. "I suspect that the Warner Brothers have another hit on their hands in the nature of *Dodge City*, and a better picture into the bargain."

My Favorite Wife (RKO, May 1940, 88 minutes)

CREDITS   Director: Garson Kanin; Producer: Leo McCarey; Screenplay: Bella and Samuel Spewack

CAST   Irene Dunne (Helen Arden), Cary Grant (Nicky Arden), Randolph Scott (Stephen Burkett), Gail Patrick (Bianca), Ann Shoemaker (Ma), Mary Lou Harrington (Chinch), Scotty Beckett (Tim), Granville Bates (Judge), Donald MacBride (Hotel Clerk)

Synopsis: Nicky Arden has a lot to fret about. On his wedding day to his second wife, he discovers that his first wife, long believed dead, had actually spent seven years on a tropical island with good-looking hunk Stephen Burkett.

My Favorite Wife is an agreeable comedy from the screwball era that is now somewhat over rated. It opens with a hilarious courtroom sequence in which Cary Grant, playing lawyer Nicky Arden, tries to explain to an addle-headed judge (Granville Bates, who steals the film) that his first wife should be declared legally dead so that he can marry his second wife. Little does Nicky know that wife number one will return within the hour.

Among the complications is third-billed Scott, who positively shines in a wonderful comic role as the other man. This is no Ralph Bellamy type; Scott's Stephen Burkett is the sort who truly threatens to steal a woman away from her husband. His first appearance is about half way through this 88 minute comedy. Clad in a bathrobe and sitting by the club pool

Cary Grant doesn't seem too pleased with Scott's wisecracking in the 1940 comedy *My Favorite Wife* (1940). That's Irene Dunne, a favorite leading lady of both men, in the center. (JC Archives, Inc.)

with a pair of comely brunettes, he chatters on seductively for a moment before deciding to show off his physique by going for a swim. As he mounts the diving board, a matronly woman approaches Grant, who has come to the club to find Scott, and (indicating Scott) asks, "Is that Johnny Weissmuller?" "No," replies Grant in perfect deadpan timing, "but I wish it were." Scott was probably happy not to have to carry the entire weight of the film on his shoulders.

Those curious about the Scott-Grant relationship can store up a lot of ammunition from watching this film. It's full of homoerotic symbolism, from the scene where Grant, trying to work, finds himself haunted by the image of a near-naked Scott diving into the pool, to the sequence where Grant, asked by wife Irene Dunne to bring her some clothes (she got pushed into the pool), tries on her attire in front of the mirror and gets caught in the act by a doctor who is convinced that Grant is gay or impotent. "They're for a friend of mine … he's waiting downstairs," Grant matter-of-factly explains to the befuddled doctor. The friend is Scott, who is supposed to take the clothes back to Dunne, but of course the doctor thinks otherwise.

"*My Favorite Wife* is one of those films that was a hugely popular success at the time of its release, but that for reasons not immediately apparent falls far short of expectations (and memories) today," accurately noted William K. Everson in his 1994 book *Hollywood Bedlam*, "Basically *My Favorite Wife* has no surprises and takes no chances." Everson noted that *Too Many Husbands*, a similar film from the same year with the same theme done in reverse (dead husband shows up unexpect-edly), is better than *My Favorite Wife*.

Leo McCarey to Peter Bogdanovich (*Who the Devil Made It?*): "We finished (*My Favorite Wife*) and then found in a sneak (preview) that after about five reels the picture took a dip, and for about two reels or more it wasn't as funny as what preceded it — it didn't come up to it; it was a lot of unraveling of a tricky plot. So the cast was dismissed, the writers went home, the director went back to New York and I sat there with the cutter trying to figure out what to do to save the picture. We sneaked it out once more to be sure and were right that something had to be done and sure enough, right in the same place, it dipped — was very unfunny.

"Then I got the wildest idea I ever had. There was a judge in the opening who was very funny, and he dropped out of the picture, and I decided to bring him back. What we actually did was to tell the judge our story problems in the picture and have him comment on them. And it was truly great. It became the outstanding thing in the picture."

Grant blew his lines 17 times in the courtroom scene because he kept breaking up at Granville Bates' performance.

The film's working title was *Woman Overboard*; filming took place between December 1939 and March 1940, with Scott taking home $28,333.34 for his efforts. (Grant got $112,500 and Dunne $100,000.) The film was remade in 1963 by Fox as *Move Over Darling* after their abortive 1962 attempt, *Something's Got to Give*, folded due to star Marilyn Monroe's death.

The Boston Post (6/21/1940): "Slick, smart and sophisticated. The plot is pre-posterous, of course, but there is a laugh a minute." *The New York Post* (5/31/1940): "It is comedy, skillfully made, but not as original in synopsis as one would prefer. Randolph Scott as a muscular vegetarian is a pleasing departure from type-casting."

When the Daltons Rode (Universal, August 1940, 80 minutes)

CREDITS   Director: George Marshall; Screen-play: Harold Shumate, based on the book *When the Daltons Rode* by Emmett Dalton and Jack Jungmeyer, Sr.

CAST   Randolph Scott (Todd Jackson), Kay Francis (Julie King), Brian Donlevy (Grat Dal-ton), Broderick Crawford (Bob Dalton), Stu-art Erwin (Ben Dalton), Frank Albertson (Em-mett Dalton), Andy Devine (Ozark), George Bancroft (Caleb Winters), Mary Gordon (Ma Dalton), Harvey Stephens (Rigby), Edgar Dear-ing (Sheriff), Edgar Buchanan (Blacksmith)

Synopsis: The Dalton Brothers are driven to a life of crime thanks to the under-handed machinations of crooked political bosses.

When the Daltons Rode is a rip-roar-ing, good-humored Western with tip-top direction and tight ensemble playing. It may best be described as rambunctious — a term one wouldn't immediately apply to most Randolph Scott films — and it bene-fits from a really effective one-two punch from the team of director George Marshall and scenarist Harold Shumate. How faith-ful it is to real-life events may not be im-portant; the film's creators wisely throw in a introductory title card stating that "No man can say where fact ends and fancy be-gins," which is good enough for me.

Taking an obvious cue from 20th Century–Fox's *Jesse James*, Shumate's script sees unscrupulous government regulators illegally taking land from Kansas farmers, including the Daltons. This leads the Dal-ton boys to rebel, first through legal routes, and then via robbery. Scott plays the gang's lawyer, a childhood friend who falls in love with Bob Dalton's gal Julie (Kay Francis). The film ends with the Dalton gang going down in a blaze of gunfire as they attempt to rob two banks at the same time.

I love watching Scott play opposite old-time raconteurs like George "Gabby" Hayes and Edgar Buchanan. He always seems bemused as these characters take center stage and launch into long-winded monologues about this or that or nothing. In the first scene of *When the Daltons Rode*, Scott tries in vain to suppress a genuine smile when Buchanan recites a lengthy diatribe about the history of pioneering — and all this nonsense in response to a simple question as to where the Daltons live!

Scott knew how to use his eyes to convey a longing — for a place to call home, for love, for revenge, or even lust — which he does here in a scene where Francis tells him her heart is bound to Broderick Crawford's Bob Dalton. Scott and Francis enjoy a nice give-and-take relationship that is hearty and real; it's too bad they fade into the background once the Dalton boys take up arms and start shooting up the territory.

Marshall knew how to get his actors to commit to physical shtick. The first reel of this film is pure slapstick, with normally somber actors like Crawford, Brian Donlevy and Scott taking the buffoonery to the limits. The comic byplay between the Daltons and an unknowing counter man at a diner is a gem of a scene. Shumate's screenplay offers up surprises, and Marshall delivers on them. The lynch mob scene is among the most terrifying I've seen on film; a chase sequence wherein the outlaws use a stagecoach to escape a posse is novel, and the ensuing train robbery chapter — where the Dalton Boys (make that the stuntmen doubling for the actors playing the Dalton Boys) ride their horses off of a moving train after stealing the payroll — remains surprising and suspenseful today.

Memorable dialogue: Crawford to comrade Andy Devine, as they and their gang ride hell-bent-for-leather in an effort to escape a posse: "How we doin'?"

Devine takes a look at the posse, which is fast closing in, and responds, "Not so good."

The Frank Skinner score is of immense help, complementing the flow of action throughout. The gunfights, chase scenes and simple one-on-one dialogue sequences are all handled with a brisk sense of energy and commitment that confirms Marshall's status as a "get in there and show them how to do it" director.*

As is portrayed in the film, in real life the Dalton Gang did attempt to rob two banks at once in their home town of Coffeyville, Kansas. Bob and Grat Dalton, as well as two non-family accomplices, were shot dead in the raid. Emmett Dalton was severely wounded but survived to tell his story. (*When the Daltons Rode* is based on his book, even though Shumate's script sees Emmett killed.) There was no Ben Dalton (Stuart Erwin plays Ben in the film), but there was a Frank Dalton, a law-abiding brother who as a federal deputy marshal was killed by bootleggers in 1887. A fifth brother, Bill Dalton, died in a shootout following a bank robbery with the Doolin gang in Longview, Texas.

The credits for *When the Daltons Rode* do not include a stunt coordinator, but whoever was in charge of all those fantastic physical feats deserves credit. Apparently the four actors portraying the Daltons were unskilled at even the basics of horsemanship. Two months before the picture was released, Crawford annoyed

---

*Stuntwoman Polly Burson relates a telling story about Marshall's directorial personality that took place on the set of the 1947 Betty Hutton film *The Perils of Pauline*. While doubling for Hutton (playing Pearl White), Burson had to gallop alongside a train and board it before moving along the coal car towards the engine, where she was to shoot at some pursuing outlaws. Marshall made Burson do the stunt three times, even though the stuntwoman felt she had done it perfectly the first time. On the last take Burson happened to look into the engineer's cabin and she noticed Marshall, his head covered by an engineer's cap, driving the train. Beaming, he turned to Burson and said, "Ever since I was a little boy, I wanted to be an engineer." That was the only reason he made her do the stunt three times — he wasn't done playing "choo choo" yet.

Edgar Buchanan seems to be in the middle of a double-take as he reacts to the sight of Kay Francis and Randolph Scott, arm in arm, at the conclusion of *When the Daltons Rode* (1940). (JC Archives, Inc.)

Universal by telling *New York World-Telegram* reporter Frederick C. Othman that, "If the truth should come out, this picture would be titled, 'When the Daltons' Doubles Rode.' None of the Daltons knows how to ride a horse. You'll see us climbing on horses and climbing off, but in between you'll see stuntmen." Journalist Paul Harrison's on-set visit confirmed Crawford's assertion. Harrison noted that Donlevy needed a ladder to mount, that Crawford had ruined an escape scene by putting his right foot in the stirrup, and that Erwin was terrified while shooting a scene where Crawford, Donlevy and Devine ride to his rescue while he lay in the street. Marshall assured Erwin that horses wouldn't step on a man, but the frightened actor came back with, "Of course the

horses know better, but I don't trust Devine and Crawford and Donlevy." Watch closely in the first scene where Donlevy has to get off of his horse and you'll see he practically falls off of it. Most of the close-ups of the Daltons on horseback were done amidst rear-projection material and look pretty phony, but the film is so good you probably won't care.

Reviews were mostly positive; box office was healthy, and Scott, though seen in a secondary role, had once again hitched his wagon to a hit. The year 1940 was a very good one for the actor; all three of his films garnered critical and commercial success and all three showcased him in somewhat different roles.

"The picture does amazingly well what Westerns ever since the 1903 *Great*

Train Robbery have aimed at," wrote *Cue* magazine's reviewer (8/24/1940), "It packs in 81 minutes of running time with hammering action … mixed with appropriate doses of comedy, romance and atmosphere." *The New York Post* (8/23/1940): "The action is fairly convincing, although the ability of the Daltons to pass unwounded through hails of bullets becomes increasingly difficult to accept. This is particularly noticeable because, when the picture comes to its appointed end, the Daltons lose their invulnerability with startling suddenness." *The New York Times*' (8/23/1940) Bosley Crowther, in his tongue-in-cheek but thumbs-up review, called the film a "titanic Western," adding that "the picture itself is straight, fast Western fare, and for folks who like plenty of shootin', here is your gunpowder." Crowther, incidentally, stated that Universal would never be able to make a sequel to the film, as all of its hero outlaws were killed at the end. But the studio did manage to remake the film before war's end, turning out an inferior imitation, *The Daltons Ride Again* (1945), featuring Lon Chaney, Jr., Noah Beery, Jr., Alan Curtis and Kent Taylor as the Daltons.

Western Union (20th Century–Fox, February 1941, 94 minutes)

CREDITS   Director : Fritz Lang; Producer: Harry Joe Brown; Screenplay: Robert Carson, based on Zane Grey's book *Western Union*

CAST   Robert Young (Richard Blake), Randolph Scott (Vance Shaw), Dean Jagger (Edward Creighton), Virginia Gilmore (Sue Creighton), John Carradine (Doc Murdoch), Slim Summerville (Herman), Chill Wills (Homer), Barton MacLane (Jack Slade), Russell Hicks (Governor), Victor Killan (Charlie), Minor Watson (Pat Grogan), George Chandler (Herb)

Synopsis: Edward Creighton builds the Western Union line between Omaha and Salt Lake City with the assistance of telegrapher Richard Blake and scout Vance Shaw. Unbeknownst to Creighton, Shaw is an outlaw, and his brother is none other than the infamous Jack Slade.

Western Union opens with a beautiful shot of a rugged (and ragged) cowpoke silhouetted against the spectacular Utah scenery. Zane Grey's novels knew how to make the landscape a character in itself, and in this shot we really get a feel for how a man can be lost in hell — or happy in heaven — in the heart of the country. The cowpoke is Scott's Vance Shaw, an outlaw on the run from a bank robbery with a posse on his trail. And from then on, though he doesn't have top billing or the largest part, *Western Union* belongs lock, stock and barrel (double barrel, in fact) to Randolph Scott. It may not be his best overall film, but along with the role of Gil Westrum in *Ride the High Country*, I think it's among his finest acting work.

Scott had learned to do a lot with a little, expressing fear, love, anger and self-doubt with the slightest facial expressions. His eyes do all the talking for him in this film; in fact, he probably has less dialogue in *Western Union* than any other Western he appeared in. Scott is playing the odd man out in the love triangle again, vying with Easterner Richard Blake (Robert Young) for the hand of Sue Creighton (lovely Virginia Gilmore, who was director Lang's girlfriend at the time). Shaw at least fights for his place with the girl, giving the role an inner strength and nobility that surprises the viewer. Virile, lively and determined, Scott's Vance Shaw is a man who knows he has run up his last box canyon. There's something tragic about his character here — more tragic than the Boetticher heroes, or even Gil Westrum — as Shaw is a man who realizes the choices he has made in life will never bring him happiness.

> SHAW (to Sue Creighton): "I should have met you a couple of years ago."

A lobby card for *Western Union* (1941), in which Scott, playing good-bad guy Vince Shaw, gives an Academy Award–worthy performance.

SUE: "Why?"

SHAW: "Since then I've made some mistakes."

SUE: "Mistakes can be corrected."

SHAW: "Not always."

Like Westrum, Shaw has a shot at redemption in the form of an odds-against-living shoot-out against his outlaw brother's gang but, unlike Westrum, Shaw dies, buying a return ticket to self-respect in the process. It's a beautiful performance that was honored by critics, and I think it's the one film where Scott should have been Oscar-nominated as Best Supporting Actor. (Look at who was nominated: Sydney Greenstreet for *The Maltese Falcon*, Walter Brennan for *Sergeant York*, Charles Coburn

for *The Devil and Miss Jones*, James Gleason for *Here Comes Mr. Jordan* and Donald Crisp for *How Green Was My Valley*. Crisp won.)

Scott truly suffered for his art in this film. "Pioneering was no doubt a fine and noble calling, but compared to this job, Daniel Boone had a snap," he told visiting journalist John Franchey. In one scene Scott had to hold his bound hands over a campfire to burn off the rope. John Ford's daughter Barbara recalled watching the film on television with her dad in the early 1970s as the elder Ford said to her, "Those are Randy's wrists, that is real rope, that is a real fire...."

Lang believed in realism, all right. He and assistant director Otto Brower started a bona fide forest fire. The mock 15-acre forest was built on the back lot of Fox with wood and trees taken from Los Angeles property owners who were trying to clear their land. Reportedly all the actors had asbestos clothing on for the scene, but even at that it was dangerous. "Robert Young lost his eyebrows in one scene," Brower explained to a journalist. "The heat singed them off before he realized what was happening. Dean Jagger and Randolph Scott also suffered minor burns."

Scott was Zane Grey's personal choice for the role of Vance; *Western Union* was the author's last book and he sold the rights to Fox in 1939 for $40,000 (Grey died of heart disease in the autumn of 1939). Fox's head of production, Darryl F. Zanuck, had a lot to say to the screenwriters about the character of Shaw. "Shaw should be a character like the boy (John Wayne) in *Stagecoach*," he wrote producer Harry Joe Brown late in 1939. "Quiet, doesn't say much, but we know he is deadly. He should never regenerate, but remain to the end a renegade, but a hell of a nice guy, but never a hint of noble regeneration." By the following autumn, when director Fritz Lang read the script, the Shaw character was still somewhat undefined, according to a memo Lang sent Brown. "Shaw I feel I do not know," he noted. "I must recognize the fact that Randolph Scott is playing Shaw and I want to get it clearly set in the audience's mind who he is—an outlaw! I am thinking how I want to play my scenes with Shaw and I feel I can play them best if they know he is a bad man whom I am going to make into a good man before the picture is over."

Zanuck, in the interim, paid close attention to the development of the story, asking his writers and producer to make it a personal odyssey rather than the history of Western Union. In the spring of 1940 he offered six pages of criticism of the latest draft, writing, "Every other page we are bounced into a hokey melodramatic situation. I wager we have more hoks than they had in *Union Pacific*." He went on about building up the characters and eliminating some of the action sequences: "We should forget about making this a history of Western Union … make it a great story about a group of people who happen to be engaged in this enterprise. *This should be a man's story about men.*" Zanuck suggested writing out all the female characters and asked his team to eliminate a bizarre subplot involving some Mormons who save the day at the last minute.

The ending kept changing. Scott's Shaw character was killed by Dean Jagger's Edward Creighton in one draft; in another, Scott killed all the bad men, including his evil brother Jack Slade (Barton MacLane), before expiring. Brown, in the interim, kept pushing Lang to get more visuals and more violence into the film. Lang and/or Zanuck then forced ingénue Virginia Gilmore on Brown. All the added interest and suggestions probably made *Western Union* a better film, but they also slowed up the shooting schedule, and the film went over budget by at least $60,000, which infuriated Zanuck. However, his personal touch made all the difference in the finished product. Unfortunately, he didn't — or couldn't — put the same sort of effort into Scott's next Western entry, *Belle Starr.*

"The film was made after a book by Zane Grey but nothing from it was used in the picture but the title," director Fritz Lang told Peter Bogdanovich. "I forget who wrote the script, but they had to invent many things because in reality, nothing happened during the entire building of the line except that they ran out of wood for the telegraph poles … and the only other thing that disturbed the laying of the line was the ticks on the buffalos; the buffalos got itchy and rubbed themselves against the poles, and the poles tumbled. And that was all that happened. Naturally much more happened in the picture. Anyway when the film was finished, I found out that the laying of the line did not take half as long as the shooting of the picture!" (It only took Western Union between three and four months— accounts vary— to lay the line at a cost of $212,000, whereas it cost Fox about a million dollars and ten months to make the film.)

Harry Joe Brown, Jr. (to author, on his father's penchant for finding proper locales): "He knew a lot about Westerns, having made them from about 1920 almost up until his death [April 1972]. He knew stuff like where the right cliffs and deserts were, where to get the horses and getting people up to location and working. And the whole idea of the location — the natural beauty of the land, the red cliffs, the streams— that was very important to the Western and my father. Some time later a lot of those wide open spaces weren't there any more." Two years later, Brown and Scott would reteam for *The Desperadoes*, again shooting in Kanub, Utah.

Western Union was a major hit for 20th Century–Fox and reviews were almost unanimously positive, with particular praise for Scott's work. *New York Herald Tribune* (2/9/41): "Randolph Scott is especially fine as the reformed bad man." *New York World Telegram* (2/7/41): "No matter how many Westerns you may have seen, *Western Union* is certainly one of the best of them…. Randolph Scott's performance could scarcely be improved upon." *The New York Times*: "A bang-up outdoor action picture. Randolph Scott, who is getting to look and act more and more like William S. Hart, herein shapes one of the truest and most appreciable characters of his career as the party's scout." *New York Morning-Telegraph* (2/7/41): "If memory serves, this is one of the few occasions on record where Mr. Scott loses the girl and gets himself killed in a shooting affair. He's so good-looking it usually turns out that

somebody else gets killed. But that's progress, or art, or something, and there can be no quarrel with that."

Belle Starr (20th Century–Fox, November 1941, 87 minutes)

CREDITS   Directed by Irving Cummings; Producer: Darryl F. Zanuck; Screenplay: Lamar Trotti, based on a story by Niven Busch and Cameron Rogers

CAST   Randolph Scott (Sam Starr), Gene Tierney (Belle Starr), Dana Andrews (Major Thomas Crail), John Shepperd [Sheppherd Strudwick] (Ed Shirley), Elizabeth Patterson (Sarah), Chill Wills (Blue Duck), Louise Beavers (Mammy Lou), Olin Howland (Jasper Trench), Paul Burns (Sergeant), Joe Sawyer (John Cole), Joseph Downing (Jim Cole)

Synopsis: Angry because the South lost the Civil War, Belle Starr, aided by her husband Sam Starr, goes on the warpath.

Ugly as a bucket of mud, Belle Starr, the so-called Bandit Queen, was known for her outlandish dress, which included velvet skirts and plumed hats with matching six-guns. She was born on a farm near Carthage, Missouri, in 1848 and had an array of outlaw lovers ranging from Cole Younger to Jim Reed to one Sam Starr, a Cherokee Indian. Belle stole horses, money and whatever she could get her mitts on, riding the range from central Texas to the Oklahoma Strip territory. She settled down with Sam in the late 1870s, and after he was killed in a gunfight (some time around 1886), she took on another Cherokee beau, one Jim July. Three years later, Starr, 41, accompanied July part-way to Fort Smith, where he was to face larceny charges. She was shot in the back on the ride home by an unknown assailant. Some blamed her son, one Ed Reed (father was Jim Reed), but her killer was never found. "I regard myself as a woman who has seen much of life," she was reported to have said.

Somewhere along the Hollywood trail to this film, hatchet-faced Belle became

Southern officer Scott avoiding Union fire in 20th Century–Fox's mess of a biography, *Belle Starr* (1941). (JC Archives, Inc.)

glamorous Gene Tierney, the first of many liberties to be taken with Belle's story. The outlaw queen was turned into a Southern hellcat who wages war with the Union rather than engage in hold-ups, horse-stealing and other felonies. Tierney had talent, but in this film she seems to be auditioning for the role of Scarlett O'Hara in *Gone with the Wind* two years too late. Tierney plays Belle as a bitter, hysterical woman, one ugly in personality rather than physical presence; the sort of girl you'd like to take a switch to— repeatedly.

Belle Starr is a disappointing Western all around. It's done in by its script, which is by turns tedious, absurd and inaccurate. It's set in the 1860s, when Belle would have been about 15 or 16, and presents her as an amateur Confederate guerrilla rather than a hold-up artist. Belle's story is presented

as a flashback narration by black share-croppers, and the film's depiction of blacks probably kept the film off television for many years. They are shown to be cowardly, superstitious and greedy, ravenously delighting in the Confederates' defeat. They're referred to as old darkies, told to shut their black lips, and in one sequence Scott's Sam Starr condescendingly pats a young black boy on the head before referring to the obese Louise Beavers as an "Ethiopian elephant."

You can be a fan of Scott's and yet not be a fan of all his movies. I don't think he does enough in this film to convey either the strength or the ambition of outlaw leader Sam Starr (who here is shown as a gallant Southern officer rather than a Cherokee criminal). He has a few early moments of Southern charm, but they give way to a rather nondescript performance that suggests the actor realized he was up against a stacked deck — or script. The action scenes lack a personal scope. That is, they come off as a bunch of tableaux involving stuntmen who shoot and ride and hoot and holler. And while one of the characters in the film refers to the title character as "a legend," there's nothing legendary about this film.

The idea for the film had been kicking around the Fox studio since 1938, but everyone on the lot was waiting to see how *Jesse James* came off first. When that picture took off at the box office, Fox began working and reworking the Belle Starr script to death, even turning out a version where she lives happily ever after at the end. Studio head Darryl F. Zanuck wanted a bigger scope to the picture; his memos urged those working on the film to add carpetbaggers, martial law, the Civil War and the whole works to the script. (He also suggested Claudette Colbert, Ida Lupino, Paulette Goddard or Loretta Young for Belle in November 1940, while he favored using Fred MacMurray or George Brent for Sam Shaw. As for Scott, Zanuck, apparently not thinking much of the actor, recommended him for Dana Andrews' role as a Union officer!) With *Western Union*, Zanuck wanted the overall history of the line cut back in favor of focusing on the men who made the line. Here, he downplayed the personal characterizations in favor of a grander scope of history, and his approach failed.

Belle Starr historian Burton Rascoe got a sneak preview of the film in October 1941 and wrote a scathing and very amusing pre-critique of the picture for *The New York World-Telegram*. "The truth is that the picture ought to be good, because it's made up of the best shots and best gags from *Gone with the Wind*, *Show Boat*, *When the Daltons Rode* and *The Return of Frank James*," Rascoe wrote. "A good film

editor could have assembled the picture from cuttings from those features." Rascoe, who said he saw the original script Lamar Trotti wrote, wondered why publicity posters showed Belle robbing banks and such when no such scenes could be found in the film. "You would think that the only excuse for a picture about Belle Starr is that she was a consort of bandits, and yet every reference to the fact that she was knowingly associated with desperadoes is cut out of the film," Rascoe continued. "I have seen the script Lamar Trotti wrote. He had stuff in there about Belle, showing her as a gang leader, knowingly participating in hold-ups. It has all been cut out. Belle is made out to be a mere sentimental moron who thinks she can carry out the Confederate cause entirely by herself and 20 Hollywood extras."

Rascoe also noted that Scott seemed to be having a tough time keeping a straight face while Tierney butchered her Southern accent to pieces in an attempt to be Vivien Leigh: "Scott is a Southerner and his Southern speech is natural; and there is nothing funnier to a Southerner than to hear a tin-eared Northerner give an imitation of what he or she thinks Southerners talk like."

"In a closeup," Rascoe continued, "Randolph Scott had fallen into a wicked burlesque of Miss Tierney's Southern accent. It didn't sound like Scott's voice, of course. It sounded as though Edgar Bergen had given a corny imitation of Southern speech to the sound track man, who had synchronized it with the movements of Scott's lips. It's marvelous. I have rarely seen or heard anything funnier on the screen." Most of the other critics saw very little humor in the whole thing, and the film, as a whole, was roundly condemned as both inaccurate and ineffective.

Dallas Morning News (9/28/1941): "Randolph Scott is dry and wooden as Sam Starr." *New York World Telegram* (11/1/

1941): "Randolph Scott is supposed to be a dashing Captain Starr. He doesn't fool anybody, not even himself, with his performance, because he goes through it with obvious tongue-in-cheek." *Variety* (8/27/1941): "Twentieth-Fox makes a good job of completely botching up the historical character it pretends to portray. This is a weak-kneed and thoroughly false biography." *New York Sun* (11/1/1941): "The acting is far from good. The men — Randolph Scott, Dana Andrews, John Shepperd — are also pretty wooden. In fact, it is a wooden picture." *The New York Times* (11/1/1941): "It matters not so much what has been done to history as what has been done to the film. Continually it tries to flavor its outright bunkum with real emotion and out of a Wild West junket it has tried to squeeze the liebestod Romeo and Juliet. This Belle Starr was never a scourge and legend in the West. She is a cantankerous school child fighting over jacks and marbles, not life and death. When you're playing at hokum it's best not to fudge. You get caught too easily."

Paris Calling (Universal, January 1942, 108 minutes)

CREDITS   Director: Edwin L. Marin; Producer: Benjamin Glazer; Screenplay: Benjamin Glazer and Charles K. Kaufman, based on a story by John S. Toldy

CAST   Elisabeth Bergner (Marianne), Randolph Scott (Lt. Nick Jordan), Basil Rathbone (Andre Benoit), Gale Sondergaard (Colette), Lee J. Cobb (Schwabe), Charles Arnt (Lantz), Eduardo Ciannelli (Mouche), Elisabeth Risdon (Madame Jannetier), Pat O'Malley (McAvoy)

Synopsis: French socialite Marianne reluctantly aids the French Resistance during World War II, getting involved with Nazi sympathizer Andre Benoit and downed American airman Nick Jordan along the way.

For diehard Western film fans, part of the challenge of focusing on Randolph Scott's film canon is sitting through the melodramatic misfires and embarrassing epics he made outside of the sagebrush genre. On the other hand, there's considerable joy to be had in discovering some offbeat "B"s that give a larger scope of Scott's career while providing unintentional amusement. *Paris Calling* is one diverting dud of an example.

Scott is Nick Jordan, a carefree American pilot flying for RAF (the part has Errol Flynn written all over it). His character, like just about everyone in the film (except Elisabeth Bergner's Marianne) is an absolute idiot. Told by headquarters that the airfield he was to land at has been bombed out and that he'll have to hang out at a French village, Jordan smiles and responds, "Nothing could be sweeter." There, he and his aerial pal McAvoy get drunk, fall asleep and allow a German prisoner to escape. A German patrol hears Jordan and McAvoy singing loudly and investigate, only to be told by a friendly Frenchwoman that all they heard was her radio (though there's no radio in sight). Jordan and McAvoy escape by hitching a ride on a hay truck, unaware that it's a camouflaged German troop truck. They turn this to their advantage when they discover a nearby hay field is a cover for a German air field. The duo set fire to the joint to tip off approaching British bombers, only to have to outrun the falling bombs that their colleagues in the air are dropping around them! McAvoy is killed but Jordan escapes.

Jordan, now on the run, casually wanders the streets of a nearby Nazi-occupied French town and ends up in the cafe where Marianne works. (Note: As a former military intelligence analyst who flew on reconnaissance missions, I assure you that none of Jordan's actions follow the survival training I received in the early 1980s. Perhaps things had changed for the better over 40 years, due to real-life goof-ups like the type Jordan pulls off in the film.) The cafe owners figure Jordan to be an undercover

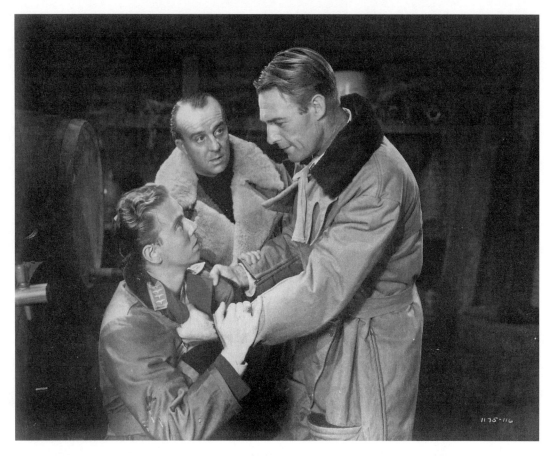

Scott and J. Pat O'Malley give the once-over to German pilot Gene Garrick in 1942's *Paris Calling*, a diverting misfire from Scott's career. (JC Archives, Inc.)

Nazi and order Marianne to seduce him. From here on out, everyone acts like buffoons of the grandest order: Marianne takes Jordan at his word that he's an American pilot, the French believe he is a member of the Gestapo while the real Gestapo, led by Schwabe (Lee. J. Cobb, who sports a derby and cigar and talks like a Brooklyn police detective), pay him little mind at all.

Ridiculous plot coincidences continue. Jordan is picked up by the Germans and imprisoned, and the German prisoner Jordan let loose ends up being the jail guard (the German had been a bomber pilot so how he got demoted is beyond me). Jordan, sensing the Heinie's an okay guy, approaches him in his cell with the solicitous line, "May I talk to you please?" He knocks the guy out, steals his uniform and makes it back to the underground hideout before Schwabe and his men do—and they had left the jail a good half-hour before Jordan! The plot gets crazier: Marianne plays a song at the piano which has an underground code-line tied to the keys, and the Nazis arrest her, while Jordan, still dressed as a German soldier, contacts the RAF, who send a sea plane of commandos to land in occupied territory. The commandos take the Germans in a short flurry of action, then the French resistance fighters join Jordan, Marianne and the commandoes aboard the plane. They all take to the skies as bystanders cheerfully wave, saying, "Bye-bye, bye-bye…" Finally, the strains of "La Marseilles" play over the closing credits.

Paris Calling is not a very good movie. But at least Scott is animated, delighting in a naughty scene wherein he entices Bergner into his bed where he's hiding. We get a hint of his past when his Nick Jordan says in a short monologue that he flew for the Chinese against Japan aggressors and against Franco in the Spanish Civil War. "I never seem to get on the winning side," he tells Bergner. "This was started years ago. It's been fought in lots of places all over the world — it's the same war, though." That's as in-depth as the script gets.

Far-fetched but undeniably entertaining, *Paris Calling* receives a slight boost from its talented cast, who refused to give up on the absurd material and gave it all they could. Elisabeth Bergner, the Viennese-born stage actress, never attained cinematic success despite an impressive array of solid German and English films (including the 1936 film version of Shakespeare's *As You Like It*). She was reaching the end of her screen career by the time Universal cast her in this anti–Nazi picture. She's quite good, though she lacks the sensuality of Marlene Dietrich, who had just been signed to a multi-picture deal by Universal.

The critics were not impressed. *The New York Times* (1/20/1942): "It is all mechanically contrived melodrama, and neither the direction nor most of the performances have made it seem less so. Miss Bergner, with her lost and frightened look, her small, haunted voice, is always more believable than her lines." *New York World-Telegram* (1/19/1942): "The director keeps the action moving at breakneck speed. In this way you don't have much opportunity to think about all the flaws in the narrative. This speed also helps to make you forget the acting of the principals. Randolph Scott makes one more than just a little unhappy as the gay, dashing aviator." *The Daily Worker*'s Milton Meltzer (1/20/1942) wrote that the film had "all the elements of powerful drama except a good script … Randolph Scott plays the American flyer almost entirely for laughs."

My recommendation is watch it — it's an obscure and absurd melodrama, but enjoyable enough, and Scott, playing it for laughs, is a joy to behold.

To the Shores of Tripoli (20th Century–Fox, March 1942, 86 minutes)

CREDITS   Director: Bruce Humberstone; Produced by Darryl F. Zanuck; Screenplay: Lamar Trotti, from an original story by Steve Fisher

CAST   John Payne (Chris Winters), Maureen O'Hara (Mary Carter), Randolph Scott (Sgt. Dixie Smith), Nancy Kelly (Helen Hunt), Maxie Rosenbloom (Okay Jones), Henry Morgan (Mouthy), Edmund MacDonald (Butch), Russell Hicks (Major Wilson), Alan Hale, Jr. (Tom)

Synopsis: Chris Winters, a spoiled rich kid, is sent into the Marines by his father. Chris' nemesis is Sgt. Dixie Smith, who served with Chris' father in World War I. Complicating matters is the presence of a pretty nurse, Mary Carter.

To the Shores of Tripoli, completed late in 1941 just before the attack on Pearl Harbor, opens with a rather stern Scott lecturing some rube recruits with a history lesson about the first Marine leathernecks who fought in Tripoli in the early 1800s. Described by one onlooker as "a guy who's about to break a blood vessel," Scott's Dixie Smith is a fairly humorless leader, but he did remind me of the drill sergeants I had when I was in basic training (U.S. Air Force). He also has a strong male actor to play opposite in John Payne (as Chris Winters). Payne, eyebrows perpetually raised in defiance, was 20th Century–Fox's equivalent of John Garfield, the tough guy who has a heart somewhere beneath all the steel. Payne was one of those actors who committed whole-heartedly to everything — sometimes too much so — but he was, like

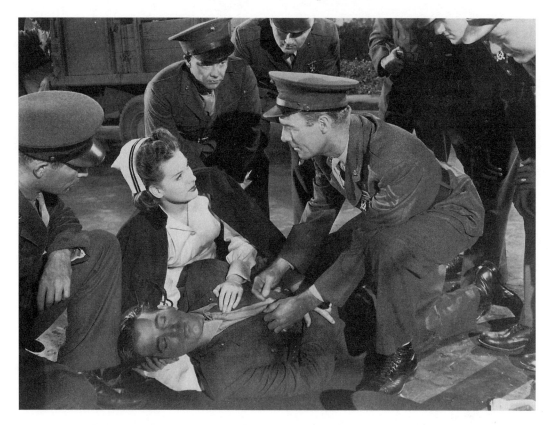

Maureen O'Hara and Scott over the prone body of John Payne (who is faking injury) in 1942's *To the Halls of Tripoli*, 20th Century–Fox's paean to the Marine Corps. (JC Archives, Inc.)

Scott, a truthful performer. He didn't really hit his stride in films until the postwar years, when he left Fox to freelance. Then, like Scott, he carved out a niche for himself in well-mounted "B" productions; mostly Westerns and film noirs.

What plot there is here has been seen in dozens of similar films before and since. Dixie Smith has to turn Chris Winters into a real man while Winters attempts to woo the rather cold and calculating Mary Carter (Maureen O'Hara). Interestingly, Scott's character is presented as a man pushing 50, too set in his ways to pursue women — a unique characterization for the actor.

The first hour of the film is painless, enjoyable propaganda. But the corn-laden climax borrows from *20,000 Men a Year* and *Coast Guard* with Chris proving his worth by rescuing his nemesis Smith from a life-threatening barrage of shells during a training exercise at sea. When war breaks out, Dixie, Chris and Mary all happily board a troop ship heading overseas to take on the Axis, and that's the end of that.

To the Shores of Tripoli moves quickly and harmlessly past the viewer, like cascading blank shells that have enough blast to keep you awake but little other impact. Scott would later work with director Bruce Humberstone in an interesting misfire of a Western, Columbia's *Ten Wanted Men*, while Payne and O'Hara would reteam three more times, most notably in the 1947 Christmas classic *Miracle on 34th Street*.

In his book *Encounters with Filmmakers*, author Jon Tuska maintains that Scott's Fox contract was just about up when director Humberstone began casting, and that while Fox wanted to let Scott go,

Humberstone fought for Scott in the role. (Scott would repay the favor by hiring Humberstone for *Ten Wanted Men*.) 20th Century–Fox studio files indicate that Darryl F. Zanuck originally wanted Pat O'Brien for the role of Sgt. O'Brien and Dana Andrews or George Montgomery for the John Payne role. Once Humberstone got Scott, Zanuck changed the name of his character from O'Brien to Smith ("Why make him Irish?" the studio head wrote in one note.) According to Tuska, the film was the first 20th Century–Fox release to gross one million dollars, which lead the company to give Humberstone a $25,000 bonus check.

Note: The strawberry blonde who ends up with Payne's pants near the end of the film (he discards them during a military parade) is none other than Hillary Brooke, later to make her mark as a "B" film ingénue at Paramount and as a comic foil for Abbott and Costello on their television show. A naughty story about Brooke that has nothing to do with Randolph Scott: During her screen test for Paramount in the early 1940s she was asked to read a scene in a period dress once worn by Claudette Colbert—a dress that was way too small. While the cameras rolled, Brooke's breasts spilled out of the dress, and this "baring all" test film was screened by male executives and movie stars at Paramount for years afterwards. Brooke got the studio contract, by the way.

"If this film is a fair estimation of Marine discipline and tradition, then wire Congress," wrote Bosley Crowther in *The New York Times* (3/26/1942). "Randolph Scott makes a doughty drill-sergeant, despite the humiliating restrictions the script impels." *The New York Post* (3/26/1942): "Randolph Scott is the hard-bitten top sergeant. Don't ask me what bit him."

The Spoilers (Universal, May 1942, 87 minutes)

CREDITS   Director: Ray Enright; Producer: Frank Lloyd; Screenplay: Lawrence Hazard and Tom Reed, based on the novel by Rex Beach
CAST   Marlene Dietrich (Cherry Malotte), Randolph Scott (McNamara), John Wayne (Roy Glennister), Margaret Lindsay (Helen Chester), Harry Carey (Dextry), Richard Barthelmess (Bronco Kid), George Cleveland (Banty), Samuel S. Hinds (Judge Stillman), Russell Simpson (Flapjack), William Farnum (Wheaton)

Synopsis: Crooked gold commissioner McNamara joins forces with a cadre of con men to cheat honest miners out of their claim in turn-of-the-century Yukon territory.

The Spoilers, based on the Rex Beach novel of 1905 and stage play of 1907, features Scott as an out-and-out bad guy, unlike the "good bad man" roles he played in *Western Union*, *The Doolins of Oklahoma* and *Ride the High Country*. Playing a sarcastic and cynical sexual predator, Scott revels in the hearty double entendre humor of the script, as when he asks Marlene Dietrich's Cherry character to show him around—and he's not talking about her saloon. I always enjoy watching a Hollywood hero play a villain, whether it's Humphrey Bogart in *The Treasure of the Sierra Madre* or Audie Murphy in *Night Passage*. McNamara is the most cold-blooded character Scott ever portrayed, although he peppers the persona with his usual Southern charm. It's pretty obvious what he wants: to get into both rival Roy Glennister's mine and Cherry's pants. This film proves that Scott had the capability of projecting a darker side to his personality, and while he does add a hard edge to his performance late in the film, for the most part he doesn't go quite far enough to suggest he's really an evil man. (His character does attempt to orchestrate the back-shooting of Glennister.) In any event, the picture is worth seeing just to watch Scott play the Duke's antagonist and for the now-famous five-minute fistfight.

Scott and Marlene Dietrich exchange sly smiles in *The Spoilers* (1942) while a dubious John Wayne looks on. The fisticuffs come later.

That brawl remains impressive, even with stuntmen Eddie Parker and Alan Pomeroy doubling for our boys much of the time. Scott and John Wayne did as much of the swinging and falling as they could for closeups and medium shots, and it's obvious that they sweated and bled during the filming. Scott, not a man known for telling Hollywood tales or exaggerating the truth, later said that he and Wayne sustained considerable damage from the fight, and that some of the blows were thrown in earnest due to an off-set rivalry for both billing and the lead role. Scott wanted to play Glennister but Wayne, then one of Dietrich's paramours, reportedly got her to intervene for him. Still, Scott held onto second billing below Dietrich and above Wayne — a fact that rankled the Duke for years. Scott was, in fact, on the verge of rising stardom in the early 1940s, his rank increasing due to select property choices like *Western Union* and *The Spoilers*. Unfortunately, his chance to rise into the sphere of superstardom — as Wayne was then doing — was offset by some mediocre film choices in this period, including *Paris Calling* and *Belle of the Yukon*. Still, *The Spoilers* remains one of Scott's best-known films. It is an above-average Western, considerably enlivened by a great supporting cast including Harry Carey and Richard Barthelmess (as a faro dealer who is in love with Dietrich) and the spirited direction of Ray Enright. The fight sequence took about five days to lay out and film, according to the production's continuity report.

Dietrich wrote at length about Wayne in her autobiography but only mentioned

Scott in passing, although her comment indicates that he took his work seriously. "Wayne was not a bright or exciting type," the actress wrote in *Marlene*. "He confessed to me that he never read books. But that didn't prevent him from accumulating a nice pile of money over the years. It proves you don't have to be terribly brilliant to become a great film star. In 1942, when we were working together in *The Spoilers*, he had become a little more sure of himself but had not increased his talent. Randolph Scott, also a member of the cast, concerned himself with the quality of the acting. [Scott] performed the same function in *Pittsburgh*, which we made shortly thereafter."

Rex Beach lived in the Yukon for sev-

eral years, panning for gold and studying the men around him. *The Spoilers* had been filmed three times before and would be filmed one more time, in 1956, with Jeff Chandler and Rory Calhoun in the Wayne and Scott roles.

Daily News (5/22/1942): "Movies come and movies go, but *The Spoilers* goes on forever. The big moment is the climaxing fight between Wayne and Scott. It puts to shame any fight you've ever seen anywhere at any time between two mad men and is the film's redeeming feature. Without it, this would be just another dullish movie." *Baltimore Sun*, (4/13/1942): "It is a forthright melodrama, with no more subtlety than a fresh-picked nugget, and its problems are solved with a right hook, a

Scott had a rare bad guy role in *The Spoilers* (1942). Here John Wayne tries to prevent Harry Carey from shooting Scott (hand in pocket) as Samuel S. Hinds looks on. (JC Archives, Inc.)

hunk of lead or a come-up-and-see-me-sometime dialogue. When it is stated that Mr. Scott knocks down Mr. Wayne thirty times and Mr. Wayne knocks down Mr. Scott thirty-one times, that about covers it."

Pittsburgh (Universal, December 1942, 90 minutes)

CREDITS   Director: Lewis Seiler; Producer: Robert Fellows; Screenplay: Kenneth Gamet, Tom Reed and John Twist; story by George Owen and Tom Reed

CAST: Marlene Dietrich (Josie "Hunky" Winters), Randolph Scott (Cash Evans), John Wayne (Charles "Pittsburgh" Markham), Frank Craven (J.M. "Doc" Powers), Louise Allbritton (Shannon Prentiss), Shemp Howard (Shorty), Thomas Gomez (Joe Malneck), Ludwig Stossel (Dr. Grazlich), Samuel S. Hinds (Morgan Prentiss)

Synopsis: Coal workers Cash Evans and Charles "Pittsburgh" Markham work their way up to positions of power in the industry, only to find their friendship breaking apart when their moral paths begin to disconnect.

The Spoilers was enough of a success to encourage Universal to reteam its three stars in *Pittsburgh*. The film, a saga of the rise and fall of both an industry and a man (John Wayne), was shot in the autumn of 1942 on the Universal lot. Wayne portrays the title character, an initially generous man who loses his way once power and money infect him. Scott is Wayne's loyal pal Cash, who stays true to his friend until he can stand no more, and then he engages Wayne in a big brawl. Scott had the more interesting role in *The Spoilers*, but in *Pittsburgh* it's Wayne who gets not only the lion's share of the footage, but the meatier part. In some ways, Wayne's Pittsburgh Markham is a predecessor to his Tom Dunson character in Howard Hawks' *Red River* (1948).

Pittsburgh was not considered a bet-ter film than *The Spoilers* when it was released in December 1942, but I would argue that it is a superior film in that the characterizations of the two heroes are fleshed out more. The moral changes that overcome Pittsburgh as he moves on and up in the world are both realistic and involving. Character development, rather than action, drives this film, but it's a worthy effort to touch on both the indestructible nature of the country (this was made during World War II, remember) and the potential pitfalls of capitalism.

Pittsburgh opens with an elder Cash extolling the virtues of the steel industry in a speech to a horde of mining employees (stock footage of some real-life rally), circa 1942, before segueing into flashbacks. These flashbacks are built around the idea that mining executive "Doc" Powers (Frank Craven) can hold the attention of both Cash and Pittsburgh — as well as the audience — with the most long-winded drivel ever written. "You two were gay young blades of coal town," Powers cheerfully recalls as he begins his tale. The film races back to the 1920s, where Cash and Pittsburgh are seen as friendly adversaries pursuing earthy pleasures like women and beer. Dietrich shows up as Hunky (!), the rather regal daughter of a long-deceased miner. The three meet up in a theater where Pittsburgh tricks Cash into a boxing ring to take on a brutish brawler. Scott is a little Lou Costello to Wayne's Bud Abbott here, reluctantly entering the ring to take on the bruiser, but he acquits himself well with his fists as his pal cooks up trouble backstage.

There's some funny scenes early in the film, suggesting that Scott and Wayne could have carried a full-length situation comedy on their own if given the chance. The boys tear out of the theater, leaving a major riot in their wake, and then hijack Dietrich's car as they race off to a mine cave-in. She veers around in the backseat

A publicity photograph of Scott, Dietrich and the Duke in 1942's *Pittsburgh*, which is arguably a better film than *The Spoilers*.

as the duo swerve through traffic like slapstick stewards. Dietrich helps out at the cave-in site, and within moments both Scott and Wayne are hitting on her. She gets off a great line at Wayne's expense: "It's guys like you that make me change my phone number." Thrown into this entire early mix of comedy is a chance encounter with Shemp Howard, sporting a pencil-thin mustache and acting like brother Moe.

From here, the film slowly segues into drama. Wayne's Pittsburgh pretty much dominates the film, making audacious plans to transport coal at a discount for mining companies and stooping to forgery to get the contract. ("Sing-Sing, here we come," Cash good-naturedly intones.) Scott is an amiable second lead, and as an actor and a character doesn't seem to care that Wayne steals both the film and Dietrich's heart. Scott even performs a telling

monologue wherein he acknowledges his position as second best — an apt commentary on his film career, perhaps. He also engages in some daring sexual byplay with Dietrich, with her making references to the size of his "shaft" (he's a miner, remember). Later, she tells Scott that "The man I marry must have both feet on the ground." "About a size 12?" Scott responds, flashing a lascivious smile.

Wayne's Pittsburgh becomes the bad guy in this one; turning on his colleagues, friends, employees and wife (Louise Allbritton, wasted once again). It's up to Scott to set him straight with a good right hook, and so the audience gets another brawl, this one set in the dark recesses of one of the mines. This fight will forever be compared to the one in *The Spoilers*, which is both unfortunate and accurate. It's not a bad fight, but it is constrained by the

Scott and John Wayne slug it out in *Pittsburgh*. **Wayne never thought much of Scott as an actor —
maybe the Southern gentleman hit the Duke a bit too hard in the fight scenes.** (JC Archives, Inc.)

environment. After all, a mineshaft with a freight elevator isn't quite as interesting as a two-story saloon. Dietrich brings the two men together again after she takes a one-way trip on a faulty freight elevator that leaves her hospitalized. It's hokum, to be sure, but well-produced hokum.

The film could have ended here, with Pittsburgh regaining his senses. But it has 20 minutes left to go, and in that time Pittsburgh loses his wife, his friend Cash and the respect of his co-workers and employees. But he doesn't lose his self-respect, so he begins again, starting at the bottom and working in an entry position at Cash's new mining organization. (Remember that Craven's character is reciting all this in a monotonous recitation — as if

Cash and Pittsburgh really want to hear *this* windbag recapping their lives' work. Around this point, the old chatterbox notes that when World War II began, "the laughter went out of the world.") Cash and Hunky marry while Pittsburgh works the steel mill fires below. Hunky brings the boys together with a patriotic speech that extols the virtues of America and cooperation and capitalism and everything. "You need each other! Your country needs you!" she commands, and the boys listen. Cash hires Pittsburgh as his new production manager, and how does the Duke respond? He immediately begins answering Cash's phone and barks out orders to everyone within hearing range. Now *this* is a film that merits a sequel.

Despite its shortcomings, some ludicrous moments and Craven's deadening monologue, *Pittsburgh* is better than *The Spoilers*. It belongs more to Wayne than Dietrich or Scott, but Randy holds his own and plays with an honest introspection that is admirable. In fact, it strikes me that even when Scott isn't an exciting actor, he's always honest, and you never suspect he's pushing for the emotions. In the shadow of a John Wayne, Scott could be low-key, but there's a confidence to that approach that suggests he was going to stay in the game for the long run, even if it mean he'd have to come in second a lot of the time.

The film was both a commercial and critical failure, and Universal squelched all plans to reunite Scott, Wayne and Dietrich.

Washington Evening Star, (12/16/1942): "With the Messrs. Scott and Wayne in the vicinity, *Pittsburgh*, the movie, would have been nigh ridiculous if blasting fists had not been written generously into the script."

The Desperadoes (Columbia, May 1943, 85 minutes)

CREDITS   Director: Charles Vidor; Producer: Harry Joe Brown; Screenplay by Robert Carson, from a story by Max Brand

CAST   Randolph Scott (Steve Upton), Glenn Ford (Cheyenne Rogers), Claire Trevor (Countess Maletta), Evelyn Keyes (Allison MacLeod), Edgar Buchanan (Uncle Willie MacLeod), Guinn "Big Boy" Williams (Nitro Rankin), Porter Hall (Stanley Clanton)

Synopsis: Utah, 1863. Former saddlepals, one an outlaw, the other a sheriff, band together to fight bank robbers and crooked town leaders in a mining town.

The Desperadoes, Columbia's first entry in Technicolor, belongs to Glenn Ford and Evelyn Keyes. Scott has top billing but the third — or maybe, in retrospect, the fourth — most interesting part (behind Edgar Buchanan), but he seems content to play the soft-spoken, good-hearted sheriff, Steve Upton. Although the main thrust of the film is supposed to be Scott's efforts to find the bad guys, much more footage is devoted to Ford's efforts to reform and his romantic pursuit of Keyes. When Columbia released a promotional comic book in conjunction with the film, the lion's share of the footage — er, uh, strippage — went to Ford and Guinn "Big Boy" Williams.

If anyone ever earned the label "bedroom eyes" it was Evelyn Keyes, another in a long line of Columbia Studio heroines who were under-utilized by the studio in the 1940s. She was married to director Vidor at the time; shortly thereafter, she would leave him to marry John Huston. She's sultry and scrappy in this film, chipping in to help Scott overcome an opponent in a fistfight by first tripping the miscreant and then cracking him over the head with a bucket. It's refreshing to see a leading lady getting involved in the action stuff every now and then.

The film is enjoyably routine, the color sure looks good and it moves fairly quickly. Harry Joe Brown knew the importance of good locale shooting; the Utah scenery is breathtaking. The film is helped along by good ensemble playing, impressive comic energy and some amusing dialogue. Example: Porter Hall and Claire Trevor are dancing on a ballroom floor when she stops to take note of Ford (who she's clearly enamored of) moving in on Keyes. Hall, concerned that she has stopped in mid-waltz, innocently asks, "Something wrong, Countess?" "No," Trevor responds. "I thought I stepped on your foot," Hall says. "No, but you probably will," replies Trevor — and off they go again.

Guinn "Big Boy" Williams is introduced as a nitroglycerin expert with a penchant for blowing up rooms. ("A lamp exploded," Trevor explains to some curious onlookers after one such episode.) He is

Scott keeps badman Bernard Nedell in line while Raymond Walburn looks on in *The Desperadoes* (1943), Columbia's first Technicolor film. Guinn "Big Boy" Williams and Glenn Ford are seated in the far background.

the usual "Big Boy" buffoon and has his moment in the sun when he comes to Ford's aid in a good saloon brawl marked by impressive stunt work and comic business. The saloon keeper, after spending considerable time trying to stop the carnage in vain, is reduced to giving the camera Oliver Hardy–like looks as beer glasses fly by, wrecking the bar's ornate trimmings.

The film, set in 1863, features at least two anachronisms: Trevor calls Williams a zombie in one scene; the term did not come into popular use until well after the turn of the next century. And one oldtimer casually mentions Custer's Last Stand to a compatriot — an event that did not take place for another 13 years!

The Desperadoes is adequate action fare, but never quite funny or action-packed enough to be a total success.

Evelyn Keyes (to author): "Charles (Vidor), despite being from Hungary, was determined to make *the* American movie. It was a helluva Western. God, I remember that stampede of the horses going through town, and it was thrilling. I don't remember much about Randy. He was such a big star and I was shy. I didn't know how to reach out then. If he was as private as I was, not reaching out either, we wouldn't have had much contact off the set. I remember much more about Glenn Ford, who I worked with so much and who was so helpful. We were under contract to Columbia and it was like our home."

Scott reloads while Guinn "Big Boy" Williams and Glenn Ford keep the bad guys busy in the rather ridiculous finale to *The Desperadoes* (1943). (JC Archives, Inc.)

"For painted mesas, and broad green range land, and men and horses and lean, sun-browned blondes like Evelyn Keyes— I guess that's why Technicolor was born," John T. McManus wrote of the film in *PM* (5/13/1943). More telling was Leo Mishkin's review in the *Morning Telegraph* (5/13/1943): "Put a 10-gallon hat on Randolph Scott, put Randolph Scott on a horse, and it's a cinch you know what will happen."

Bombardier (RKO, June 1943, 99 minutes)

CREDITS   Director: Richard Wallace; Producer: Robert Fellows; Screenplay: John Twist, story by John Twist and Martin Rackin

CAST   Pat O'Brien (Major Chic Davis), Randolph Scott (Capt. Buck Oliver), Anne Shirley (Burton Hughes), Eddie Albert (Tom Hughes), Walter Reed (James Carter), Richard Martin ("Chito" Rafferty), Robert Ryan (Joe Conners), Barton MacLane (Sergeant)

Synopsis: Army Air Force officers Chic Davis and Buck Oliver argue over whether bombardiers or fighter pilots are the most important personnel when it comes to aerial combat. They also vie for the attention of secretary Burton Hughes (that's a girl).

Another propaganda-driven, cornball war film that is fun to watch, *Bombardier* features Scott as a fast-talking, fun-loving ladies' man, not unlike his aerial counterpart in 1939's *Coast Guard*. He plays second fiddle to Pat O'Brien, who dominates the film as a determined proponent of bombardier training. One of the film's strengths is also one of its weaknesses: It doesn't set its sights on a target as clearly as the bombardiers do in the course of their training, instead veering from comedy to drama to romance to inter-service conflict to training documentary. It's never dull, but it does lose perspective at times. Perhaps the film's jumpy narrative is due to uncredited scenarist Jack Wagner, who reportedly rewrote the script day by day as it was being shot (on location at Kirtland Air Base in Albuquerque, New Mexico) over the course of three months.

Scott not only relinquishes footage to O'Brien, but to Eddie Albert and Walter Reed as well. Scott's character is supposedly a good pilot, but his planes sure do have problems—a parachute flare gets stuck on the rear wheels of the first plane, the steering wheel jams on the second plane, and his oxygen equipment fails to work on the third, leading to a student's death. Watch closely in that early scene where Scott is trying to prove that low-altitude runs are more efficient than bombardier-driven attacks and you'll see him silently mouth the words, "Damn it."

Barton MacLane doesn't have a big part, but he's amusing as a likable lout of a sergeant, and he gets the most memorable shtick in the film. After reading a headline stating that Hitler is up to more mayhem, MacLane gripes, "That guy burns me up!" before spitting a stream of tobacco juice at a flying insect, bringing it down. Heroine Anne Shirley gives him a disapproving look, but MacLane makes no bones about this cold-blooded murder: "German moth," he explains.

Scott suffers the fourth of five screen deaths of his film career in *Bombardier*, going out in a far-fetched but flamboyantly fiery manner in an effort to save the day. It's almost as good as James Cagney's explosive death in *White Heat* (1949).

In an era when a half-million dollars' profit was considered a success story, *Bombardier* scored big at the box office, in part due to its strong male ensemble cast. The story was loosely based on the real-life character Col. John P. Ryan (known as "Paddy"), then a proponent of the newly developed Norden Bombsight. The film was shot in late 1942; O'Brien earned $55,000 for eight weeks' work while Scott took home $35,000. The Irish actor was still enjoying the peak of his popularity, thanks in part to his 1940 film *Knute Rockne — All American*, so he was considered the bigger box office draw. Incidentally, the stand-in for O'Brien listed on the call sheets is one Burt Kennedy. Could this be the same Burt Kennedy who later scripted some of the best Randolph Scott films?

Walter Reed (to author): "Randy was a wonderful guy. He was a very competent actor, but I don't think he was Marlon Brando. When we were doing *Bombardier* we all stayed in a hotel on location in Albuquerque. Pat [O'Brien] was on one side of my room, and Randy was on the other. And every morning, before dawn, I could hear Randy getting up to exercise, counting off 'One, two, three, four…' as he did sit-ups or whatever. And at about the same time, Pat would just be rolling in from a party from the night before! And we'd go out on the set and do the scene and Pat wouldn't miss a line — and here's Randy being a health nut!"

New York Morning-Telegraph: (7/2/1943): "We have had dozens of pictures about Air Force pilots during the past several years. Now we have *Bombardier* paying its tribute to another guy in the plane. Next thing you'll know somebody will come up with a pictured called *Navigator* or *Waist Gunner* or even *Tail End Charlie*."

Corvette K-225 (Universal, November 1943, 99 minutes)

CREDITS Director: Richard Rosson; Producer: Howard Hawks; Screenplay: John Rhodes Sturdy

CAST Randolph Scott (Lt. Commander MacClain), James Brown (Lt. Paul Cartwright), Ella Raines (Joyce Cartwright), Barry Fitzgerald (Stookey O'Meara), Andy Devine (Walsh), Fuzzy Knight (Crickett), Noah Beery, Jr. (Stone), Thomas Gomez (Smithy), Richard Lane (Vice-Admiral), David Bruce (Rawlings), Robert Mitchum (Shephard), Matt Willis (Rogers), Charles McGraw (American Engineer), Peter Lawford (British Naval Office)

Synopsis: A Canadian naval warship (corvette) lead by Lt. Commander Mac-Clain is ordered to escort a convoy of tankers to England and back.

The best of Randolph Scott's handful of war films, *Corvette K-225* is probably one of the few seafaring battle films to show how a storm at sea can be just as terrifying as a German submarine. The second half of the film maintains suspense as Scott's commander and his convoy encounter German subs and fighter pilots in a convincing mix of documentary footage and miniature models. The film's best scene has a German sub surfacing to engage Scott's corvette in a cannon battle; like a pair of conflicting pirate ships, the two vessels let loose at each other in a terrifying volley of gunfire during which Scott is severely wounded while his craft is pretty much torn to pieces.

It's unfortunate that the film sometimes veers away from the drama at sea to focus on its myriad of human characters: Matt Willis as a greenhorn prone to seasickness, Noah Beery, Jr., as a gabby know-it-all, Fuzzy Knight as a dog-loving lug, Thomas Mitchell as a cynical legal expert and Barry Fitzgerald as Barry Fitzgerald. Still, the narrative doesn't stay on these sea-bound saps too long, and all these characters do come to life when the shooting starts.

As a man who has no time for anything in his life except, seemingly, his job,

Scott gives a tight performance. He's particularly effective in a sequence where he confronts a dead comrade's angry sister (Ella Raines), with both players keeping the encounter simple and honest. Later, a romance begins to blossom between the two (her other brother, played by James Brown, ends up on Scott's ship) and it's to the film's credit that it never lets this relationship go anywhere. Their first real date is foiled by the war: she is called away to work as a nurse and Scott is duty-bound to sail, even though both of them would probably much rather sneak off to a dockside hotel to fulfill their mutual passion. Watch Scott's face while he views Raines driving off in her car at scene's end; he reveals pain and loss with nothing more than a subtle change in his facial expression.

Scott's salary kept going up. Here he was guaranteed $45,000 for eight weeks of work. He fell ill for five days in mid–February 1943, shortly after filming began, costing the studio some time and leading them to consider filing an insurance claim against the actor. Robert Rosson was a minor-league director who was active during the silent era and made a handful of "B" Westerns during the 1930s. *Corvette K-225* was his last and best film; he died a decade later, just before his sixtieth birthday. Howard Hawks produced the film as a favor to the Canadian Navy; apparently he had full say in casting and chose both Scott and Raines (who was then Hawks' lover). "I did the story and got it all ready, and Dick Rosson did the shooting during an actual trip to England and back," Hawks told interviewer Peter Bogdanovich (*Who the Devil Made It*), going on to suggest that because it didn't have *his* creative directorial touch, it wasn't a very good film. "It's very hard to make a good movie out of anything like that because you are always bound by limits laid down by the Army and Navy and so forth. There are too many people who have an idea of what

A pensive Scott, with James Flavin, in the underrated and obscure war drama *Corvette K-225* (1943). (JC Archives, Inc.)

it should be." Still, I would argue that *Corvette K-225* is as good a film as Hawks' *Air Force*, made the same year and featuring the same sort of set-up, right down to a dog-loving crew member (John Garfield).

Rosson filmed much of the action aboard corvettes on patrol in the North Atlantic earlier that year, giving the film's documentary style an extra shot of realism. The film's planned six-week shooting schedule dragged on to nearly 50 days, and the initial $736,670 budget spiraled up to $1,030,630. Universal could not have been too happy with this—and perhaps this is why Rosson never directed another film — but the film was popular enough to break

even, so the company didn't lose money on the venture.

"Randolph Scott gives a beautiful performance as the skipper of the corvette — a restrained and authoritative master, you can tell by the cut of his jib," wrote Bosley Crowther in his *New York Times* review (11/21/1943), "The film lacks the scope and compassion of Noel Coward's *In Which We Serve*, but in its purely graphic marshalling of sea warfare, it compares most favorable with that film." *New York Journal American* (11/21/43): "The picture is expertly handled on all counts, and a well-chosen cast acquits itself admirably. Randolph Scott does one of his best jobs as the hard-bitten commander." Archer

Winsten of *The New York Post* (11/21/43) noted that a veteran sailor of one of the corvettes showed up for a personal appearance for the film at Loew's Criterion Theatre in Brooklyn, deeming the film "true." Winsten wrote in his review, "It's also thrilling, authentic, fascinating, inspirational and touching. Randolph Scott is perfect as the tight-lipped skipper."

Scott remained friends with Canadian writer John Rhodes Sturdy, who later worked as technical advisor on *Canadian Pacific* (1949) and provided the story for Scott's 1950 Western *The Cariboo Trail*. Scott used Ella Raines again for the 1949 Western *The Walking Hills*, and gave James Brown, a decent actor with considerable screen presence whose career never quite took off, bit roles in two of his 1950s Westerns, *Man Behind the Gun* and *Thunder Over the Plains*.

Gung-Ho! (Universal, December 1943, 88 minutes)

CREDITS   Director: Ray Enright; Producer: Walter Wanger; Screenplay: Lucien Hubbard, based on a factual story by Capt. W.S. LeFrancois, U.S.M.C.

CAST   Randolph Scott (Col. Thorwald), Grace McDonald (Kathleen Corrigan), Alan Curtis (John Harbison), Noah Beery, Jr. (Kurt Richter), J. Carrol Naish (Lt. Christoforos), David Bruce (Larry O'Ryan), Peter Coe (Kozzarowski), Robert Mitchum (Pig Iron Matthews), Rod Cameron (Rube Tedrow), Louis-Jean Heydt (Lt. Roland Browning), Sam Levene (Transport), Richard Lane (Capt. Dunphy)

Synopsis: In this not-too-loosely based story on the celebrated August 1942 Marine assault on the Japanese-held Mackin Island by Col. Evans Carlson's raiders (forerunners of the Green Berets), Col. Thorwald leads a 200-strong Marine battalion against a Japanese-dominated island in the early months of World War II.

Typical World War II film fare, *Gung-Ho!* showcases a predominantly male cast enacting the usual array of lovable louts: Rod Cameron is a hillbilly recruit, Alan Curtis is an ordained minister who doesn't want to kill, Robert Mitchum is an ex-con boxer named Pig Iron and Noah Beery, Jr., and David Bruce are a pair of quarreling brothers who spend more time thinking about their mutual girlfriend (Grace McDonald) than they do about the attack. So there's a Brooklyn bum, a slaphappy sap, a hick hillbilly, a mousy minister—the works. Scott, who is repeatedly referred to as "the old man," is the group's kindly but determined leader, a man who fought with the Chinese and uses the word Gung-Ho! ("work in harmony") to inspire his men. Aside from a moment of stunned silence upon hearing about the death of a good friend, Scott is given little chance to act, though he holds his own in the battle scenes. While given top billing, he has a relatively small role.

Director Ray Enright stages a suspenseful sniper attack with Japanese marksmen firing from tall palm trees in the jungle. Scott, firing furiously with a tommy gun, brings a couple of the bad guys down, but his actions are not the focus of the scene. Likewise, the director and company pull off a thrilling sequence in which Scott's group attacks a Japanese radio station deep on the island. This is followed by a horrifying scene wherein the Japanese soldiers pursuing the Marines are inadvertently shot down by their own fighter pilots thanks to a trap set by the ingenious Scott. As is usual in these World War II era films, the Japanese are shown to be deceptive, evil and ever-grinning, but at least in this case they're also presented as brave soldiers.

Robert Mitchum, appearing in the second of two films with Scott that year (he made nearly 20 movies in 1943, his first year in motion pictures), gets a great scene where he sends a Japanese sniper to his grave with a knife to the back. "I played just about everything," Mitchum later recalled, tongue-in-cheek, of this period in his career. "Chinese laundrymen, midgets, Irish washerwomen, faggots. I even played a journalist once. I don't know what I was like. I never *saw* the pictures." Five years later, *Gung-Ho!* was re-released on a double-bill with *Corvette K-225* to cinemas nationwide, and Mitchum was elevated to co-starring status opposite Scott. In the case of *Corvette K-225*, Mitchum wasn't deserving of the promotion. But given his prominence—and Scott's lack of footage—the step-up is understandable with *Gung-Ho!*

"*Gung-Ho!* is for folks with strong stomachs and a taste for the sub-machine gun," wrote Bosley Crowther of *The New York Times* (1/26/1944).

Follow the Boys (Universal, March 1944, 110 minutes)

CREDITS   Director: Edward Sutherland; Producer: Charles K. Feldman; Screenplay: Lou Breslow and Gertrude Purcell

CAST   George Raft (Tony West), Vera Zorina (Gloria Vance), Charley Grapewin (Nick West), Grace McDonald (Kitty West). With guest stars W.C. Fields, Orson Welles, Marlene Dietrich, Donald O'Connor, Peggy Ryan, Sophie Tucker, Dinah Shore, Randolph Scott and others.

Synopsis: Movie star Tony West organizes an array of all-star troupes to entertain the boys during World War II.

A lower-level all-star extravaganza, *Follow the Boys* provides mindless entertainment for nearly two hours. The film's main selling point is the specialty bits done by then-popular stars: W.C. Fields does his famous pool hall routine, Dinah Shore belts out "I Promise You," Orson Welles saws Marlene Dietrich in half, and so on. One of the highlights, for me, is Sophie Tucker's rendition of "The Bigger the Army and the Navy, The Better the Lovin'," in which the brassy diva extols American

women to prove their patriotism by bedding down lusty servicemen! Also good is Louis Jordan's band's swing version of "Is You Is or Is You Ain't?" and George Raft's jaunty dancing-in-the-rain number to the tune of "Sweet Georgia Brown."

Scott has a one-line cameo appearance about 30 minutes into the film, in the Hollywood Victory Committee sequence. Leaning against a wall, clad in a stylish three-piece suit, he says, "How about me goin' overseas?" in response to Raft's request for volunteers to entertain the boys. We never see Scott again—I guess he went overseas. Scott shot his scene in less than one hour on the evening of Tuesday, December 14, 1943, just before he did embark on a entertainment tour of the South Pacific. There is no record of how much the studio paid him, but I suspect Scott did this as both a contribution to the war effort and as a favor for Universal, especially if he felt he owed them something for the days he missed on *Corvette K-225*. This was the actor's last appearance in a Universal film. His only other cameo appearance would be in 1951's *Starlift*, a similarly-minded "let's put on a show for the boys" saga.

Vera Zorina (to author): "I really can't remember the plot of [*Follow the Boys*]. I just did what I had to do and the day it was finished, I got out. You're not supposed to speak ill of the dead, but George Raft was so ... icky. It was towards the end of his career and I had to dance a tango with him. He just wasn't a nice man."

Belle of the Yukon (An RKO release of an International Pictures film, March 1945, 83 minutes)

CREDITS   Directed and produced by William A. Seiter; Screenplay: James Edward Grant; Music: Johnny Burke and Jimmy Van Huesen.

CAST   Randolph Scott (Honest John Calhoun), Gypsy Rose Lee (Belle DeValle), Dinah Shore (Lettie Candless), Bob Burns (Sam Slade), Charles Winninger (Pop Candless), William

Marshall (Steve), Guinn "Big Boy" Williams (Mervyn), Robert Armstrong (George)

Synopsis: Honest John Calhoun (Scott) romances Belle DeValle (Gypsy Rose Lee) and contends with double-dealing partners in the turn-of-the-century Yukon.

> *If it's blood you want*
> *and cold you want*
> *And the call of the Klondike Night*
> *If it's mud you want*
> *and gold you want*
> *or what Robert Service would write…*
> *You're in the wrong theater, brother!*

This amusing opening caption (accompanied by voiceover narration) to *Belle of the Yukon* suggests a snappy satire on Alaskan action pics. Alas, nothing else in this roughly 80-minute musical comedy is nearly as humorous. *Belle of the Yukon* provides a bizarre mix of comedy, music and Klondike capers in which lots of guns are drawn but nobody actually fires them. "I'm confused," says Charles Winninger, playing Scott's partner, late in the film when it's revealed that one double-cross has pre-empted another. That line pretty much sums up the film, a real oddity in which Scott plays off of two of the most unlikely leading ladies in film history: virginal belle Dinah Shore and stripper Gypsy Rose Lee, the latter wearing more layers of clothes than she was probably accustomed to.

As Honest John Calhoun, Scott has little to do but smile and say he'll take care of the town's problems, be they financial or artistic, even though he acts like he's about to hightail it out of town with the collection plate at any moment. The film has lots of lame in-jokes to other, better films, including *The Spoilers* and *To Have and Have Not* (Gypsy tells Scott that if she wants him, she'll whistle). The plot veers about like an out-of-control ore car wheeling through a Yukon mine, jumping from comedy to musical to Western and yet finding room for everything from a shang-

hai attempt to a crazy footchase. Much of the film is taken up by scenes with characters socking each other in the jaw, crashing vases over each other's heads and getting handcuffed together. It sounds funny; it looks funny, but it's *not* funny. Good comedy should be played straight, but in this film, everyone plays it *too* straight. The one truly comical line in the whole film is delivered by Gypsy Rose Lee when she informs the stage manager that she's calling off the show in an attempt to stop Scott from leaving town. "But the show must go on," the stage manager implores. "Why?" rejoins Lee after the perfect pause, leaving the poor sap speechless. I wonder if Scott suggested this bit; it was a line he had nearly ten years before in 1936's *Follow the Fleet*. Shore knocks off a couple of enjoyable standards, including the hit "Like Being in Love," but it's difficult to see why the saloon's rough-and-tumble Klondike killers would be so docile in her presence when she's warbling such mushy ballads as "A Sleigh Ride in July" (nominated for an Academy Award).

The New York Times (4/30/45): "It takes neither itself nor the audience too seriously, with the result that this serio-comic musical about confidence men, double-dealing and young love in the Klondike of the gold rush era never quite makes up its mind whether to be satiric or just plain musical narrative. Randolph Scott gives a literal portrayal of Honest John while the comedy, which is not inspired, is handled by Bob Burns, Charles Winninger and Guinn Big Boy Williams. Despite its Technicolor glitter, *Belle of the Yukon* yields few nuggets. It's fool's gold, after all."

China Sky (RKO, May 1945, 78 minutes)

CREDITS   Director: Ray Enright; Producer: Maurice Geraghty; Screenplay: Brenda Weisberg and Joseph Hoffman, based on the novel by Pearl S. Buck (that's what the credits say, but it was actually a magazine serialization in *Collier's* that caught RKO's attention.)

CAST   Randolph Scott (Dr. Gray Thompson), Ruth Warrick (Dr. Sara Durand), Ellen Drew (Louise Thompson), Anthony Quinn (Chen Ta), Richard Loo (Colo. Yamada), Ducky Louie (Little Goat), Philip Ahn (Dr. Kim), Benson Fong (Chung)

Synopsis: Pearl S. Buck's story about budding friendships between the Chinese and Americans during World War II becomes a typical Hollywood love triangle between an American doctor, his wife and his comely colleague.

I can't say that *China Sky* is a good film. In fact, what's even more disappointing is that it's also not bad enough to be unintentionally funny (well, maybe in a few places). The Chinese are stereotyped as simple buffoons who are honored to be in the presence of a great American doctor, played by Scott. He is Dr. Grey Thompson, a medic who mans a hospital in the mountain village of Wan Li in China. Wan Li is a strategic military outpost which acts as a shelter for tons of munitions, yet the town has literally no defense and for reasons not explained in the script, the Japanese only attack by air via bombing raids. Dr. Sarah Durand (Warrick) is Scott's peer — a woman devoted to both her duty and her fellow doctor. Scott's wife Louise, played by Ellen Drew, is a selfish, skittish and shrewish gal who wears a mink stole around the tiny village, which could hardly endear her to the poverty-stricken locals. Nor does Scott exude a doctorly air with his wardrobe: he dons a tweed suit and hat in one scene, an evening jacket in another and a trench coat in yet a third — hardly the attire I'd figure a mountain medic to wear.

Sometimes the dialogue *is* downright hilarious. Scott deposits Drew at a bomb shelter during an attack and light-heart-edly says, "I'll pick you up after the air raid." Anthony Quinn, playing a Chinese guerrilla leader in love with a Chinese nurse, sees the dame coming to his hideout and cries out, "I've got to comb my hair!" Later still, after Scott declares his true love for Warrick with a kiss, he tells her, "I loved the sound of your voice when you called me 'Doc.'"

In Drew's defense, while she may not be much of a wife, Scott's pretty unsympathetic to her plight, preferring instead to work late or hang out with Warrick. Even when Scott comes home from the office to discover the fetching Drew taking a shower in the living room, he passes on an opportunity for romantic byplay in favor of returning to work. Frankly, I think there are some things that should keep a man at home. Incidentally, this scene was originally set up with Scott in the living room and Drew in the bathroom, but Joseph Breen, then head of the industry's Production Code (in other words, he was the head censor), wrote a memo to RKO stating that "there can be no suggestion at any time that Gray (Scott) can look into the bathroom where Louise (Drew) is bathing." Amazing — married men couldn't even watch their wives take baths in films of the 1940s. Someone at the studio obviously had a good sense of humor and simply moved the shower into the living room so Scott didn't have to look into the bathroom to see her.

The film ends with a brief but well-staged battle between Japanese soldiers and the Chinese peasants, the latter egged on by a machine-gun touting Scott (who has taken a bullet to the chest at close range, but that doesn't faze him one bit). Ray Enright's handling of the scene helps bring the film to life here, but it's way too late to help the film earn more than a mediocre rating. Scott is adequate, which is a nice way of saying he pretty much stepped back into the sort of bland leading man roles he perfected back in the 1930s. The year 1945 was not a good year for Scott, film-wise, and it's easy to see why he decided to go west forever.

Pearl S. Buck never saw the film, but she didn't hear good things about it. In a June 1945 letter to her friend Edward C. Carter, she said she had reason to believe *China Sky,* the movie, was "pretty bad … I am getting more and more disgusted, in fact, with what comes out of Hollywood. It doesn't matter what one sends in…what comes out is pretty much the same old stuff."

The New York Times, (5/25/1945): "It is hard indeed to believe that the scenarists paid much attention to Mrs. Buck's narrative. Mr. Scott and Miss Warrick are competent, and Ellen Drew is satisfactory as the nasty wife. The Chinese characters are the typical, self-effacing types to be found on the screen and who probably would be looked upon as curious in Chungking."

Captain Kidd (United Artists, November 1945, 89 minutes)

CREDITS   Director: Rowland V. Lee; Producer: Benedict Bogeaus; Screenplay: Norman Reilly Raine

CAST   Charles Laughton (Captain Kidd), Randolph Scott (Adam Mercy), Barbara Britton (Lady Anne Falconer), Reginald Owen (Cary Shadwell), John Carradine (Orange Povy), Gilbert Roland (William Moore), John Qualen (Bart Blivens), Sheldon Leonard (Boyle), Abner Biberman (Blades), Ian Keith (Lord Albemarie)

Synopsis: England, 1699: Captain William Kidd plots to gain hold of the treasure aboard the ship *Quedagh Merchant* while scheming to double-deal his three partners.

According to Bob Furmanek and Ron Palumbo's book *Abbott & Costello in Hollywood,* when director Charles Barton was casting about for someone to play Captain Kidd in the 1952 comedy *Abbott and Cos-* *tello Meet Captain Kidd,* Lou Costello sent the director to Boston to ask actor Charles Laughton (who was appearing in a play there) to enact the role. Barton visited Laughton backstage and offered him the part. To the director's surprise, the actor accepted. "Why?" Barton asked Laughton. "You want to know why, honestly?" Laughton replied. "I don't know how to do a double-take. I think I can learn from Lou."

Alas, while *Abbott and Costello Meet Captain Kidd* is an enjoyable spoof of swashbucklers, 1945's *Captain Kidd* could benefit from some double-takes and comic wordplay, for as soon as the bland narration and stock footage appear right after the opening credits, you know you're in for a cheesy cheapie. *Captain Kidd,* the first film of a three-picture package deal Scott made with United Artists, opens with Kidd and a quartet of seafaring scumbags (John Carradine, Gilbert Roland, Sheldon Leonard and Abner Biberman) burying treasure in Madagascar. Biberman's Blades challenges Laughton's Captain Kidd and ends up buried along with the treasure. Kidd tells his three remaining partners that the English government is hiring him to protect the King's galleons from pirates (!). From then on the plot gets rather complicated—for a low-budget, simple-minded pirate film, that is—with Scott coming on board as a former prisoner trying to redeem his family name while Kidd tries to outwit his three partners. The film suffers from both a lack of humor and action, and must have bored even the most undiscriminating six-year-old back in 1945. The swashbuckling highlight, in fact, is a roughly one-minute long duel between Scott and Gilbert Roland, with Scott acquitting himself well in the fencing department.

Scott, as Adam Mercy, is once again the resolute man of action seeking revenge, and as in his cowboy films, he goes undercover to ferret out the bad guys. Kidd is

Scott, in his only swashbuckler, happily poses with leading lady Barbara Britton on the set of *Captain Kidd* (1945). The two have little reason to be smiling—the film is pretty bad.

simply an annoying obstacle to him and has little to do with this not-too-interesting subplot. The film remains another weak oddity in the Randolph Scott film canon, and another reason for him to get in the saddle and stay there full-time. The year 1945 just kept getting worse for the actor.

In the film's favor is Laughton's performance—the aging ham was clearly having a ball (as he did again in the Abbott

Sheldon Leonard, Charles Laughton and Scott all look bemused in this shot from *Captain Kidd* (1945). (JC Archives, Inc.)

and Costello comedy)—and it's almost sad to see his character go to the gallows in the last scene. For the record, the real Captain Kidd was a Scottish sea captain who started out as a legalized privateer in 1695 before turning to piracy with his ship *Adventure Galley*. At first he was not a very good pirate leader, and some 90 members of his original 150-man crew deserted him in Madagascar. In 1698 he did capture the *Quedagh Merchant*, renamed *Adventure Prize*, but the cargo, while impressive (money, silk, sugar, opium, iron and saltpeter), belonged to the British East India Company and his looting of it put him at odds with the English government. He reportedly buried much of this treasure in several places, enhancing his notoriety. Kidd fell in love with a woman named Amanda and decided to leave piracy, stealing treasure from his own crew to finance

his wedding. Soon he had the English government *and* his own men pursuing him, and he sailed into New York in a vain effort to clear himself. Instead he was captured and sent back to England, where he was tried for piracy and murder (he had killed one of his gunners, William Moore, when the latter insisted they fire upon every ship they encountered). Kidd was hanged on May 23, 1701, in London. The rope broke on the first attempt (Abbott and Costello would have loved that), but his resolute executioners simply strung him up again until he was dead. In retrospect, his seems a sad life full of poor choices, but that didn't make for good cinematic storytelling in 1945, so who can blame the filmmakers for taking license with it?

Scott had a few teeth knocked loose after an extra playing a pirate inadvertently kicked the star in the mouth during a rope-climbing scene. ("That fellow acts just like a producer," Scott told visiting journalist Jerry Dale of the incident. "Kicks people on the way up.") To promote the film, United Artists gave kiddie filmgoers Captain Kidd keys with Charles Laughton's likeness on them for "big box-office treasures." They were probably good for a box of popcorn.

Man in the Saddle: 1946–1955

As early as 1935, Randolph Scott seemed to understand certain truisms about Hollywood and the way the industry used and then discarded talent. "It's half luck and half ability," he said in the *Screenland* magazine piece "I Won't Be a Hollywood Hero." "In the end the hullabaloo fades, the town forgets. And you're left with only what you've managed to keep through your own smartness. I don't mean just money either. But your integrity." Scott aimed to keep his integrity. He also aimed to keep his career going.

Despite his sometimes contradictory comments regarding his profession (Jon Tuska, for one, believes Scott cared very much about his work in films but was resigned to the fact that no one took him seriously as an actor), Scott began taking the reins of his career, branching out into film production to gain firmer control over his material. Unlike his tough guy colleagues Humphrey Bogart, James Cagney and John Garfield, all of whom did the same thing in the late 1940s with mixed results, Scott had no illusions about creating great cinematic art pieces. He just wanted to make good Westerns. Most of the time, he succeeded.

"Westerns always make money," Scott told one reporter, acknowledging that he liked to make cowboy films but that he worked even harder in between film productions on such outside interests as oil well investments and golf. "One thing about Westerns is that they're never dated," he told Hedda Hopper in 1952. "They can be played over and over without the worry of changes in fashions and hair styles that date other types of films." Indeed, Scott's 1940 Warner Bros. Western *Virginia City* was re-released in 1951, when the actor was making new films for the studio. The re-release performed moderately well when paired on a double-bill with *Dodge City*.

In 1946 Scott started up two production partnerships, one with Nat Holt, an independent producer who had worked mainly in film distribution, and the other with Harry Joe Brown. The Holt connection led to a series of seven co-productions with RKO and 20th Century–Fox. These movies, while generally entertaining, fail to measure up to the level of the Scott-Brown productions. Holt, however, often utilized one of Scott's favorite directors, Edwin L. Marin (1899–1951), an underrated assembly line journeyman who knew how to make a film exciting. Marin began as an assistant cameraman for Paramount's Famous Players Studio on Long Island in the mid–1920s and worked his way up to the director's chair at MGM by the 1930s (he had several Ann Sothern *Massie* films under his belt). Marin made more films with Scott than any other director; eight in all, but this output, like much of Marin's work, has been overlooked. "Marin never managed to make a decent film," writes film historian David Quinlan, "but he had a sure visual eye that often produced pleasing results, notably in some of the Scott Westerns." (I think Quinlan should re-examine *Abilene Town*.) Sometime in the 1940s, Marin's brother Ned became Scott's agent, though it's unlikely the actor really needed an agent, as he developed strong personal and professional friendships with movie moguls Jack L. Warner and Harry Cohn. Edwin L. Marin was just one of many film technicians hired by Scott because he knew they were dependable and easy to work with. One can rarely find a story of behind-the-scenes conflict or personality problems on the set of a Scott film; the actor and his producer partners made it a point to hire sure and steady actors, technicians, directors and musicians— Paul Sawtell being a favorite of Scott's in this last category.

Another regular Scott director in this time period was Andre DeToth, a one-eyed Hungarian refugee who worked his way into and up the Hollywood talent chain relatively quickly. DeToth, like many studio directors of the era, made some good pictures (*Ramrod*, *Pitfall*, Scott's *Man in the Saddle*) and some not-so-good pictures (Scott's *The Stranger Wore a Gun* and the jungle thriller *Tanganyika*), making him one of several Scott directors whose overall body of work is difficult to gauge (the same must be said of Marin and Ray Enright). DeToth pushed his actors towards giving grittier performances, reveling in repeated takes, something that probably did not endear him to budget-conscious producers. Still, two of Scott's best Westerns from the early 1950s were helmed by DeToth, who had a penchant for detail. And the director held his own with three out of four of the other six Scotts he directed between 1951 and 1954. Unlike Budd Boetticher, however, DeToth would not look back at his Scott Westerns with fondness.

With the exception of two films that were leftover contractual obligations— 1946's *Home Sweet Homicide* and 1947's *Christmas Eve*—Scott pretty much chose his own material, all of it Western-themed, for the remainder of his film career. To some degree, the actor did look to vary that cinematic personality. He played a cynical gunman (*Gunfighters*), a dead-hearted cowpoke seeking vengeance (*Coroner Creek*), an ex-killer turned sheriff (*Fighting Man of the Plains*), an emotionally lost outlaw (*The Doolins of Oklahoma*), an amiable idiot trying to run cattle in gold country (*The Cariboo Trail*), a greenhorn trying to learn the ways of the West (*Sugarfoot*), a newspaper man who makes noise with both his six-shooters and his printing press (*Fort Worth*), a Confederate officer (*Hangman's Knot*), a Union officer (*Thunder Over the Plains*), a heartless bounty hunter (*The Bounty Hunter*), and a resigned and slightly fearful town marshal (*A Lawless Street*). And yet, much to the delight of audiences and exhibitors, he was still Randolph Scott.

"The Scott hero in many Scott Westerns (not just those for Ranown) was always more complex and projected with greater depth than anything John Wayne did, or could ever achieve, but Randy's oblique ability to resonate his characters from within was no doubt wasted on the audiences for a Scott Western," film historian Jon Tuska accurately noted. Scott could and would inject more character work into most of these films roles (though perhaps not all of them; here and there he seems to be just going through the motions, especially when he knows he's acting in a dud). But the actor must have realized that most audience members, and certainly critics, wouldn't give his work much more thought after the closing credits ran.

In comparison to the Nat Holt productions, the pictures Scott made with Harry Joe Brown for Columbia under his own production banner, Producers-Actors Corporation, were shot in 12 to 18 days on budgets that probably didn't exceed $500,000, a much smaller figure than the budgets of the films Scott made for Warner Bros. in the 1950s. (Compare this to the Audie Murphy and Joel McCrea Universal Westerns of the early 1950s, which were budgeted somewhere in the $750,000 to $800,000 range.) Scott and Brown put up half the costs and took in half the profits; Columbia was their partner, and both parties profited from this deal, often sharing in grosses of several million dollars, thanks in part to Scott's popularity in Europe. Scott's deal with Holt and RKO–Fox was somewhat different, and it's unlikely the actor put any money into these productions. They were shot over a longer period of time (upwards of two months) with budgets nearing the million dollar mark.

On top of all of this, Scott became a contract player again — and this in the uncertain Hollywood climate of the 1950s. This is doubly amazing given that he was nearing 52 years of age when it happened. But Jack L. Warner, head of Warner Bros., always had a fondness for Westerns and thus looked for ways to work his contract stars, from James Cagney to Errol Flynn to Dennis Morgan, into the genre. The story has it that Jack Warner was on vacation in Southern California sometime in the late 1940s when he noticed a string of movie marquees with Scott's name on them. "This guy must be making money for somebody," Warner reportedly mused. He offered Scott a ten-picture contract at

$10,000 per week with a guarantee of ten weeks' work per film. Scott agreed, and though there is nothing in the Warner Bros. studio files (housed at the University of Southern California in Los Angeles) to suggest that Scott had production power, the actor could and would suggest character actors, technicians and musical directors (Paul Sawtell, for instance) from time to time. As Scott's popularity grew in the early 1950s, he renegotiated the contract, increasing his salary and ensuring that all of the films would be made in color (though 1957's *Shoot-Out at Medicine Bend* was shot in black-and-white). It's fascinating to consider that Scott actually landed a long-term studio contract at a time when most of the studios, including Warners, were paring back their contract players list. Scott wouldn't be the only actor making Westerns at Warners in the 1950s — Errol Flynn and Dennis Morgan managed two each, and Gary Cooper made several — but the Southern gentleman's films drew larger audiences, and he stayed with the studio until 1959, when the studio system was all but dead and Westerns were slowly making their way out of the corral towards the last sunset.

Scott was one of a very few number of film stars who never made a television appearance. However, he did agree to appear briefly to narrate a television pilot called "Theater of the West" for Harry Joe Brown. The pilot, entitled "Officer's Choice," featured Scott Brady as an outlaw turned sheriff forced to confront his past when a federal marshal, played by Paul Kelly, catches up with him. The pilot, which was probably never aired, was strong on storyline and acting but weak on production values and action scenes. Ralph Murphy directed the show, which was likely shot sometime between 1955 and 1958.

Somebody was sure enjoying Scott's Western films. From 1950 through 1953 he made the list of the Quigley Poll of Exhibitors Top Ten Box Office Draws—and this in the era of Marlon Brando, Dean Martin–Jerry Lewis and Doris Day. He was also in the top ten of the Motion Picture Herald Poll during this period. "His pictures rate with exhibitors the way A.T.&T. does with Wall Street," columnist Sidney Skolsky wrote in 1952. "His movies may not play the class theaters like the Music Hall, but they manage to lure people away from their television sets and make money." Nat Holt echoed Skolsky's statement: "Scott is a fine actor. Customers come to see him knowing exactly what to expect. They are never disappointed." Scott's son Chris would agree, writing of his father's film persona, "For the great majority of the roles which Randolph Scott brought to the screen, he was less an actor and more a man who simply portrayed himself."

In 1952, while he was filming *Man Behind the Gun*, Scott was asked by a visiting journalist whether he was concerned that Westerns would go out of style. "I've been making Westerns for 20 years," the actor replied. "And every year I hear they're cutting them down. I've never forgotten a lesson I learned when I was in a small Arizona town years ago. The theater there was playing *One Way Passage* with Kay Francis and William Powell, on the same bill with a Buck Jones Western. Well, sir, when *One Way Passage* came on, all those Buck Jones fans walked out." Audiences didn't walk out of a Randolph Scott Western.

From the mid–1940s on, Scott gave fewer interviews, partially because he felt uncomfortable revealing much about himself ("It's no one's business," he once told his son Chris) and partially because he figured that his films would sell well on their own accord. They did. He didn't play the cowboy hero at home, and when columnist Hedda Hopper visited the actor in Beverly Hills in 1952 she noted, "There

Studio portrait of Scott, circa 1955. He always looked older when wearing non–Western garb. (JC Archives, Inc.)

was not one item about his place to suggest that he'd ever appeared in a Western or that he ever knew what a pair of chaps or a spur looked like." Hopper said she saw Scott as "a nice guy in semi-retirement." Scott was prouder of showing off his house and putting green than talking about his films, telling Hopper that he was "a great believer in fate. I think things happen in spite of—and despite—yourself."

By that time the Scotts had adopted two children, Christopher in 1950 and Sandra in 1952. While Chris Scott's memoir suggests that the elder Scott was a remote father, he also wrote of his father and mother's marriage, "In all the time I watched my parents, the only thing I ever saw or felt from them was love and trust for each other." Why the Scotts didn't conceive is unknown, but actress Jane Wyatt suspects that one or the other was infertile. While Scott was filming *Home Sweet Homi-*

cide on the 20th Century–Fox lot, he paid a visit to Wyatt on the set of Elia Kazan's *Boomerang* (released in 1947). Wyatt had just found out that she was pregnant. "So just how does this 'making babies' business work?" Scott asked her, explaining that he and Pat were unable to conceive. Wyatt said she suggested adoption, and Scott replied that they were looking into the prospect — making the actor's participation in 1947's mediocre film *Christmas Eve* somewhat understandable.

The Randolph Scott of this period is comfortable, popular and financially successful. He wasn't looking to prove he was a great actor, nor did he seek to expand his range *that* much. He did lose some close industry friends in the early 1950s: Edwin L. Marin died in 1951 after completing the superior Scott entry *Fort Worth*, Ned Marin died in 1955, and pal Irving Pichel, who worked with Scott on *Last of the Mohicans* and later on *Santa Fe* (1951), passed away in 1954. Other film friends, like "Gabby" Hayes and director Ray Enright, retired or faded out of the business. Scott was incredibly loyal to some industry acquaintances — he used actor Robert Barrat, a colleague from is Paramount years, in his

Columbia and Warner Bros. Westerns through the 1950s. (Barrat died in 1970; one of his last film roles was in Scott's *Tall Man Riding* in 1955.) Scott's health, wealth and popularity continued unabated, although his career was not always blessed with solid critical hits—*Canadian Pacific* (1949), *Colt .45* (1950), *The Stranger Wore a Gun* (1953) and *Tall Man Riding* (1955), among others, are far from good films.

But perhaps it didn't matter, as screenwriter Burt Kennedy would note, because by the mid–1950s Scott had established himself as one of the most popular Western heroes on film. "Randy could wear the hat," Kennedy said, summing up Scott's appeal. "Fred MacMurray made Westerns, but he could never wear the hat. James Cagney couldn't either. But Randy could wear the hat."

He wore that hat through an array of films, probably not aware that as he approached his senior citizenship, he would top everything he had done before in Hollywood with a series of superior Western films that hinted at something darker and more determined within the Randolph Scott persona. But that part is around the next bend.

FILM ROLES: 1946–1955

Abilene Town (United Artists, January 1946, 91 minutes)

CREDITS   Director: Edwin L. Marin; Producer: Jules Levey; Screenplay: Harold Shumate, based on the novel *Trail Town* by Ernest Haycox

CAST   Randolph Scott (Dan Mitchell), Ann Dvorak (Rita), Rhonda Fleming (Sherry), Jack Lambert (Jeff Younger), Edgar Buchanan (Bravo), Lloyd Bridges (Henry Dreiser), Dick Curtis (Ryker), Helen Boyce (Big Annie)

Synopsis: Abilene, 1870: Marshal Dan Mitchell tries to keep law and order.

As *Abilene Town* opens, it's Sunday morning and the main saloon in Abilene is full of rowdy patrons who are skipping church in favor of female cheesecake in the form of comely Rita (Ann Dvorak), a saloon singer who is rendering a saucy can-can number called "I Love It Out Here in the West." Scott's town marshal, Dan Mitchell, is trying to enjoy the church sermon, but he gets called over to the saloon thanks to some promiscuous shooting. He enters the joint, takes care of the matter at hand, and gets distracted by the sexually free Rita. Following her to her dressing room, he peppers her with questions as she prepares to change clothes.

"Now that you've found out everything you wanted to know," she curtly tells Mitchell, "would you mind leaving while I change?"

Without missing a beat, Scott's Dan Mitchell casts an appreciative eye over her lithe body and replies, "I haven't found out everything ... yet."

What an opening. *Abilene Town*, in my view, is the closest thing to a masterpiece that director Edwin L. Marin ever made. I bet if Henry Fonda and Barbara Stanwyck had been in this film instead of Scott and Dvorak, it would be considered a classic. It stands as one of a handful of outstanding Westerns Scott made between 1946 and 1956, and it was the perfect film to kick off his "all Westerns" career. The actor's enthusiasm for the script shows throughout the film; Scott gives an energetic and forceful performance as a marshal who enjoys his job, including the killing. He's a four-dollar-a-day lawman in love with both his work and the saloon gal. He has no remorse over shooting a man in the back, he likes the violence that comes with the job and he makes no excuses for it. Still he has to wonder what sort of life he can possibly have in terms of a future and a family when his badge and gun are always calling to him.

The storyline is complicated. The townsfolk don't mind the marauding cattlemen who shoot up their streets because the rowdies spend a lot of dough in town. Likewise, though the town has a sheriff (Edgar Buchanan), he's the sort of lawman that would just as soon debauch as defend, and as such he's constantly at odds with Scott's town marshal. Guns are allowed to be worn on one side of the street but not the other, adding some confusion to the mix. And when homesteaders, lead by Lloyd Bridges, move in, they initiate a three-way battle between cattlemen, townspeople and settlers.

Made right after World War II came to a close, *Abilene Town* has a lot to say about the themes of reconciliation and cooperation in times of uncertainty. The complexities of the plot give the film an intelligence most studio Westerns of the time lacked, but that doesn't mean these points get in the way of the action. The film, in fact, is quite violent for its time (another reflection of the era, perhaps), with a good number of shootouts, outlaw raids, casual killings and the like. Little touches abound, adding realism: Scott takes his spurs off before sneaking up on one villain and later, after a rousing fistfight which he just barely wins, he takes a moment to wipe the sweat from his forehead and let out a sigh of relief.

The dialogue is great. "Why don't you let this town shoot it out and die?" one cynical observer asks of Marshal Mitchell early on. "There's people in it," Mitchell solemnly explains. Another so-called buddy tells Mitchell, "The only pals you got are on the wrong side of the street," but the marshal doesn't buy into it. "Nothing makes me cheaper than wearing a badge that don't mean anything," he says, trying to make sense of his efforts to keep law in a town that clearly doesn't want it. Rita is impressed by Mitchell's verve, but she still thinks he's just a dumb, handsome stud. At one point, perhaps in reference to Scott's 1930s screen image, she calls him a "big blonde baboon."

Edgar Buchanan has fun in a role that would have suited W.C. Fields. A train passenger complains that outlaws stole $50 from him; Buchanan chides the man for carrying so much money on his person! Later still, in an effort to stop Scott from pursuing outlaw Jeff Younger (Jack Lambert), Buchanan knocks Scott out and ties him up, leaving him on the prairie floor. "Poor fellow," Buchanan muses with just a

Abilene Town (1946), a superior Randolph Scott offering that's still considered just another assembly-line Western but which probably would be called a classic if Henry Fonda and Barbara Stanwyck starred in it instead of Scott and Ann Dvorak. (JC Archives, Inc.)

tinge of regret as he rides away. "Hope the ants don't crawl all over him."

The film climaxes with a superb sequence wherein Scott's marshal moves through town closing up all the saloons in the face of an army of gun-wielding cowboys. *Abilene Town* is a top Scott Western, one the actor could be proud of.

Trail Town, the Ernest Haycox novel that this film was based on, paralleled the story of former New York City policeman and Western lawman Tom Smith. United Artists approached Abilene, Kansas, about publicizing their town with the title, capitalizing on Abilene's plans to honor homecoming hero Dwight D. Eisenhower. The ploy worked and the film was a huge hit early in 1946, with *Variety* accurately stating (1/9/46) "word of mouth will likely snowball this when given proper advance bally ... it's that sort of picture." *Time* (1/28/1946) was more sanguine about the film's prospects, calling *Abilene Town* "just one more in a current series of Western omelettes." I like omelettes myself, and think *Abilene Town* is a superior one, so there.

Rhonda Fleming (to author): "Randy was a polite, reserved guy who couldn't have been nicer. I was just starting out as an ingénue. If you get somebody [opposite you] who gives you something in a scene, then you can do something with it. I thought I did a better job in that picture because he gave me more than usual to work with. He was a very unusual actor. It was not ego that drove him. He had a natural quality about him. He sold tickets. Watching him, he never had a lot to say. He had a stoicism to his posture. He had a good sense of humor and was charming. I only did that one picture with him, but everyone who was around him thought he was a charming, nice, wholesome man. You really didn't get to know more about him than that.

"But that's the film where the red ants got all over me. [Fleming slept in an ant-invested trailer on the set.] It was the night before my first big shot, and the doctor gave me an antihistamine for it and within an hour the swelling went down."

Badman's Territory (RKO, April 1946, 98 minutes)

CREDITS   Director: Tim Whelan; Producer: Nat Holt; Screenplay: Jack Natleford and Luci Ward, based on a story by Clarence Upson Young and Bess Taffer

CAST   Randolph Scott (Mark Rowley), Ann Richards (Henryette Alcott), George "Gabby" Hayes (Coyote), James Warren (John Rowley), Ray Collins (Col. Farwell), Virginia Sale (Meg), John Halloran (Hank McGee), Andrew Tombes (Doc Grant), Chief Thundercloud (Chief Tablequah), Lawrence Tierney (Jesse James), Tom Tyler (Frank James), Steve Brodie (Bob Dalton), Phil Warren (Grat Dalton), William Moss (Bill Dalton), Nestor Paiva (Sam Bass), Isabel Jewell (Belle Starr)

Synopsis: Lawman Mark Rowley has nothing but problems: His brother gets involved with an outlaw gang, he finds himself stuck in a veritable no-man's land of lawlessness, and the only people who seem to like him are the bad guys.

The preceding synopsis of *Badman's Territory* is not meant to be flippant. *Badman's Territory* is a weak Scott Western, one that is overlong, dull and devoid of logic. It opens with a confusing series of events in which just about the entire cast of characters are introduced in comic-book fashion. Unfortunately this bizarre opening sets the tone for the remainder of this sub par Western.

Mark Rowley (Scott) and his brother John Rowley (Scott and James Warren, who enjoyed — or perhaps didn't enjoy — a short three-film series of "B" Westerns at RKO during Tim Holt's absence) are railroaded by a crooked lawman (John Halloran), and soon find themselves fleeing the town of Quinto — the *Badman's Territory* of the title — in the Oklahoma Strip. There the brothers befriend an entire canon of Western badmen while attempting to help newspaper editor Henryette Alcott (Ann Richards) expose corruption.

The film goes nowhere for a considerable amount of time, despite the plethora of gunmen, rowdy cowboys, equally rowdy Indians, a horse race and "Gabby" Hayes. Throw in an effort to gain statehood for Oklahoma, the infamous Coffeeville Raid, a love story between Scott and Richards—the latter portraying an amazingly pouty paramour who needs a good spanking—and you've got quite the Mulligan's stew of frontier foolery. How this film merited three stars from Leonard Maltin and company is beyond me. It's pretty slow going and ends with a weak and implausible shoot-out in a saloon.

Isabel Jewell scores in a brief but effective cameo as a blonde Belle Starr. She's not as glamourous as Gene Tierney, but I think she's more earthy, and though she is way too good-looking to physically impersonate Belle, I suspect her portrayal is closer to the truth than Tierney's. She's a hell of a sexpot to boot, and I wonder why her film career never went anywhere.

Most film historians believe RKO was simply borrowing an idea from Universal when it grouped all these famous outlaws together for the film. Universal's *House of Frankenstein* (1944) and *House of Dracula* (1945) managed to find a way to cram Dracula, Frankenstein, the Wolf Man, a hunchback and a mad doctor into the proceedings, and RKO, perhaps figuring that fiercesome outlaws would be as terrifyingly attractive as horrific monsters, pretty much followed suit, pairing the James Brothers with the Dalton Brothers, Sam Bass and Belle Starr. The studio would repeat this formula, with better results, in 1948's *Return of the Badmen*, an in-name sequel only. Still, along with *Gunfighters*, *Canadian Pacific* and *Shoot-Out at Medicine Bend*, *Badman's Territory* remains one

of the weaker postwar Randolph Scott Westerns, and one that probably isn't worth watching more than once.

Australian actress Ann Richards was on board the *Mariposa*, the last ship out of Australia to America, when World War II broke out. The *Mariposa* was reported to have been sunk at sea by the Japanese, so when Richards arrived in Hollywood everyone thought she was dead. She maintained a brief but unspectacular career at MGM during the war years, but was dissatisfied there: "MGM kept promising me pictures but gave me nothing. I felt that if I could get away from MGM I could do more things." So she did *Badman's Territory* after her MGM tenure and not much else.

New York Daily News (5/31/1946): "The quantity of events is not marked by quality; in most of the conflicts the participants are too obviously a group of actors going rather awkwardly through the paces of a motion-picture scene." *The New York Times* (4/31/1946): "A lumbering action melodrama. Westerns seem to have a lot more life when told rapidly and concisely."

Home Sweet Homicide (20th Century–Fox, September 1946, 85 minutes)

CREDITS Director: Lloyd Bacon; Producer: Louis D. Lighton; Screenplay: F. Hugh Herbert, based on the novel *Home Sweet Homicide* by Craig Rice

CAST Peggy Ann Garner (Dinah Carstairs), Randolph Scott (Lt. Bill Smith), Lynn Bari (Marian Carstairs), Dean Stockwell (Archie Carstairs), Connie Marshall (April Carstairs), James Gleason (Sgt. O'Hare), Anabel Shaw (Polly Walker), Barbara Whiting (Jo-Ella)

Synopsis: The three Carstairs children, offspring of mystery novelist Marian Carstairs, decide to solve the murder of a neighbor in an effort to help their mom's reputation and love life.

When *Home Sweet Homicide* came out in September 1946, Kate Cameron of

The New York Daily News wrote, "The antics of the young ones are amusing, and while the suspense of the manhunt has been slighted and there is only one exciting sequence in the film, adults will not be bored by the juvenile chatter."

I can't speak for how adults viewed the film 50-some years ago, but I assure you that today's adult audience will be bored, not just by the juvenile chatter but by the entire film. *Home Sweet Homicide* is plagued by a lifeless, overly loquacious script devoid of suspense or laughs. In addition, the antics of those young ones—played by Peggy Ann Garner, Dean Stockwell and Connie Marshall — are enough to make you wish that the murderer had gotten to them in the first ten minutes.

For Scott, the role of Lt. Bill Smith is a return to his Richard Denning years at Paramount. He and Lynn Bari (as Marian Carstairs) both disappear for long periods of screen time, and their characters are superfluous to the activities of the children. Bill Smith is an innocuous part in an innocuous film, and it's easy to see why the actor wanted out of such bland modern-day roles. Unfortunately, he had one more non–Western stinker, 1947's *Christmas Eve*, in front of him before he could ride the cinematic trail full-time.

Home Sweet Homicide was produced by Fox as an "A" picture by Louis D. Lighton, who had an impressive track record including the 1945 hit *A Tree Grows in Brooklyn* (featuring Garner) and 1946's *Anna and the King of Siam*. The book *Home Sweet Homicide* was based on author Craig Rice's experiences trying to make a living as a writer while raising three children, and she had first crack at the screenplay (apparently her version wasn't good enough to use). Let's hope that in real life she had a brood more pleasant than the trio of kids in this movie, for I agree with *Newsweek*'s reviewer, who wrote, "Few, if any, of the audience would want these brats in their own home."

Studio publicity claimed that when Scott walked onto Stage 3 on the Fox lot, where much of *Home Sweet Homicide* was shot, he recognized the set as the same one where he had appeared in his first film back in 1928. Scott couldn't recall the title of that epic —*Sharp Shooters*. Fox's contract files suggest that, as of 1946, the actor still owed the studio two films on his 1938 contract. He shot *Home Sweet Homicide*, and then Fox negotiated a new two-picture deal which would kick off with *Canadian Pacific* (filmed in 1948 and released in 1949) for which Scott would be paid $130,000 per picture. (The other two Fox films are *Fighting Man of the Plains* and *The Cariboo Trail*.)

Trail Street (RKO, February 1947, 84 minutes)

CREDITS   Director: Ray Enright; Producer: Nat Holt; Screenplay: Norman Houston and Gene Lewis, based on the *Cosmopolitan* story by William Corcoran

CAST   Randolph Scott (Bat Masterson), Robert Ryan (Allan Harper), Anne Jeffreys (Ruby Stone), George "Gabby" Hayes (Billy Burns), Madge Meredith (Susan Pritchard), Steve Brodie (Logan Maury), Billy House (Camody), Virginia Sale (Hannah), Harry Woods (Lance)

Synopsis: Bat Masterson brings law and order to Liberal, Kansas— with the help of land office agent Allan Harper.

Dapper, intelligent Bat Masterson was a buffalo hunter, railroad man, lawman, gambler, bodyguard and journalist. Bat helped tame such tough towns as Dodge City and Tombstone, though whether he ever played a role in the development of wheat in Kansas, as *Trail Street* tells it, is not recorded. He died of a heart attack at his desk at the *New York Morning Telegraph*, where he worked as a sports writer, in October 1921 at the age of 66. He was probably not quite the rascal of a lawman that Wyatt Earp or Pat Garrett or Wild Bill Hickok were, and to the credit of *Trail Street*'s filmmakers, the script alludes to Masterson's journalistic ambitions.

Trail Street looks like a build-up for RKO's contract player Robert Ryan, much as *The Desperadoes* seems specifically crafted for the talents of Glenn Ford. Scott's Bat Masterson doesn't appear in *Trail Street* until about the 15-minute mark, when he pulls up in a stagecoach and uses his gun to knock out a bad guy who's planning to shoot Allan Harper (Ryan) in the back. Scott plays Masterson as a slow-speaking and soft-moving lawman, a guy confidently willing to let bullets fly past him as he takes his time aiming and shooting at badmen. The film stresses plot and character development over action, reiterating the old "cattlemen vs. farmers" conflict, with Ryan as a guy who wants to turn Kansas into the "bread basket of the world." Several murders and gunfights later, he, with the help of Scott, succeeds.

Trail Street is a compact Western that places little demand on anyone involved, including the viewing audience. You have to wade through some pretty stale dialogue to get to the fighting, but the compelling cast of characters, including Billy House as a walking puppet of a villain and "Gabby" Hayes as a teller of tall tales, keep you watching. The film ends with an exciting night-time street battle, with the villain (Steve Brodie) marshaling the forces of evil in an all-out assault on the jail where Ryan, Scott, Hayes and second female lead Madge Meredith seek refuge. Anne Jeffreys, as a bad girl who's got the hots for Scott, turns in another sterling performance, and gets herself a bullet in the back, courtesy of bad guy Logan Maury (Brodie), who, in a surprising twist, is then shot down by his own men, who don't cotton to any man who'd do such a dastardly deed.

Shot in the summer of 1946 at the RKO ranch, *Trail Street* was one of three Nat Holt–produced Westerns with nearly the same cast and crew. The film's budget was $745,800. Scott received $70,000 for his work in the film; compare that to Ryan's $22,850, Hayes' $8,750 and director Enright's $750-per-week salary. Kermit Maynard, younger brother of Ken Maynard and once the star of low-budget 1930s Westerns, has a relatively small role as a gunman; an interesting memo in the RKO studio files suggests that he refused to take part in stunts that were hazardous beyond the scope of the $16.50 daily fee paid to extras! Another memo hints that Hayes suffered a heart attack during shooting, but the RKO files are not nearly as detailed as the Universal or Warner Bros. files so there's little more information on this incident. Hayes was past 60 when he filmed *Trail Street*; perhaps mounting health concerns led him to retire from films just three years later after appearing with Scott in *The Cariboo Trail.* The two men got along well enough to make four films together. Hayes' nephew Clark once said of their relationship, "Randolph Scott was really one of the finest gentlemen he ["Gabby"] ever had any dealings with. They not only worked together on screen, but they were close friends off screen." Hayes died of a heart attack in February 1969.

Anne Jeffreys on Randolph Scott (to author): "He was a very private person and kept to himself. He was a thorough gentleman, pleasant and easy to work with."

The New York Times (4/10/1947): "It is just another pistol drama in which the good marshal, played by Randolph Scott, cleans out a nest of cowboy villains who are making life miserable on the Kansas range."

Gunfighters (Columbia, July 1947, 87 minutes. A Producers-Actors Production)

CREDITS   Director: George Waggner; Producer: Harry Joe Brown; Screenplay: Alan Le May (also dialogue director); based on Zane Grey's *Twin Sombreros*; U.K. title: *The Assassin*

A rare off-camera shot of Scott (right) with his partner Harry Joe Brown and Brown's son Harry Joe, Jr., on the set of *The Gunfighters* (1947), the first official Scott-Brown production. (JC Archives, Inc.)

CAST Randolph Scott (Brazos Kane), Barbara Britton (Bess Banner), Dorothy Hart (Jane Banner), Bruce Cabot (Bard Mackie), Forrest Tucker (Ken Alcott), Charley Grapewin (Mr. Inskeep), Steven Geray (Joe), Charles Kemper (Sheriff Klaceden), Grant Withers (Sheriff Bill Yount), John Miles (Johnny O'Neill)

Synopsis: Gunfighter Brazos Kane vows to hang up his guns, but once his pal is killed in a range war, he straps them on again.

"You got your choice of getting famous or getting rigor mortis," Scott's Brazos Kane tells fledging gunman Johnny

O'Neill (played by John Miles) in a memorable scene from *Gunfighters*. Up to this point the film is an agreeable story of yet another tired gunman (Scott) hoping to quit the business. But shortly thereafter, *Gunfighters* starts to drift rather aimlessly into a pretentious and fairly dull saga involving two ranchers, two twin daughters (one good, one bad), two sheriffs (one good, one bad) and two gunmen. Scott sets things right by killing off the bad guys in a rather unexciting finale.

Gunfighters, the first official Brown-Scott production, kicks off with a compelling opening credits sequence featuring Scott leaning against a piano in a smoke-filled saloon. The cast, the color cinematography and the location shooting (Lone Pine) are good, and while the film's story predates themes found in such later classics as *The Gunfighter* (1950) and *Shane* (1953), the scripting is not as complex and the direction and character development are weak. The film's pacing is slowed by lengthy fade-out sequences, extended camera closeups on characters who have nothing to say, and long patches of uninteresting dialogue. Nor is it helped by actor Steven Geray's stereotypical portrayal of a Mexican cook (Scott calls him an "old jumping bean") or by a lackluster fight scene between Scott and evil sheriff Grant Withers, which in itself is marred even further by obtrusive comedy relief from Geray. *Gunfighters* remains a passably watchable oater that promises much more than it delivers, but compared to almost every other Brown-Scott production, it's pretty tepid. Writer Burt Kennedy, who later scripted several Scott films in the late 1950s, recalled Scott telling him that *Gunfighters* was the only Scott-Brown film *not* to make money, which must have made Columbia Studio head Harry Cohn nervous, for he had just inked a deal to co-produce a series of Scott-Brown films with the understanding that they would equally share in both the budgeting and profits. Fortunately, the next Scott-Brown film, *Coroner Creek*, was both a commercial and critical success, and most of the ensuing Columbia Scott films made a profit.

The New York Times (7/25/1947): "The film is too long, the sound track is often blurry and a pair of twin girls confuse things immensely. It is average fare for the inveterate Western addicts."

Christmas Eve (United Artists, November 1947, 90 minutes)

CREDITS Director: Edwin L. Marin; Producer: Benedict Bogeaus; Screenplay: Lawrence Stallings; story by Lawrence Stallings and Richard H. Landau

CAST George Raft (Mario Volpi), George Brent (Michael Brook), Randolph Scott (Jonathan), Ann Harding (Aunt Matilda), Reginald Denny (Phillip Hastings), Joan Blondell (Ann Nelson), Dolores Moran (Jean), Molly Lamont (Harriet), Douglass Dumbrille (Dr. Bunyon), John Litel (FBI Agent Bland), Joe Sawyer (Detective Gimlet)

Synopsis: Aunt Matilda is about to be confined to the loony bin and have her fortune turned over to her greedy nephew Phillip. The only way she'll be saved is if her three surrogate sons show up on Christmas Eve.

Here's one holiday movie you likely won't be rushing to see come Christmas time. *Christmas Eve* (retitled *Sinner's Holiday*) is not a Christmas-themed movie at all, per se, but rather a collection of three short subjects hastily tied together into the biggest mishmash of comedy, drama and comedy-drama that you've ever encountered. It sports a film buff's dream cast list, to be sure, but most of the actors appear in two-shots: Joan Blondell with George Brent, Scott with Dolores Moran, Joe Sawyer with Ann Harding, etc. Imagining Randolph Scott, George Raft and George Brent as brothers—even foster brothers—is difficult, and the fact that actress Ann Harding

Dipsomaniac rodeo star Randolph Scott orders yet another shot of whiskey from bartender Al Hill while perplexed butler Dennis Hoey looks on in the ill-titled *Christmas Eve* (1947), another oddity from Scott's film canon. (JC Archives, Inc.)

was younger than Scott and Raft and about the same age as Brent doesn't make it easy to accept her as their doddering old stepmom (one character refers to her as "a lovely old heirloom").

Brent is a dissolute playboy trying to escape a life of debt, Raft is an exiled gangster fighting ex–Nazis in South America and Scott is a rodeo rider who finds himself involved in an illegal adoption racket. Raft has the showiest role, and the picture only comes alive in a brief but exciting scene in which he slugs his way across a Nazi-infested yacht.

Scott does get to poke some fun at his own cowboy image as a hard-drinking, woman-chasing, dim-witted man of the saddle. "You look the part of a big, tender-hearted hero," says Jean (Dolores Moran),

a comely brunette who leads Scott's cow-poke into a ring of intrigue. He goes with her to the home of a shady doctor (Douglass Dumbrille) who is selling unwanted babies for a price. When the doc refuses to cough up a babe for Scott and his gal, our hero draws a six-gun (this in 1947!) and says, "Sorry, doc, but you know how it is with expectant fathers." Through a series of convoluted circumstances, Scott separates from Moran (who turns out to be an undercover cop) and corrals three errant baby girls from the home, bringing them to his mom on Christmas Eve. Brent and Raft show up on time too, the latter realizing he'll have to serve time for his crimes.

Interestingly, the character Raft plays mirrors a real-life counterpart. During shooting of *Christmas Eve*, Raft's criminal pal Bugsy Siegel was killed in his home in Beverly Hills by gangland associates unhappy with Bugs' lack of success in turning the Las Vegas–based casino, the Flamingo, into the gambling Mecca of the country. Raft later said that when Siegel died, part of him died too, which was true because the gangster kicked off owing Raft something like a quarter of a million dollars. Raft's career is interesting to compare to Scott's, in that both men sort of stumbled into filmmaking, both became Paramount contract stars in the early 1930s, and both worked with big-name directors without seeing their careers advance. Likewise both men left Paramount in 1938 to freelance. But Raft never shrugged off his wooden approach to acting, and unlike Scott he did not take creative control of his career. Nor did he pick good scripts— Raft turned down *Dead End* (1937), *High Sierra, The Maltese Falcon* (both 1941) and *Double Indemnity* (1944), for instance. By 1947 Raft's career was in serious trouble; he floundered around in "B" productions and European cheapies through the early 1950s, and by the end of that decade his film career was pretty much over. When Scott retired from filmmaking in 1962, he was a wealthy man, while Raft was playing cameo parts in Jerry Lewis films.

As for Scott, excluding a cameo appearance in 1951's *Starlift, Christmas Eve* was his final non–Western role. No wonder he threw in the towel — as a non–Western entity he was not "box office" enough to ensure good roles in good films. He probably did the film because it was easy work (he's only in a third of it, more or less), because Edwin Marin was directing, and because the theme appealed to him, given he and wife Pat were then considering adoption themselves.

The Big Reel (February 1980): "The plot is implausible and the ending is too pat for modern tastes. It might have been interesting back in 1947, but now it's passé

and stilted." *The New York Times* (11/28/47): "This episodic potpourri … only succeeds in being transparent, plodding and occasionally confusing. Merely adequate are George Raft, George Brent, Reginald Denny and Randolph Scott."

Albuquerque (A Clarion Production, released by Paramount, January 1948, 89 minutes)

CREDITS   Director: Ray Enright; Producer: William Pine and William Thomas; Screenplay: Gene Lewis and Clarence Upson Young, based on the Luke Short novel *Dead Freight for Piute*

CAST   Randolph Scott (Cole Armin), Barbara Britton (Letty Tyler), George "Gabby" Hayes (Juke), Lon Chaney, Jr. (Steve Murkill), Russell Hayden (Ted Wallace), Catherine Craig (Celia Wallace), George Cleveland (John Armin), Karolyn Grimes (Myrtle Walton), Bernard Nedell (Sheriff Linton)

Synopsis: Ex–Texas Ranger Cole Armin takes on his crooked uncle John in a fight to gain control of the freighting industry in Albuquerque.

A still-obscure Scott Western, *Albuquerque* is well-produced and colorful. It is also dull, flabbily constructed and illogical, lacking in both excitement and character development. Those anxious to see it (it was only recently released on DVD) may be more generous with their praise than I am, but for my money it merits no more than the two-star rating that Leonard Maltin gives it in his *Movie and Video Guide.*

The plot sees Scott coming to the title town to take a job with his long-lost uncle John (a wheelchair-bound George Cleveland), little realizing his kin is a skunk of the worst odor. Cleveland has some grand Napoleonic scheme to take over the entire Southwest with his freighting business, but it seems to me that he doesn't have much of a chance, being he can't even keep Albuquerque under his thumb. His only reliable henchmen are a weak-willed sheriff (Bernard Nedell) and a brutish gunman (Lon Chaney, Jr.). Scott quickly turns against his uncle and sides with the competition, the brother and sister freighting team of Ted and Celia Wallace (Russell Hayden and Catherine Craig). Scott is no stern avenger of justice here; rather, he's a laid-back cowpoke drawn into a conflict he hadn't reckoned on. The abrupt change of character only works because he's Randolph Scott, for the scripting gives him little backstory. We only find out he was a Texas Ranger when Hayden off-handedly mentions it late in the story.

Having set up this basic conflict, the film plugs along, or chugs along, with little energy or excitement, until Barbara Britton shows up as a good-bad girl in Cleveland's pay. Her character is under-developed, but her physique isn't, and hence male viewers won't mind being distracted when she's around. "Gabby" Hayes is his usual delightful comic raconteur, but Chaney and Hayden are wasted. In fact, the latter gets shot in the knee half-way through the film and the spends the rest of the footage in bed sipping coffee and commenting on the action.

On the plus side, the production's Cinecolor is vividly impressive. Scott's character does get to engage in some novel comic shtick, from a bit of sock puppetry to a dead-on Cary Grant facial impersonation to a Shemp Howard–like take after he breaks some dishes in the kitchen. His Cole Armin often seems more interested in getting laughs than getting the bad guy, but at least it's a different sort of cowboy hero.

Director Ray Enright apparently wasn't too happy working for the Pine-Thomas unit, according to the late William C. Thomas' unpublished memoir *Hollywood's Famous Dollar Bills, or How to Make Money Making Movies* by Thelma King. Thomas and his partner William Pine were the

producers of *Albuquerque*, as well as a slew of other second-feature Paramount films. "They had a unit at Paramount," explained A.C. Lyles of the duo, who were known as the Dollar Bills due to their cost-cutting efficiency. "They were both heads of the publicity department at Paramount at one time, and Bill Pine had been an associate producer for Cecil B. DeMille. They got together in 1940 and did a series of pictures with people like Richard Arlen, Chester Morris and Jean Parker. I don't like to classify films by 'A' or 'B.' I prefer to call them program pictures. They were inexpensive, and they made about 70 of them."

The Pine-Thomas films showcased second-grade stars, although now and then the duo landed a first-class actor like James Cagney (1955's *Run for Cover*). They only got Scott by agreeing to give him $75,000 up front and a third of the profits, as well as the director of his choice and star billing above the title. "The idea of a star selecting the director appalled me," Thomas recalled in his memoir. "I fought the idea of relinquishing *any* power like a tiger, but lost. If *Albuquerque* was to eclipse everything we'd done previously, we needed Randolph Scott." Scott, in turn, felt he needed Ray Enright.

While Enright has been categorized as a pussycat by others, to Thomas and Pine he was a hellion. According to Thomas, the director wasn't happy with actor Russell Hayden, whom the producers had chosen as he was under contract to the studio. Enright wanted actor Robert Oliver for the role. "In time, Enright made a sly innuendo, insinuating Russ didn't have the ability to carry the part," Thomas recalled in his book. "That sent my temper to the boiling point. It was easy to see the route the unpleasant director was going to take. Before mid-morning he was yelling at Russ. His blood-curdling shouts sent the crew into huddles. Russ was visibly shaken, but tried to please. It was impossible."

Pine and Thomas, accustomed to working under family-like environments, grew to dislike Enright. They began looking for ways to get rid of him while lining up director Frank McDonald to take over, if necessary. With McDonald committed as back-up, Thomas pulled Enright aside and said, "You're going to get along with Russ Hayden or *get the hell off the picture.* Don't try going to Randy. He's just as interested in getting this picture under budget as we are." Enright backed down and played ball, according to Thomas, giving the company trivial trouble along the way. "Ray Enright was a good director, and we got a good picture along with the headaches," Thomas acknowledged. I think Enright was a good director, but I don't think *Albuquerque* is a good picture, and Enright may have been right about Hayden — the actor gives a nondescript performance that could have been done by any third-rate contract player.

Perhaps Enright's dissatisfaction with the way things were going diluted his enthusiasm for the project. His direction is weak, as is the script, and the animated portrayals given by Scott, Hayes and Britton can't overcome these strikes against the film. Chaney, who is in a lot of scenes but probably doesn't have ten lines of dialogue, remains an unworthy adversary for Scott throughout the entire piece. The first half of the film is nearly devoid of action, and the second half is full of half-loaded fight scenes, including a bland bit of fisticuffs between Chaney and Scott. Chaney does have a fantastic (if unbelievable) death scene: After being loaded with lead by Randy, he runs out of a saloon, hurls himself over a hitching post and flips into the street to die!

The climax, involving some runaway freight wagons heading hell-bent-for-destruction down a mountain pass with Scott at the reins of the last one, sounds exciting but is unfortunately played against obvious rear projection footage. And then the final gun duel, in which Scott and Hayes take on Cleveland, Chaney and their gunmen, also promises to be exciting but is short and unimpressive. Pine and Thomas must have learned from this disappointing ending, however, for they achieved much better results with the same set-up in the following year's *El Paso* (starring John Payne) which ends with a humdinger of a gunfight amidst a dust storm. No disaster, *Albuquerque* remains a disappointment, which won't stop diehard Randolph Scott fans from wanting to see it.

The producers came up against another annoyance once the film was completed when Britton (who has a showier, but smaller, role than Craig) slapped a lawsuit on them, demanding star billing. The Dollar Bills managed to get Paramount to pay her off ("some small amount like five thousand dollars," Thomas wrote) and most of their problems were over by the time the film was released early in 1948. "There was a bittersweetness about *Albuquerque* that began the first morning of shooting and continued until the premieres, but once it was on the marquees, it brought nothing but money into the tills and acclaim from the critics," Thomas noted. "We made it for $728,000 and grossed over two million in the U.S. and Canada alone!"

Actress Karolyn Grimes (to author): "Most of my part was shot on location at the Paramount Western ranch. When I was a little girl I used to faint a lot at high altitudes. I recall being in a big log cabin with a big wood stove in it, and it was hot. And one morning I went through the process of make up, hair and wardrobe all morning before the shoot, and the next thing I know I was lying outside and there were people looking over me. I had fainted [in the cabin], and Randolph Scott had carried me outside to revive me! And he was leaning over me and the whole cast and crew was there to see if I was okay. He really did rescue me!

"He was a very gentle man. A lot of the guys—John Wayne, for example—were men's men types of guys. But Randy was more of a Cary Grant character in person; elegant in a way. Most of the stars I worked with did joke around, but Randolph Scott never joked around. He was a little aloof. But you also ran into a lot of stars who they warned you from the get-go to stay away from. David Niven and George Sanders, people like that; they told me, 'Don't go near them.' But Randolph Scott wasn't one of them. He was accessible, and he did carry me out when I fainted!"

Grimes also recalled the backstreet brawl between Scott and Lon Chaney, Jr.: "They had a fight scene, and I watched it and was really fascinated by the whole thing. They did quite a bit of that themselves. Randolph Scott assured me that everything would be okay, that it was all pretend. And later Lon Chaney, Jr., showed me how the blood came from the blood capsule in his mouth. But in retrospect, as I look at the fight scene today, Randolph Scott doesn't even have a hair out of place in the battle! He looks like he came off the cover of *GQ*!"

A.C. Lyles (to author): "Randy came back to Paramount to make one film in 1948—*Albuquerque*. I was publicity man on the picture. Lon Chaney, Jr., was in it, "Gabby" Hayes was in it, and Catherine Craig—who was married to my friend Robert Preston—was in it. *Albuquerque* has never gotten much play or attention. I'm not sure why. You don't know how many people call me to ask what happened to that film or where it is. It's disappeared."

Variety (1/12/1948): "With all the basic ingredients to be an exciting Western filmfare, *Albuquerque* nevertheless misses. The story lacks punch. Scott and Hayes bolster the doings considerably." *Daily Variety* (1/20/1948) went a step further "*Albuquerque* is one galloper that never breaks into a gallop."

Coroner Creek (Columbia, July 1948, 90 minutes)

CREDITS   Director: Ray Enright; Producer: Harry Joe Brown; Screenplay: Kenneth Gamet, from the book *Coroner Creek* by Luke Short

CAST   Randolph Scott (Chris Danning), Margerite Chapman (Kate Hardison), George Macready (Younger Miles), Barbara Reed (Abby Miles), Forrest Tucker (Ernie Coons), Edgar Buchanan (Sheriff O'Haly), Wallace Ford (Andy West), William Bishop (Leech Conover), Sally Eilers (Della Harms), Russell Simpson (Walt Hardison), Joe Sawyer (Frank Yordy)

Synopsis: Chris Danning seeks the man responsible for his fiancée's death. The trail leads him to Coroner Creek.

> "I know all I need to know about you ... except the beginning. I know the ending."—Kate Hardison (Margerite Chapman) to Chris Danning (Randolph Scott) in *Coroner Creek*.

Nearly a decade before Scott worked with Budd Boetticher and Burt Kennedy to fashion the first of an array of vengeance-driven cowpokes who were prepared to ride to hell to get their man, the actor crafted a finely tuned predecessor to those characters in Chris Danning, the protagonist of *Coroner Creek*, just about the best Western Scott made in between *Western Union* (1941) and *Seven Men from Now* (1956). Scott is a single-minded man bent on revenge who can not see how his hate can hurt those around him. He's in no hurry to exact his revenge and he has no room for romance either, even though two vibrant women are pretty much shoving it in his face (romance, I mean). Chapman, as a hotel owner who wants to help Scott overcome his personal demons, can't quite comprehend what drives Scott. She asks her Bible-toting father, played by Russell Simpson, "Dad, what's wrong with him?" "The spirit is dead," Simpson replies. "You can see it in his eyes. They're ugly. But his face isn't. He just doesn't care."

It's easy to take Scott for granted as an

Forrest Tucker and his pals are about to give Scott a good going-over in the excellent *Coroner Creek* (1948). They'll be sorry.

actor. After all, from the mid-war years on he began making formula films with the emphasis on Westerns. But if Scott was stiff or unsure of himself in his films of the 1930s, then the combination of time, growing confidence and a willingness to take risks on performances that stressed economy (like William S. Hart or Gary Cooper) worked to suggest an inner turmoil that the actor conveyed with the subtlest of gestures and emotions. This is not true in every Scott Western, but it's highlighted in *Coroner Creek*, a minor masterpiece of the genre. I wonder if Burt Kennedy saw the film when it came out — it's opening is not too far removed from the beginning of *Comanche Station*.

Scott's Chris Danning is casual, confident, cunning. He's willing to shoot a man full of holes to get what he wants, and he's willing to take chances a man just oughtn't take on the frontier. The men he confronts along the way — played by the likes of Joe Sawyer, Douglas Fowley and William Bishop — are weaker than he is; not just physically but morally and psychologically. You really feel Scott doesn't care if he dies, which means he obviously doesn't give a damn if anyone else around him dies. "There are some things a man can't ride around," a character says in *Ride Lonesome*, scripted by Kennedy. In *Coroner Creek*, most of the men — and women — learn how to ride around Scott fast. As Younger Miles, the man Scott seeks, George Macready doesn't have a choice. He can't ride around Scott. In the late 1940s and early 1950s, Macready pretty much patented the cold automaton-like villain at Columbia, eschewing the devious charm of a Zachary Scott or the comical cynicism of a Dan Duryea. As time went on, Macready tackled each new bad guy role with a minimum of change, but here, appearing opposite Scott for the first time, he brings a fresh interpretation of a walking dead man who is still determined to make his mark in the world. The difference between he and his antagonist is simple: Scott's Chris Danning knows he is dead. Younger Miles does not.

Ray Enright — or perhaps Kenneth Gamet's script — gives two to three minutes of silent footage to Scott's pursuit early on, adding tension to the film in an innovative manner. Enright may be dismissed as a hack director of the old school, but he, like Marin, DeToth and Boetticher, obviously earned Scott's trust, and I'm willing to give Enright credit for his ability to work with actors. The entire ensemble in *Coroner Creek* give performances that suggest that someone was exhorting them to work a little harder. All of them add an extra edge to their playing, including Sally Eilers (the wife of Harry Joe Brown), who packs her role as an aging widow with sexual energy. Also good is overlooked character actor Wallace Ford as an ambivalent cowhand who regains his self-respect under Scott's leadership.

During the course of the film, Scott takes as much physical abuse as any James Stewart character in the Anthony Mann series. First he's beat senseless by Forrest Tucker while the latter's henchmen hold him; then, still unconscious, he has his gun hand smashed by Tucker. The fight is not

Scott and Forrest Tucker share a smoke in *Coroner Creek* (1948). They'll be trading bullets later on in the film.

over, for Scott revives and takes Tucker on in one of the best-staged brawls in Western film history, with our hero inflicting pain on both his adversary and himself whenever he inadvertently uses his broken hand. Enright knew how to make Scott look good in a fight (see *The Spoilers* and *Return of the Badmen*). Having not read the actual script, I'm wondering how much of the little moments within the fight (Scott head-butting Tucker, biting him, etc.) were in the script and how many were suggested by Enright and/or the actors.

Coroner Creek never fails to surprise. I'm reluctant to put together a list of Top Ten Randolph Scott films, or Top Ten Randolph Scott performances, but *Coroner Creek* belongs up there in both lists all the same. I'll go a step further and risk being run out of town: In terms of packing an emotional wallop, it may be just as good as the movies Scott made with Budd Boetticher and Burt Kennedy a decade later.

Jon Tuska (letter to author): "As an actor in Westerns, Scott's character was never on the surface, but came forth from within his depths, and so you can only discern it if you do what most viewers did not do—watch his films over and over until, slowly but persuasively, you see what it was he was doing."

Return of the Bad Men (RKO, August 1948, 90 minutes)

CREDITS   Director: Ray Enright; Producer: Nat Holt; Screenplay: Charles O'Neal, Jack Natteford and Luci Ward

CAST   Randolph Scott (Vance Cordell), Robert Ryan (The Sundance Kid), Anne Jeffreys (Cheyenne), Jacqueline White (Madge Allen), George "Gabby" Hayes (John Petit), Gary Gray (Johnny), Steve Brodie (Cole Younger), Richard Powers (Jim Younger), Robert Bray (John Younger), Lex Barker (Emmett Dalton), Walter Reed (Bob Dalton), Michael Harvey (Grat Dalton), Robert Armstrong (Bill Doolin), Tom Tyler (Wild Bill Yeager)

Synopsis: A gang of outlaws headed by Bill Doolin terrorize homesteaders in 1889 Oklahoma. Former Texas Ranger Vance Cordell comes out of retirement to track the gang down.

Return of the Bad Men is one of those Scott films that I've altered my perception about. I now think it's the best of the trio of RKO films Scott did with Nat Holt in the late 1940s, contradicting my view in *Last of the Cowboy Heroes* that *Trail Street* is the best film. *Return of the Bad Men* is a good oater with a good cast, enough action to satisfy fans and a dark tone that almost qualifies it for *noir* status. Scott is his usual good-humored, determined self; a man of action who would just as soon be a man of inaction but who, if pushed far enough, will buckle on his six-gun and go to work shooting down ornery outlaws. The actor seems content to let "Gabby" Hayes, Robert Ryan and Anne Jeffreys take the film away from him.

Hayes plays the town banker, a cantankerous old raconteur with a comic edge whose catch phrase is "Yes sir-ey Bob!" Whether you'd trust such a lovable but absent-minded old galoot to run your bank is another thing altogether; Hayes is the sort of financial officer who proudly gives away the bank's security secrets to the outlaws (who are posing as cattlemen), leading to the expected comic bank robbery. Later still, the old coot gets some laughs by mentally calculating how many years Scott is subtracting from his life by taking time out to shave! Scott, obviously amused at Hayes' vaudeville-like antics, gives the veteran actor his moment in the spotlight here.

Ryan was still finding his way at RKO, but here is an actor who gave consistently good performances no matter how weak the material was. He plays the Sundance Kid as a sadistic, angry, cynical killer, acting at times as if he has just stepped out of a *noir* film. His cold-blooded murder of both Scott's pal Gray Eagle and Jeffreys' Cheyenne character are presented with style and restraint, making them all the more chilling.

As for Jeffreys, to me she remains one of the unsung heroines of 1940s cinema. She was an opera singer and model before RKO put her under contract during the war years. There, she was pretty much wasted in such grade-B claptrap as *Step Lively* (1944), *Nevada* (1944), *Genius at Work* (1946) and *Vacation in Reno* (1947). Now and then the studio gave her a good role, as in the underrated Pat O'Brien drama *Riff-Raff* (1947). *Return of the Bad Men* was her last film under her RKO contract; sad to say, no other studio picked up on her talents and she drifted into television and stage work. In this Western she looks downright ravishing clad in tight jeans and wearing a gun belt slung seductively over her pelvis, giving a thoughtful portrayal as a good-bad girl.

The woman's touch in the script is evident: Jeffreys and Jacqueline White play rivals for Scott's hand, and in one quick scene, we see them both standing in front of separate mirrors, fixing their hair and appraising their own figures. Later still the duo have a feisty vocal confrontation in the marshal's office during Scott's absence, with each one giving the other as good as she gets.

The best scene in the film remains the posse's raid on the ghost town where Doolin's gang is hiding out. The bandits are enjoying a candlelit ball in the deserted saloon, dancing about like ghosts, when Scott and his men mount their raid. What follows is a splendid night-time shootout with crashing windows, flying bullets, shadowy figures and a raging fire all working in tandem to ensure that nobody's quite sure who is shooting at anyone else. The final climax has Scott and Ryan fighting it out in same deserted saloon, Scott apparently doing all of his own fight

scenes. (One can imagine Enright egging him on with, "Come on Randy ... remember how good it looked on *The Spoilers*?")

Some fun is to be had in watching how the studio assembled such diverse outlaw characters as Billy the Kid, the Sundance Kid, the Dalton and Younger Brothers and Bill Doolin in one place and one time. The Daltons, at least, were pure-bred Oklahoma outlaws. But Billy the Kid basically roamed the New Mexico range, and he died not far from Fort Sumner, New Mexico, in the summer of 1881—eight years before *Return of the Bad Men* is set! The Younger Brothers mostly terrorized Missouri, Minnesota, Iowa and points Midwest, and in any event whoever was left of the gang following the infamous Northfield, Minnesota, raid (September 7, 1876) were serving prison time by 1881 (Bob Younger died in prison in 1889; Jim later committed suicide). As for the Sundance Kid, most closely associated with Butch Cassidy and his "Hole-in-the-Wall" gang, he was a criminal byproduct of the mountain states before disappearing with Cassidy into South America, where they are believed to have been killed by Bolivian troops following a bank robbery. Obviously historical accuracy was not important to the scenarists of this film.

The film was shot between May and July 1947 at the RKO Ranch. Scott got $87,500 for his work, an increase of nearly $20,000 from *Trail Street*, the previous RKO Scott Western. While the RKO film files are not particularly in-depth for this film, they do reveal that airplanes flying overhead cost the production a day or two of work and that Jeffreys' horse had to have his mouth stitched up after a reflector fell on him.

Gary Gray (to author): "*Return of the Bad Men* was a good movie. Randolph Scott was really a very nice guy but he kept very much to himself and I was a little kid so of course I wasn't spending a whole lot

Scott's characters often spoke in lead when words failed to do the job. *Return of the Badmen* (1948).

of time with him. He was extremely nice and well-mannered. The only thing I can tell you about him is that he is what I consider the true Southern gentleman. He was a lot of what you saw on the screen. I don't think that there was a whole lot of acting

for him. That was his character; the way he did things.

"The thing I remember most about him was his horse, White Dust. This horse would follow him around like a dog. I can remember him throwing the reins up over that horse's neck and walking away and that horse would follow right behind him. That was amazing to me — I've had lots of horses and I never had one that would follow me around unless I had sugar or apples."

Jacqueline White (to author): "A lot of the dialogue was written day by day. The general plot stayed the same, but you'd come in ready to work and they'd have something new for you that day. Randy was a lovely man to work with — a gentleman. When you worked one on one with him, he was a very good actor. He took the picture all in stride. It's something he was used to doing; more or less the same character he'd played before, and he did it very well. (*What memories do you have of director Ray Enright?*) He was a very jolly, outgoing kind of guy. But he wasn't the sort that sat and talked about the character with you."

The New York Times (8/5/1948): "Another creaky and endless saga of the tumbleweeds."

The Walking Hills (Columbia, March 1949, 78 minutes)

CREDITS   Director: John Sturges; Producer: Harry Joe Brown; Screenplay: Alan Le May, additional dialogue by Virginia Roddick

CAST   Randolph Scott (Jim Carey), Ella Raines (Chris Jackson), William Bishop (Dave), John Ireland (Frazee), Arthur Kennedy (Chalk), Jerome Courtland (Johnny), Edgar Buchanan (Willie), Josh White (Josh), Russell Collins (Bibbs), Charles Stevens (Cleve)

Synopsis: Gold fever strikes nine men and one women in Death Valley as they seek to uncover a wagon train of gold buried in the sand.

In the wake of the success of Warner Bros.' 1948 classic *The Treasure of the Sierra Madre*, gold fever struck Hollywood. In 1949 Columbia put out two films obviously inspired by the John Huston picture: *Lust for Gold* (with Glenn Ford and Ida Lupino) and *The Walking Hills*. The latter, shot largely on locale in Death Valley, boasts a fine ensemble cast and an impressive sandstorm sequence, as well as some offbeat plot devices.

Unfortunately some of these plot devices also work against the film. *The Walking Hills* gets to its point quickly: A disparate group of losers, drifters, has-beens and wannabes band together to track down a buried wagon train full of gold in Death Valley. But once the group reaches their destination, the narrative winds here, there and yonder like a dry arroyo looking for water. Redundant flashbacks establishing a relationship between the William Bishop and Ella Raines characters (she left Scott for Bishop) are among the least interesting, and a trio of songs by troubadour Josh White, while not without merit, slow down the narrative.

Still, director John Sturges was quite good in establishing particular characters within an ensemble — think of *Bad Day at Black Rock*, *The Magnificent Seven*, and *The Great Escape* — and to that end *The Walking Hills* succeeds in delineating the desires of its ten protagonists, including John Ireland's Frazee, a private detective on the trail of killer Dave (Bishop) but who is willing to chuck the job for a share in the five million. Bishop isn't the only one involved with the digging party who has a criminal past, as it turns out — both Johnny (Jerome Courtland) and Chalk (Arthur Kennedy) have something to hide as well.

The ensemble performances are good, with Scott giving yet another understated performance as Jim Carey, a former rodeo star more interested in his foaling mare than he is in the girl or the gold. He is the conscience of the group, keeping them in line without overstepping his boundaries. When Chalk becomes hysterical for no apparent reason, Carey slaps him out of it. "What didya' do that for?" Frazee asks. "I ran out of words," replies Carey, casually rolling a cigarette for emphasis. Later, after

Left to right: Actor Jerome Courtland, Major Robin Olds (Ella Raines' husband), Ella Raines (back), Raines' stand-in Valerie Hall (front), Randolph Scott, park ranger Stanley Jones and his wife Olive relax during a break in the filming of *The Walking Hills* (1949).

Ireland's Frazee has mortally shot Johnny, Carey turns to the armed detective and, with a threatening sense of quiet intones, "If he dies, you better hold onto that gun." It's interesting to see how Scott manages to overpower all of the other actors with his work by simply underplaying. He has less screen time than Bishop or Raines, but the film still belongs to him (though Edgar Buchanan, as always, demands viewer attention in his scenes as a talkative old dreamer). The last shot of the film, showing Scott's character riding off into the distance with the new foal, and *not* the girl, cradled in his arms, is just beautiful.

Sturges, like Budd Boetticher, learned how to direct the fast and hard way under Columbia's "B" unit, turning out a dozen quickies between 1946 and 1950. He wasn't known for working closely with actors to create characters, and once said, "I believe in Take One for spontaneity. If I feel it doesn't come off, I move the camera to another viewpoint. Freshness is paramount." Actors either admired Sturges or hated him. Jerome Courtland liked him, but said he was a director who expected his actors to know their stuff: "He didn't give you much one-on-one direction. He expected you to have the character down and know what you were doing. I think everybody in that cast really did."

Courtland recalled one amusing incident during the filming: "We shot it in

Death Valley, where it was often 140 degrees. It was miserable, but I never heard anyone, including Randy, complain. Ella Raines was the leading lady, and she was married to Air Force pilot Robin Olds, who was later Commandant of the Air Force Academy and a flying ace in World War II, Korea and Vietnam — which means he shot down at least five planes in every conflict. We were out in the sand dunes doing a scene one day when this fighter plane came up over the dune, went into a vertical climb up doing rolls all the way, then turned and dived right at the entire company. The horses all stampeded. Ella was the only one who stayed on her feet when the plane pulled over our heads about ten feet above us. She yelled out, 'You son of a bitch! Stop that!' It was Robin. We all knew who it was because he had visited the set. Everybody was hoping that nobody would find out, but Louella Parsons broke the news in her column, and [Robin] got in trouble with the Air Force. We lost a little bit of production time that day because the wranglers had to go round up all the horses in the desert and bring them back, but we all thought it was funny — even Randy laughed."

Unfortunately, Scott would never work with Sturges again. The director left Columbia for MGM the following year, so even if Brown and Scott wanted to use him again, they probably couldn't due to contractual obligations. The duo hired Gordon Douglas to direct the next two films Scott made for Columbia.

Courtland maintains that the blonde bombshell adorning the pin-up poster in the backroom of the bar in an early scene is none other than Marilyn Monroe, then a Columbia contract player. It doesn't quite look like Marilyn to me, but if it is her that'd be the only time she appeared with Scott in a film, I guess.

Variety (3/2/1949): "The main kick derives from its gallery of sharp portraits of an assorted group on the prowl for a buried treasure in Death Valley."

Canadian Pacific (20th Century–Fox, May 1949, 94 minutes)

CREDITS   Director: Edwin L. Marin; Producer: Nat Holt; Screenplay: Jack DeWitt and Kenneth Gamet

CAST   Randolph Scott (Tom Andrews), Jane Wyatt (Dr. Edith Cabot), J. Carrol Naish (Dynamite Dawson), Nancy Olson (Cecille Gautier), Victor Jory (Dirk Rourke), Robert Barrat (Cornelius Van Horne), Walter Sande (Mike Brannigan), Don Haggarty (Cagle)

Synopsis: Railroad surveyor and troubleshooter Tom Andrews faces the usual slew of obstacles in his efforts to get the Canadian Pacific built.

For someone who was a pretty astute judge of Western film scripts (despite director Andre DeToth's assertion to the contrary), Scott certainly blew it when he agreed to do *Canadian Pacific*. It may not be Scott's overall worst film, but I rate it as his overall worst Western. Which is not to say that it isn't worth watching — though I'm not sure it is.

The "building the railroad" plot is one Scott would return to twice more in the next few years (*Santa Fe* and *Carson City*) so I wonder if it appealed to the engineer in him. Plot and character development are not just sketchy; they're nearly invisible. "From now on I'm a man of peace," Scott says about ten minutes into the film. Literally two minutes later, while strapping on a six-gun, he tells his sultry fiancée Cecille (Nancy Olson, who gives a fine performance), "In this country, if I draw faster, I keep living." A half-hour later he's given up his guns again, forsaking a life of violence for the love of cold, sexless Dr. Edith (Jane Wyatt, haplessly cast as the other woman).

Victor Jory is Dirk Rourke, the anti-railroad villain who convinces his neighbors that getting the Indians drunk and

Scott (center), J. Carrol Naish (left) and Frank Faylen prepare for an Indian attack in *Canadian Pacific* (1949), probably Scott's worst Western.

angry will help their cause. I must say Rourke does have a good argument when he suggests the railroad will bring not just progress, but people, and the sort of people who will change the environment for the worse. Rourke's henchmen are nameless characters devoid of personality who fire the Indians up in an effort to get them to launch a raid against Scott and his men.

One ridiculous scene has Scott blown up by dynamite (five boxes worth, for the record) by Jory. We expect that to be the end of Scott, but there he is in the next scene, lying in bed, pretty animated and no worse for the wear, except for the bandage draped across his forehead. Scott's pal Dynamite (Naish in a role that seems to have been written for "Gabby" Hayes) tells Wyatt that Scott "was standing too close. If he'd been standing a few feet away, he'd been blown to bits." Wyatt muses on this for a moment before replying, "I didn't know that."

The whole film is full of such absurd set pieces. *Canadian Pacific* is an unexciting series of baloney chunks strung together by a railroad line. For instance, Naish drives an out-of-control wagon full of dynamite through the railroad camp simply to get Scott's attention. A moment later, Scott notices a band of suspicious-looking Indians sauntering through camp and easily picks out two white men hidden among them. The men run, so Scott shoots them down — in the back, to boot. Five seconds later there's a dynamite explosion on the tracks, and we get no further mention of who the two white men were or why Scott shot them. The plotline is hung on a thread, and a tenuous thread at that.

The film does boast a fairly decent climactic Indian attack, with Scott and his comrades holding out from inside one lone railroad car. The Indians here are clever and cunning, utilizing snipers and flaming arrows to inflict damage. Unfortunately, this one almost-good scene is marred by a ridiculous bit wherein Naish, riding off for reinforcements, is waylaid by six Indians. They don't kill him immediately; rather, they draw straws to see who will get his scalp. "Mind if I smoke?" Naish asks the sextet of Indians, pulling forth six sticks of dynamite that he happens to be carrying on his person. "Finest smokes you ever had," he says, handing over the lit dynamite sticks to the six stooges. "Just puff away there." Naish sneaks off and mounts his horse, leaving the Indians amiably puffing away, and an off-screen explosion signals their fate. This is pure cartoon imagery; unfunny and insulting to boot.

The film has a few traces of dark humor that are of note: Drunken patrons of a tent bar force a dead comrade to ingest a shot of whiskey ("This'll fix you up!") while later a dying man, his belly full of bullets, falls back laughing in delight. But when Wyatt's doctor character gives Scott a blood transfusion on a moving train with no discernible medical equipment at hand, well, it's just about time to tell the projectionist to stop the film. The film boasts superb color and gorgeous Canadian scenery, but I haven't changed my mind about *Canadian Pacific*: Randolph Scott or no Randolph Scott, it stinks.

Nancy Olson, who was about 20 years old when she made *Canadian Pacific*, is young, sultry and vivacious and gives the film more than it deserves. Her next film was the classic *Sunset Boulevard*.

Jane Wyatt (to author): "Randy was underrated [as an actor]. Think of how good he was in that comedy *My Favorite Wife*. He enjoyed doing Westerns. One day on the set he showed me his [rust-colored] jacket and

told me, 'I always have a little touch of rust in my costume. I find that when you're doing an outdoor picture, you must have a touch of rust—a hankie, a tie or something.' He was very good-humored, on-screen and off.

"Once we were sitting outside our tents on location, and he was doing something with a pair of scissors and I asked, 'Randy, what are you doing?' And he said, 'Clipping coupons.' He was always thinking about saving or investing money. But he was a real gent; fun to act with. He was always self-deprecating about his talent, but I have to say he was a very ingratiating fellow, and rather attractive. But what was the point of that picture anyway?"

The New York Times (5/20/1949): "Vaudeville wasn't the only thing exhumed at the Palace yesterday. The picture that went along with it brought a whiff of the late departed, too. *Canadian Pacific* is the title, and the best to be said for it is that it rounded out a program of mediocrity." *Variety*, (5/9/1949): "The picture needs plenty of tightening ... and some of the romantic fiction with which factual circumstances are glossed puts too much strain on credence."

Fighting Man of the Plains (20th Century–Fox, October 1949, 94 minutes)

CREDITS   Director: Edwin L. Marin; Producer: Nat Holt; Screenplay: Frank Gruber

CAST   Randolph Scott (Jim Dancer), Victor Jory (Dave Oldham), Jane Nigh (Florence Peel), Bill Williams (Johnny Tancred), Barry Kelley (Slocum), Joan Taylor (Evelyn Slocum), Douglas Kennedy (Ken Vedder), Berry Kroeger (Cliff Bailey), Rhys Williams (Chandler Leach), James Todd (Hobson), James Griffith (Quantrill), Paul Fix (Yancy), James Millican (Cummings), Dale Robertson (Jesse James)

Synopsis: Jim Dancer, former guerrilla and outlaw, tries to make a new life for himself as a railroad worker in Lanyard, Kansas. Instead he ends up as marshal of the town.

Within the first minute or so of *Fighting Man of the Plains*, a sturdy Western boasting some superb sequences and a stupid title, Scott's Jim Dancer cold-bloodedly shoots down an unarmed man during the infamous Quantrill raid on Lawrence, Kansas (August 21, 1863). This is perhaps the only time in his Western film career that Scott is shown to be an outright killer and not just a good bad guy forced to turn to outlawry thanks to society. Nearly a decade later (in the film, that is), he is tracked down by a private detective, Cummings, and captured. He prepares to face a lengthy prison term when a ferryboat mishap gives him a second chance. Cummings drowns and Dancer assumes the dead man's identity, which causes trouble when his prowess with a gun impresses the townspeople of Lanyard so much that they insist he become marshal.

The premise of *Fighting Man of the Plains* is intriguing, and the story is helped considerably by some fine performances by Scott, Jane Nigh and Victor Jory. But it is also a film heavy on coincidence: The brother of the man Scott shot down hires his own gunman (Bill Williams) to get Scott, and they both reside in Lanyard, as does the dead man's daughter, who doesn't recognize Scott because ten years have gone by. (This bothers me somewhat: According to the script, the girl was about 15 when she saw her father killed. Now, at 25, she can't remember the murderer's face?) Barry Kelley's Slocum, the main villain of the piece, also benefits from a lot of scripting coincidences that allow him to buy up all of the land around the town, which means he can charge exorbitant prices to anyone wanting to pass through to reach the railroad station.

The film does have its share of suspenseful and well-played scenes, even if they are stock situations: Scott's Jim Dancer, shotgun in hand, calmly lets nine ornery gunmen know that he intends to die, but that he'll get at least half of them first before he goes — unless they put down their guns, which they do. Dancer, silently taking on a would-be rapist in a street showdown, strides towards the man with such determination that the poor guy, realizing he's made a mistake in calling Dancer's hand, suddenly shouts out, "Wait … wait …" before unwisely reaching for his pistol. Dancer shoots him down and then turns to the man's pals with an accusatory, "Was it a fair fight?" They remain silent, realizing that this is one gun hand to be reckoned with.

With a couple of days' worth of stubble on his chin and a look of perpetual sorrow in his eyes, Scott gives a thoughtful performance as a man torn by guilt but bound by honor. Like another underrated cinematic cowboy, Audie Murphy, Scott could convey a myriad of emotion with economy. When confronted by saloon girl Flo (Jane Nigh) about his true identity, Scott reacts with a silent look that reveals guilt, fear, sorrow and even a little relief all at once. No words were necessary.

Dale Robertson, on the verge of second-string stardom, plays Jesse James as an agreeable, good-humored cuss. He turns out to be a hero in the film, by the way, and preview cards and letters to 20th Century–Fox indicated that the actor was on his way to the big time. The studio signed him to a contract and put him in lower-grade Western films. He could never quite be Randolph Scott (not that he should have tried) but he did all right in a number of action pics.

Variety (10/12/1949): "The plot is hackneyed…direction is generally satisfactory."

The Doolins of Oklahoma (Columbia — A Scott-Brown Production, July 1949, 90 minutes)

CREDITS   Director: Gordon Douglas; Producer: Harry Joe Brown; Screenplay: Kenneth Gamet

CAST   Randolph Scott (Bill Doolin), Louise Allbritton (Elaine Burton), George Macready (Sam Hughes), John Ireland (Bitter Creek), Charles Kemper (Arkansas Tom Jones), Noah Berry, Jr. (Little Bill), Frank Fenton (Red Buck), Jock Mahoney (Tulsa Jack Blake), Griff Barnett (Deacon Burton), Dona Drake (Cattle Annie), Virginia Huston (Rose)

Synopsis: In 1890s Oklahoma, the Doolin Gang race against fate, the law and encroaching civilization to leave their stamp on outlaw history.

Films like *The Doolins of Oklahoma* glorified the outlaw lifestyle much in the manner that the Warner Bros. gangster films of the 1930s did. And if you can get past the usual Hollywood sugar coating of frontier badmen, then *The Doolins of Oklahoma* should please you. It's a well-made, slightly different Western showcasing Scott as a man who demands respect from the get-go. But like many of its predecessors — *Jesse James*, *When the Daltons Rode* and *Bad Men of Missouri*, for example — *The Doolins of Oklahoma* paints its badmen characters with broad, white-washed strokes of sentimentality and sympathy.

Scott's Bill Doolin is a good man turned bad, thanks to federal regulators and crooked politicians, but his heart never seems to be in his criminal work. He's more interested in breaking free of his crooked cohorts and settling down with his loving wife Elaine (Louise Allbritton, another underrated actress from the period) to start a family and a farm. The section of the film dealing with Doolin's attempt to go straight are quite well done. Unfortunately for Doolin, his pals railroad him back into action, and the film takes a dead end turn towards tragedy. "You're dead, Bill," Elaine's deacon dad tells a pensive Scott. "And I don't want my daughter married to a dead man." Doolin leaves his wife and resumes his life of crime, only to be shot down by a posse outside a church — providing Scott with his fifth and last screen death.

Scott cuts a tragic silhouette as a man who has nothing in his life but a career he doesn't want, but the film's outlaw psychology goes no deeper than the surface. Scott brings warmth, humor and nuance to the role, but as in that year's *The Walking Hills*, he's also confident enough to let the other players take center stage so that *The Doolins of Oklahoma* plays as more of an ensemble piece rather than a star turn.

Yakima Canutt is credited with the second unit action, and between he and director Gordon Douglas they set up an impressive array of action scenes, including a great night-time chase through a narrow mountain passage with Scott and company eluding a posse (led by George Macready, playing a hero part for once) and an intense street shoot-out between the Doolins and the posse. Kenneth Gamet's script successfully details the passing of the Old West — and one of the last outlaw gangs of that West — while offering some witty lines for the company players to revel in. Douglas was weaned on comedies, including some Little Rascals shorts and a couple of Alan Carney-Wally Brown films, so he knew how to pepper his films with humorous touches.

The real-life Bill Doolin (1858–96) was a bank and train robber who was shot down by a posse, as in the film, though he never achieved the sort of notoriety that his peers did. Robert Armstrong played the same character in Scott's 1948 Western *Return of the Badmen*.

According to stuntwoman Polly Burson, who worked on the film, Jock Mahoney, one of the Doolin gang members, doubled for Scott on this film.

The Nevadan (Columbia–A Scott-Brown Production, January 1950, 81 minutes)

CREDITS   Director: Gordon Douglas; Producer: Harry Joe Brown; Screenplay by George

W. George, George F. Slavin and Roland Brown.

CAST Randolph Scott (Andrew Barkley), Dorothy Malone (Karen Galt), Forrest Tucker (Tom Tanner), Frank Faylen (Jeff), Jeff Corey (Bart), George Macready (Edward Galt), Charles Kemper (Dyke Merrick), Tom Powers (Bill Martin), Jock Mahoney (Sandy)

Synopsis: Undercover agent Andrew Barkley befriends bandit Tom Tanner in an effort to find out where Tanner hid some stolen gold. Little does Barkley know that another gang is after the loot as well.

A tight and compelling Scott-Brown Columbia Western, *The Nevadan* opens with a safe being blown up over the opening credits and segues into an amusing scene wherein Scott's Andrew Barkley, clad in Eastern dude garb, naively (or so it seems) pursues fleeing bank robber Tom Tanner (Forrest Tucker), who is responsible for the $200,000 gold robbery. It's a film with so many small surprises that I don't want to relate much more about the plot, except to say that along the way Scott has to deal with a broncing buck of a horse, a myriad of double-crosses and a feisty forewoman in the persona of Karen Galt (Dorothy Malone). In a nice touch, Malone is shown to care for crippled horses that no one else wants. The film is well-acted and loaded with humor, and is one of those few movies from the golden age of Hollywood that segues successfully from comedy to drama without jolting the audience too much.

A humorous scene sees Barkley contending with an overly flirtatious, matronly hotel-keeper who seductively croons, "You know, men didn't always call me Mama." A moment later she offers to sell Barkley a suit of clothes from her hotel closet. The price is $600.

"$600?" Scott asks incredulously.

"That's what the man owed me," the grande dame replies without batting an eye.

The main villain is not Tanner, but ranch owner Edward Galt (George Macready), who wants the $200,000 for himself. In his employ are a pair of quarreling brothers (played by Jeff Corey and Frank Faylen) who nonetheless display a true affection for each other. The script's attention to these bickering siblings lifts the film several more notches above the norm.

Little touches of originality surface throughout. For instance, the final gunfight amidst rocky terrain of Lone Pine is offbeat, with Scott and Tucker, armed only with pistols, waiting for the trio of rifle-toting gunmen to come for them. This is topped by a brawl in a collapsing mine between Scott and Tucker amidst falling rock, sand and timber. Fast and fun, *The Nevadan* is one of the best Scott-Brown offerings of the pre–Boetticher-Kennedy years. Gordon Douglas was never considered one of the top tier directors in Hollywood, but many of his films are respectably drawn, and several of the Westerns stand out from the crowd, including this one and *Rio Conchos* (1964). Jeff Corey thought Douglas had a better way with actors than most film directors of the era. "I like the oldtimers like Vic Fleming and Henry Hathaway and Bill Wellman, for whom I worked a couple of times," Corey told interviewer Patrick McGilligan for the book *Tender Comrades: A Back Story of the Hollywood Blacklist* (St. Martin's Press, 1997). "Guys like Gordon Douglas, who was wonderful at action stuff and who had a wonderful feeling about characterization. God, they had such presence. In the best sense of the word, they were ballsy."

Variety (1/11/1950): "Easy to take ... Scott is up to his usual good standard." *The New York Times* (1/13/1950): "A better than run-of-mill Western ... and the margin by which this horse-and-gun show rises above the commonplace is in a couple of minor characters whom Jeff Corey and Frank Faylen play. They're just a couple of fellows and could be complete nonentities. But here, at least, someone with humor — the desperate script-writers, perhaps — endowed them with individuality and some very acid lines."

Colt .45 (Warner Bros., April 1950, 74 minutes)

CREDITS   Director: Edwin L. Marin; Producer: Saul Elkins; Screenplay: Thomas Blackburn

CAST   Randolph Scott (Steve Farrell), Ruth Roman (Beth Donovan), Zachary Scott (Jason Brett), Lloyd Bridges (Paul Donovan), Alan Hale (Sheriff Harris), Ian MacDonald (Miller), Chief Thundercloud (Walking Bear), Lute Crockett (Judge Tucker)

Synopsis: Killer Jason Brett steals a pair of gun salesman Steve Farrell's Colt .45s, leading to a chase and a lot of shooting.

Whenever someone uses the term "intelligent" to describe a Western, I always hope that doesn't mean it's slow-moving and dull. *The Nevadan*, for example, is an intelligent Western. But it's not dull. *Colt .45*, Scott's first film under his new Warner Bros. contract, is *not* an intelligent Western. It is, however, incredibly fast-moving as well as far-fetched, making one wish that it were more intelligent, even if that meant it would also be dull. In a nutshell, *Colt .45* is action-packed but stupid, and in retrospect it stands as one of Scott's weaker Warner Bros. offerings.

An excessively violent film, *Colt .45* piles one hard-to-swallow sequence on top of another, filling in the holes with gunplay and horseback chases and leaving the viewer no time to consider plot logic. The characters are not just badly drawn, they're not drawn at all, so it's up to the actors to connect the dots. Ruth Roman, a feisty talent in her day, comes through. I can't say any of the other actors, including Scott, succeed. Scott is a revenge-driven hero, but his Steve Farrell lacks the complexity of his Columbia film protagonists, and he is

a far cry from the Boetticher-Kennedy vengeance-seekers of *Seven Men from Now* and *Ride Lonesome*. I don't think Scott has more than three or four lines of dialogue in a row at any given time in this film, and we don't get to know much about this man, other than that he was once an officer in the Mexican-American War and is now selling Colt .45s. Better developed — but unfortunately badly acted — is villain Jason Brett, played over-the-top as a psychotic by Zachary Scott. I keep thinking how much more effective it would have been had Dan Duryea played Brett, as he would have added humor, cynicism and a real menace to the role. (Incidentally, for those of you familiar with Universal's *Winchester .73*, a 1950 Western which is also about a stolen gun and a man seeking revenge on the guy who stole it, compare the Dan Duryea-Charles Drake relationship in that film to the Zachary Scott-Lloyd Bridges alliance in *Colt .45*.)

So what does *Colt .45* have going for it? Director Edwin Marin kept the action going so fast that the 74 minutes flies by, the Technicolor is gorgeous, and William Lava's music score suggests a much grander epic than this (roughly) $800,000 film is. Warners did provide Scott with a really strong supporting cast on his initial outing, including reliable Alan Hale, but the actors can't do much with the one-dimensional personae assigned to them by screenwriter Thomas Blackburn and company. I say "and company" because this Warner Bros. Scott, like several others, went through a dozen or so rewrites before production began, and I doubt the continual tinkering with the script helped. Marin, to his credit, gave the film the proper "let's keep it moving" pacing. *Abilene Town*'s script, in comparison, gave the director room for reflection. *Colt .45* doesn't ask viewers to do anything but strap themselves tightly into the saddle and hold on fast. To that end, it succeeds as a matinee crowd pleaser. But more discriminating Western film fans are bound to be let down by it.

Variety (4/18/1950): "It never lives up to the promising title … the histrionic antics of Zachary Scott are ludicrous to the extreme." *The New York Times* (5/1/1950): "One thing is fairly obvious: the Warners weren't in a high-brow mood when they rounded up all the fellows and banged out *Colt .45*. This Technicolored Western is as intellectually simple as one and one are two. It is such a hackneyed picture that it is actually a lot of fun."

The Cariboo Trail

(20th Century–Fox, June 1950, 80 minutes)

CREDITS Director: Edwin L. Marin; Producer: Nat Holt; Screenplay: Frank Gruber, from a story by John Rhodes Sturdy

Scott's not sure that the job of marshal will pay dividends in *Colt .45* (1950), the first Western the actor made under a long-term contract with Warner Bros.

CAST Randolph Scott (Jim Redfern), George "Gabby" Hayes (Griz), Bill Williams (Mike Evans), Karin Booth (Francie Harrison), Victor Jory (Frank Walsh), Douglas Kennedy (Murphy), Jim Davis (Miller), Dale Robertson (Will Gray), Mary Stuart (Jane Winters), Lee Tung Foo (Ling), James Griffith (Higgins), Mary Kent (Marthy Winters)

Synopsis: Partners Jim Redfern and Mike Evans run cattle to the remote Canadian town of Carson Creek but run afoul of town boss Frank Walsh.

The Cariboo Trail is a film with a lot

of potential that suffers from an under-developed script and a ridiculous middle sequence involving an Indian raid.

Scott is Jim Redfern, a Montana cowpoke who wants to run cattle in the Canadian Rockies. Bill Williams is Mike Evans, his partner turned enemy who wants to mine for gold. Both actors are effective in a grim early scene wherein Scott has to amputate Williams' arm with a Bowie knife; this sequence is memorably unsettling. Redfern is an interesting and somewhat risky role for Scott at this point in his career in that the character, while determined and honest, is also flaw-ridden. He almost always does the wrong thing when it comes to running cattle, relating to his partner, romancing the girl, dealing with the villain or fighting off the Indians. The role calls for a lot of nuance, and Scott tries to give it his all, though he injects the character with a happy-go-lucky attitude that is not always in sync with the events of the storyline. His best moment has him consoling his dying partner in a near-silent bit of insightful performing. As a saloon keeper who keeps a totem pole in her bar, Karin Booth is more animated than the usual Western heroine, while Victor Jory gives a different perspective on the town tyrant character, playing him as a mousy, frightened man.

The Cariboo Trail is somewhat renowned for a ludicrous scene involving Scott, "Gabby" Hayes and a kicking burro. When the Indians surround Scott and Hayes in their camp, Scott tugs on the creature's ears and it lets loose with a succession of high-powered kicks, knocking a slew of surrounding warriors this way and that and allowing our heroes to escape. Scott then mounts a horse and arms himself with a rifle, shooting down another half-dozen braves as their arrows and bullets whiz harmlessly past him. I can only guess that these Indians are kin to the ones who smoked the dynamite sticks in *Canadian Pacific*. This entire bit is condescending and smug, and aside from six-year-old children, I can't imagine anyone found it amusing in 1950.

The Canadian location shooting is a great asset — though apparently none of the principal actors took the journey north to shoot, for the film is full of rear projection shots — as is Paul Sawtell's lyrical score, which is almost too good for a "B+" Western like this one. The cast does well with the material, including Lee Tung Foo as Scott's Chinese cook (who Hayes refers to as Confucius!) and Douglas Kennedy as one of Jory's gunmen. Edwin Marin, as always, does the action scenes justice (aside from the Indian attacks), but while all three Fox Scott films of this era show promise, they don't quite come together as well as the trio of RKO films Holt produced for Scott. *The Cariboo Trail*, like *Fighting Man of the Plains*, holds its own in the Scott canon, but neither film comes up to the standard of the Columbia Scotts or the better Warner Bros. offerings of the early 1950s.

The story was by John Rhodes Sturdy, who also provided the scenario for the excellent *Corvette K-225*. An inside visual joke shows a doctor's sign with the name John S. Rhodes hanging behind Scott's head at one point — an oblique reference to Sturdy, no doubt.

Variety (7/5/1950): "A scenic outdoor action feature that shapes up well."

Starlift (Warner Bros., November 1950, 103 minutes)

CREDITS Director: Roy Del Ruth; Producer: Robert Arthur; Screenplay: John Klorer and Karl Kamb, based on a story by John Klorer

CAST Janice Rule (Nell Wayne), Dick Wesson (Sgt. Mike Nolan), Ron Haggerty (Corp. Rick Williams), Richard Webb (Capt. Joe Callan), Hayden Rorke (Chaplain). With guest stars Doris Day, Gordon MacRae, Virginia Mayo, Ruth Roman, Gene Nelson, James Cagney, Gary Cooper, Phil Harris, Frank Lovejoy, Lucille Norman, Louella Parsons, Randolph Scott, Jane Wyman and Patrice Wymore

Synopsis: A little *Hollywood Canteen*, a little *Hail the Conquering Hero* as a brash GI convinces everyone that his shy pal is involved with glamourous movie star Nell Wayne. Complications develop, but all ends well when Warner Bros.' echelon of stars show up to entertain the servicemen via "Operation Starlift."

An obscure but okay musical that suffers from having no build-up and no real climax, *Starlift* comes to life in its song and dance numbers but struggles to stay airborne every time the romantic subplot takes center stage. A throwback to the era of all-star "let's put on a show" films of the 1940s, *Starlift*, like *Follow the Boys* (1944), utilizes Scott in a fairly ineffective cameo role. Here he temporarily plays emcee for the all-star revue, filling in for Phil Harris, who has been sidetracked by a gin rummy game with servicemen. Wearing what seems to be a sideshow carny's suit and bow tie, Scott grins amiably and throws out such forgettable lines as, "I'm Randy Scott, pinch-hitting for Phil Harris." In all due respect to Scott, would you choose him to replace a brash comedian as master of ceremonies? Shot against a backdrop of a curtain, Scott's scenes seem like an afterthought, and it's unfortunate that the creators of this film failed to take the opportunity to team him up with fellow *Starlift* guest star Gary Cooper. Cooper is seen to slightly better advantage in the spoof number, "Look Out Stranger, I'm a Texas Ranger," but even that bit fails to register. The film is watchable fare, uplifted by several top-notch musical numbers, including Doris Day's bouncy rendition of "S'Wonderful." But of all the guest stars, Scott has the least to do, and it probably took him about an hour of shooting time to do it.

Sugarfoot (Warner Bros., January 1951, 80 minutes)

CREDITS   Director: Edwin L. Marin; Producer: Saul Elkins; Screenplay: Russell Hughes, from the novel by Clarence Buddington Kelland
CAST   Randolph Scott (Sugarfoot), Adele Jergens (Reva), Raymond Massey (Jacob Stint), S.Z. Sakall (Don Miguel), Robert Warwick (J.C. Crane), Arthur Hunnicutt (Fly-Up-the-Creek Jones), Hugh Sanders (Asa Goodhue), Gene Evans (Billings), Hank Worden (Johnny-Behind-the-Stove)

Synopsis: Jackson "Sugarfoot" Roden attempts to start a freight line in Prescott,

Arizona, while battling arch-rival Jacob Stint.

Sugarfoot is an offbeat misfire that nonetheless provides Scott with a different type of Western hero role. It is more complex than Scott's initial Warner Bros. outing, *Colt .45*, but it is also considerably duller. Scott plays another ex–Confederate officer, but he's no gunhand; he's nicknamed "Sugarfoot" for his greenhorn manner and gentlemanly ways. One of the film's best scenes has frontier veteran Arthur Hunnicutt giving Sugarfoot tips in preparation for a gun duel.

On the one hand, Scott is tackling an interesting role in that his Sugarfoot is often uncertain of himself. Conversely, the actor isn't quite suited to the role of an ambiguous greenhorn; the sort of part seemingly tailored for a younger man such as Audie Murphy. But one of Scott's talents as an actor is in making poorly scripted scenes work, as in a brief but suspenseful moment when his Sugarfoot strides into a saloon, gun drawn, to confront the villainous Jacob Stint (Raymond Massey).

The actor is not helped by the script or direction. *Sugarfoot* is a film full of action set pieces that make no sense. For example, Massey leads a coterie of five gunmen in a near-suicidal attack on a freight train guarded by a cavalry company of a dozen men. When their efforts fail, they take flight. Scott and Hunnicutt (who helped the cavalry in the fight) pursue the bad guys. Only then the cavalry mistake Scott and Hunnicutt for Massey's gang, leading to a pointless chase scene. Later still, Scott and Hunnicutt come across Massey and Gene Evans, who are under siege from Apaches. Scott refuses to let the Apaches kill off Massey, arguing that he wants to do the job himself, so he and Hunnicutt help the bad guys route the Indians. Then Scott engages in a gunfight with Massey and Evans while a third bad guy shows up behind Scott to cause more mayhem. If it reads confusing, believe me, it *is* confusing, and Scott and Hunnicutt play the scene like a couple of Rat Packers enjoying their third martini and oblivious to the danger around them.

Sugarfoot has its moments, and Scott gives his character considerable nuance and depth, but it remains an offbeat failure. Incidentally, Patricia Neal refused Adele Jergens' role of Reva, choosing to go on suspension rather than appear in a Randolph Scott Western.

During filming, Scott built his new house on Copley Drive in Beverly Hills. He would live there for the rest of his life.

Variety (1/30/51): "It is disappointing Western filmfare that uses talk instead of action over most of its 80 minutes ... most adult audiences will find much to laugh at in the way the story is played off." *The New York Times* (2/12/51): "*Sugarfoot* ... holds no surprises. In fact, it holds no entertainment, despite the ammunition expended and the exciting complexion of the countryside in Technicolor." *Hollywood Reporter* (1/30/1951): "The comfortable rating that Randolph Scott possesses in the box office polls is going to be put seriously to the test when this inane adaptation of Clarence Buddington Kelland's *Sugarfoot* reaches the screen ... the performances are downright dreadful."

Santa Fe (Columbia–A Scott-Brown Production, April 1951, 85 minutes)

CREDITS   Director: Irving Pichel; Producer: Harry Joe Brown; Screenplay: Kenneth Gamet, based on the novel by James Marshall and a story by Louis Stevens

CAST   Randolph Scott (Britt Canfield), Janis Carter (Judith Chandler), Jerome Courtland (Terry Canfield), Peter Thompson (Tom Canfield), John Archer (Clint Canfield), Warner Anderson (Dove Baxter), Roy Roberts (Cole Sanders), Billy House (Luke Plummer), Olin Howlin (Dan Duran), Jock Mahoney (Crake), Frank Ferguson (Bat Masterson), Chief Thundercloud (Chief Longfeather), Irving Pichel (Harned)

Synopsis: Confederate Civil War vet Britt Canfield agrees to help build the Atchinson, Topeka and Santa Fe railroad, but his three outlaw brothers have other plans.

A routine railroad saga, *Santa Fe* does not hold up as well as the majority of the Columbia Scott films of the era because it doesn't boast one original thought. The building of the railroad, the conflict between the North and South and the contrast between good and bad brothers had all been done before in more inspired fashion. Scott's Britt Canfield faces the usual array of railroad conflicts: fighting a bullying trouble-maker (Jock Mahoney, who Scott runs out of camp in a wheelbarrow), threatening Indians (Scott gives the Chief a ride in the engine and promises to name a railroad after him) and a rival railroad line. The character development is extremely weak when it comes to the villains and Scott's three brothers, and the acting is a little lazy all around. The scripting remains loose, and the stakes do not seem very high for anybody, despite heroine Janis Carter's grandiose statement that this thing (the railroad) is "bigger than all of us." Still, it's certainly better than *Canadian Pacific* and boasts one good fistfight between Scott and Jock Mahoney. The color and scenery are beautiful, though the Santa Fe train depot in the film looks nothing like the one here in downtown Santa Fe where I live.

Scott sure is one looks-conscious cowboy. In one tense action scene, the actor uninhibitedly pauses to smooth out a few strands of hair that have fallen out of place. It's a hoot to see.

John Archer on director Irving Pichel (to Tom Weaver): "A very easygoing, swell guy. He had an actor's approach because he was an actor. In fact, he appeared in *Santa Fe*. Very protective of his actors, very understanding and very good. He could give you a lot. From being an actor, he knew the kind of stuff we wanted from him and we appreciated it."

Variety (4/4/1951): "Scott gives a first rate account…" *The New York Times* (5/4/1951): "As for the audience, all that it gets is a lot of muscular action, Western style, including a fist fight aboard a rolling flat car, and some pretty Technicolored outdoors."

Fort Worth (Warner Bros., May 1951, 80 minutes)

CREDITS   Director: Edwin L. Marin; Producer: Anthony Veiler; Screenplay: John Twist

CAST   Randolph Scott (Ned Britt), David Brian (Blair Lunsford), Phyllis Thaxter (Flora Talbot), Helena Carter (Amy Brooks), Dick Jones (Luther Wick), Ray Teal (Gabe Clevenger), Lawrence Tolan (Mort), Paul Picerni (Castro), Emerson Treacy (Ben), Bob Steele (Shorty)

Synopsis: Newspaper editor Ned Britt imprints the power of the press on lawless Fort Worth.

"He rode into Texas alone. His only friend was a gun." So says Phyllis Thaxter's frontier woman of Randolph Scott's trouble-shooting newspaper man early in *Fort Worth*, a superior WB Scott. The film is a solid testament to the studio system of the time, and bears lengthier discussion as an example of what the WB Scotts should have been: tight, action-packed, well-scripted and slightly complex films featuring impressive ensemble acting.

In *Fort Worth*, Scott plays yet another ex–Confederate soldier. (Why not? It helped to explain his character's strength, courage and integrity.) He once cleaned up Abilene and Dodge City with his editorials. Thaxter is presented as a much younger woman who exhorts Scott to take up six-guns to clean up the town, and fortunately this May-December romance is played up for what it is, with a knowing wink at Scott's aging but still potent romantic status.

The early 1950s WB Scotts appear to be efforts to recapture the excitement of the studio's late 1930s mini-epics, such as *Dodge City* (1939). *Fort Worth* is not quite as good as the next WB Scott, *Carson City*, but it is enjoyable enough. It's easy to see why these films put Scott in the top ten of box office draws, for there's enough attention paid to both character development and action to keep men, women and children interested.

The film has a fair number of clichés, but clichés make the Western genre what it is, and there are some raw doses of reality, as when a small boy gets trampled in a cattle stampede. The film boasts some arch dialogue ("You're right out of a dime store novel," Scott says with bemusement to one of villain Ray Teal's polished gunmen), and some wonderfully unexpected moments, as when Scott brusquely shoots down a trio of gunmen without giving them a chance to draw. The plot is also a bit more complicated than usual, with Scott facing a multi-faceted villain-hero in David Brian while trying to finagle his way out of some rather intricate romantic entanglements. The film is also an early example of the "buddy" picture, with Scott and Brian teaming up at just the right time to take on larger bands of outlaws who lay siege to both of them.

Brian, who may strike you as being a little bit Sonny Tufts, a little bit Broderick Crawford, exudes confidence and cunning as Scott's rival-partner, and he was probably the strongest of the Warners contract players to challenge Scott on screen. In fact, after the next WB Scott, *Carson City*, the studio no longer gave Scott colorful character actors like Zachary Scott or Raymond Massey or David Brian to test his strength against. Rather he was saddled with the likes of Lex Barker, James Millican and Roy Roberts, with diminishing results.

With six or seven good gunfights, a burning train sequence (partially lifted from *Dodge City*) and some better-than-average plotting, *Fort Worth* remains a

Scott with Phyllis Thaxter (back to camera) and Helena Carter in a rare non-action sequence from *Fort Worth* (1951).

noteworthy Randolph Scott outing. The film premiered at three cinemas in Fort Worth, and Scott and his wife Pat went out to Texas to help publicize the film. While in Fort Worth, the actor took part in a horse race, judged a beauty contest and acted in a re-creation of a train robbery at the railyard. I, for one, would have liked to have seen any of those events.

David Brian complained to the press that Warners had no advice for helping him adjust to the genre, as this was his first Western. "Randy Scott gave me a few directions on the quick draw, correct dueling stances and the most graceful way to shoot backwards while riding horseback. But most of the tricks I had to pick up myself," he told a U.P. reporter.

William Campbell, who worked with David Brian in several Warner films of the period, tells a funny story about Brian and John Wayne:

Wayne wasn't an alcoholic, but he liked to drink. And he used to stop at an Italian restaurant, I think it was called Sorentino's, on the way home from the studio. He went in one day and sat down and was talking to the bartender when he realizes that there's some guy singing very badly in the next room.

Wayne says to the bartender, "Who the hell is that?"

The bartender says, "That's David Brian, the actor."

Wayne said, "Well, go in and tell Mr. Brian that he's a lousy singer and that Mr. Wayne wants him to shut up."

The bartender goes into the next room, which was kind of dark, and says to Brian, "Listen, there's a customer at the bar who doesn't think your singing is very good. I think it's best if you stop singing."

Brian says, "Who the hell is that?"

"John Wayne."

"Tell Mr. Wayne to kiss my ass."

So the bartender goes in to tell Wayne — and David Brian told me this story so I know it's true — and as David Brian is sitting in the next room he sees this huge body, six foot four inches tall, coming in through the doorway, and Brian's mind started working fast to turn this situation around, and he remembered that he knew a makeup man who knew Wayne. So before Wayne could speak, Brian said, "Duke, I was just talking to so-and-so about you and..." And Duke said, 'Yeah?' and bingo, they sit down and start drinking together.

David drank himself to sleep. Wayne goes to the bartender and says, "Do you know where the hell he lives?" The bartender gives him the address; they load Brian in Wayne's car and Wayne drives him home. Wayne goes to the front door, and nobody's home. So Wayne gets Brian over his shoulder and carries him around back down the stairs to the swimming pool area, and there was a cabana there. Wayne throws Brian on a couch and starts to walk away, and then he stops and thinks, "Wait a minute. If he wakes up, he could stagger into the pool and drown." So Wayne goes back, picks Brian up, opens this pool equipment closet near the cabana with brooms and a pool sweep and all this crap in it, and sticks Brian in there and locks the door. And David Brian woke up a couple of hours later, finds himself in total darkness, and thinks he's dead!"

Paul Picerni (to author): "I loved working with Randy. He was just a nice man — but he didn't take any bullshit from anybody, including the producers. One day Henry Blanke [a major executive at Warners] came on the set and said something to him about the way a shot should be done, and Randy stood his ground and said, 'No, we're gonna do it this way.'

"Another thing: Gordon MacRae gave me an old set of golf clubs. I started playing, mostly slicing the ball to the right. I

mentioned that to Randy — he was a very good golfer — and he told me, 'Line up your ball, pick a tree on the right side of the fairway and concentrate on throwing your club head toward that tree. That forces the club head to go inside out and when you hit the ball you'll split to the left. So instead of slicing, you'll hook. I followed that advice and never sliced again.'"

This was director Marin's last Scott film; he died in May 1951 at the age of 52.

The New York Times (7/13/1951): "What's the latest Randolph Scott Western all about? Need anyone ask? Mr. Brian, incidentally, has no business in or near a saddle. In fact, he'd better go back to cuffing Joan Crawford around or next time he may see a horse laugh."

Man in the Saddle (Columbia., November 1951, 87 minutes)

CREDITS Director: Andre DeToth; Producer: Harry Joe Brown (Randolph Scott credited as Associate Producer); Screenplay by Kenneth Gamet, based on the story by Ernest Haycox

CAST Randolph Scott (Owen Merritt), Joan Leslie (Laurie Bidwell), Ellen Drew (Nan Melotte), Alexander Knox (Will Isham), Richard Rober (Fay Dutcher), John Russell (Hugh Clagg), Alfonso Bedoya (Cultus Charley), Guinn "Big Boy" Williams (Bourke Prine), Clem Bevans (Pay Lankershim), Cameron Mitchell (George Virk), Richard Crane (Juke Virk)

Synopsis: Ranch owner Owen Merritt finds himself being crowded by power-hungry neighbor Will Isham — the man who also stole Merritt's girl and hired a Texas gunslinger to enforce his own brand of range law.

An excellent offering from the Brown-Scott company, *Man in the Saddle* benefits from refined character studies, a high-caliber cast and a first-rate script. Andre DeToth, directing the actor for the first time, demonstrates a real affinity for the action scenes, which are played out with a genuine sense of excitement. DeToth's trademark, to some degree, was in bringing the action up close and personal for the audience, giving a sense of imminent danger within the scope of a vast environment. Though most of the actual action bits offer nothing new in terms of concept — the cattle stampede, the shoot-out in a darkened saloon and the gunfight in a dust storm had all been done before — DeToth makes you feel like you're seeing them for the first time, particularly in a wonderfully satisfying scene in which Scott finally takes up arms to shoot up an isolated line cabin that is chock full of rival Alexander Knox's men.

"Stay away from trouble, Owen — it comes easy to you," platonic gal pal Nan Melotte (Ellen Drew) cautions Scott. She may as well have asked the actor to stop making Westerns. Owen Merritt is an unusual Scott characterization in that he is a man who is very reluctant to get involved in the range war surrounding him. Likewise, he starts the film as a man who has just lost his woman (Joan Leslie) to his arch-rival because, we sense, he doesn't know how to say or do the proper thing. It's interesting to see Scott playing an emotionally detached man who is nonetheless *not* prone to violence or revenge; he is not so much a forerunner of the Boetticher-Kennedy protagonists as a distant cousin to Owen Wister's Virginian or Alan Ladd's Shane — men who'd just rather get along with the world but who find they've got to get involved or become obsolete. You get little sense that Scott's hero is satisfied when he does start fighting back, although I love the exchange between his character and evil gunman Fay Dutcher (Richard Rober), when Owen has the drop on the latter. Dutcher says, nervously, "You wouldn't shoot a man in the back, would you?" "I could you," Owen replies, and you realize that, in this one case, he would.

The film is helped by a top-notch cast. Both John Russell and Cameron Mitchell bring a sense of violent intensity to their roles. Alexander Knox, a low-key player who never quite achieved film stardom, is a deliciously cold villain, while Clem Bevans, Guinn "Big Boy" Williams and Alfonso Bedoya — all Brown-Scott favorites — come through with satisfying (if by now familiarly patented) roles. Joan Leslie, as Knox's ambitious but detached wife, also gives a strong performance, as does Ellen Drew as a sympathetic friend of Scott's who is not afraid to open up with a Winchester on any man who goes after Scott. This higher level of acting attracted critical notice. *Variety* said, "The playing is featured by better characterizations than is usually found in Westerns. Scott, the two femmes and Knox are excellent."

Joan Leslie (to author): "I enjoyed working with Scott. He was very professional, very on top of his portrayal and very giving in the acting. He would help you, correct you, persuade the scene to come around a little more to take it to an interesting ending. There is a tendency to take actors who work simply in Westerns for granted, and there's no question that Scott was taken for granted. He *was* a good actor. He had that All-American rugged look. He was handsome as ever — that's for sure!

"A man like Scott — and I'd have to put him in a category with Gary Cooper and Joel McCrea — was a total professional, and a real Southern gentleman. His manners were like a lovely host in his own house. He was charming, he was at ease. He knew what he had [to offer]. He was self-confident, and he was very secure within himself and the studio system of the time. On the set, between shots, we spoke about our children: my dear twin daughters and his brand new baby son [Chris]. He talked proudly and lovingly about the little boy and how he was pro-

Scott (left) watches as Guinn "Big Bog" Williams plays knife with bad guy Frank Sully in the superior Andre DeToth–directed Western *Man in the Saddle* (1951). (JC Archives, Inc.)

gressing so rapidly, showing intelligence and personality. Then he said, 'I can say this without seeming braggadocio because it's not due to me; he is my adopted son and we are so happy and grateful for him.' Nice, huh? A gracious man."

Andre DeToth gave his initial Scott outings a fresh shot of vitality and originality. However, the director never seemed to be as proud of the films he made with Scott as Budd Boetticher would be. Some 40 years later, while speaking to Anthony Slide for the book *DeToth on DeToth*, the director said, "Harry Joe Brown was a very good, down-to-earth, nickel and dime producer. He was a rough Pop Sherman with mundane taste. He made a lot of films and drank a lot. Scott drank a lot too — sarsaparilla — and they understood each other

because instead of reading scripts, they read *The Wall Street Journal*. Neither of them knew much about stories. They didn't fight about story points. They cared about money, all right, but unfortunately they didn't care enough about films."

This is DeToth's view, and he was there and I wasn't, but I would argue that Brown certainly knew story values, which doesn't mean he and Scott didn't miss the mark now and then when it came to choosing scripts. The films Brown purchased for Scott were generally written specifically for the actor by reliable scenarists (including Kenneth Gamet) and they offered Scott room for character change and development — even though the range those characters rode was, figuratively speaking, small. Even the non–Scott films that Brown produced for Columbia have the merit of originality and thought: *The Guns of Fort Petticoat* (1957, with Audie Murphy), *Three Hours to Kill* (1954, with Dana Andrews) and *The Last Posse* (1953, with Broderick Crawford) are three such examples. (*The Restless Breed*, a 1948 Brown-produced Western starring Sonny Tufts, is an exception to this rule; it's pretty bad.) "Making those epics, I felt no difference whether Scott-Brown or Warner Brothers or Columbia produced them," DeToth told Slide of the Scott canon as a whole. I still maintain Brown's production hand was firmer and he generated tighter, more thought-provoking scripts than the Warners' studio system did.

For Leslie, who acknowledges that she only worked with Scott once and didn't know him on a personal level, Scott gave off the aura of a casually detached man who loved the Western and all it stood for, but who had little desire to reach past that genre at this point in his life (a view DeToth shares). "I don't think he was an overly ambitious person," Leslie noted. "He loved doing [Westerns] and wanted to keep doing them, but some people are guided by managers and agents and told what to do, and others have their own drive to achieve, and I think quite possibly he didn't have either. Scott was very smart, very shrewd, but I don't think he had to seek out material or compete for a particularly provocative script or worry about a studio taking care of him."

Contemplate these thoughts all you like — Scott and Brown knew what worked and how to keep audiences interested in a genre that was already showing signs of wear and tear. At Columbia, Scott was the Cowboy King in the 1950s, and with a handful of exceptions the films he made with Brown remain memorable samples of the Western genre.

Carson City (Warner Bros., May 1952, 86 minutes)

CREDITS   Director: Andre DeToth; Producer: David Weisbart; Screenplay by Sloan Nibley and Winston Miller; story by Sloan Nibley

CAST   Randolph Scott (Silent Jeff Kincaid), Raymond Massey (Big Jack Davis), Lucille Norman (Susan Mitchell), Don Beddoe (Zeke Mitchell), Richard Webb (Alan Kincaid), James Millican (Jim Squires), Larry Keating (William Sharon), George Cleveland (Henry Dodson)

Synopsis: Railroad engineer Jeff Kincaid plans to build a railroad through Carson City against severe opposition and an outlaw gang lead by the infamous "Champagne Bandit."

Carson City, the absolute best Warner Bros. Scott Western of the period,* is the only hand-me-down Scott received during his tenure at WB. The film was supposed to reunite director Michael Curtiz and star Errol Flynn, who had teamed so well on such Western epics as *Dodge City* and *Virginia City*. But Flynn, then in his last year of contractual servitude to Warner Bros. and anxious to avoid making any more Westerns, turned the film down, and Curtiz then passed on the project as well. The beneficiaries were Scott and Andre DeToth. Interestingly, while many of Scott's films were based on Western novels or magazine stories, *Carson City*'s origins were in a February 1951 *Master Detective* magazine story (the mag cost 25 cents then).

A title card opening the film tells us that "no state blazed a more colorful path across the pages of Western history than Nevada," but I bet if the film were titled *Tucson* you could replace Nevada with Arizona. The film opens with a wonderfully comic scene in which a stagecoach is held up at gunpoint by the infamous Champagne Bandit and his gang. "That strongbox

---

*I'm not including 1956's *Seven Men from Now*, produced by John Wayne for Warner Bros.

belongs to the bank," passenger-banker Larry Keating protests as the gang takes the goods. "They can have it back after we bust it open," one masked outlaw wisecracks. The outlaws keep the passengers happy by treating them to a champagne brunch. "Never saw lunch like this in Boston," one matronly passenger says, impressed by the culinary goods. "Never saw men like this there either," says her equally elderly companion, lustfully eyeing the bad men! *Carson City* sports a great sense of humor.

Raymond Massey (in a role intended for Charles Ruggles) plays the Champagne Bandit, who fancies himself something of a Robin Hood of the West. He robs from the rich, but he doesn't give it to the poor — he keeps it to himself. Unlike his one-dimensional villainous character in *Sugarfoot*, here Massey is given a meaty part to sink his teeth into, and he has a ball.

Keating's banker finances a railroad simply in an effort to circumvent the Champagne Bandit — a rather ambitious and absurd plan — and that's where Scott comes in. Scott is Silent Jeff Kincaid (who sure talks a lot), and he's introduced in a good saloon brawl scene combining fun with fisticuffs and crashing bottles with collapsing chairs. Scott does a nice job projecting a world-weary indifference as a man who would rather brawl than build yet another railroad — but build it he does.

The Champagne Bandit (Raymond Massey, left) is amused with the Scott hero's easygoing manner in another good DeToth effort, *Carson City* (1952). (JC Archives, Inc.)

It's interesting to note how the film's pro-progress view fell into step with America's postwar optimism, and some intelligent scripting touching on this issue lifts the film above the usual run-of-the-mill Westerns of the time.

Ah, another railroad, another newspaper. This time the local rag is run by Lucille Norman, another in a long line of Warner Bros. starlets thrust into a Scott film. Norman was an opera singer who flirted with Hollywood for about a year, and in my view she had a lot more potential as a screen actress than the studio gave her credit for. She's sexy, she's savvy and she has good comic timing, and Scott's rescuing of Norman from a dynamite blast is enacted with comic and sexual energy. (An interesting casting note: other actresses considered for the part were Donna Reed, Dorothy Malone, Jane Wyatt and Gail Russell.)

The film also has more than its fair share of shocking sequences: the murder of a freight wagon driver (sent unconscious over a cliff to his death), the back-shooting of the newspaper editor, a bloody saloon brawl (which leads to a newspaper headline "Railroad Crew Terrorizes Town" — and Scott's half-brother is the editor!) and a tunnel collapse. Each action scene successively builds towards the next, culminating in a dual climax: First Scott and a relatively anonymous gunman shoot it out in an abandoned mining town, and then Scott, the bandits, the horses, the train and the camera all come together in an action-packed finale involving a robbery and a shoot-out. The script and direction combine to top *that* sequence with yet another climax in which Scott and Massey shoot it out in a rocky canyon.

I love the film's attention to detail: A trombone player, late for a music concert, rushes in to play "catch up" midstream, the bit player enacting the role of gunman who shoots it out with Scott casts cautious

looks about as he attempts to move in on his adversary; the bit player doing the freight wagon driver gives a nervous glance at his outlaw captors as he realizes death is approaching, and so on.

Some of the assembly line studio offerings were bound to come out better than the rest, and *Carson City* is a prime sample. It's an incredibly enjoyable, top-notch testament to the power of the studio system of the 1950s. The film premiered in Carson City (of course) and made a lot of money for the studio. At a time of a changing cultural climate in Hollywood, this leathery-faced guy in his mid–50s, who was never considered much of an actor, was somehow gaining in box office popularity. Neither Warner Bros. nor Columbia cared to analyze why. They just sat back and counted the profits.

Hangman's Knot (Columbia, October 1952, 80 minutes)

CREDITS　Director/screenplay: Roy Huggins; Producer: Harry Joe Brown

CAST　Randolph Scott (Matt Stewart), Donna Reed (Molly Hull), Claude Jarman, Jr. (Jamie Grovers), Frank Faylen (Cass Browne), Richard Denning (Lee Kemper), Lee Marvin (Rolph Bainter), Jeanette Nolan (Mrs. Harris), Clem Bevans (Plunkett), Ray Teal (Quincey), Guinn "Big Boy" Williams (Smitty), Monte Blue (Maxwell), John Coll (Egan Walsh), Glenn Langan (Capt. Peterson)

Synopsis: During the Civil War, Confederate officer Matt Stewart and his men ambush a Union patrol to gain hold of a gold shipment that could help the South. Only after the dust has cleared does Stewart discover that the war is over, making him and his compatriots outlaws.

A taut Western that emphasizes human relationships and unexpected plot twists as much as slam-bang action, *Hangman's Knot* is another top-notch Randolph Scott Western from the 1946–55 period. The film boasts an unusual pre-credits sequence in

Donna Reed gives Scott a concerned hug at the end of *Hangman's Knot* (1952), another top Scott entry. Most of the rest of the cast is dead by this point.

which Scott and his men quietly lay out an ambush for an approaching Union patrol in a mountain canyon, and follows up on this tense prologue with a well-staged gunfight between the two gangs. The film benefits greatly from both Roy Huggins' script and his direction (it was the only film the producer-writer directed) and tight ensemble playing from the likes of Lee Marvin (in the first of three Scott Westerns), Frank Faylen, Clem Bevans, Ray Teal, Claude Jarman, Jr., and Donna Reed.

Huggins sets the majority of the action in a relay station in the mountains, where Scott and his surviving men — played by Marvin, Faylen, Jarman, Jr., and John Coll — attempt to stave off a gold-crazed posse of drifters lead by Ray Teal and Guinn "Big Boy" Williams (appearing in his last Scott film). As such, it's the most claustrophobic of Scott's Westerns, and relies on the in-house conflict between Scott and Marvin and between the outlaws and their captives, including Reed's Union nurse and Richard Denning's ambivalent and cowardly Indian agent.

Huggins knew how to pepper a story with tension and humor. At one point, Faylen innocently asks Scott whether the latter has a plan for escaping the relay station. "Umm, hmmm," Scott casually replies. "We go out shooting sometime tomorrow." Scott saunters off, leaving Faylen to contemplate the notion: "Wish I hadn't asked."

Huggins and company set up a terrific climactic confrontation in the wind- and rain-swept darkness of night in which the bad guys turn on each other while Scott and Jarman wait them out. The film is marred only by some clumsy editing choices during the interior action scenes between Marvin and Scott.

A few years before his death in April 2002, Huggins recalled (to the author) his memories of *Hangman's Knot*, a film he wrote for Scott to do at Warner Bros. Scott showed the script to partner Harry Joe Brown, who agreed that Columbia would do the better job with the script (he was no doubt right) and so the duo made a bid for the screenplay, offering Huggins less money for the story but the opportunity to direct — an offer Huggins didn't refuse.

"I wanted to produce," Huggins recalled, "But I directed that film to prove I could do it. Directors are a strange group. They like to make the world feel that directing is a very difficult thing to do, and it isn't at all, so I wanted to prove I could do it so directors would no longer talk down to me. But I had no ambition to be a director. If I had known that directors would be running the industry [one day], I might have decided to be a director."

The film was shot on location in Lone Pine for a budget that was, by Huggins' estimate, less than $400,000. He was given an 18-day schedule and recalled finishing the film in 17 days. Brown did most of the casting, Huggins said, including Scott perennials Frank Faylen, Clem Bevans and Guinn "Big Boy" Williams. Scott suggested Donna Reed, who was then suffering a pre–*From Here to Eternity* career slump, and he may have also put in a good word for Richard Denning, who started his film career at Paramount in 1937 (Denning has an unbilled bit in Scott's *The Texans*). Harry Joe Brown brought in stage actor John Coll, who had played the role of the leprechaun in the Broadway music *Finian's Rainbow*, to play one of Scott's men — much to Huggins' dismay.

"[Coll] couldn't act his way out of a sack," Huggins said. "I wasn't even sure he could read. He only had one scene of importance, where he talks to the woman in the cabin about this boy — Claude Jarman, Jr. — and he couldn't do it. He didn't know what it was about. We were coming close to lunch and everyone was getting very uneasy, so I called a lunch break, took him into another room, and did what I had been told by several well-known directors to do, which is to give [him] line-readings. I read the lines for him, and went through the whole scene with him, seven words at a time. Whatever Harry Joe saw in him must have been not just something he could do — a leprauchan — but all he could do! Well, he came out and did the scene, and he did it well, and when he finished it, the whole damn set broke into applause, and he took a bow!"

Reed, Huggins recalled, was the only one in the cast who wanted to rehearse. Everyone else was willing to do it with no rehearsal, relying on the spontaneity of the moment to carry them through. Marvin in particular seemed happy with this approach, telling a bemused Huggins, "Dialogue isn't important with an actor — it's body language that matters." Huggins came to respect Marvin's talent, but he never did come to appreciate Denning, an actor he felt only had one note to play. Huggins did like and respect Scott. "I'm sure [Scott] was a limited actor," Huggins explained. "He didn't have any feeling for acting except he wanted to do his best, and it was a good way to make a living. Randy was a very realistic man — a businessman. But he had some attitudes about the Western hero that were very hard to get out of him. Some of them I was able to change rather easily. For example, once he grabbed [Donna] Reed and kissed her, and there were eight inches between their pelvic areas. I knew I couldn't say, 'Randy, hold her tight against you! He would say no. He was the Southern gentleman, very much the same on the set as off. But he never talked down to me. He treated me as if I had made 80 pictures, and when we were through he said, 'I hope we can do another picture together.'

"I just had to direct him from being Randolph Scott too much. Whenever a heroic line would come up, he would play it with Randolph Scott zeal, and I would say to him quietly, 'Randy, throw that line away.' He was very receptive — he was wonderful. I was astonished at how easily he went with the elimination of that heroic zeal to just throwing it away. I didn't have to give him much direction — he gave me direction!"

Huggins maintained that *Hangman's Knot* made 20 percent more than all previous Scott films for Columbia. If *Hangman's Knot* did outgross its predecessors, it may have been in part to good reviews. *The New York Times* (12/11/1952) called the film a "taut, action-filled adventure sensibly designed to keep the devotees— especially the older ones—from yawning. Harry Joe Brown and Randolph Scott, who also stars, obviously were aware that motion pictures should move, and their robust drama wastes few words and very often digs into the character of its principals to give genuine substance to the brisk action of the story."

It's of some interest to compare Scott's career at this point to that of Richard Denning. The latter, like Scott, started off as a light-haired, well-built athletic leading man in bit parts at Paramount, but Denning didn't seem to have the talent or the ambition to go further. By the late 1940s Denning was appearing in double-bill dreck like *Unknown Island*, but he did work steadily, and was apparently quite well-liked by his peers. Anne Gwynne, who knew Denning's wife Evelyn Ankers, once told a story about Denning's fondness for alcohol. "One night the police found him butt naked in the middle of the street," she told Michael Fitzgerald (*Western Clippings* #26 November-December 1998). "They asked what he was doing, and he told them the world is constantly moving and he was waiting for his house to come by so he could go in."

Columbia contract player Glenn Langan receives fifth billing in the film, which is curious since he only has about a dozen lines before getting shot down by Marvin in the first reel.

Man Behind the Gun (Warner Bros., December 1952, 82 minutes)

CREDITS   Director: Felix Feist; Producer: Robert Sirk; Screenplay: John Twist

CAST   Randolph Scott (Ransome Callicut/ Rick Brice), Philip Carey (Capt. Roy Giles), Patrice Wymore (Lora Roberts), Lina Romay (Chona Degnon), Roy Roberts (Senator Mark Shelton), Morris Ankrum (Bram Creegan), Anthony Caruso (Vic Sutro), Alan Hale, Jr. (Olof Swensen), Dick Wesson (Monk Walker), Katherine Warren (Phoebe Sheldon), Robert Cabal (Joaquin Murietta)

Synopsis: Union officer Ransome Callicut (Scott) poses as a gun-shy schoolteacher to foil revolutionists in pre–Civil War Southern California.

In my book *Last of the Cowboy Heroes* I call *Man Behind the Gun* "empty-headed nonsense." I should have added, "but very entertaining." This Warners effort holds up quite well after repeated viewings, thanks to a delightful sense of humor. The film opens with a direct steal from *Virginia City* with suave bandit Anthony Caruso surprising his fellow passengers by holding them up at gunpoint. (A similar scene was played out with Humphrey Bogart in the earlier film.) Scott, however, manages to divest the villain's gun of its bullets, thus saving the group, which includes pretty Patrice Wymore. Scott gives Wymore a gun to protect herself and later, in a naughty

Phil Carey, Lina Romay and Randolph Scott spice up the empty-headed but entertaining Warner Bros. Western *The Man Behind the Gun* (1953). (JC Archives, Inc.)

scene tinged with double entendres, asks her where she's hidden it, since it's not obvious to the naked eye. Wymore shifts about uncomfortably before responding, "Don't be rude, Major," leaving the audience wondering *just* where that gosh-darn pistol is! It turns out to be in her muff, and you can interpret that description any way you want to.

Scott, relying more and more on his Southern charm and grace, clearly enjoys himself in the early sequences as a bookish nebbish who pretends to be afraid of guns. "I'm just a man who's lived an uneventful life among his books," he sighs sadly, adding just a pinch of hamminess to the line. As a cowardly greenhorn who can't shoot (or so he claims), Scott makes you wonder what he would have done with the title role of *Destry*.

The plot is both fascinating and confusingly complex. Senator Sheldon and his rival, Graham Creegan, are in opposition over access to the state's water rights (this 20 years before the film *Chinatown*) in an effort to turn it into a slave state. Somehow the film's storyline makes room for slavery issues, gunrunning, racism, buffoonery, adultery, explosions, chases through foggy backstreets and enough shootouts and fistfights to fill five Westerns. The plotting, in fact, is somewhat crazy, but that only adds to the film's fun, and *Man Behind the Gun* benefits from solid production values, sterling color and good ensemble work under the direction of Felix Feist.

The women characters are particularly strong. Wymore, a lively actress, is sincere as a naive Easterner, while the fiery Lina Romay, in her last film of an all-too-brief movie career, is spunky as a saloon entertainer who is also the leader of the gunrunners. At one point she engages Scott in a firefight in a dark alley in an effort to give her gang of men a chance to get away. Her boys hightail it fast, leaving her behind to hold the good guys off—which she does!

There's also comic relief a-plenty (maybe *too* plenty) in the form of Alan Hale, Jr., and Dick Wesson. Wesson, who was sort of the Frank McHugh of the 1950s, plays a Lash LaRue–type character who goes about cracking a whip (at one point he uses it to tear away a dress from a passing saloon girl!). Later, Wesson disguises himself in women's clothing for some cross-dressing humor. A couple of amazing double entendres got past the censors, including some visual buffoonery where Wesson considers using a couple of oranges as breasts, and a joke wherein Wesson warns Scott to stay away from rival Philip Carey's harem or he'll end up "eunich" (unique).

The film climaxes with a no-holds-barred gunfight amid the rocks of coastal California. Roy Roberts' senator, revealed to be the bad guy, takes flight on a horse and Scott follows. The gunfight is fine, but as for the horse chase, Warners chose to utilize stock footage from the 1945 Errol Flynn Western *San Antonio*. Sharp-eyed observers will note that the dry Texas plains of that first film do not in any way resemble the green coastal landscape of California.

Anthony Caruso (to author, on Randolph Scott). "He was the gentleman actor. How he became an actor I'll never know. But he wasn't as bad as he said he was. That story about him trying to join the L.A. Country Club and being told, 'We don't take actors,' and him replying, 'I'm no actor, and I have 100 pictures to prove it,' really sums him up."

Romay, once a singer in Xavier Cugat's band, did bit parts at MGM 1942–50. *Man Behind the Gun* afforded her the largest role of her career, but she retired from films shortly thereafter upon marrying Jay Gould III, grandson of a railroad financier. Romay later became sports announcer at Hollywood Park Race Track. "I know I looked like hot stuff in my movies," she said years later. "And I *was* hot stuff!" And how.

Scott reportedly fell with his horse during a relatively simple dialogue scene while riding in between actors Phil Carey and Robert Cabal. "I have fallen many times during riding scenes," he told the press. "What horseman hasn't? When a horse goes down, there's no other place to go but to the ground."

The film's original title was *City of Angels*. Warners changed it to *Man with the Gun* but discovered that RKO had registered a title by that name, so they switched it to *Man Behind the Gun*— the best title of the three, in my opinion.

Los Angeles Times (1/31/1953): "Randy Scott imparts a certain quizzical humor to his portrayal which, while scarcely tongue-in-cheek, does make it easier for you to go along with him."

The Stranger Wore a Gun (Columbia, July 1953, 82 minutes)

CREDITS Director: Andre DeToth; Producer: Harry Joe Brown; Executive Producer: Randolph Scott; Screenplay: Kenneth Gamet, based on John M. Cunningham's *Yankee Gold*

CAST Randolph Scott (Jeff Travis/Mark Stone), Claire Trevor (Josie Sullivan), Joan Weldon (Shelby Conroy), George Macready (Jules Mourret), Alfonso Bedoya (Degas), Lee Marvin (Dan Kurth), Ernest Borgnine (Bull Slager), Joseph Vitale (Dutch Mueller), Clem Bevans (Jim Martin), Pierre Watkin (Conroy), James Millican (Quantrill), Roscoe Ates (Jake Hooper)

Synopsis: Ex-Quantrill guerrilla Jeff Travis tries to make a new life for himself in the desert town of Prescott, Arizona, but runs into more trouble when he finds he owes a debt to a criminal — and all this in 3D!

A fast-moving piece of Western blarney, *The Stranger Wore a Gun* remains one of the weaker Columbia Scotts. Perhaps Harry Joe Brown and company felt that the novelty of 3-D would enliven the proceedings, and it probably did back in 1953 when viewers saw it through tinted glasses on the big screen. I don't mind a Western being simple, but *The Stranger Wore a Gun* is simple-minded, with all the hard-to-swallow plot points rapidly thrown at the audience within the first five minutes. Scott is Jeff Travis, an ex–Confederate officer involved with Quantrill's famous raid on Lawrence, Kansas (shades of *Fighting Man of the Plains*), who turns riverboat gambler, then frontier outlaw, then stage shotgun rider, all through a series of events that have to do with his believing he owes his life to town boss Jules Mourrett (George Macready, conveying a touch more humor than usual). The failure here is in the scripting, for Kenneth Gamet's screenplay just doesn't do enough to build the necessary transitions for Scott's character to act upon. I for one get used to seeing Scott in superior Western fare, which is why I'm probably doubly hard on him when he's stuck in a weak but watchable film like this one.

Other factors hurt the film as well. Scott's Jeff Travis holds down two jobs in Prescott — one legal, one illegal — and everyone seems to know about both careers except for the heroine Shelby (Joan Weldon) and her father. The acting among the supporting ensemble is quite bad, with the exception of Ernest Borgnine and Lee Marvin. The action scenes are uninspired, and one hotel room brawl between Borgnine and Scott is really bland, with way too obvious use of doubles for both men. And with the exception of Marvin (who gives his customary professionally rendered performance), when the bad guys kick the bucket, they die ludicrously, like five year olds enacting "shoot-'em-up" on the playground. Watch it and decide for yourself whether I'm right.

There are a handful of memorable sequences in the picture. The gun duel between Scott and Marvin is a highlight, as is the final shootout between Scott and Macready in a burning saloon. When Macready riles up the townsfolk to lynch Scott (it's too complicated to explain why here), Scott's gal pal Claire Trevor runs to a nearby deputy. "Quick, there's a lynching!" she screams. "Oh, is that what all the ruckus is about?" the lackadaisical lawman replies.

And though Weldon was never a great actress, in both this film and *Riding Shotgun* she and Scott exude a very warm chemistry suggesting that she had a crush on the older man and that maybe the sentiment was returned. I'm not suggesting an affair between the two, but Weldon is one of the few actresses to appear opposite Scott twice in the postwar years (excluding Karen Steele, Budd Boetticher's girlfriend, who did three Scott films in the late 1950s), and to this day she speaks with both reverence and awe of Scott. It's sort of like the schoolgirl crush on the older teacher who probably doesn't mind the attention. Scott goes off with the Claire Trevor character at film's end, which is a more realistic touch.

Andre DeToth (*DeToth on DeToth*): "I believe Randolph Scott could have gone further as a performer. But he did not have the ambition to step up, to be better in anything except golf. Golf was all that mattered. He was a handsome man; took showers twice a day. He was a man whose shoes shined. But he had a tremendous inferiority complex about his acting ability and that made him stiff."

One day on the set DeToth asked Borgnine if he could ride.

"Can I ride? Like the wind!" the actor replied.

Borgnine mounted a horse and, with a slew of other riders, did a scene in which they had to come riding down a hill fast. According to DeToth, Scott's double, who was riding next to Borgnine, missed his mark.

"Once more, please," DeToth said.

"Why? Didn't I ride like the wind?" Borgnine asked.

"You did great. Ride like the wind again."

"Yeah?" Borgnine replied incredulously. "Well, I have no idea what I did that was great. This was the first time in my life that I was on a damned horse."

Lee Marvin, who made three films with Scott, enjoyed telling a typical Scott-on-the-set story: "There was a flaming stagecoach in one scene, racing along while the cameras rolled in the driver's seat. Holding the reins sat the stunt man while 20 yards away, sitting in a canvas chair, sat Scott, all dressed in his cowboy outfit, with legs crossed, reading *The Wall Street Journal.*"

Joan Weldon (to author): "It was rather A-B-C dialogue, as I remember. It was forgettable. I have more vivid memories of *Riding Shotgun*, which was done first. Warners had nothing scheduled for me so they decided to put me on suspension without pay. I ran into Randy somewhere, and he heard I was on suspension and called my agent and said he had a part in a picture at Columbia and would I consider doing it…. It was three weeks' work; six days a week. Then Warner Bros. said, 'She's under contract to us, we want the money from the loan-out.' My agent said, 'No way. You put her on suspension; she can do what she wants with the money.' So I did get the money."

Some 30 years after *The Stranger Wore a Gun* was released, Weldon ran into co-star Claire Trevor at a dinner party. Trevor didn't recognize the younger actress. "Don't you remember me?" Weldon asked.

"We did a film together — *The Stranger Wore a Gun.*"

"Remember you?" Trevor responded. "I don't even remember the film."

Weldon couldn't blame her.

Variety (8/5/1953): "Okay entry for the general action market … Scott delivers in his usual style. *The New York Times* (7/30/1953): "The story is as cliché-cluttered as some of the staged bouts and the attempted hold-ups of the stagecoaches that abound in this muscular drama. It's hard to tell this Randolph Scott from the scores of heroes he's played before."

Film audiences taking in Columbia feature films of the time may have seen Scott in Ralph Staub's Columbia short subject *Screen Snapshots: Men of the West*, in which the actor plugs *The Stranger Wore a Gun*. Staub was adept at utilizing stock footage from the Columbia vaults and silent film footage to weave together ten-minute shorts celebrating Hollywood's legends. In his book *The Great Movie Shorts*, Leonard Maltin wrote of these *Screen Snapshot* shorts, "Not that there was much time or effort involved for (Columbia) stars to make these appearances. Each appearance consisted of the star standing or sitting somewhere on the Columbia lot, smiling, as Ralph Staub entered. Then the two exchanged amenities. The star would say something like, 'Gee, Ralph, I'd love to see some of that old footage of yours,' and Staub would genially reply, 'Well, I've got some right here!' and the film would jump into stock footage, returning to Staub and his guests every few minutes for some unnecessary comments." In Scott's case, this consisted of sitting in a Columbia screening room while Staub ran silent film footage of Tom Mix and Will Rogers. Incidentally, I only know of two short subjects that Scott appeared in — this one and 1936's *Pirate Party on Catalina Island*. Film historian John Cocchi believes Scott also shows up in the 1941 20th Century–Fox short *Three of a Kind* but I've been unable to confirm this. In addition, Leonard Maltin, in his book *The Great Movie Shorts*, writes that Scott can be seen taking part in a country-western quartet with Barton MacLane, Buster Crabbe and Fuzzy Knight in one of Paramount's *Hollywood on Parade* shorts from the 1933-34 season.

Thunder Over the Plains (Warner Bros., October 1953, 82 minutes)

CREDITS Director: Andre DeToth; Producer: David Weisbert; Screenplay: Russell Hughes

CAST Randolph Scott (Capt. Dave Porter), Phyllis Kirk (Norah Porter), Lex Barker (Bill Hodges), Charles McGraw (Ben Westman), Henry Hull (Lt. Col. Chandler), Elisha Cook, Jr. (Standish), Hugh Sanders (Balfour), Lane Chandler (Faraday), James Brown (Conrad), Fess Parker (Kirby), Mark Dana (Lt. Williams)

Synopsis: Carpetbaggers vs. homesteaders vs. cavalry vs. outlaws in postwar Texas, with Union officer Dave Porter doing his best to quell the disturbances and deal with an unhappy wife.

An adequate Warner Bros. Western that I've come to like more and more as time goes by, *Thunder Over the Plains* is full of brief but well-paced action scenes that are adroitly handled by Andre DeToth, and an interesting romantic subplot involving our hero's lonely (but loyal) wife. Scott plays a duty-bound Texan reluctant to pursue the outlaw gang headed by Charles McGraw. Scott gives a subdued, warm — you might even say soft — performance as an officer torn between duty and conscience, and his acting style gels well with heroine Phyllis Kirk's. Also good is McGraw as the outlaw leader who is willing to give up his own life if Scott will let the rest of his band go. The film succeeds at balancing action scenes with tableau focusing on the home life of Scott and Kirk, and it gives a pretty realistic view of married life and the different ways in which

men and women define their priorities in life.

Some of the action scenes are superb, including a sequence wherein an informer makes his way through the darkened streets of town while a slow-moving but determined mob of vengeance-driven cowhands follow him. Also good is a fistfight between Scott and Lex Barker, the latter playing a junior officer who forces his attentions on Kirk. But *Thunder Over the Plains*, like several of the Warner Scotts, is tarnished by inconsistent scripting, an overly simplistic approach to a rather complex chapter in Texas history, and downright dumb voice-over narration ("The situation became worse ... a powderkeg waiting to blow up," the solemn narrator intones at one point. This sort of banal exposition helped dim the impact of the films Audie Murphy made at Columbia in the 1960s.) The entire setup is often reduced to sequences of the cavalry pursuing outlaws through dense brush, with the actors giving the film a little extra punch along the way. The film climaxes with a well-done shootout, with Scott's officer blasting it out with three bad guys amidst the deserted streets of town. Scott makes an admirable crashing leap through a window of glass in this scene; close-ups reveal that it is not the work of a stuntman.

James Brown, Scott's co-star in *Corvette K-225* back in 1943, has a small role as an evil carpetbagger, but his star had diminished considerably since the war years. Barker gives a one-dimensional performance as a one-dimensional character, and he seems to have been brought in to needlessly complicate matters, a point not overlooked by some critics. "Barker's West Pointer role ... seems dragged in without much purpose other than to get an outright cad in the picture," *Variety* noted (11/11/1953). Still, *Thunder Over the Plains* offers a steady diet of solid action well served up by DeToth, and Scott gives a more varied performance than usual as an officer who can no longer see things in strict shades of black and white.

Phyllis Kirk (to author): "Randy was very present for me; very generous as an actor. He was also incredibly good-looking, even as old as he was when we made that film — he must have been 55. I knew a lot of people in that town [Hollywood] and never heard one unpleasant or unkind thing said about him. Everyone liked him a lot. He was much more interested in finances than films, and by the time we did that picture I think he figured out that his career was not half-bad. The picture was the usual not-very-complicated Western. Andre [DeToth] lifted it a little bit above the normal. It wasn't a great film. In fact, if I hadn't been under contract, I wouldn't have done it!"

Riding Shotgun (Warner Bros., March 1954, 75 minutes)

CREDITS   Director: Andre DeToth; Producer: Ted Sherdeman; Screenplay: Tom Blackburn, from a story by Kenneth Perkins

CAST   Randolph Scott (Larry DeLong), Wayne Morris (Tub Murphy), Joan Weldon (Orissa Flynn), James Millican (Dan Maraday), Joe Sawyer (Tom Bigger), Charles Bronson (Pinto), Paul Picerni (Bob Purdey), James Bell (Doc Winkler)

Synopsis: When stage shotgun rider Larry Delong tries to warn his townspeople of an impending attack by outlaws, they turn on him.

A fairly short, fast-paced Western, *Riding Shotgun* strives to be a little different in its complex and unorthodox plotting. At times, however, the set-up is presented in an unbelievable manner. For example, early in the film when Scott's Larry DeLong character rides back into town after having been ambushed on the trail, he comments via voiceover narration that the streets are empty and that the only men left behind to defend the place are "old and ineffectual." Yet within minutes there are at least two dozen armed and ready men prepared to capture DeLong (who they believe is guilty of a stagecoach robbery and murder). Throughout the film, DeLong continually expresses concern that the townsfolk will not be up to the task of taking on outlaw Dan Maraday's gang of nine, but it seems to me that the gunmen are the ones who should be worried.

Andre DeToth noticed this nonsensical touch when he first read the script, and wrote a lengthy letter to producer Ted Sherdeman, suggesting changes and improvements. Some were accepted; some were ignored. The Warner Bros. file for this film is chock full of memos suggesting that the studio initially saw *Riding Shotgun* as a vehicle that would rival *High Noon*, with Scott's hero standing alone against both the outlaw gang and his own town. Everyone on the lot was more or less invited to chime in with an opinion on this film, and various Warners executives read the script and made suggestions (probably a big mistake), although one nameless executive did state that it seemed ridiculous that the outlaw gang would leave hero Larry DeLong alive, his hands tied, with a derringer within reach (which he uses to blow the ropes off his hands). The film went through a lengthy pre-production period starting late in 1952, but by the time the cameras started rolling in March of 1953, all Jack Warner wanted was another assembly line Randolph Scott picture. When DeToth began playing with the dialogue during shooting in an attempt to improve the scenario, Warner chided him: "There will not be any changes of dialogue or scenes in *Riding Shotgun* without my personal okay. The script is very good and you should shoot it without any changes."

Two days later, apparently unhappy with the fact that DeToth took nine takes to get a scene between Scott and actor Fritz

Feld right, Warner fired off another memo: "We do not want any more nine takes. Stop at one if it is okay and go right on to the next one." So much for producing high-level entertainment. DeToth responded by moving like gangbusters, finishing the film seven days ahead of schedule, one take per scene, in about 15 days. No wonder the Warner Bros. Scotts generally don't hold up as well as the Columbia Scotts of the period.

As for the film itself, Scott's DeLong is another man bent on revenge, riding the stagecoach routes as shotgun man in an effort to find the man who killed his brother. The killer is Dan Maraday (James Millican), an outlaw known for his prowess with a derringer — probably a first in Western cinema, and typical of the script's outlandish but not unwelcome touches. Maraday and his men rob DeLong's stage and kill the driver (Paul Picerni) and leave DeLong tied up in the hills, even though they've vowed to kill him on sight. Our hero escapes and heads back to the town of Deep Water to warn the townspeople of an impending raid by the gang. Unfortunately, Deep Water's denizens have already gotten wind of the raid and believe De-Long was in on it, despite having no evidence to back up their claim. He's forced to take refuge in the cantina where he waits out a siege by his former friends while Maraday's gang saunters into town to pull off a casino robbery.

I'm not sure that *Riding Shotgun* should be considered a good Western, but the film does touch on McCarthyite themes (1954 was Joe McCarthy's Waterloo, the year he lost favor on national television with the Army Hearings). DeLong notes, "The town had already tried and found me guilty." The widow of the stagecoach driver attacks him, a little boy hits him with a slingshot and, to top things off, a cantankerous old buzzard takes potshots at DeLong when the latter isn't looking. Why

would anybody want to live in a town like this?

On DeLong's side are the doctor, the daughter of the man who runs the casino, and the ambivalent debuty, Tub (Wayne Morris). The townsfolk have no respect for Tub. One of them calls him "Jelly Belly" and it's easy to see why. The former Warner Bros. star and World War II aviation hero had put on considerable poundage by this time, and his character continually saunters off to the local diner to grab a cup of coffee and piece of pie ("I didn't have time for dessert!" he explains to some complaining citizens at one point when they catch him eating a pastry rather than corraling outlaws). Morris was really overweight and jowly in this film; he looks and acts a lot like Alan Hale, Jr., in the old *Gilligan's Island* series. Still, he gives an honest portrayal of a basically decent man who tries to maintain order in an atmosphere of chaos.

DeToth did what he could with the script, eliciting solid performances out of most of the cast, including ingenue Joan Weldon. I like that the script doesn't do more than hint at a romance between Weldon and Scott; they're more like platonic pals. DeToth ends things on an energetic note with a slam bang shootout and brawl in the darkened casino.

The film boasts one line that I'm still trying to make sense of. In one scene, a streetwalker eyes a silent lynch mob leader fingering a long rope and says, "What are you doin' fiddlin' around with that rope for, honey? Don't you like me any more?" If there are strange sexual rituals involving men and ropes — past the usual bondage routine, that is — I, for one, am clueless as to what they are.

Joan Weldon (to author): "When I went under contract to Warner Bros. I had to sign a piece of paper that said I was not, and had never been, a Communist. I knew about McCarthy but I didn't really realize

Joan Weldon is just about the only character to offer a besieged Scott moral support in *Riding Shotgun* (1954), a decent assembly-line offering from Warner Bros. (JC Archives, Inc.)

what I was signing. I was a kid. I do remember *not* wanting to sign it, but I couldn't go under contract if I didn't. I never considered that *Riding Shotgun* might have some [McCarthy] themes like that.

"Randy was a lovely man and a generous actor. He would put me facing to the camera and almost upstage himself, with his back to it. I never found another actor who did that. When we were doing *Riding Shotgun* he said, 'Want to go riding?' I said, 'I've never been on a horse.' So we got on the horses and took off and he's proceeding to give me a lesson in riding a horse and the first thing he said was make sure to keep an eye out for gopher holes, because it's the most dangerous thing; the horse can go down and bring you down and possibly go on top of you. So we hit a

couple of gopher holes and he told me to pull up the reins tightly and so on.

"We went out about a half hour and he says, 'We better get back to the set; they may call the shot early,' so we go back. He goes into a scene but they didn't need me for another hour. I thought, 'Well I've had a lesson. I can ride now.' So I go off on the horse by myself. I took the same route we had gone and about 15 minutes out I hit a gopher hole and I pulled up on the reins and got out of it and thought, 'I did the right thing.' But then I said to the horse, 'You know something, I better take you back. That's enough gopher holes for one day.'"

During shooting, Warner Bros. issued a press release that stated that Scott's first feature film was 1935's *So Red the Rose*. It probably sounded better than *Women Men Marry*.

Variety (3/10/1954): "The pattern is strange for a star of Scott's stature, whose heroics in the past always have been good for considerable violent action and money in the till for exhibitors. It's a far cry from the standard Scott epic." *The New York Times* (4/2/1954): "Mr. Scott plays a man among men, a stalwart citizen, mistaken for an outlaw, who has to prove his innocence by wiping out the real varmints single-handed. In case anybody wonders, for Mr. Scott, it's a cinch." *Des Moines Tribune* (5/5/1954): "Real standout is [Wayne] Morris as the paunchy, burping deputy, trying to keep order without spilling blood."

The Bounty Hunter (Warner Bros., August 1954, 79 minutes)

CREDITS Director: Andre DeToth; Producer: Sam Bischoff; Screenplay: Winston Miller; story by Winston Miller and Finlay McDermid

CAST Randolph Scott (Jim Kipp), Dolores Dorn (Julie Spencer), Marie Windsor (Alice Williams), Howard Petrie (Sheriff Brand), Harry Antrim (Dr. Spencer), Robert Keys (George Williams), Ernest Borgnine (Bill Rachin), Dub Taylor (Eli Danvers), Paul Picerni (Judd)

Synopsis: Bounty hunter Jim Kipp arrives in the desert town of Twin Forks to find three outlaws who robbed a train. His presence leads to paranoia, distrust and some shooting.

The Bounty Hunter, the last of the Andre DeToth–directed Randolph Scott films, benefits from an intelligent and unpredictable screenplay by Winston Miller and a hard-driving performance by Scott as Jim Kipp, a determined and almost arrogant bounty man indifferent to the feelings of those he hurts. "You'd turn your grandmother in on her birthday if there was a reward for her," one town sheriff chides Kipp, but his argument doesn't

make a dent in the bounty hunter's hide. Kip cheerfully acknowledges this is true, and refuses to pitch in $10 to pay for his latest victim's coffin!

The opening is very similar to Sergio Leone's *For a Few Dollars More* (1967), in which bounty hunter Lee Van Cleef lines his gunsight on a moving target in the desert valley below — only in this film it is the outlaw who targets Scott's Jim Kipp. The wanted man misses, and Kipp, clad all in black (a favorite color of Scott's), gets his man with his six-gun. Shortly thereafter, the Pinkerton Detective Agency approaches Kipp with an offer he can't refuse: They want him to track down three surviving outlaws who disappeared a year ago with $100,000 in stolen money from a train robbery. Kipp agrees, and using his wits and his gun, picks up the trail in Twin Forks. There he waits out his three foes, who slowly but surely reveal themselves to him — as do a handful of other outlaws hiding out in the town. What makes *The Bounty Hunter* so compelling is the fact that the film doesn't give the viewer much of a clue as to who the real bad guys are. All the red herrings are potential targets, and the entire town falls prey to paranoia, much as the townspeople in the later Audie Murphy film *No Name on the Bullet* (1959) do when Murphy, as a killer, comes to town to hit one man, but won't say who that man is. Scott's Kipp is willing to just sit back and wait out his prey. And pretty soon they come out of hiding, caught up in an emotional whirlwind of distrust, fear and revenge.

The screenplay and actors work well together in setting up tension, but while DeToth does well with the dialogue scenes, including the semi-romantic byplay between Scott and Dolores Dorn, this time around the director lets the film down when it comes to the actual action scenes. The first shoot-out in the hills is made up of one-shots, never giving the viewer a larger sense of where Scott and his adversary are. The one fistfight in the film is ludicrous, though it's possible that it was intended to be funny: Kipp comes across four ornery cusses in a remote relay station. He grabs the most portly of the quartet and sticks the man's behind on a potbelly stuff, where the would-be bully wiggles about like Lou Costello, howling "Whoa whoa whoa whoa!" while wildly firing his gun at the other three varmints, who quickly vamoose. Two later gun duels, both of which have Kipp cornering his man in a dead end alley, are not only repetitive but unbelievable and badly staged. Kipp shoots the hat off of one bad guy, and it flies up at the camera in comical fashion, as if set on a trick wire. Some similar items are thrown at the camera here and there throughout, as the film was intended as a 3-D picture.

Still, there's much to like in the film, and it's the most anti-heroic role Scott played in the Warner Bros. series, as a cold killer who won't let anything get in his way. In retrospect, *The Bounty Hunter* wasn't a bad one for DeToth and Scott to end their six-film relationship with.

Of note is the fact that Frank Mattison, a long-time unit manager at the Warners lot, was hired as assistant director on this film. Mattison was accustomed to filing daily reports to Jack Warner and his underlings as to what was happening on the set, including notes on whether the stars were acting up. I wonder if Mattison really was helping DeToth, or simply put there to keep an eye on Scott, who liked to have a hand in the producing even when he wasn't listed as producer. Paul Picerni and Anthony Caruso have testified that Scott threw Warner Bros. executives off the set when they came down to see how the films were progressing. In any event, the Warner studio files do not indicate that there were any problems during the shoot, which took place from mid–July through early September in 1953 — a period of about six weeks, twice the time Scott and company usually spent on the Columbia Westerns.

DeToth (on why he left the Scott series at this time): "I had the feeling that I was at a dead end. There was less and less left in me to give. I had to get some fresh air. [Scott] was a nice, brittle old gentleman and I couldn't get blood out of an abacus any more." More pointedly, DeToth once said he couldn't "stand the horseshit" any longer.

While DeToth, like so many directors, probably let Scott pretty much direct himself, he had a feel for crowd scenes and building tension that other directors, including Budd Boetticher, didn't have. I don't think DeToth was always as capable at staging the actual action scenes as Boetticher or even Ray Enright, nor do I think he gave the actors as much to work with, performance-wise, when it came to intimate two-shots (Boetticher's forte). Still, two of his Scott films—*Man in the Saddle* and *Carson City*— are very good; three — *Riding Shotgun, The Bounty Man* and *Thunder Over the Plains*— are respectable, and as for *The Stranger Wore a Gun*, well, we're all allowed one miss now and then, aren't we?

Hollywood Reporter (8/25/1954): "Scott gives a driving, hard-boiled performance that makes you hope this film will do for him what *High Noon* did for Gary Cooper."

Ten Wanted Men (Columbia, February 1955, 80 minutes)

CREDITS Director: Bruce Humberstone; Producer: Harry Joe Brown (Associate Producer: Randolph Scott); Screenplay: Kenneth Gamet; story by Irving Revetch and Harriet Frank, Jr.

CAST Randolph Scott (John Stewart), Jocelyn Brando (Corinne Michaels), Richard Boone (Wick Campbell), Skip Homeier (Howie Stewart), Alfonso Bedoya (Hermando), Donna Martell (Maria Segura), Leo Gordon (Frank

Scavo), Clem Bevans (Todd Grinnel), Minor Watson (Jason Carr), Dennis Weaver (Sheriff Gibbons), Lee Van Cleef (Al Ducker), Denver Pyle (Dave Weed), Louis Jean Heydt (Tom Baines), Kathleen Crowley (Marva Gibbons)

Synopsis: Arizona rancher John Stewart finds his cattle empire under siege thanks to the machinations of vengeance-driven Wick Campbell and his ten hired gunmen.

The ten wanted men of this film's title are a cadre of infamous gunmen brought in by Richard Boone's lust-crazed rancher to win back his girl Maria (Donna Martell) and bring down anyone who stands in the way of his plan — including Scott's John Stewart. The title is something of a misnomer since Boone seems to hire more than ten men. The film is an interesting and ambitious misfire that shows Scott's willingness to test the boundaries of the conventional Western. Scott plays the sort of determined (almost ruthless) land owner who would have been the villain in any other film, who goes up against the equally determined but more violent Boone character. Scott has the law and the church on his side, but they're not much help when Boone's gunmen, led by the physically imposing Leo Gordon, start shooting up the town. The film is more about Boone's desire for respect and vengeance than it is about Scott's efforts to defend himself, and even more focus is given to Skip Homeier, as Scott's hot-headed but inexperienced Eastern nephew Howie. As such, *Ten Wanted Men* is interesting in that it is unafraid to show Scott in a less than totally positive light (he has more in common with the Alexander Knox character in *Man in the Saddle* than with any other Scott hero).

Still, the picture is repeatedly brought down by stilted direction and a less than stellar script from the normally reliable Kenneth Gamet. Bruce Humberstone, who directed Scott in 1942's *To the Shores of Tripoli*, seems out of his element here, failing to bring the necessary level of excitement to this endeavor; even the dialogue sequences lack punch and are sometimes downright painful to sit through. The cast is an odd mix of familiar Western performers, studio contract players and people like Jocelyn Brando, Marlon's sister and not a particularly good actress. Clumsy editing doesn't help matters. Scott's gun does not fire in one closeup in which he sends an adversary to boot hill, making the loud gunshot even more incongruous. And yes, I like to keep track of people in chases. If 12 riders set out to pursue Homeier and his pal Alfonso Bedoya in a night-time chase scene, I get annoyed when the number drops to nine by scene's end (and no, nobody got shot off their horse). Later, Boone leads eight men in pursuit of Scott's brother (played by Lester Matthews); seven men finish the ride. And the ten wanted men never see their ranks thinned despite continued losses throughout the film until Scott puts them away with some well-aimed dynamite tosses — an idea Howard Hawks would appropriate for the superior *Rio Bravo*, also shot on the Old Tucson set.

The final fistfight between Scott and Leo Gordon is really poor, with ill-staged choreography and Scott's double sticking out like *two* sore thumbs. One reviewer noted this in his critique of the film, stating, "The doubling done for Scott in the big climactic fight is painfully obvious."

Jon Tuska on *Ten Wanted Men* (from his book *Encounters with Filmmakers*): "Brown wanted Lucky [Humberstone] to direct *Ten Wanted Men*. It was a cut above the typical high budget Western, but for one reason or another Lucky was unable to achieve the effects with Scott and the storyline that Budd Boetticher would in the splendid entries he would later direct in the Scott series in the late Fifties. Westerns somehow did not tap the creative responses in Lucky that musicals and detective stories could." (Humberstone was accustomed to working with the likes of Betty Grable and Charlie Chan at 20th Century–Fox in the 1940s.)

Donna Martell (to author): "In those days I would not fly. Randolph Scott got wind of it and gave me his compartment on a train (to Tucson) and he flew. He was a great guy. It was a pretty happy cast and crew. Bruce Humberstone was very congenial and things went smoothly. Harry Joe Brown was a colorful character. And he loved the pretty women. I had to show him the dress I wore for the wedding scene, and when I walked in he said, 'Oh my God!'— He was breathless. I guess I was a looker back then."

Denver Pyle (to author): "Randolph Scott was a much better actor than he got jobs for. By that I mean he was versatile, but nobody seemed to know that. I thought he was a marvelous actor. The job he did in *Western Union* was just outstanding. The people who do Westerns are really working and people — the critics— don't think they are. That's the secret of good acting — some of those guys were so great that people insisted that's who they were off the screen, like Randolph Scott and Walter Brennan."

Variety (2/9/1955): "The entertainment content isn't up to the level usually reached in the action fare bearing the Scott-Brown production brand. There is a pretentiousness … to which the story development is not equal."

Scott and Brown liked Richard Boone and would hire the actor again for *The Tall T* (1957). In his book *Riding the Video Range: The Rise and Fall of the Western on Television* (McFarland 1995), author Garry N. Yoggy writes that in the late 1950s, "Boone was reportedly given a crack at the role of Paladin [in *Have Gun, Will Travel*] because Randolph Scott, the creators' first choice, was not available." In 1952 Scott told the press he would never tackle a television series, saying, "I don't want to reach

that saturation point where people are tired of looking at you."

Rage at Dawn a.k.a. *Seven Wanted Men* (RKO, March 1955, 86 minutes)

CREDITS   Director: Tim Whelan; Producer: Nat Holt; Screenplay: Horace McCoy, based on a story by Frank Gruber

CAST   Randolph Scott (James Barlow), Forrest Tucker (Frank Reno), Mala Powers (Laura Reno), J. Carrol Naish (Sim Reno), Myron Healey (John Reno), Denver Pyle (Clint Reno), Edgar Buchanan (Judge Hawkins), Howard Petrie (Lattimore), Ray Teal (Sheriff), Kenneth Tobey (Monk Claxton), William Forrest (Amos Peterson)

Synopsis: Undercover detective James Barlow infiltrates the infamous Reno Gang in an effort to bring the gang to justice.

A poor Western and a disappointing end to Scott's relationship with RKO, a studio that gave him some good breaks in the 1930s, *Rage at Dawn* suffers from a loose screenplay, indifferent direction and less than stellar production values, although it does boast fine location shooting at Columbia Historic State Park in Sonora, California.

The film has as much to do with family obligations as it does with the actual saga of the Reno Brothers, who are credited with pulling off the very first train robbery in American history in October 1866 near Seymor, Indiana. The outlaws are drawn less heroicly than in similarly minded Hollywood films. I like how the script shows the three main brothers— Frank, Sim and John — as flawed men who are, on the one hand, quite capable of burning a man to death, and yet loyal and caring towards their two law-abiding siblings (played here by Mala Powers and Denver Pyle). But the film fails to register on almost any other level.

J. Carrol Naish gives a good turn as the conscience of the family, and Mala Powers adds a shot of vitality as the law-abiding but fiercely independent Reno sister who doesn't want any man — including Scott's James Barlow — telling her what to do. The rest of the actors, including Scott, pretty much stroll through their roles without giving them much thought or nuance. Scott is posing as an artist in this one, which is an interesting but ultimately laughable idea as he is never once shown creating art or even buying art supplies. A nosy storekeeper who turns out to know more about art history than one would expect throws Scott for a loop when he asks, "Oh, like Greco, Van Gogh, Rembrandt?" "No, not quite," replies Scott, throwing out a wan smile that suggests he couldn't paint the side of a barn.

The action scenes are tame and unconvincing. Scott seems slower and less sure of himself in this film than in any other of the period, and his on-screen cohort Kenneth Tobey has to finish off two tough guys in one fight scene. The final shoot-out has a lot of "bang-bang" to it but no real sense of panache. Nor is the love story between Scott and Powers well-developed, leaving the finale, in which they end up in each other's arms, hard to take. The film does end with a striking lynch mob sequence in which a calm but determined group of vigilantes hang the Renos. Scott tries to help the trio, to no avail; his silent reaction as he watches the Renos hang (off-screen) is really something to see. You have to wonder whether the actor didn't pull off some "method" acting here, reaching back to his past in World War I for an influential experience to color the scene. It's a nice moment of acting. The climactic lynching scene was based on fact; the brothers, with the exception of John (who got 40 years in prison), were indeed hanged by a mob.

Of some help is another fine Paul Sawtell musical score. Nat Holt, Jr., worked on the film as production supervisor, and the entire thing was a co-production between a fading RKO and Nat Holt. Films like this sure weren't going to help RKO in its death throes. The studio struggled on for a few more years before Lucille Ball and Desi Arnaz, both former RKO contract players, bought the place for television production purposes.

Mala Powers on Scott (to author): "As an actor, he seemed to have a lot of confidence. He was very much connected with you. I teach acting so I try to get actors to do more than just look at the other actors and read the scene. I urge them to find a connection; and he was someone who did connect. Obviously he never had a tremendous range of emotion in films. He pretty much always underplayed: the strong and silent type. The characters he played got into trouble but he didn't go with the range of emotions that other actors who don't do Westerns have the chance to do. I don't recall any films I've seen of his in which Randy Scott had that range of emotions to play."

According to actor Myron Healey, he, Forrest Tucker and J. Carrol Naish, who played the Reno Brothers, were mischief-makers off the set as well. One night the trio used Naish's limousine to visit a nearby brothel because they were, in Healey's words, hungry: "They had a big colored lady who was the cook and she made us bacon and eggs, fried potatoes, everything that was greasy but good. But she wasn't too happy with our behavior so we decided to get going." Without elaborating on what *that* behavior was, Healey said the trio had to buy their way out of the place as the cook screamed bloody murder, with Tucker passing out five and ten dollar bills to the girls while the chef pursued them down the hallway. Somebody called the cops, and the trio fled to Naish's car. But they couldn't find the keys. "Finally Tuck hit the visor and the keys dropped down in his lap and we started driving that car and we drove down this country road heading back to Sonora," Healey recalled. "As we came up to first rise of this hill, we could hear a siren and we saw a red light coming up the road past us and right on to the whorehouse. We got back into Sonora about 15 to 20 minutes later. We parked the car and ran like hell for the inn." (*What if you had been just five minutes more getting out of that place?*) Then Nat Holt would have been putting up a lot of bail money the next morning!"

This was not the sort of behavior Scott would go for. On the set he remained the perfect gentleman, according to Healey: "Randolph Scott falls into a league with two other actors I worked with — Joel McCrea and Bill Elliott. Those three gentleman all sat in the saddle the same way — straight up and down. Their backs were like ramrods when they rode and it was beautiful to watch — graceful and strong. All three were strong, polite men. And none of them used profanity, especially around the ladies. In fact if somebody on the set said something profane and there was a lady on the set, that person was set for a scolding."

Tall Man Riding (Warner Bros., May 1955, 82 minutes)

CREDITS   Director: Lesley Selander; Producer: David Weisbart; Screenplay: Joseph Hoffman, based on the novel by Norman A. Fox

CAST   Randolph Scott (Larry Madden), Dorothy Malone (Corinna Ordway), Peggie Castle (Reva), Bill Ching (Rex), John Baragrey (Sebo Pearlo), Robert Barrat (Tuck Ordway), John Dehner (Ames Luddington), Paul Richards (The Peso Kid), Lane Chandler (Hap Sutton)

Synopsis: Larry Madden returns home seeking revenge on the man who ruined him.

> "You lookin' for trouble?" — Deputy Barclay (Mickey Simpson)
>
> "You'll know when I am." — Larry Madden (Randolph Scott)

Tall Man Riding is a bland horse opera featuring Scott as yet another vengeance-driven cowpoke who uses a lawyer to get back at his nemesis, a rancher (played by Robert Barrat) who ran him out of town and drove him away from his lover (Dorothy Malone). To director Lesley Selander's credit, *Tall Man Riding* has several decent action scenes, though most of them have little point — people shoot at each other but keep missing in botched ambushes, for example. Scott's Larry Madden is a little different from the slew of vengeful riders the actor had played before in that he wants to do things nice and legal, saving up his hard-earned cash to hire a respected lawyer (John Dehner) to bring down Barrat. However, if Dehner is such a fine upstanding sample of the legal profession, why is it he turns against Scott late in the film? The Scott character here turns out to be a poor judge of character, though little is made of this personality trait.

The supporting cast for this one is weaker than the usual Warners Western, with Dorothy Malone (finishing off her Warner Bros. contract) giving an annoying and tiresome performance as a bitter widow. Better is Peggie Castle as a naughty saloon girl who throws in with Scott to undo main villain John Baragrey; also effective is Lane Chandler as Barrat's sympathetic foreman. The film boasts a good land rush sequence with both Scott and Malone getting in on the action before some anticlimactic gunfights ensue. The laughable fade-out has Scott, a bloody bullet hole in his chest, casually walking into the sunset with Malone, who has spent the entire film loathing and distrusting him. Not good.

The behind-the-scenes off-camera antics are much more interesting to consider than the film itself. Scott engages in a good fistfight with burly Mickey Simpson about halfway through the film; studio files indicate that during the shooting, the two men fell under a wagon in the street, leading the nervous horses to bolt and nearly sever Scott's head in the proceedings. The wagon wheels reportedly crushed the actor's Stetson Chapeau, a hat he claimed to have worn in over 25 films. I can believe it; the fight is better staged and more realistic than some of the brawls in the Columbia Scotts of the period.

An interesting studio memo to the research department from scenarist Joseph Hoffman asked, "If a soldier swims a river in 1892 does he have to keep his bullets dry so he can fire them again right away?" The answer was no; bullets are insulated against water. At least Hoffman thought to ask, though there's no scene in the film in which a character swims a river and then has to fire his gun, making me think Hoffman never wrote the sequence or it got cut.

One day Selander, fed up with losing so much time and footage due to passing planes overhead, borrowed some six-guns loaded with blanks from the prop department and opened up on one offending aircraft as it flew overhead, amusing the cast and crew.

Finally, during the shooting of the film (the summer of 1954), Warner Bros. released its highly touted Biblical epic *The Silver Chalice*. The film was a bomb, but it was Paul Newman's film debut. Scott attended a premiere of the picture at the studio's request and predicted to the studio that Newman would be a big star *despite* the film. He was right.

Tall Man Riding was shot on the Warners lot, at Iverson Ranch and in California's Hidden Valley. It didn't impress the few critics who chose to write about it. "A Western in which so much corn gets mixed with the oats that the audience, if not the horses, get indigestion," *The Hollywood Reporter* wrote (5/11/1955). *Variety*'s review of the same day noted, "It's quite talky and slow moving for a Scott Western."

Paul Sawtell provided the musical score.

A Lawless Street (Columbia, November 1955, 78 minutes)

CREDITS   Director: Joseph H. Lewis; Producer: Harry Joe Brown (Associate Producer: Randolph Scott); Screenplay: Kenneth Gamet; Story: Brad Ward, from his book *Marshal of Medicine Bend*

CAST   Randolph Scott (Marshal Calem Ware), Angela Lansbury (Tally Dickenson), Jean Wallace (Cora Dean), Warner Anderson (Hamer Thorne), Wallace Ford (Dr. Amos Wynn), John Emery (Cody Clark), James Bell (Asaph Dean), Michael Pate (Harley Baskam), Ruth Donnelly (Molly Higgins), Jeanette Nolan (Mrs. Dingo Brion), Don Megowan (Dooly Brion)

Synopsis: Marshal Calem Ware knows that one day the lawless street outside his office will explode — and thanks to the machinations of two power-bent villains and their gunsel Harley Baskam, it does.

One of the most interesting aspects about *A Lawless Street*, a just-misses-the-mark Scott offering, is comparing it to the Warner Bros. Scott films of the period. The films Scott made at Warner Bros. during this time strove to present him as a mature but still-youthful lover dealing with cardboard-cutout villains and wimpy and weepy women. *A Lawless Street*, like several of the Columbia Scotts of the mid–1950s, presents our hero as an obviously aging lawman, older, not necessarily wiser, but surely more tired. "I've got just one chance, only one," Scott's resigned lawman says early on in the film. "To outlive the times." His hope, of course, is that the dying frontier West, as he knows it, will take its gun-happy killers with it before they take him down. Scott's Calem Ware, a not-too-distant cousin of Gary Cooper's Will Kane from *High Noon*, realizes that with each showdown his chances for survival decrease — he is a man who is way past his prime, winning gun battles on his reputation rather than his speed. "No matter how hard it was this time, the next time it will be worse," he notes after somehow besting a younger foe in a street duel. To get a good night's sleep, Ware is reduced to locking himself in his own jail.

I think Ware is the more interesting of the two marshals. Kane goes around town literally pleading for help; Ware suggests that the townspeople get behind him but he's still willing to go it alone with the town's two top bad guys, Hamer Thorne and Cody Clark. Thorne and Clark begin plotting to bring him down with the help of assassin Harley Baskam (Michael Pate, one of those actors I always enjoy watching). A novel touch about the bad guys in this film is the fact that one of them, Clark, is the manager of a theater group (an artistic despot!), while the other, a saloon keeper, has a wonderfully open and humor-filled relationship with Ware.

Angela Lansbury plays a dance hall girl who has enjoyed a romantic relationship with Scott in the past. "I do know the marshal's gun has quite the reputation," Lansbury tells the townspeople with pride, injecting sexual innuendo into the line. Aside from one or two similar witticisms and the song "Mother Says I Mustn't" (in which she is backed by four deliciously plump chorines who are adorned in red sequin Batgirl-type outfits!), Lansbury doesn't really register, overacting badly in many of the scenes in an effort to make up for Scott's subtle underplaying. That was her mistake, for Scott knew, like Gary Cooper, that less is often more, and probably in one-to-one playing with other actors he didn't strike them as being magnetic. Years later, Lansbury would dismiss the film and her work in it, saying, "I once rode off into the sunset on a backboard with Randolph Scott — another low point."

The rest of the cast, including Pate as the gunman who abides by his own set of rules, Wallace Ford as a feisty frontier doctor and Warner Anderson as the lead villain, give the film an added shot of life, often taking the static out of the storyline.

Andre DeToth would claim that neither Scott nor Harry Joe Brown paid much attention to storylines, but somebody — Brown, I'm sure — was purchasing some pretty solid screenplays for the actor, and these films, including *A Lawless Street*, really are superior to the majority of the B+ oaters being put out at the time. Kenneth Gamet's script is more cutting and insightful than his *Ten Wanted Men*; and Joseph H. Lewis was adept at inspiring actors to do character work and setting up suspense for the action scenes.

Lewis handles Pate's shooting of Scott well. Yes, Scott gets shot down in this one — but he's not dead. And that's where *A Lawless Street* starts to go astray. The bad guys, believing the marshal is dead (Ford has spirited his wounded body away), began taking over the town to the tune of circus music, forcing an endless string of saloon owners to sell their property. The dialogue throughout all of this is unintelligent and sometimes downright ludicrous, and the potentially exciting sequence of Scott's marshal coming back from the dead to reclaim the town is handled almost entirely offscreen in a misplaced attempt to build suspense or be "arty" or just do something different. I for one would rather have seen Scott marching into all of the saloons along the way, routing the bad guys as he moves down the lawless street to face Pate again.

As such, *A Lawless Street* is running on empty pistols by the last ten minutes, but up until then it's a pip, and Scott seems to have put some extra effort into this one, either because he sensed the script was offering him something a little different in terms of characterization, or because Lewis prodded him. Like *Ten Wanted Men*, *A Lawless Street* tries to be something more than just another run-of-the-mill Western. Its ambition does not mark it for failure, nor does Lewis' direction, necessarily — certainly he was better at staging action

Aging marshal Calem Ware (Scott) engages in some playful flirtation with his landlady (Ruth Donnelly) in Joseph H. Lewis' *A Lawless Street* (1955).

scenes than Bruce Humberstone. Rather, *A Lawless Street* fails — but only by a gunsight — because its finale can not live up to all the promise that comes before it. But for three-quarters of the way, it's a tight and tense adult Western that showcases Scott at the top of his craft.

A nice in-joke: The calendar in Scott's room has Gamet's Vegetable Company inscribed upon it in reference to the film's author.

It's unfortunate that most of the major newspapers had stopped reviewing middle-class Westerns by 1955; *A Lawless Street* deserved more mention and praise than *Variety*'s (11/23/55) comment that it was "an okay offering. Scott gives a robust account of himself in a role that has become similar to stereotyping."

Michael Pate (in Boyd Magers' *Western Clippings* #20, December 1997): "I was called in to see the always friendly, very modest director Joseph H. Lewis at Columbia. Sitting in his office, I was amazed when he told me he'd seen me in *Hondo* and had decided right there and then I'd be a good bet for Harley Bascom. Oh boy — was I nervous about getting that part! I borrowed a gunbelt and a Colt .45 from the Columbia property department and practiced and practiced in front of a full-length mirror until I got so fast on the draw I could almost out-draw myself! We came to the scene in the bar where Randy dives under the batwing doors to gun down Bascom. In the first rehearsal, I was so fast on the draw I got off three shots before Randy had hardly hit the floorboards as he slid under the batwings and into the bar. His six-gun *never* got to blaze! Randy got slowly to his feet, very thoughtfully holstered his six-shooter, carefully brushed a speck or two of dust from his trousers and drawled, as only he could, 'Son, that was a *mighty* fast draw you did there — but keep in mind *I'm* supposed to win this one!'"

The Last Round-Up: 1956–1962

"I have always been a fatalist about my career," Scott once said. "What was to be, was to be." Scott's Hollywood career had to a large degree been the combined result of luck, chance, fortune, fate; however you wish to describe it. And once again, in the mid–1950s, at a time when his career was sagging (though hardly sinking), Scott was to be blessed with a double stroke of luck in the form of writer Burt Kennedy and director Budd Boetticher. Kennedy should probably deserve just a little bit more of the credit when it comes to Scott's late comeback, because he's the one who wrote the screenplay for *Seven Men from Now*, the film that kicked it all off.

Kennedy, who'd been eking out a living around Hollywood for some time as a stuntman, stunt coordinator, actor and writer, had tied up with John Wayne's production company, Batjac, sometime in the early 1950s. Kennedy did rewrites and fix-ups on other Wayne-produced films of the period, and one day someone in the company suggested the writer pen a script for Wayne. So Kennedy wrote *Seven Men from Now*, a searing revenge drama set in the Old West, on a pad with pencil in eight weeks time, for $1,500.

According to Kennedy's autobiography, *Hollywood Trail Boss*, nobody wanted to even look at the darn thing. It got stuck on a shelf somewhere ("along with about 30 or 40 other scripts," Kennedy noted) until Kennedy heard that Robert Mitchum was looking for a good Western script. Kennedy brought the script to Mitchum's agent, who offered the screenwriter $15,000 for it. Kennedy then went back to Wayne to ask permission to sell it. Wayne decided he wanted to read it. He liked it — as did studio head Jack L. Warner — but since the Duke was involved in the making of *The Searchers*, they needed another actor to play the protagonist, Ben Stride.

Wayne and company offered the script to Joel McCrea, who turned it down. Then they offered it to Robert Preston, who, Kennedy suspects, never even read the script. Kennedy and Boetticher both claim that Wayne suggested Randolph Scott in a disparaging tone. Scott read the screenplay and agreed to do it. Wayne then cast Gail Russell, an alcoholic beauty whose career had dried up, as the heroine (Wayne had done two pictures with Russell in the 1940s; it was rumored that they had been lovers). The film was released by Warner Bros. in the summer of 1956 and did surprisingly well, earning some unexpected critical praise along the way. Scott, who knew this Western was of higher quality than the films he was making under the Warner Bros. banner, immediately got his partner Harry Joe Brown to hire Boetticher and Kennedy away from Wayne. Someone — possibly Boetticher; possibly Brown — also netted a couple of screen properties that the Duke owned, *The Tall T* and *Buchanan Rides Alone*, for Scott. Brown produced both of those works for Columbia with Boetticher directing and Kennedy rewriting.

And so began the Brown-Scott-Boetticher-Kennedy films, commonly known as the Ranown Series even though only the last two — *Ride Lonesome* and *Comanche Station* — are official Ranown films. All six films benefit from tight-fisted Randolph Scott performances, a colorful array of supporting cast members, dynamic and dark-humored villains and austere settings — usually desert locales featuring isolated way stations and rocky terrains that half-resembled Scott's trail-worn face. Rarely can it be said that an aging matinee idol concluded his film career with a good, let alone great, film, but Scott finished out his movie canon with an impressive round-up of *seven* superb Westerns: *Seven Men from Now, The Tall T, Decision at Sundown, Buchanan Rides Alone, Ride Lonesome, Comanche Station* and the Sam Peckinpah–directed MGM film *Ride the High Country*. It should be pointed out that Scott also made three routine Westerns during this time period: *7th Cavalry* for Columbia and *Shoot-Out at Medicine Bend* and *Westbound* for Warner Bros. They're not dreadful films, but it'd be nice if someone could find a way to erase them from Scott's filmography. All in all, these ten films constitute Scott's last cinematic round-up.

Who should take the credit for the Ranown series? Frankly, all four film artists — Brown, Scott, Boetticher and Kennedy. Still, Western film historians are bound to feel that Kennedy and/or Boetticher deserve the most accolades. "The Scott character — as Jim Kitses characterized the roles Randy played in these films — was very much a co-creation of Budd, Burt and Randy," Jon Tuska noted, giving screenwriter Kennedy extra credit by adding, "What the Scott Westerns directed by Budd had that they didn't have with [Andre] DeToth or [Bruce] Humberstone comes to this — Burt Kennedy. To an amazing degree, in retrospect, the Scott character was reinvented in the Kennedy scripts, and Scott was inspired because he could see how the added depth had a powerful effect on him and on his screen work." Boetticher, who liked to boast, did give a lot of credit for the success of the series to Kennedy, later saying with some bemusement that Scott enjoyed Kennedy's company more than his own. "I think he liked Burt better than he liked me," Boetticher remarked of the actor. "Burt's very charming and I was more down to business and argued a lot about what I wanted."

Boetticher has been characterized as a bragging nutcase by more than one of his associates. Kennedy himself would often decline to refute Boetticher's claims about the Scott films (let's face it — Boetticher still gets the most credit for their success). By most accounts, Kennedy was the quietest and most easy going of the quartet, but he apparently worked side by side with Boetticher on most of the sets, reworking scenes as called for. This left Boetticher to bask in the glow of acclaim that began to descend upon the Ranown series in the late 1960s. And most of the film artists who worked on those films, despite a personal dislike of Boetticher, admired the director. L.Q. Jones called Boetticher "a mad man, a blithering idiot, a talented man. He came along at a time when you couldn't be an individual, but he was." Rand Brooks, who knew Boetticher on a personal basis, said,

"He had qualities that were exceptional. Things that would stop anybody else never stopped him." Ultimately, however, Boetticher's self-destructive nature stopped him before he could really make the "A" grade. Actor-stuntman Roydon Clark summed up the reasons for Boetticher's lack of post–Ranown success: "As a director, Budd was a balls-out guy; one of the big names of Western action directors. Budd probably could have gotten bigger. But he had a fairly hot temper and was not beyond telling people off if he thought he was right, and there's nothing wrong with that, but a lot of times when you're working in the motion picture business you can't tell off the people who have the money."

Oscar Boetticher was born in July 1916 in Chicago. Kevin Thomas, a *Los Angeles Times* writer who knew Boetticher, said, "Budd cast a larger than life shadow. His life was more colorful and adventuresome than many of the heroes of his own films." That life included attending Culver Military Academy, boxing, playing football, bull fighting in Mexico and working in Hollywood, thanks to his family's connection to producer-director Hal Roach. Because of his bullfighting skills, Boetticher worked as technical advisor on the 1941 20th Century–Fox production of *Blood and Sand*, and this experience gave him the opportunity to work his way up to directing films at Columbia in 1944. Most of his films of the 1940s—*One Mysterious Night*, *Escape in the Fog* and *Youth on Trial*, for instance—are mediocre, and when he moved to Universal Studios in the early 1950s, they only got a little bit better, though 1953's *The Man from the Alamo* has a considerable reputation. The best picture Boetticher did during this period was 1951's *The Bullfighter and the Lady* (for Republic), a bullfighting drama starring Robert Stack and produced by John Wayne. It was Wayne who reportedly gave Boetticher the nickname "Budd," which stuck.

Though his directing was generally only as good as the material, Boetticher did manage to create suspenseful and exciting moments in standard films: the swamp ambush in *Seminole*, the voodoo ceremony in *City Beneath the Sea* and the one-sided boxing match between Tor Johnson and Richard Carlson in *Behind Locked Doors*, for example. Likewise, he had a talent for staging action scenes, such as Wendell Corey's shooting of John Larch in *The Killer Is Loose* (the bullet passes through the milk bottle Larch is holding) and the railyard gunfight in the Audie Murphy Western *The Cimarron Kid*. Boetticher learned how to work with up-and-coming talent and fading stars, a trait that would come in handy on the Ranown series. And even in routine fare, the actors in Boetticher movies tend to give intense performances, perhaps because the fast-moving, risk-taking director kept everyone on edge. "With Budd you never knew what was going to happen," recalled L.Q. Jones, who co-starred with Scott in Boetticher's *Buchanan Rides Alone*. "He just went bonkers when he shot. Budd worked from the seat of his pants which is one thing that made him so good." Asked to sum up Boetticher's directing style, actor Steve Mitchell drew a parallel between the director's cinematic approach and his personal lifestyle. "I was in the back seat of a car with Alan Hale, Jr., and Budd was driving, with John Hubbard up front," Mitchell recalled. "And Budd never went slower than 95 miles an hour. We kept looking at each other with the thought, 'Who the hell do we have to go to bed with to get out of this car?' What more can I say about him?"

Nancy Gates, however, recalled Boetticher handling her with kid gloves on the set of 1960's *Comanche Station*. "He had the greatest sense of humor and he would let me do anything," she recalled of Boetticher. "For the most part he was very easy going. If you did something one way he'd say, 'Give me a little more,' or 'Try this instead.' He was the best.'"*

Rand Brooks said Boetticher "had the ability to keep everybody alive and happy on the set. He did a few things, possibly, that were a little 'over the line' but he was a gutsy and imaginative man. He had a great talent for dialogue — where he got it, I don't know. And he listened to his actors. If an actor said, 'I'd like to try it this way,' he'd say 'Let's try it.' And film crews liked to work for him. I think they all knew he was a special character."

Boetticher, described by several male actors who worked with him as "macho," also got his performers to do their own stunts — including Scott. "Randy did most of his own stunts for Budd," recalled Steve Mitchell of the *Seven Men from Now* shoot. "That's [Scott] being dragged behind the horse. I liked it because it made for a better picture, but I was amazed that somebody would let a star stick his neck out like that." Egged on by both Boetticher and Scott, Mitchell jumped off a rock onto his own horse for an action scene in film. L.Q. Jones recalled that Boetticher coerced Scott into doing his own stunts during the shooting of *Buchanan Rides Alone*. "Randy had no business doing that, but Budd would talk him into it and off we'd go," Jones said. Chris Scott, in his biography of his father, insists that Scott did mount and briefly ride a Brahma Bull for the 1957 Boetticher-Kennedy film *The Tall T*, though that is clearly *not* Scott taking the fall from the bull at ride's end.

Though Boetticher may not have worked that closely with Scott in shaping his on-screen character for these films,† Scott still respected the director's unpredictable, 95 miles per hour "let's-push-this-thing-as-far-as-we-can" attitude. "Budd was a madman," said Mitchell. "But he was a good director. He let Randy alone. I didn't see him ever jumping on Randy. Why did Randy and Budd get along? I can't answer that question directly. I can only surmise that Randy knew Budd made him look good, and when you have a guy who makes you look good, you ride with a winner."

Scott may not have needed much direction from Boetticher at this point. He understood the complex underscoring within Kennedy's script, and he'd been around long enough to know how to color a scene with subtle nuance. "Scott wasn't a great actor by any means, but when you go back and look at all the stuff he did, he was all right," said Burt Kennedy. "Scott was very real. He didn't really act. He was very much a Southern gentleman. He didn't have the stature that the Duke [Wayne] had, but he had great dignity."

Boetticher continues to heap the most praise, posthumously of course, for the films. Certainly they embody the director's finest work, for he was never as good before or after the Randolph Scott films.‡ Typical of the praiseworthy analysis (over-analysis, perhaps) of these films is film historian Dave Kehr's comment that, "For Boetticher, the Western landscape is both abstract and concrete, an arena for stylized philosophical action and a place of pressing physical presence — a highly textured, tactile environment, which must be attended to with the utmost sensitivity and intelligence in order to master its dangers.

---

*Gates, who Boetticher once referred to as his favorite actress, said she shot some behind-the-scenes film footage of *Comanche Station* that I would love to see.

†Boetticher himself, rarely at a loss for words, never could articulate what sort of director/actor relationship he had with Scott. "The only trouble with Randy was, he was perfect," Boetticher told me the first time I met him. "He never did anything wrong." The director's favorite phrase regarding Scott was always, "If the South had had just forty Randolph Scotts, they would have won the Civil War." He was probably right.

‡I don't think Burt Kennedy's film career was ever as good after the Ranown Series came to a close, either, though he directed and/or wrote a couple of pretty good films in the late 1960s.

Boetticher's dual vision of the West is the key to the unique temper of his work, which gives the sense of being at once immensely detailed and thematically generalized, dramatically alive and formally distant, consistently entertaining and deeply serious." Reading that statement, you'd think Kehr was discussing Tolstoy, and you'd never know that Burt Kennedy wrote most of those scripts or that Harry Joe Brown chose the landscapes. Boetticher himself would dismiss such heady praise, stating that he and Kennedy were just trying to make good Westerns.

Producer Harry Joe Brown is probably the most under-appreciated of the quartet, but Harry Joe Brown, Jr., has a valid point when he notes, "My father's job as producer was to find a great team, and getting Kennedy and Boetticher together on those later films was his doing. The formula of the films was all my father's doing, and the basic finding of stories, setting them up and getting good actors, was his job." It's interesting to examine the dynamics within the quartet in terms of their independent work. For instance, without Brown and Kennedy helping them, Boetticher and Scott floundered with the Warner Bros. film *Westbound*. Working with Brown and Scott but without the benefit of a Burt Kennedy script, Boetticher's work as a director was only adequate with *Decision at Sundown*. Burt Kennedy, providing a fascinating Ranown-like script for the Audie Murphy Western *Six Black Horses*, just didn't seem like such a hot screenwriter when journeyman Harry Keller directed that film for producer Gordon Kay at Universal. But when Scott, Brown, Boetticher and Kennedy got all their pistols blasting together, they produced Western

wonders (shot on 12–18-day schedules) with budgets in the $400,000 to $500,000 range (and maybe even less). Actor-stuntman Jack Williams, who worked with Scott, Boetticher and Kennedy over the years, put the relationship between the quartet like this: "If they wanted to do a movie, they had all those guys—Harry Joe Brown, Budd, Randy, and Burt Kennedy who wrote them, plus guys like Claude Akins and Skip Homeier to act in them. It was like building a house. You hire a carpenter, a plumber and a framer, and you get the house built."

What was Columbia's attitude towards the films? "They didn't think anything about them," Boetticher said. "They didn't give a damn. They didn't expect what they got. We were left alone because we weren't really anybody." The studio was, however, happy with the commercial and critical response to the films. "We were making second features as far as the price was concerned," Boetticher noted. "But they became A pictures in quality."

Quality or not, the studio system was changing in the late 1950s and the days of the medium-budget Western were starting to fade away. By 1960 it was felt that only a major star like John Wayne could anchor a Western production, though Universal did a good job maintaining the quality of its Audie Murphy series through the mid–1960s.* Scott, who turned 62 when *Comanche Station* was released in 1960, was considered over the hill by Columbia, particularly by younger executives who were running the joint in the shadow of studio chieftain Harry Cohn's death in 1958. "According to Harry Joe, Columbia began to regard [Scott] as old-fashioned in the kind of Westerns he wanted to produce," Jon

*Murphy's 1964 oater *Bullet for a Badman* is fairly good, although his final film for the studio, 1966's *Gunpoint*, shows a marked decline in care and quality. According to Jon Tuska, Western novelist Ray Hogan was disappointed when Universal cast Murphy in a very Randolph Scott–type part in 1960's *Hell Bent for Leather*, based on the author's novel *Outlaw Marshal*. "What Audie had for the time, as you no doubt realize, was relative youthfulness compared to Randolph Scott," Tuska noted.

Tuska explained. "And it was felt Randy was too old to be playing a Western hero. It was also a source of resentment that Brown and Scott were getting an override on their films. Scott, Brown, Boetticher and Kennedy were a good team, but former Columbia executives I talked with felt there was too much sameness to the films."

Scott's Warner Bros. contract came to an end in 1959, although he still owed the studio one more film. (Warners paid him off—see the section on *Westbound*.) He continued to make wise investment choices, building his financial fortune. Likewise he eschewed giving interviews, although he would still make public appearances to promote his films. But the end of Randolph Scott's film career was in sight by the time the decade closed out, and the actor rode it out with his dignity intact. After completing one last beauty of a film, *Ride the High Country*, he hung up his six gun, corraled his horse for the last time and, rather than ride off into the sunset, he decided to go play golf.

FILM ROLES: 1956–1962

Seven Men from Now (Warner Bros., July 1956, 77 minutes)

CREDITS   Director: Budd Boetticher; Producers: Andrew V. McLaglen and Robert E. Morrison; Story and Screenplay: Burt Kennedy

CAST   Randolph Scott (Ben Stride), Gail Russell (Annie Greer), Walter Reed (John Greer), Lee Marvin (Masters), Don "Red" Barry (Clete), John Larch (Bodeen), Stuart Whitman (Lt. Collins), John Berradino (Clint), Chuck Roberson (Mason), Steve Mitchell (Fowler)

Synopsis: Ex-sheriff Ben Stride seeks the seven men who killed his wife in a Wells Fargo robbery.

Sometimes there's nothing more satisfying than watching a Randolph Scott Western on a Saturday afternoon. *Seven Men from Now*, which rates alongside *Ride the High Country* and *Western Union* as among the star's best, is an ideal candidate for that sort of afternoon viewing. The first in a series of films made with director Budd Boetticher and screenwriter Burt Kennedy, *Seven Men from Now* displays an older, deadlier Scott, a man whose face resembles a Western landscape where men brawled, killed, rode and fell in love. Scott's Ben Stride is not just a Westerner to respect and reckon with—as so many previous Scott heroes were—but a man to fear. Unlike the James Stewart character in the Anthony Mann Westerns of the era, Scott's Ben Stride is a man who hasn't quite gone over the edge yet. His fury and determination are still restrained, though like the Mann heroes, he's set on revenge and not too interested in letting anything stand in his way. In this case, though Stride is hot on the trail of the seven desperadoes who did in his wife (or five desperadoes, since he sends two of them to their maker in the film's first scene), he takes time out of his mission to guide a naive pioneer couple (Gail Russell and Walter Reed). Stride may have an ulterior motive, for he's a man consumed with a longing—including an understated love for Russell's Annie Greer.

Scott and company are joined by a pair of roving gunmen (Lee Marvin and Don "Red" Barry) who are willing to aid Scott in his mission—provided they get the Wells Fargo strong box, which contains $20,000. Invariably, there's going to be a showdown, or maybe two or three. Marvin is a joy to watch as a big kid who shouldn't be allowed to play with guns. He's the first in a line of colorfully ambivalent good-bad

The Scott Westerns just kept getting better and better, due in part to the involvement of director Budd Boetticher and screenwriter Burt Kennedy. Here rifleman Scott evades death in the rocky hills of Lone Pine, California, in *Seven Men from Now* (1956), a Boetticher-Kennedy effort for Warner Bros.

"Chiricahua jumped me 'bout ten miles back," Stride curtly replies.

"They stole him?" the jumpy cowhand asks of Stride's horse.

"They ate him."

A moment later the second man, more in tune to Stride's intent than his compatriot, casually asks about a hold-up in nearby Silver Springs involving the robbery of a Wells Fargo box that led to the death of a woman clerk. Seven men were responsible.

"That killing — they ever catch up to them fellas that done it?" the man asks.

"Two of 'em," Stride replies, fixing his gaze on the guilty pair.

Gunshots in the dark tell the rest of the story, and an amusing follow-up scene has Stride blithely riding across the desert — with two horses!

Kennedy's script has a nice dose of realism to it. The men tuck their pants in after trysts with bar room prostitutes, horses get washed down in a shallow river, the wind kicks dust into the face of the participants and the protagonists end up sleeping in the rain quite a bit. Russell's character even takes time out to wash everyone's clothes and hang them on an impromptu clothesline. If Kennedy deserves the most credit for making the story as good as it is, give Boetticher merit for not only building suspense throughout the film, but giving the viewers a satisfying payoff in terms of the climactic action scenes. The supporting cast includes veterans Walter Reed and John Larch and newcomers Stuart Whitman and Pamela Duncan. Henry Vars' theme music is hauntingly beautiful and should be better known as a classic Western film soundtrack.

Seven Men from Now, shot in the autumn of 1955 in Lone Pine, remains a fairly obscure Scott Western in the sense that it's still difficult to track down a copy. Michael

guys, or bad good-guys, that Kennedy created. Kennedy's dialogue is excellent. "You move like you're all-over alive," Marvin says to Russell with just the right amount of salicious intent. Scott, realizing a showdown with Marvin is nearly impossible to avoid, tells his adversary, "I'd hate to have to kill you." "I'd hate to see you try," the ever-grinning Marvin replies. You just know these two are going to face off by film's end.

Comically striking is the film's opening sequence, in which Scott's Ben Stride abruptly invades the rainswept campsite of two cowpokes. Stride informs the men that he's been walking for some time. The more nervous of the duo innocently asks Stride why he doesn't have a horse.

Wayne's Batjac Corporation still retains the rights (though Michael Wayne is deceased), and as of this writing there are no plans to release the film to video. However, the University of California has a newly restored print that has made its way around the country. If you're real lucky, you can find passably watchable prints via pirate video companies. It remains one of Scott's top performances and is surely one of his best films.

Boetticher took credit for suggesting to Marvin that the actor continually practice his fast-draw throughout the film for the character of Masters. This could be true, but Claude Jarman, Jr., recalled Marvin practicing his fast draw in between scenes of *Hangman's Knot*, and there's a brief scene of Marvin's character doing this same bit of business in the 1954 film *Bad Day at Black Rock*. I bet Marvin, rather than Boetticher or Kennedy, came up with this business.

Don "Red" Barry's own Western series for Republic had come to an end in the late 1940s; by the mid–1950s he was freelancing as an actor. Boetticher had contempt for the actor, though he never explained why. "He was lucky to get the part," the director recalled years later. Barry was then involved in an affair with actress Susan Hayward, who surprised Burt Kennedy with a visit to the set one day. By way of introduction to the writer, Hayward said, "Burt, do you have any idea how many paper bags are used in Los Angeles in one day? I'm giving up the picture business and going into the paper bag business."

Budd Boetticher (to author): "Randy loved an ensemble. Duke wouldn't have wanted one! [Laughs] I loved the Duke, particularly what he did for me, but he was wrong 75 percent of the time. There's a scene where [Reed and Scott] bathe the horses in a river, and when Duke saw the rushes he called Burt and me — he didn't know that I knew more about horses than

he would ever know — and he said, 'How can you do a thing like that in a river? We'll get letters (protesting) from every good horse-man in the United States.' Well, we got letters. Letters that said, 'What a great idea!' If you had a river nearby, why in the hell shouldn't you fill up a bucket to wash a horse there? It was common sense.

"Gail (Russell) was a complete alcoholic. About two-thirds of the way through the picture, she was going to play a love scene where she was hanging clothes and talking to Randy, and she said, 'Budd, I want to go back to the hotel, I'm not feeling very well.' And I knew she was going to go back and drink. I said, 'Gail, if you get in your car to head back to the hotel, I'm gonna pull you out of the car and spank you in front of the whole crew.' And she played the scene, and she was great. The night we got home from Lone Pine I had a big party at my house and she got drunk, and [assistant director] Andy McLaglen, who fell in love with her, couldn't find her for three days."

Burt Kennedy (to author): "Randy had enormous respect for the script. I recall a scene in *Seven Men from Now* in which they came upon an abandoned relay station, and Scott says to Walter Reed and Gail Russell, 'Stay here, I'll go take a look.' Randy takes off and heads for the station, and then suddenly he pulls up, turns around and rides back. Budd was screaming, 'Keep going, keep going!' Scott came back and said, 'I said, "I'll go take a look" but Burt had written, 'I'll go have a look.' He wouldn't change a word. I liked him an awful lot."

Steve Mitchell (to author): "Randy was very quiet and unassuming. He had a reserve about him. I don't think he was distant — that was just him by nature. We didn't discuss what he did offstage. We counted scrapes and cuts. He did most of his own stunts for Budd. I bet you didn't know that. I think [Scott] was probably under-rated. He didn't just do a 'yep' or a 'no.' He was always very believable."

Stuart Whitman (to author): "It was a dusty, dirty location — just the kind I like. Both Budd and Randy were standup guys — so was the Duke, whose company produced the film."

Seven Men from Now, made for about $700,000, earned back that much overseas and made nearly another million in the United States, making it a surprise financial success for Warner Bros. The film also received far greater critical acclaim than any other WB Scott film. Scott, sensing a good thing, put Boetticher and Kennedy under contract to make more films for him at Columbia. Warners announced that Boetticher and Kennedy would reteam to make *The Captives* for the studio, but Scott and Harry Joe Brown got the property *and* Boetticher and Kennedy away from Warners and made the film for Columbia under the title *The Tall T*.

Variety (7/11/1956): "One of Randolph Scott's better Western entries. Scott delivers a first-rate performance." *Motion Picture Daily*, (7/10/1956): "You've got to go back to the late William S. Hart, greatest of the motion picture West's strong, silent men, for a full precedent with which to compare this story and its star, Randolph Scott. Like all Hart heroes, Randolph Scott is stern, unsmiling straight-shooting avenger who makes no apology for killing his men." *The Los Angeles Times* (8/9/1956): "*Seven Men from Now* is one of Randolph Scott's better entries in the giddy-ap field." *The Hollywood Reporter* (7/11/1956): "Scott is a master at the dead-pan approach but he always manages, as he does here, to suggest humor and warmth so that his characterizations never seem flat. A good Western, well played and well directed, with an excellent story."

I particularly like the *Cincinnati Time Star*'s review (8/3/1956), which stated, "Randolph Scott is the greatest living phe-nomenon in motion pictures. The man must be at least 200 years old and he still looks young enough to be John Wayne's son." Wayne must have *loved* that review.

In 1964, Warner Bros./7 Arts got into a lengthy legal dispute with Michael Wayne of Batjac Films over who would own the subsidiary and television rights to *Seven Men from Now*. I don't know for sure who won, but I'm betting on Batjac, which is why, I think, the film has pretty much disappeared from public view.

7th Cavalry *a.k.a.* Seventh Cavalry
(Columbia, October 1956, 76 minutes)

CREDITS   Director: Joseph H. Lewis; Producer: Harry Joe Brown; Associate Producer: Randolph Scott; Screenplay: Peter Packer; story by Glendon F. Swarthout

CAST   Randolph Scott (Capt. Tom Benson), Barbara Hale (Martha Kellogg), Jay C. Flippen (Sgt. Bates), Jeanette Nolan (Mrs. Reynolds), Frank Faylen (Kruger), Leo Gordon (Vogel), Denver Pyle (Dixon), Harry Carey, Jr. (Corp. Morrison), Michael Pate (Capt. Benteen), Donald Curtis (Lt. Fitch), Frank Wilcox (Major Reno), Russell Hicks (Col. Kellogg), Pat Hogan (Young Hawk)

Synopsis: Accused of cowardice and desertion in the wake of Gen. Custer's last stand, 7th Cavalry officer Tom Benson volunteers to command a burial detail for Custer and company.

7th Cavalry may be the only one of countless films about Gen. Custer that deals with the immediate aftermath of the battle and the burial detail. It opens with a great scene (borrowed from *Beau Geste*) in which Scott and his bride-to-be (Barbara Hale) come across a deserted fort in the middle of North Dakota territory. Director Joseph H. Lewis' forte was in establishing tension, as witnessed by this tense, nearly silent sequence.

Unfortunately, neither Lewis nor the scenarist, Peter Packer, deliver the promised goods throughout the rest of the film. *7th Cavalry* is talky, and that talk is not only uninteresting but often repetitive. The film suffers from a static script and the miscasting of Scott (in terms of his age) as a junior officer who is sentimentally obsessed with the memory of Custer. I can guess what aspects of the script appealed to Scott, because for once he's not a Southern gentleman but rather a riffraff character who once gambled, brawled and scouted for the Army before working his way up the ranks through sheer determination and guts. His hero worship of Custer is understandable if misguided.

The film's offbeat plotting and stunning scenery (kudos to Ray Rennahan, director of photography, and Henri Jaffa, the film's Technicolor consultant, on this last score) aren't strong enough in themselves to overcome the film's scripting flaws. Scott volunteering to head the burial detail is one thing, but why does he insist on taking the company's worst soldiers—an array of deadbeats, drunks and criminals—with him? Story-wise, it does provide good tension as at least two of these misfits, played by Leo Gordon and Denver Pyle, attempt to kill Scott. Otherwise it does little to add accuracy or movement to the film.

The climax hints at a big battle that never comes. Scott and his rag-tag battalion are surrounded by Sioux warriors at the battle site. An affable sub-chief, Young Hawk, approaches Scott and gives a long-winded and unintentionally humorous speech about spirits, symbolism, etc. He invokes such hoary Indian myths as the belief that Custer's spirit is "transmitting" (that's the word he uses) itself into the Sioux warriors, which means the Sioux can't allow Scott to remove Custer's body from the site. Scott holds his ground, knowing he and his men will be wiped out, but the group is saved when Dandy, Custer's second horse (the other was Comanche), shows up. The Sioux mistake the horse for a ghost and scram out of there like five-year-old children running out of the spook house at Coney Island. Scott brings Custer's body back to Fort Lincoln and is exonerated of his supposed crimes.

The film isn't afraid to suggest that Custer was an egotistical, power-crazed leader. The on-location photography in Mexico is breathtaking at times. Sometimes, in fact, the vistas are almost distracting from the main thrust of the story. And though he just isn't right as Capt. Benson, at least Scott shows he was willing to tackle different roles within the Western genre. The movie *7th Cavalry* remains a misfire, although it is an ambitious misfire.

For the record, Custer and his command of over 200 men were wiped out on June 25, 1876. They were given a rather hasty burial at the battle site on June 28. The following year, Custer's remains were moved to West Point, New York. The 7th Cavalry, activated in 1866, took part in various Indian campaigns, border skirmishes with Pancho Villa, World War II, the Korean and Vietnam Wars and, as recently as 2002, in the invasion of Iraq.

Joseph H. Lewis (to Peter Bogdanovich, *Who the Devil Made It?*): "I became terribly confused because I found out what a horrible man Colonel [*sic*] Custer was. Jiminy cricket! This was really a maniac — despicable man. And *that* truly interfered with my work, because I couldn't tell a true story. And I couldn't make a hero out of this man because of what I knew about him, and you *had* to in this film."

Harry Carey, Jr.: (to author): "We shot the film outside of Mexico City. Columbia had built the fort for a previous Western, and it was located on a volcanic mountain. I had one big scene with Scott and I remember I did it nursing a horrible hangover! (*Laughs*) I liked Joe Lewis. He was patient and he knew what he was doing and he could shoot fast. On those little pictures, they tended to compact all of your work into a certain amount of days to get you off of salary. I did all my scenes for *7th Cavalry* in three days. Randolph Scott was Randolph Scott just like John Wayne was John Wayne. He was very easy to work with. The Duke worked so hard at his trade, he developed this persona that the American public bought. Scott did the same thing to a lesser degree. I've seen some of his non–Western stuff, like *My Favorite Wife* and *Go West, Young Man*. He was terrific then. But then Westerns typed him into a different kind of role."

Barbara Hale (to Michael Fitzgerald, *Western Clippings* #45, January-February 2002): "We shot [*7th Cavalry*] in Mexico, and the area residents cooked their tortillas, or whatever, for us on a huge rock. Every day, ten extras who were very sweet, I would try to talk to them. One day, we were sitting at the table and four of the extras appeared with a bowl of soup [for me]. I looked down and a hog snout was staring back at me! Oh wonders. You can imagine what I thought!"

Burt Kennedy, to Thomas McNulty of *Classic Images* (1998): "When the material was good, [Scott] was excellent. *7th Cavalry*, which he made for Columbia, wasn't too hot, but he believed in everything he did, so it worked."

Variety (10/23/1956): "Film is burdened with an overage of dialogue and carries little exciting action until the last reel. Scott is none too happily cast, suffering through contrived plottage ineptly developed."

The Tall T (Columbia, April 1957, 78 minutes)

CREDITS   Director: Budd Boetticher; Producer: Harry Joe Brown (Randolph Scott, Associate Producer); Screenplay: Burt Kennedy, based on Elmore Leonard's *The Captives*.

CAST   Randolph Scott (Pat Brennan), Richard Boone (Frank Usher), Maureen O'Sullivan (Doretta Mims), Arthur Hunnicutt (Ed Rintoon), Skip Homeier (Billy Jack), Henry Silva (Chink), John Hubbard (Willard Mims), Robert Burton (Tenvoorde)

Synopsis: A trio of killers take newlyweds Doretta and Willard Mims hostage in hopes of collecting a ransom for Doretta. Unfortunately, the kidnappers make the mistake of taking rancher Pat Brennan hostage too.

Perhaps the most viciously violent of the Ranown series (not because of the number of killings but rather the way in which they are committed), *The Tall T* is a taut Western that seems like two films in one. The first 20 minutes serves as a lengthy prologue in which Scott's Pat Brennan is shown to be a happy-go-lucky man of dreams hoping to get a prize bull to mate with his stock. These early scenes seem to do little other than to introduce Brennan, stagecoach driver Ed Rintoon and newlyweds Doretta and Willard Mims—but they do throw the audience off-guard in terms of what comes next.

What comes next is Richard Boone, Henry Silva and Skip Homeier as a trio of murderous bandits out to make some fast dough over some bloody bodies. In the span of a minute, the audience is thrust from a seemingly good-natured Western of ranching into a tense struggle for survival. The trio, initially out to nab a stage payroll, end up taking Doretta hostage while her cowardly husband tries to wring some ransom money from her copper tycoon father. The threesome kill off Rintoon (who was reaching for a shotgun with which to cause some serious mischief) but they keep Brennan alive, bringing him along to their hideout — which turns out to be a big mistake on their part.

Boetticher, by many accounts a wild and unpredictable man, probably had a ball letting Boone and company go to town with equally unpredictable acting antics. Boetticher was at his best when lassoing moments of unexpected tension and ac-

Scott and Arthur Hunnicutt in another Boetticher-Brown-Kennedy gem, *The Tall T* (1957). Somebody's about to get shot. (JC Archives, Inc.)

tion within a story; likewise he knew how to highlight the interplay between two people who know each other even though they've never met (Scott and Boone). There's a great, nearly silent scene between Scott and Boone wherein the latter, with gun drawn on the unarmed Scott, sizes up his antagonist as a man to be reckoned with. Boone's Frank Usher has the upper hand, but he has more to fear than he realizes.

"You know what's gonna happen to you?" Usher asks Brennan.

"I think so," Brennan replies.

"You scared?"

"Yeah."

"At least you're honest about it."

Usher connects to Brennan — or tries to connect, despite their differences. He likes his captive's attitude, his sense of self, and his acceptance of life and death. "A man should have something of his own, something to belong to," Usher tells Brennan, who already has those things and now wants to hold onto his life. These two are bound to face off against one another by film's end — and they do.

Once the meek Willard volunteers to ride off to nab the ransom money (he's clearly more interested in saving his own neck than that of his wife), the film pretty much settles on the relationship between Brennan and Usher and, to a lesser degree, Brennan and Doretta. The latter two don't really fall in love, but they do fall in lust, and it's pretty clear that Brennan has his way with her (the lady *is* willing) during one of their three nights in captivity. Still, there's little else to suggest that the Scott character is falling for her, and a cynic might imply that he's simply building her up, sexually and romantically, in order to use her to escape when the time is ripe. The time does get ripe and Doretta *is* of great help, distracting one of the bad men long enough for Brennan to get his hands on a shotgun. And then the shooting starts.

The film features some darkly hilarious lines courtesy of Kennedy. Boone, upon surveying the bloody damage Scott has done to his fallen comrades, simply muses, "You been busy, ain't you?" And Scott, having finished off his captors, silences a hysterical O'Sullivan with the calming line, "Come on now, it's gonna be a nice day."

The Tall T is one of the best of the Boetticher-Kennedy-Brown-Scott Westerns and a far superior film to Scott's *Shoot-Out at Medicine Bend*, released by Warner Bros. the same month. According to both Boetticher and Kennedy, Scott was much more animated and outgoing on the set of this film because he enjoyed working with Maureen O'Sullivan, an actress whose career dated back as far as his. The duo would often have dinner at night after a day's work and talk about "the old days."

Budd Boetticher (to author): "I liked Maureen [O'Sullivan] from the *Tarzan* films on and I needed a girl that wasn't glamourous. She was the kind that nobody's going to marry. And John Hubbard was a friend of mine, and I wanted a weak actor to play that guy because he was a bum. Henry Silva I just loved. He came down to play the part, and he had never seen a horse up close before, and he put the wrong foot in the stirrup! [*Laughs*] But he rode fairly well, I thought.

"Nobody knows how to finish pictures today. We did. When Randy says to her, 'Come on now, it's gonna be a nice day,' you think to yourself, 'God, I hope so!'"

Burt Kennedy (to author): "I think *The Tall T* was done for just over a half

million [dollars]. They were all done cheaply. I designed them so there were no interiors for budgetary reasons. We had a magic number and it had to be cheap. So there's lots of scenes where people just sit around and talk. We just didn't have a lot of money."

Variety (4/3/1957): "There's a wealth of suspense in the Burt Kennedy screenplay. Scott impresses as the strong, silent type. Film's title, incidentally, is rather obscure since there's nothing in the action to explain it." That title, according to Boetticher and Kennedy, referred to the Tenvoorde Ranch Scott visits in the early part of the film, and was given to the film by some executive at Columbia.

Shoot-Out at Medicine Bend (Warner Bros., April 1957, 86 minutes)

CREDITS　Director: Richard Bare; Producer: Richard Whorf; Screenplay: John Tucker Battle and D.D. Beauchamp

CAST　Randolph Scott (Capt. Devlin), James Craig (Ep Clark), Angie Dickinson (Priscilla), James Garner (John Maitland), Gordon Jones (Wilbur Clegg), Dani Crayne (Nell), Myron Healey (Rafe Sanders)

Synopsis: Army officer Capt. Devlin goes undercover as a Quaker in order to track down the man responsible for his brother's death.

Shoot-Out at Medicine Bend, a disappointing blend of comedy and action that features an oddball cast of has-beens and gonna-bes, remains one of the oddest Westerns of Scott's career. Like *Canadian Pacific*, it is something of an embarrassment in terms of plot structure and direction, but unlike that earlier film, it possesses a sense of humor that makes it watchable. Opening with a lackluster action sequence in which Scott's brother tries in vain to fend off an Indian attack with faulty ammunition (shells comprised of coal dust) and ending with an unexciting brawl between Scott and villain James Craig, the film really demonstrates how far and fast Scott's star was falling at Warner Bros. No wonder Scott and director Budd Boetticher were worried when Warner Bros. insisted Scott make one more film for them — 1959's *Westbound*.

The script is a big culprit here. It's not exciting, it's not funny and it makes little sense, stripping most of its characters of motivation. The bad guy just wants to sell faulty goods at high prices (imagine a crooked Woolworth's and you get the picture). As played by James Craig, a second-string leading man of MGM "B" films of the 1940s, the villain, Ep Clark, lacks the rakish charm of John Carroll, who did much more with a similar role in Scott's *Decision at Sundown*. Craig gives a lazy performance (though it's a poorly written character to start with), robbing Scott of a firm adversary to play against.

But it can hardly be said that Scott gives a good account. He's Randolph Scott, which will always please his fans, but he doesn't even try to invest the character with nuance. There's not a moment of remorse after his brother is killed, and his protagonist has none of the inner torment or the determined sense of vengeance that marked Scott's best Western work in the 1940s and 1950s. He does make the most of such deadpan lines as "This is my evening for meditation" and "Violence is against my creed" (this said while he's clad in Quaker garb), but it's probably one of the few uninteresting performances the actor gave in his post–Paramount years.

The entire storyline is hard to swallow. Scott and Army pals Gordon Jones and James Garner decide to head to Medicine Bend to even the score with the scoundrel who sold Scott's brother bad ammo. They go skinny-dipping, have their clothes stolen by Craig's men and are forced to wear Quaker attire to fulfill their goal. (There is one amusing visual gag when the trio, clad in skirts made from bushes, appear over the crest of a hill while the Quakers are engaged in a religious service.) Once in Medicine Bend, the trio of heroes do Quaker shtick while working to unveil the true villain of the piece, adding a few "thee"s and "thou"s to their speech to give themselves some extra credibility. At night Scott plays a frontier Robin Hood, dressing all in black and beating up the bad guys while stealing their ill-gotten goods (which he returns to the victims). In the climax, Jones and Garner are nearly hanged before being rescued by Scott and the Quakers, who poke, punch and kick the bad guys while spouting proverbs. Then Scott and Craig have it out, the latter getting his after an unconvincing fight sequence. Scott and Garner get the girls (Angie Dickinson and Dani Crayne) while Jones uncharacteristically joins the Quakers.

As a Western, *Shoot-Out at Medicine Bend* fails on almost every level. The characters are like soggy cardboard cut-outs while the action scenes are performed without focus or innovation (and, in some cases, probably without the principal actors, for much of the final fight between Scott and Craig is done in long shot in the dark, suggesting the work of stuntmen). Richard L. Bare, the director, was not accustomed to action pictures, and the lack of excitement and energy in these sequences is most likely his fault. That said, Bare, an accomplished comedy director (he directed and/or co-wrote the studio's funny Joe McDoakes short subjects of the era), did get his actors to give comic zest to a script desperately in need of laughs. The story itself is not necessarily funny; the actors make it humorous with performances that suggest they all knew they were in a stinker. So maybe it smelled bad, but it didn't have to look bad, and that's what makes *Shoot-Out* worth sitting through. The facial mugging and forced vaudeville-type acting indicates an attempt to make the thing a little more interesting than it was on paper, and to some degree it succeeds. In any event, it's something different, and at this point perhaps Scott was willing to do the film just to finish up his Warners contract. Scott's father was a Quaker, so perhaps this aspect of the script interested him as well.

Richard Bare (to author): "Randolph Scott had face lifts, and I never saw a man do that, but I guess he was kind of vain. They did make him look younger. Years later I directed *Green Acres* and I would watch as Eva Gabor received these instant face lifts. They were gummed attachments to tiny wires that went under the hair; they moved the jowls up, but you couldn't see them.

"I think the reason Warners shot the film in black-and-white was because it was Scott's last commitment to them [*sic*]. Jack Warner probably figured, 'He's got to do it, let's just shoot it in black-and-white and save money.' Scott was a good soldier, reporting on time, knowing his lines. He probably figured, 'The money's good.' I bet he was getting about a hundred grand for that picture. Years before I had directed one other Western, in Technicolor, with Gordon MacRae, called *Return of the Frontiersman* [1950], and there's the difference between Warners putting money into a guy coming up and a guy working on his last picture. I assume Randy Scott's popularity had been dropping off a little bit, and that's why it was done cheaply." (Contractual documentation in Scott's Warner Bros. file at USC suggests that there was some confusion as to how many films he still owed the studio at this point.)

Myron Healey (to author): "I never saw the film. I'll have to watch it around three o'clock in the morning sometime. People always ask me, 'Why do you stay up all night?' and I say, 'Because I get to see the stuff I didn't see 35 years ago.'"

Variety (3/10/1957): "Okay actioner … it's in austere black and white, as contrasted to Scott's usual tinted entries." *New York Daily News* (4/13/1957): "*Shoot-Out* was designed to be a Western as funny as it is active. But the humor is painfully unfunny and the comic performances are pitifully inadequate."

The film, shot in 19 days under the title *The Marshal of Independence*, was made for about $640,000 and barely recouped its production expenses, leading Jack Warner to reconsider Scott's worth to the studio.

Decision at Sundown (Columbia, November 1957, 77 minutes)

CREDITS Director: Budd Boetticher; Producer: Harry Joe Brown; Executive Producer: Randolph Scott; Screenplay: Charles Lang, Jr., from a story by Vernon L. Fluherty

CAST Randolph Scott (Bart Allison), John Carroll (Tate Kimbrough), Karen Steele (Lucy Summerton), Valerie French (Ruby James), Noah Beery, Jr. (Sam), John Archer (Doc Sorrow), Andrew Duggan (Sheriff Swede Hanson), John Litel (Charles Summerton), Ray Teal (Morley Chase), James Westerfield (Otis), Richard Deacon (Zaron)

Synopsis: In this reverse take on *High Noon*, town boss Tate Kimbrough finds his wedding ceremony interrupted by the arrival of gunman Bart Allison, who vows vengeance for unexplained reasons.

A claustrophobic Western, *Decision at Sundown*, while the weakest of the Boetticher-Brown-Scott films, nonetheless has much going for it, primarily Scott's performance. His character, Bart Allison, is perhaps the most unsympathetic hero the actor ever played. He's stubborn, single-minded and blinded by rage, anger and hate. At times he seems near-suicidal. In a way it's much more difficult to empathize with this Scott hero. In the other Ranown films the Scott character, while driven towards revenge, always took time out to

Scott played against type when he rode the bitter trail of vengence in the offbeat *Decision at Sundown* (1957). (JC Archives, Inc.)

help others, be it a faltering pioneer couple or a sick horse. Here, you suspect he doesn't even give a damn about his partner, Sam (Noah Beery, Jr.), although Scott nearly breaks down in tears of fury when his pal is shot in the back by one of the town deputies.

In the other revenge-driven Ranown films, Scott's character spends much of the footage trying to find the man or men responsible for the death (or abduction, as in *Comanche Station*) of his wife. Here, he confronts the man in question (John Carroll) within the first reel or so, and then he beats a hasty retreat to the livery stable after revealing his hand. Soon Scott and Beery are surrounded by Carroll's paid lawmen, who set siege to the stable in a series of so-so action scenes. It doesn't make sense, ac-

tually, for no sooner has Scott made a dramatic appearance in the church to interrupt the wedding and threaten Carroll (who, at first, does not know what all the ruckus is about), then he turns tail and runs, choosing instead to fight his war from his own private fort. At least Charles Lang's script allows the other characters, including Beery, to comment on this lack of logic.

It turns out Carroll's Kimbrough, a notorious ladies' man (he has a mistress on the side even as he prepares to wed heroine Karen Steele), was the last in a line of men to make love to, and then abandon, Allison's wife Mary in Sabine Pass after the Civil War. Distraught, Mary committed suicide, and Allison blames Kimbrough. The set up for all this fuss is much more interesting than the actual explanation.

While the complexities of the character relationships are novel —for example, many of the townspeople, though cowed by Kimbrough and his paid gunmen, support Allison in his quest — the dialogue is not nearly as interesting as that found in the Kennedy-scripted Scotts. There is too much preaching about how good men have to act in order to fight corruption and evil. The majority of the supporting characters are reduced to stereotypical dupes who continually make the wrong decisions. Late in the film, Scott's Bart Allison cuts his right hand in a poorly scripted and directed sequence to deny him the use of his good gun hand for the final battle. Likewise the final snippets of dialogue between John Archer's Doc Sorrow and Steele's Lucy Summerton are absurdly simplistic.

Boetticher's direction doesn't help. Like John Ford or William Wyler, Boetticher knew how to capture the expanse of the land, and highlight the challenges the men within that land faced while trying to survive. But given a Western that takes place in town, Boetticher seems hard-pressed to get people to act as if they live in the place. The extras mill about with nothing to do, the streets are always deserted, and people just come together at times to face the camera and exchange dialogue. While the director did somewhat better with *Buchanan Rides Alone*, both that film and *Westbound* suffer from this deficiency as well.

Boetticher later claimed he didn't care for the film, saying it was one Scott and Harry Joe Brown planned to do before he shot *Seven Men from Now*. Perhaps some falling-out between director and screenwriter Lang lead Boetticher to put down both this film and *Buchanan Rides Alone* in later years. "It was already written, it was an old Randolph Scott picture," Boetticher recalled. "And I didn't like that he was drunk in a lot of the last scenes. That didn't befit him at all. It was also a disas-terous picture for me because that's when I met Karen Steele." (Steele and Boetticher stayed together as a couple for about four years. Contrary to rumors, they never married.)

Valerie French gives a thoughtful performance as a fallen woman who really does love Carroll, and the latter really comes through in conveying the inner strength of a man who is afraid to face the wrath of Scott but who still finds a way to do it. Carroll was a second-string leading man at MGM in the 1940s and at Republic in the 1950s, and his film career was giving out when *Decision at Sundown* was made. He's surprisingly good as a low-key town boss who seems disgusted and bemused, rather than angry or betrayed, when the townspeople turn on him. Boetticher said most of the cast was chosen by Brown and Scott but that he personally selected Carroll. "He was a character," he recalled of the actor. "I watched him lose $40,000 at a crap table one night in Las Vegas, and he never batted an eye. He could sing "Around the World" better than any singer in the world."

But it is Scott who makes *Decision at Sundown* as memorable as it is. As a man pushed so far over the brink that he cannot accept that his wife may have been the equivalent of the town whore (making you wonder what sort of husband *he* was), he plays his part with all six cylinders going, reaching for emotions that he rarely conveyed in other films. As in *High, Wide and Handsome,* he's willing to make a fool of himself (though he doesn't), taking a chance on alienating his fan base by portraying such a single-minded sap of a nemesis. His final moments, drunk and disillusioned at the bar, are handled with a sense of understated, bitter resignation. When he rides out of town for the final frame, leading his dead partner's horse behind him, you get the sense that he's planning to take his own life once he gets outside the town limits.

Whereas the Scott characters in the other Ranown films sometimes carry a badge of hope with them, here, Allison realizes his quest is insignificant and has only brought about death (although, arguably, he helped clean up the town by usurping Kimbrough's power).

Decision at Sundown is an interesting miss-the-target Scott Western that is still worth seeing, but it doesn't hold a candle to the other Columbia films directed by Boetticher.

Burt Kennedy (to author): "I saw *Decision at Sundown* recently, and I called Budd and asked him when it was shot. It's not a very good picture. I wasn't asked to do the film. In fact, I wasn't even asked to see the film!"

Variety (11/6/1957): "Role is an offbeat one for Scott, but he carries off the gunman's frustrated rage well ... this entry stacks up as one of the better of the newfangled Westerns."

Buchanan Rides Alone (Columbia, August 1958, 78 minutes)

CREDITS   Director: Budd Boetticher; Producer: Harry Joe Brown; Screenplay: Charles Lang, based on the novel by Jonas Ward

CAST   Randolph Scott (Buchanan), Craig Stevens (Carbo), Barry Kelley (Lew Agry), Tol Avery (Simon Agry), Peter Whitney (Amos Agry), Manuel Rojas (Juan), L.Q. Jones (Pecos), Robert Anderson (Waldo), Joe De Santis (Esteban Gomez), William Leslie (Roy Agry), Jennifer Holden (Katy)

Synopsis: Mercenary Buchanan returns from a profitable sojourn in war-torn Mexico to a California border town where he finds himself caught up in an interfamily struggle for control of Agrytown.

Based on Jonas Ward's 1956 Western novel *The Name's Buchanan*, *Buchanan Rides Alone* remains the most darkly comic of the Ranown series. It's a film in which just about everybody double-crosses everybody else — with Scott's Buchanan being

the only exception — in an effort to gain hold of $50,000 ransom money that would let the winner run Agrytown, a border town operated by the corrupt Agry Brothers (well played by Barry Kelley and Tol Avery). There is a third Agry brother, the opportunistic coward Amos (Peter Whitney), and all three brothers begin wrangling over who will take charge of Mexican rancher Juan Del Cuervo, who shot down Simon's son Roy after the latter raped Juan's sister. The $50,000 is the money Juan's father is willing to put up to save his son from a necktie party; Buchanan, a new ally of the boy, ends up unexpectedly figuring into the scheme of things, as does Simon's paid gunman Carbo. Unlike the rest of the Ranown films, Scott's character is not seeking revenge, nor is he simply out to survive, though obviously he wants to avoid the hangman's noose that Sheriff Lew Agry has fashioned for him.

The film was shot in Tucson, Arizona, early in 1958 and was, as such, the last Scott film made under the aegis of studio head Harry Cohn, who died in March of that year. Screenwriter Charles Lang utilized much of the action and dialogue of the book and the film follows the book's plotline, with some minor variations, for about two-thirds of the way. Boetticher, Burt Kennedy and actor Craig Stevens all intimated that much of the film was rewritten on the set, a point contested by Lang and *Western Clippings* contributor and author Michael Fitzgerald. Boetticher claimed that Lang adhered *too* faithfully to the novel, turning in a too-long opus that rambled. In Boetticher's words,

> Charlie Lang was the screenwriter, and one of my best friends. He was known as Froggy Lang. He was getting a divorce at the time, and he was drinking. And Burt and I were working out the treatment for *Buchanan* from the book. I went with Karen [Steele] to Mexico City for Christmas vacation [1957] and sent the script to

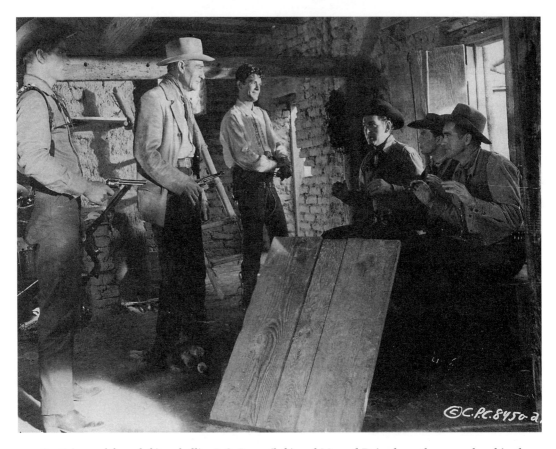

Scott (second from left) and allies L.Q. Jones (left) and Manuel Rojos have the upper hand in the darkly comic Western *Buchanan Rides Alone* (1958). But the shooting ain't over yet.

Charlie, and he was paid 25,000 dollars [for] polishing it up.

"On the way back from Mexico City— Karen had left me in a huff—I drove through Tucson because I wanted to pick locations with Lucien Ballard [the director of photography]. I was sitting there having breakfast all alone one morning when Lucien walked in and threw the rewritten script at me.

"Did you read this?" he asked.

"What do you mean, read it? I wrote it!" I said.

"Well, read *this* piece of shit," he said.

I read it and it *was* awful. We couldn't shoot a god-damned thing. I called Burt and said, "Come to Tucson. We're gonna make a piece of shit if you don't get over here." And we ad-libbed the whole god-damned picture. There was nothing for Craig [Stevens], there was no part for him. And when you see the original poster from Columbia, there are no credits because they couldn't say what we did. They couldn't say, "Written, directed, produced and ad-libbed by Budd Boetticher and Burt Kennedy." That's a true story.

It has been suggested that Boetticher, who loved to spin a story so he came out looking like gold no matter what, took extra credit for the script of *Buchanan Rides Alone*.* But there is considerable collaborative evidence for his case, if anybody cares to look into it. In a 1971 interview

*A Burt Kennedy quote about Budd Boetticher's penchant for rewriting history that I love: "Budd's told the same stories so many times that he no longer knows what the truth is—and the problem is, neither do I!"

with Leonard Maltin for the book *Behind the Camera*, Ballard pretty much echoed Boetticher's words, saying that he accosted the director with the script, "You better read it, it's the worst piece of crap I've seen in years." Ballard goes on: "So [Boetticher] started rewriting it at night, during lunch breaks, all during shooting. He was still working on it during lunch hour on the last day we were shooting."

Kennedy said he worked on the film briefly at the beginning but ceded rewrites to Boetticher. (Kennedy lists the movie in his filmography in his autobiography *Hollywood Trail Boss*.) The late Craig Stevens said that when it came to the development of his character, Boetticher did a lot of recrafting on the set: "The character was really created on the spot. It was originally a very small role, but Budd built it up on the set. We did a lot of improvising. Budd was an 'on his feet' kind of director. He had ideas, and I listened. It was fascinating to play — there were good guys and bad guys and some in between, and Budd was fascinated with that."

But to L.Q. Jones, who played the amiable deputy Pecos in the film, the script has all the earmarks of a Burt Kennedy writing job. "Budd will tell you anything," Jones said to this writer in a 2002 interview. "Burt wrote the script and kept rewriting while shooting. The reason I did *Buchanan* was because of Burt — he recommended they look at me for the part. But he wrote so many of the films for Randy that Harry Joe Brown produced that it gets hard for me to say, 'Who wrote this one?' If you pinned me in a corner and asked me, I'd say, 'Burt wrote this one (*Buchanan*).' But you don't want to take credit away from someone who did the thing. Most writers tend to repeat themselves. Something works for them and they drag them in under different guises. And Burt's signature is all over the place on those films."

Complicating matters is Boetticher's autobiography, *When in Disgrace*. Without mentioning *Buchanan Rides Alone* by title, Boetticher notes that Lang wrote it, and while he does indicate that some rewriting took place on the sets of every single Ranown film, he doesn't suggest that the original script was unworkable. But in his foreword for *When in Disgrace*, Bill Krohn states that Kennedy and Boetticher "improvised [the film] during shooting when the credited writer's script proved unsatisfactory."

In a brief phone interview with Lang in 2000, he would only say that he wrote the film while under contract to Brown, that Boetticher was lying, and that maybe some changes were made on the set while he (Lang) was away on his honeymoon (he apparently remarried in 1958).

Ultimately Jonas Ward should take credit for much of the screenplay, for the first 60 to 65 minutes of this 78-minute oater is taken from the novel, up to the point where Pecos is killed and Buchanan heads back into Agrytown to settle the score with Lew Agry. Then the film veers away from the book considerably, using 15 minutes of screen time to end the story, which, given the novel goes on for some length more, was probably necessary given the constraints of the Columbia-Brown budgets. In the book, Buchanan shoots Lew and is wounded in the exchange, Juan spirits him back to his father's hacienda in Mexico, and Carbo kills middle brother Amos before attempting a one-man assault on the hacienda, where Buchanan kills him in a knife duel. Simon escapes death but watches in stunned despair as his beloved town is burned to the ground by Mexican raiders. Buchanan romances a fiery servant girl, Lilita, before heading back to Texas. But while sitting by his campfire one night, Buchanan is surprised by the appearance of his Latin lover. "Had anything to eat?" he asks her. "Hombre, I did not come all this way to eat," Lilita responds, suggesting that a wild night of passion is about to take place.

That's how the novel ends. What was added or altered for the film is the climax, a complex, corpse-strewn shoot-out over the border bridge. Craig Stevens' Carbo is left alive to take over the town. As Scott's Buchanan rides out of town on Juan's horse, having recovered his dignity and most of his $2,000 grubstake, Carbo turns to the hapless Amos and says, "Don't just stand there — get a shovel," a line Boetticher claims to have injected in the script on the final day of shooting.

Whoever wrote the script (and keep in mind that up to this point Lang had mainly written such lower level "B" action pictures as *Call of the Klondike* and *Wolf Hunters*), Boetticher did a tight job of directing, eliciting strong comic performances out of the entire cast. The script is very funny, and Scott seems to delight in playing a man of ambiguous morals. Holes in the plot logic abound in the final 15 minutes (at one point Scott, who has sworn to get even with bully sheriff Barry Kelley, lets his man go) but it's an immensely enjoyable film, and easier to take, despite its array of killings, than the other, more violent, Ranown Westerns. Harry Joe Brown was on the Tucson set continually, complaining about the budget and the schedule (Boetticher and Stevens both said the film was shot in 12 days!).

But Harry Joe Brown didn't give Scott as much grief with his griping as did a horde of tourists who visited the set one day while Scott and Jones were relaxing in the sun. "One day for some reason we had 300 people who were visiting the set," L.Q. Jones recalled. "We got a break and Randy and I took our two chairs, went by an old barn, and sat there chewing the fat. And they released most of the crowd who were watching, and they came over the ropes and charging over to us and of course they wanted to see Randy.

"After the crowd walked off a lady walked up, dragging two children by the hand, and she said, 'Oh, this is one of the crowning moments of my life. I've always wanted to meet you, get your autograph and have my photo taken with you.'

"Randy was beginning to get tired, but he was still happy, and as he started to get up to acknowledge her, she said, 'You have no idea — I've always wanted to meet you, Joel McCrea.' And Randy just about fell back in his chair. That was the first and only time I ever saw Randy get upset."

Buchanan Rides Alone will almost inevitably be listed as the number five Ranown film — after *Seven Men from Now*, *Ride Lonesome*, *Comanche Station* and *The Tall T*, and Boetticher later referred to it as "one of the lesser films" of the canon. For my money it holds its own among the Ranowns, and is superior to *Decision at Sundown* and most everything else Scott made earlier in the decade. Like the other Ranowns, *Buchanan* made more money in Europe than it did in America, a sad financial fact that the new executives at Columbia took note of. With Harry Cohn dead, the set-up was about to change for Brown and Scott and company. Their six-shooter was running out of bullets, but they still had two shots left — and they made them count.

L.Q. Jones on Budd Boetticher's reputation as a director (to author): "Would you put Budd in with a Raoul Walsh or a Sam Peckinpah or a Don Siegel or an Eddie Dymtryck? The best pictures Budd made were with Burt and Randy. I wouldn't place him in the top tier but he'd be close behind it. It's hard to rate Budd. You can see the stuff that John Ford did, you can see the stuff that [William] Wellman did; that Sam Peckinpah did. They got shots at really big pictures. Budd, on the other hand, never really got a shot at a big picture. Look at the stuff he did with Randy and Harry Joe Brown. They were making them for spit. I think our budget on *Buchanan* was somewhere between 300,000 and 350,000. When you have that sort of budget and limitation, can you be a John Ford?"

Variety (8/6/1958): "It is an honest picture, made with skill and craftsmanship. Scott gives an understated performance."

Ride Lonesome (Columbia, February 1959, 74 minutes)

CREDITS   Director-Producer: Budd Boetticher; Executive Producer: Harry Joe Brown; Screenplay: Burt Kennedy

CAST   Randolph Scott (Ben Brigade), Karen Steele (Carrie Lane), Pernell Roberts (Sam Boone), James Best (Billy John), James Coburn (Wid), Lee Van Cleef (Frank)

Synopsis: Bounty hunter Ben Brigade captures outlaw Billy John and plans to take him back to Santa Cruz, California. Only Brigade has a secret motive in mind, as Billy John — and a pair of tagalong outcasts — discover.

The shortest and simplest of the so-called Ranown series, *Ride Lonesome* is a little beauty of a Western that holds its own quite nicely when compared against the standard for high-quality "B+" Westerns, *Seven Men from Now*. Shot in Lone Pine in the early autumn of 1958, *Ride Lonesome* features Scott as a man who rides with a confidence that states that he's got nothing more to lose. He's out to collect a bounty on outlaw Billy John (James Best, wonderful as a pouty criminal), but after he's joined by two drifting outlaws who want Billy John for themselves, it becomes clear that Brigade has something entirely different on his mind: revenge — not against Billy John, but against this older brother Frank (Lee Van Cleef), who strung Brigade's wife up years before.

Joining this male quartet is widow Carrie Lane (Steele, still Boetticher's girlfriend at the time), a woman who can hold her own when it comes to toting a rifle and riding hard. Steele was never a great actress, but she's passably effective here as a woman whose body and spirit are still alive even as she's burying her emotions. Steele's figure was just fantastic, however, and Boetticher had fun outlining it against the natural curves of the mountainous Lone Pine landscape.

Ride Lonesome is not as full of plot twists and turns as any of the other Ranown films. It's slow-moving, but never dull, and boasts perhaps Boetticher's best-choreographed Indian raid, as well as a taut climactic gun battle between Scott and Van Cleef. Boetticher kept the actors, action and camera moving just about all the time, developing a sense of constant momentum that threatens to spill outside of the film frame at times.

The film also sports some of Kennedy's best lines, including, "A man needs a reason to ride this country. You got a reason?" and "There's some things a man can't ride around." The relationship between Scott's Brigade and his desperado saddle pals is much different here than in the other films too. The Scott character respects and fears the characters that Lee Marvin, Richard Boone and Claude Akins play in *Seven Men from Now*, *The Tall T* and *Comanche Station*, but he doesn't exactly approve of them. Here, Brigade seems to actually like Sam and Wid (Pernell Roberts and James Coburn), and indeed the duo, unlike other Kennedy villains, have already found their heaven on earth in the form of a ranch. All they need is a grant of amnesty to fulfill their dream, and bringing Billy John in will earn them that amnesty. They're even willing to back Scott against Van Cleef and his gang, who are riding to free Billy John.

But the duo also have a respectful fear of the man they have to shoot out of the saddle in order to achieve their goal. "He ain't a man you can go straight at," Coburn's slow-witted but intuitive Wid tells

James Best (right) figures bounty hunter Scott is tackling more than he can handle at the start of *Ride Lonesome* (1959). But neither man is the real target in this Ranown gem.

Roberts' Sam Boone. "Can't kill a man like Brigade from behind," reasons Boone, confirming that Brigade is a man to be reckoned with no matter which side you tackle. Ultimately, as in all the Ranown films, Scott has to face off against a man he really doesn't want to kill.

Watching the film repeatedly — and *Ride Lonesome* is a film worth watching repeatedly — you can assume Kennedy, Boetticher and Scott were also paying homage and/or poking gentle barbs at John Wayne. There's a reference to the town of Rio Bravo, which is the title of Wayne's 1959 Western directed by Howard Hawks, the Indians trailing Scott and company along the desert ridge ride in a similar formation to the warriors who pursued Wayne and his posse across the river in *The Searchers*,

and Scott takes an arm-across-the-torso pose similar to the one Wayne took as he stood outside the doorway in the climactic shot of *The Searchers* (which in itself was a tribute to Harry Carey, Sr.). Scott even gets a Wayne line from that film: "That tears it," and delivers it in Wayne fashion! This could all be coincidence, but I don't think so. All three men knew, respected and sometimes disliked Wayne, so they had reason to have fun with his image, even if nobody picked up the allusions until 45 years later.

If Boetticher tended to take extra credit and excessive pride in the films he made with Scott, Brown and Kennedy, he did not, at least, buy into the pretentious analysis that many film historians have since heaped upon the Ranown cycle.

When it was suggested that the film's final shot of a burning cross–like tree was full of religious significance, Boetticher simply replied that it meant nothing of the kind and that he figured the Scott character would go off and have a drink and try to get on with his life afterwards, and that was that. Kennedy would also dismiss much of the heady praise given the films: "I would quote the great Italian filmmaker Fellini, who once said, 'I read the critics to see what I had in mind when I made the movie.' They're good pictures because we had to play character. But all the stories are the same. Basically they're morality plays."

This film and *Comanche Station* ushered in a new (and brief) relationship between the Scott-Brown company and Columbia. Harry Cohn, who died in March 1958, had a soft spot for old-time producers like Harry Joe Brown and contract players like Rita Hayworth and The Three Stooges. The new regime felt no such sense of loyalty. If a star or director or genre still made them a buck, fine. Otherwise they were shown the door. As a result, according to Boetticher, the last two pictures the Scott-Brown coterie made were done with new provisions in place. "They always call it the Ranown series," Boetticher said of all the Columbia films he made with Kennedy, Brown and Scott. "After Cohn died, Columbia gave us a two-picture deal for *Ride Lonesome* and *Comanche Station*. Those are the only Ranown pictures. You'll notice I'm the producer on both films. Harry Joe's the executive producer. Columbia Pictures didn't want Harry Joe to have anything to do with it. Here's a guy who made 100 pictures for them, millions of dollars, and this freaking studio didn't want him to be involved. They said, 'You can do it without Harry Joe.' And Burt and I said, 'Either Harry Joe is the executive producer at his usual salary or we won't make the picture.'"

Kennedy did not dispute Boetticher's

story, but noted that Randolph Scott still carried considerable weight at Columbia and that it was the actor who ultimately insisted Harry Joe remain on the payroll. That said, Boetticher did receive producer credit, and by all accounts Brown stayed off the set and out of the way on both this film and *Comanche Station*. Nancy Gates, Scott's co-star in *Comanche Station*, could not recall Brown visiting the set even once during the shooting of that film.

Boetticher assembled a superb supporting cast, probably the best of any Ranown film: Pernell Roberts, James Best, Lee Van Cleef and James Coburn (in his first film, though some sources list the Fred MacMurray Western *Face of a Fugitive*, also from Columbia, as his first). It was an agreeable ensemble, according to both Kennedy and Boetticher, but Scott, 30–40 years older than the rest of the cast, pretty much stayed to himself after the day's shooting had finished. Boetticher liked Van Cleef but said he ended up cutting a couple of the actor's scenes because the future spaghetti Western star was fond of the bottle — which, if true, could be one reason the film is shorter than the rest of the Ranowns. "He drank a lot," Boetticher recalled. "There were a couple of scenes in the picture where he opened his mouth and his tongue was absolutely white from the liquor, so we had to cut them out." (The scenes, not the tongue.)

It's unfortunate that most mainstream newspapers had long ceased paying critical attention to the "B" Westerns of the period; *Ride Lonesome* is a superb sample of the genre and better than most "A" Westerns of the time. *Variety*'s reviewer liked it, writing (2/18/1959), "Another good Western from the Ranown Production team. Budd Boetticher, who produced and directed, had a tough, honest screenplay by Burt Kennedy, and he has given it perception and tension. Kennedy has used genuine speech of the frontier and some offbeat, often rather grim, humor. Scott does a good job as the taciturn and misunderstood hero."

It remained Burt Kennedy's second favorite Scott film: "I like *Ride Lonesome* a lot ... but *Seven Men from Now* is my favorite."

The film made money overseas, as did most of the Scott films, but its domestic return was disappointing, though it likely broke even by playing the drive-in circuit. About a half-year after *Ride Lonesome*'s release, the Scott-Brown-Boetticher-Kennedy team set out to make one more Western, perhaps not realizing it would be their last. It would be a good one to go out on. Unfortunately, in the interim Warner Bros. released their final Scott film, *Westbound*.

Westbound (Warner Bros, March 1959, 72 minutes)

CREDITS   Director: Budd Boetticher; Producer: Henry Blanke; Screenplay: Berne Giler; story by Berne Giler and Albert Shelby

CAST   Randolph Scott (John Hayes), Virginia Mayo (Norma Putnam), Karen Steele (Jeannie Miller), Michael Dante (Rod Miller), Michael Pate (Mace), Andrew Duggan (Clay Putnam), Wally Brown (Stubby), John Day (Russ), Walter Barnes (Willis)

Synopsis: During the Civil War, Union officer John Hayes attempts to help the Overland Stage run gold shipments from California to the East for the Union cause.

Westbound signals an end to an era for both Scott and Warner Bros. It turned out to be the last film he made for the studio, but despite being directed by Budd Boetticher, it's not a particularly noteworthy film. (It is, however, better than *Shoot-Out at Medicine Bend*.) It also sheds some light on Boetticher's career as a director, for once again, working on a project that didn't have a determined and organized producer like Harry Joe Brown, nor a script as tight, humorous or insightful as those written by Burt Kennedy, it shows

the director didn't have the wherewithal to make much out of mediocre material. Scott, too, is less animated than usual, showing both his age and his lack of enthusiasm for the script. As such, *Westbound* is interesting only in that it marks the end of the Warner Bros. period and the one time Scott and Boetticher worked without Kennedy outside the conventions of the Columbia unit. The budget was about $700,000, based on the Warner Bros. studio records—but Boetticher, producer Henry Blanke and Scott just didn't get the same bang for their buck that Columbia did with $500,000 Scott films. *Westbound* is a firecracker in the shadow of that year's dynamite stick *Ride Lonesome.*

Westbound was shot quickly in September of 1957 before Boetticher and Scott went to work on *Buchanan Rides Alone.* Warners had sent Scott a legal notice that he was to report back to work at the studio to make another film before he returned to the Columbia lot, and the actor, reluctant to leave the security of the Brown-Boetticher-Kennedy unit, called Budd up to ask for his advice. Boetticher offered to direct the script, and Warners probably didn't mind as they saw what Scott and Boetticher were achieving with the Columbia pictures. What they didn't take into account was the creative input — or in this case the lack of creative input — of Burt Kennedy and Harry Joe Brown. And so, Boetticher and Scott were saddled with the Calabassas Ranch instead of Lone Pine, as well as an indifferent and unexciting script courtesy of Berne Giler. *Westbound* is also stuck with David Buttolph's overly jaunty musical score, which immediately lets the audience know that this is not a Ranown-style film. This score overwhelms the film and leads you to think the characters might break out into song and dance at any moment.

The plot is routine and one Scott had done before, although this time he portrays

Scott actually looks his age (60) in this unhappy scene from the equally unhappy film *Westbound* (1959), which signaled the end of the line for Scott's Warner Bros. Westerns. That's Karen Steele, then Budd Boetticher's girlfriend, pouring the coffee. (JC Archives, Inc.)

a Union officer for a change. He goes to the Colorado town of Julesberg (which many of the actors pronounce as "Jewsberg") to take over a failing stage line so he can move Union gold east. That sounds farfetched to me, and it isn't long before half the region is in on the secret. The villains are played by Andrew Duggan and Michael Pate; the latter is somewhat amusing as a laconic gunman, but the duo lack the depth and complexity of the Kennedy villains, and you tend to forget about them most of the time. Studio contract player Virginia Mayo is Duggan's wife and Scott's former paramour; she has about 10–12 minutes of footage in the entire film and I can see why she showed little enthusiasm for the project. The film is therefore left to

focus on Karen Steele, who was then Boetticher's love interest (off-screen) and not a good actress. She's beautiful to look at all the same. Boetticher ponders too long on every scene, extending them with unnecessary footage while seguing in and fading out. And he gives a *lot* of close-ups to Steele.

It was not a happy shoot. Pate would suggest that everyone had a ball and wrote of the making of the film: "It was *go, go, go, go* every minute of the day and night, which was pretty typical on a Budd Boetticher picture" ("Along the Big Trail," *Western Clippings* #41, May-June 2001). I bet it was *go, go, go, go* because Warners kept the film on a tight schedule and everyone wanted to get this low-rent imitation of the Ranown films over with fast, and not because everyone was having fun. Boetticher later said he and Steele were not getting along at the time, and Virginia Mayo was none too happy with her top-billed but secondary role as the bad guy's gal. "It wasn't a good part," Mayo recalled. "This was my last film for Warners and I was having trouble getting to work because I was having my teeth taken out due to an abscessed tooth. I did the film, but the fact is, I wasn't in the picture at all. Karen Steele was the director's girlfriend, and it was not my picture. Scott was very courteous and mannered, but I didn't get to know him at all. He was quite a commodity for Warners in the 1950s, but I think this was his last picture for them too."

Boetticher said Mayo gave him trouble, but he didn't blame her for doing it: "She needed me like a hole in the head," he said in a 1997 interview. "She was gorgeous, just beautiful, but she didn't need a Budd Boetticher–Randolph Scott Western. One day the studio called me at six o'clock and said, 'Don't come to the studio today because Miss Mayo is sick.' It was a Monday morning and she was due in the shot but I knew it was probably her way of saying, 'Fuck you!'" (In fact Mayo *was* suffering from serious teeth problems, according to Michael Pate.)

Boetticher continued, "I called the studio and said, 'I'm sending Miss Steele to wardrobe. Put her in the sheerest gown of that period—no brassiere, no panties, no nothing.' Then I called the location manager and said, 'Get the interior and exterior of the stage cottage ready—we'll have a nine o'clock shoot.' We put her [Steele] in bed—that's not in the script. We have a closeup of her and outside you hear a horse and Karen wakes up and looks out the window and here's her one-armed husband [Michael Dante] fighting this stallion. And Karen runs out the door and I put the camera on a dolly and I went all the way down the porch, and her knockers were going up and down—it's not censorable because you couldn't see a thing, but it's sexy—and I cut her in with Dante and the stallion.

"The next morning, Miss Mayo came in and she was really sweet. She said, 'Budd, I'm sorry I ruined your day yesterday.' I said, 'No, Virginia, we had a good day. You wanna see what we shot?' I took her in to the screening room, showed her the scene, and she was never late again!" One can't blame Mayo for being late, bad teeth or no bad teeth. Billed below Scott but above the title, she has a thankless role in a forgettable film.

Boetticher called *Westbound* "crap." It's better than that, though I'm hard-pressed to say it's worthy of much analysis or thought. (Boetticher, who saw several of Scott's 1950s Warner Bros. Westerns, had this to say about all of them: "Black horse, black hat, chin strap! Crap!") The director maintained that Kennedy worked uncredited on the script, but Kennedy said he only fashioned one scene, wherein the town doctor tells Scott that he and the rest of the townsmen will stand behind him to take on Duggan and Pate. It makes little sense and is no better written or directed than any other scene in the film, but at least it explains why all those anonymous guys with guns (including the doctor) show up at the end to help Scott take on Pate and his gang.

The stagecoach that goes over a cliff to its demise in one scene had been on the Warner lot for nearly 30 years and was being retired in grand fashion. Apparently the old gal, infested with termites, still had enough life in her to send one of her loose wheels flying in Steele's direction, nearly running her down. Mayo probably regretted that it didn't lay Steele out flat.

Westbound, released in March 1959, was neither a critical nor commercial success in any sense of the word. It actually lost money in the States but made a slight profit in Europe thanks to Scott's popularity. Rather than invest in another Randolph Scott Western, Warners paid the actor $110,000 in December 1959 *not* to make the one remaining film on his contract. The studio figured that the days of the budget Western were at an end and that they'd lose far more money if they produced one more film. With a few exceptions, Warner Bros. pretty much avoided making Western films for the remainder of Jack Warner's regime (until 1967). Scott really was about to face the last sunset — or maybe the last two sunsets.

Variety (3/25/59): "Boetticher's direction keeps the action at properly spaced peaks, thus bringing the chases, gun battles and ambushes right out where audiences can get lost in their excitement. All concerned handle their roles well."

Comanche Station (Columbia, January 1960, 74 minutes)

CREDITS   Director/producer: Budd Boetticher; Screenplay: Burt Kennedy; Executive Producer: Harry Joe Brown

CAST   Randolph Scott (Cody), Nancy Gates (Nancy Lowe), Claude Akins (Ben Lane), Skip Homeier (Frank), Richard Rust (Doby), Rand Brooks (Station Master)

Synopsis: Cody (Scott) has been traveling the Southwest for ten years in an attempt to find his wife, kidnapped by the Comanches in a raid. Instead he finds captive

The last of the Ranowns — *Comanche Station* (1960) — with Claude Akins and Randolph Scott. Maybe everyone involved figured it could never get better than this.

Nancy Lowe—whose presence attracts three drifting scoundrels who want her for themselves.

Comanche Station, another short and sweet wonder from the Boetticher-Kennedy team, opens with a man on horseback rambling through the rocky terrain of no man's land. It is Scott, who was over 60 when filming began (but who looks about 48), giving a wonderful "I've been in the saddle for nearly 30 years so don't cross me" performance. This would be the last time the actor played a man of silent integrity (his Gil Westrum of *Ride the High Country* being something of a rascal), and it's almost as if everyone involved in the film knew it was going to be the end of the trail for the actor. The title refers to a stage relay station where Scott and company hold up for a spell; otherwise it has little to do with the story, which ambles more than any of the other Ranowns. It is to Boetticher's strength as a film director that he can make you watch even when nothing happens, for despite a couple of brief Comanche attacks and the final gun duel between Scott and Akins, *Comanche Station* emphasizes character development and dialogue over action. The acting is superb throughout; it's probably Boetticher's best directorial effort.

Kennedy's script actually gives more attention to the trio of gunmen this time around than in any other of his Scott films, though the writer borrows a bit from both *Seven Men from Now* and *Ride Lonesome* to flesh them out. Claude Akins' Ben Lane is another grinning polecat of a killer, willing to do in both Scott and heroine Nancy Gates to get the $5,000 reward money the latter's husband has offered for her re-

turn—dead or alive. Skip Homeier's Frank tags along because he doesn't know better, but Richard Rust's Doby wants to make a better life for himself. Rust has some great lines in the film, including a monologue where he talks about how he was taught to open doors and pull out chairs for women—and not to shoot them. "A man does one thing," he tells Homeier, who doesn't quite get the logic of it all. "Just one thing he can look back on—goes proud." Homeier doesn't buy into the idea of going to your maker justified: "A man sort of gets used to a thing," he replies.*

Kennedy throws a few twists into this script to alter the by-now familiar finale between Scott and the bad guys. Homeier is killed off-screen by Comanches, Rust gets shot down by Akins, and Scott defeats Akins in a somewhat unfair final battle in that he gets the jump on the villain from behind. At the end, Scott returns Gates to her husband (who is blind, which explains why he didn't come looking for her) and heads out into the rocks on a blind quest of his own. It's an appropriately melancholy ending to the series, suggesting our cowboy hero is riding into a perpetual sunset in search of a solace he will probably never find. Scott's Cody is probably the closest thing to a Greek mythological hero that you'll come across in a Western.

The work of Nancy Gates, a fine, underrated actress (this was her last film), also raises the stakes. Neither Boetticher nor Kennedy seem overly concerned with the role of women in the West—unlike Ford, say, who at least respected women and gave them individual personalities—but in *Comanche Station* the woman character is treated with some reverence as

---

*I like Rust's work in this film, and once asked Boetticher if he knew what happened to Rust, whose career sort of lurched through the 1960s and 1970s. "He never went anywhere," Boetticher said. "Years later, I was in the Pantages theater, sitting alone watching this movie, and a kid came in wearing a cowboy hat and sat right in front of me without taking his hat off, and I was trying to see the picture and couldn't, and I thought, 'Jesus, here's a kid with no class,' and I tapped him on the shoulder and he turned around and it was Richard Rust. So that's what happened to him." The Internet Movie Database (IMDb) website says Rust died in 1994 at the age of 56.

both an object of desire and a person who can hold her own in the West. Likewise, Gates' Lowe is more intelligent and forward-thinking than any of the other Boetticher-Kennedy women, and she may just have been the best actress of the lot.

Boetticher was getting better and better as a director, his confidence no doubt inspired by having the same stable set of technicians to work with (as well as Scott). The director knew how to use the natural terrain as a backdrop for passion, hate and gunplay. As always, all the men are torn in a personal conflict that urges them to maintain their humanity while at the same time challenging them to do what they need to do—even if it's murder—to survive. It's a shame the Ranown team couldn't have stayed together for at least one more film, but for Scott, *Comanche Station* was a fitting cap to his Western film career, and there really was no way he could top it. But of course, being Randolph Scott, he did.

So why, after this beauty of a film, did the Ranown series come to an end? A lot of reasons, according to Boetticher and Kennedy, including the fact that they were all beginning to look the same to the Columbia executives. "Every year a hundred would be made, and you could count on your hand the number of great ones," Kennedy explained. "And there were so many of them. You couldn't turn on a TV set without seeing one." Plus, Kennedy maintained, Scott was getting a bit bored of it all. "Randy was tired of the business," Kennedy recalled. "He'd been around all these years and he never got recognition."

Boetticher said the films were made on a one-by-one deal, with the exception of the final two-picture deal for *Ride Lonesome* and *Comanche Station*. The team did not discuss doing another film after *Comanche Station*, the director said. While *Six Black Horses* was written by Kennedy after *Comanche Station*, the screenwriter had other plans for that film. Kennedy

wanted to direct and made a deal with Universal to do it with Richard Widmark in the lead. He later said he signed a bad contract that lost him the directing gig, and that the studio then cast Audie Murphy and Dan Duryea in the lead roles and let journeyman Harry Keller direct the film. "I got $10,000 for the script and another $5,000 *not* to direct it," Kennedy explained of *Six Black Horses*. "They took it away from me. I eventually saw the film and liked it, but not as well as the ones I made with Budd."

If Kennedy wanted to branch out on his own to direct, then Boetticher wanted to get out on his own to write *and* direct. Anxious to complete his long-planned film on Mexican matador Carlos Arruza, Boetticher agreed to direct a quickie gangster picture, *The Rise and Fall of Legs Diamond*, for Warner Bros. in 1960, with girlfriend Karen Steele in the female lead. (Boetticher married actress Debra Paget later that year, but for what it's worth, *Legs Diamond* probably represents Steele's best screen work.) Boetticher would go off on a seemingly never-ending quest to make his bullfighting film, acting a bit like Scott's Cody at the end of *Comanche Station*. He was in Mexico for nearly a decade and achieved very little, and by the time Boetticher got back to the States in the late 1960s, the cultural climate of the country had changed considerably, and his one effort at a comeback, *A Time for Dying* (1969), a fascinating failure of a film, didn't help him. Boetticher did get *Arruza* made and it received a limited release in 1972. But despite some good reviews, it wasn't enough to turn the director's fast-falling career around. He never directed another film, though he reportedly kept writing screenplays up until his death late in 2001.

Likewise, Columbia Pictures changed after Harry Cohn's death. The Ranown films were not *that* successful Stateside, although they turned a nice profit in Europe, where a cult following for Scott had developed. The new Columbia regime wanted no part of oldtimer Harry Joe Brown, so he was more or less ousted, although he kept busy through the early 1960s working in television before returning to the studio to produce one last "B," the 1967 Phil Karlson–directed *A Time for Killing* (sounds like *A Time for Dying*). "I think the Western became more and more of a metaphor and less and less of a reality," explained Harry Joe Brown, Jr. "And my father recognized it as a metaphor — the story of a man of strong character in a lawless world — but then the Western disappeared." The Western didn't disappear that quickly (it still hasn't totally faded out of view, though it's getting harder to find), but by 1960 Westerns were no longer a mainstay of Columbia. The studio did make a half-hearted attempt to resurrect the genre in the mid–1960s with a quartet of weak Audie Murphy oaters.

And then there was Scott. He turned 62 the month *Comanche Station* was released and, as Boetticher and Kennedy noted, he really didn't need to be saddling up and riding the cinematic range any more. He'd made 100 films, give or take one or two, and by 1960 he was a millionaire. Physically, he was having a hard time hearing his co-stars due to ear problems he suffered as a result of too much movie gunfire (Nancy Gates, like actor James Drury on *Ride the High Country*, recalled that she had to speak her cue lines a little louder than normal so Scott could respond), and with his long-term relationships with both Harry Cohn and Jack Warner having ended, why should he try to make new contacts in the ever-changing Hollywood climate?

Interestingly, the few trades still reviewing these Westerns seemed to know the genre was headed towards the last showdown. "The feature Western of any category grows scarcer and scarcer, and the medium budget film of the genre has practically disappeared," *Variety* accurately noted in their positive review of the film in January 1960. "*Comanche Station* … is by any standard a good picture. There must be an audience for these films, despite the plethora of such fare on television, an audience now with little from which to choose."

The *Variety* reviewer wrote as if he knew *Comanche Station* was going to be the last of the Scott Westerns. And yet Scott wasn't officially retired. If he was planning *Comanche Station* as his last picture, he didn't mention it to Kennedy, Boetticher or Gates. "Randy didn't talk about retiring," Gates recalled. "But he loved his golf. He was, I think, more interested in stocks and bonds. He was always reading *The Wall Street Journal* on the set. He was a great guy, always very quiet, he was just himself. You meet some people in the business who aren't nice, but Randy wasn't one of them. As an actor, he knew what he was doing. He'd been around a long time. And I think we made that movie in 18 days, which is absolutely incredible.

"I saw the film recently [summer 2002] at the Egyptian Theatre with about 300 people in attendance, and it's still a fabulous movie. I have one funny story not quite related to that. A few weeks before the screening, I went to an evening event at the Beverly Wilshire with some friends, and the photographers were there taking photos of everybody and one photographer, an older guy, lowered his camera, looked at me and said, 'If I didn't know she was dead, I'd swear you were Nancy Gates.' I almost died laughing — what else could I do?"

And what else, in 1960, could Scott do, but go about his business of investing, golfing and gardening and wait and see, like a patient but prudent gambler, whether one more good hand would turn up in the form of a script.

One more good hand did turn up — and it was all aces.

Ride the High Country (MGM, July 1962, 93 minutes)

CREDITS Director: Sam Peckinpah; Producer: Richard E. Lyons; Screenplay: N.B. Stone, Jr.

CAST Randolph Scott (Gil Westrum), Joel McCrea (Steve Judd), Mariette Hartley (Elsa Knudsen), Ron Starr (Heck Longtree), James Drury (Billy Hammond), John Anderson (Elder Hammond), L.Q. Jones (Silvas Hammond), Warren Oates (Henry Hammond), John Davis Chandler (Jimmy Hammond), R.G. Armstrong (Joshua Knudsen), Edgar Buchanan (Judge Tolliver), Jenie Jackson (Kate)

Synopsis: Former lawman Steve Judd reckons to end his long career with a successful transfer of gold bullion from an isolated and dangerous mining camp. But his partner, Gil Westrum, has other plans for the gold.

> "Partner, what do you think?"— Gil Westrum (Randolph Scott)
>
> "Let's meet them head on, halfway, just like always."— Steve Judd (Joel McCrea)
>
> "My sentiments exactly."— Westrum

Use the term "moving" to describe a Western — particularly a classic one — and diehard cowboy film fans are liable to run you out of town. Yet *Ride the High Country* is a moving character study that serves as a fitting finale to Randolph Scott's career. His Gil Westrum is a likable scoundrel, a man dead set on stealing even if it means going against his old friend and the Code of the West. And while he does redeem himself, siding with McCrea's Steve Judd against a trio of desperadoes in the last reel, he is more of a villain in this film than in the handful of other films in which he played "bad" guys in (*Sunset Pass, Western Union, The Spoilers* and *The Doolins of Oklahoma*)— particularly as he's continu-

ally unwilling to change his mind about the gold heist, though he has plenty of time to do so.

Yet while Scott has the flashier role (his eyes just about shine with larceny throughout), he has less range to move in than McCrea does. McCrea's Steve Judd is an honorable man of pride willing to give his life to do what's right so he can enter his house justified. The McCrea character has more nuance than Scott, and one wonders what Scott would have done with the role had the casting been in reverse (as was originally intended). As it is, McCrea gives what might be described as a heartbreaking performance, and one wishes he had chosen to retire after this film. He didn't, choosing instead to appear in two more not-very-good Western films.

The plot is simple enough. Aging lawman Steve Judd agrees to serve as a bank guard hauling gold from a mountain mining camp for $20 a day. The pay and the job are a far cry from his glory days as a Federal Marshal, but to Judd, accomplishing the task means a lot more in terms of his self-worth. To aid him, he calls on his old pal Gil Westrum, who has been reduced to playing a Wild Bill Hickok clone in a cheesy Wild West carnival exhibit. Westrum in turn enlists the help of his young comrade Heck Longtree (Ron Starr), who is as much of a tinhorn chiseler as Westrum is. These two decide to steal the gold, with Westrum hoping to convince Judd to go along with the caper, but willing to go to more desperate lengths if Judd is uncooperative. Westrum tries to persuade Judd in a roundabout manner, recounting stories from their past that suggest that law and order just doesn't pay. Both men have sacrificed love and health for their careers, and Westrum, for one, figures society owes them something. "Partner, you know what's on the back of a poor man when he dies? The clothes of pride," Westrum tells his partner on the

Two classic cinematic cowboys — Joel McCrea (second from right) and Randolph Scott — team together for the first (and last) time in Sam Peckinpah's elegy to the Western, *Ride the High Country* (1962). That's Mariette Hartley (left) and Ron Starr trailing behind. (JC Archives, Inc.)

ride up. "And they're not a bit warmer to him dead than they were when he was alive. Is that all you want, Steve?"

"All I want is to enter my house justified," Judd replies, leaving Westrum with a tough hand to gamble with.

Complicating matters is the virginal mountain girl Elsa Knudsen (Mariette Hartley, in her film debut), who takes a liking to Longtree but is mostly anxious to get out from under the overbearing religious ways of her father Joshua (R.G. Armstrong). Desperate for an escape route, she agrees to marry miner Billy Hammond (James Drury, in a role intended for Robert Culp), the least dangerous of the five Hammond brothers, an unnerving quintent of frontier hellions. What Elsa doesn't count on is the brothel wedding or gang rape the Hammonds have in store for her.

Judd and Heck come to Elsa's rescue just in time, and they're then forced to take her back down the mountain after a miner's court decides in their favor (Scott's Westrum having conveniently shanghaied the presiding judge's license at the point of a gun). On the way back, Westrum and Longtree make their move, but are headed off at the pass by Judd, who was anticipating their move. He binds the two up but frees Longtree when the Hammonds come a-calling for Elsa on the trail, leading to a gunfight in which two Hammonds are shot dead.

But there's another gunfight on the way, because the surviving trio of Hammonds, including Billy, plan an ambush at the Knudsen ranch. Westrum, in the interim, escapes, borrows a horse and gun from a dead Hammond, and pursues Judd

Scott, who at age 63 still looked like he could stare down a gaggle of gunmen, played his last role as a good-bad guy in Peckinpah's *Ride the High Country* (1962). (JC Archives, Inc.)

and company, still set on getting the gold. But when he sees his old partner caught under fire, Westrum's Code of the West prevails, and he gallops at full throttle towards the Hammonds, firing wildly. His horse shot out from under him, Westrum scrambles to the nearby ditch where a wounded Judd is sheltered with Heck and Elsa.

"Partner, what do you think?" an animated Westrum asks his old pal. "Let's meet them head on, halfway, just like always,"

Judd replies. And so the two veterans taunt the Hammonds out into the open for an old-fashioned gunfight. The bullets fly fast and it's smoky and bloody and confusing, with everyone taking at least one hit, and when it's over all three Hammonds are dead and Judd has received a couple of bullets too many in the belly. Westrum promises his partner he'll deliver the gold, and then, in one of the greatest endings of any Western, bids farewell to his dying friend. "So long, partner," Judd says. "I'll see you later," Westrum replies, aware that his own day of reckoning isn't far off.

According to Burt Kennedy, he got the script for *Ride the High Country*, originally titled *Guns in the Afternoon*, to Scott because he knew the actor was looking for a film to make with Joel McCrea: "I had done some things with Richard Lyons at Metro. He had a script by a guy by the name of Stone, about two old gunfighters, and he [Lyons] was going to be fired by Metro unless he came up with a picture. So I said, 'Jesus, Randy has always wanted to make a picture with Joel," because he [Scott] had kept talking to me about that for years.

"We all met at the Brown Derby for lunch — Randy, Joel, Dick [Lyons] and me. We told them the story and they loved the idea. And it is true that they flipped a coin to see who would get top billing; that happened right in front of me. I suggested Sam Peckinpah as a director, because he was a hell of a writer, and he rewrote much of it. I was just the David Susskind of that deal — I really had nothing else to do with it."

Lyons then gave the script to Peckinpah, who to date had only made one film and a lot of television programs (including the underrated *The Westerner*, starring Brian Keith). Peckinpah read the script and called Lyons to say, "I've been reading and re-reading this script all night. It is the finest script I have ever read in my life.

What do I have to do to direct it?" Apparently all he had to do was accept the rather paltry sum of $12,000 to direct and rewrite, which he did. Lyons and McCrea would later estimate that Peckinpah rewrote 80 percent of the dialogue, which makes one wonder how he could have thought the original script was one of the best he had ever read. Why didn't Peckinpah receive screenwriting credit? Because the Writers Guild rules stipulated that a director must be responsible for at least 50 percent of the script construction to receive credit (this is the same argument Boetticher used when explaining why he didn't get a screenwriting credit on *Buchanan Rides Alone*). Peckinpah also changed the ending, which originally had Westrum dying to save his friend, a plot device that had been used repeatedly in Westerns. At this point, according to most sources, McCrea was slated to play the double-dealing Westrum, while Scott was to play the more steadfast Judd. But neither actor was satisifed with their roles.

Kennedy claimed McCrea called Lyons about two weeks before filming began to say he didn't want to do the film: "I don't want to play the bad guy." This led Lyons to call Kennedy, who in turn called Scott to talk to him about it. He didn't have to say much, because, according to Kennedy, Scott rather coincidentally said, "I want to play the bad guy in this picture. I want to switch parts with Joel. What should I do?" Kennedy said he told Scott he could handle everything, and thus everything worked out on its own.

McCrea told a slightly different story to interviewer John Kobal. He said he told Lyons, "I'll do it, but only if I can play Steve Judd. I don't want to do the other part, I want to be the guy with integrity, because that's what I've been doing for 47 years [sic] and I might as well finish it that way. But Randy is the one who found the story, and so he should have first choice." Lyons, according to McCrea, then called Scott to explain the situation, to which the Southern gentleman replied, "I'd like to do the sono-fabitch that wants to steal the gold. It would give me a little color." McCrea altered this story for Patrick McGilligan, claiming that Lyons invited both actors to a lunch at the Brown Derby to discuss the matter, at which point McCrea said to Scott, "Randy, you're the guy who came up with the project. We're all working because you came up with a piece of property; because that's the hard thing to find any more, for us, the property. So you have the choice." And he said, "Well, I'll play either one, but if I had my choice, I'd rather play the other guy. I've played the straight honest guy so damn long and so much that this would be more interesting."

In any event, Scott won top billing (over a coin toss) and the role of Westrum. Burt Kennedy thought Scott had made the wiser casting choice: "Randy knew that all the bad guy parts in his pictures were the best parts—Lee Marvin and right down the line." Both actors deferred a good part of their salaries in return for a third of the profits (to be divided between the two of them). "We had a helluva lot of fun," McCrea told Kobal, going on to compare Scott with John Wayne. "[Scott] was the most charming Southern gentleman. Wayne was good, he was fine. But nothing got in his way and he did what was best for him. Randy was a gentleman."

McCrea, like Scott, had segued into making Westerns full-time after the war years. Unlike Scott, he made some poor script choices during the later part of the 1950s, drifting into lower-level oaters for

A rare shot of Scott and Mariette Hartley on the set of his last film, *Ride the High Country* (1962). What more did the Southern gentleman have to prove?

Allied Artists and United Artists. But he knew he had landed a good one when *Ride the High Country* fell into his hands. The two men had remained distant friends since the early 1930s, and actor Earl Holliman recalled with glee that when the two ran into each other, both men would stand on tip-toes to see who was losing more hair.

Shooting took place over 24 days in October 1961 on a budget of $813,000. Peckinpah planned to shoot the vast majority of the film in the Inyo National Forest in the High Sierras, but early winter storms curtailed filming, and after just four days he was forced to return to Los Angeles, where much of the rest of the picture was shot. (The first gunfight between the Hammonds and Judd was shot in Inyo.) Despite this setback, the filming went smoothly, and Peckinpah finished only four days past schedule and about $50,000 over-budget.

Peckinpah may have treated other cast members with disregard, but he had nothing but respect for Scott and McCrea, according to both L.Q. Jones and James Drury. He rehearsed the actors for four days before shooting started, telling Andrew Sarris, "I worked very closely with them on the set. They *want* to work, they are looking — I won't say for help, but they give a lot on the set and they expect a lot, which is exactly the way I like to work." (Scott would later say he wished he had come across a Sam Peckinpah earlier in his career.) But to Bill Catching, who doubled for Scott and took part in the brothel fight scene, Peckinpah had not just respect for Scott and McCrea, but fear. "Sam was afraid of both of them when they started," Catching recalled. "I could tell he was afraid. He had two of the biggest Western stars in the history of film. They did what they wanted to do and Sam printed it. They were themselves. Those two guys at the end of their careers— you didn't have to direct them, for God's sake."

Scott was more animated than usual on the set of this picture, moving from table to table at lunch time to share stories and conversation with cast and crew members and behaving as if he knew it would be his last movie. "They were both wonderful guys to work with," Drury recalled. "We had a very happy group of people working on that show. We all felt very honored to be working with Joel and Randy because it was their first picture together, and Randy's last picture. It was the last hurrah for both of them in a way.

"That was the perfect movie for [Scott] to go out on. He showed great range in the characterization that he did — the venal part of the guy and yet the good came out in him as well. It was all very believable.

He had such an image of being a hero that it was truly interesting to see him play a greedy person with no morality. I think Randy really enjoyed doing *Ride the High Country* because it was a stretch.The picture was made in 1962 [*sic*] and that was the end of his career. He had 30 years of films behind him, and those films are on television constantly."

According to Drury and Jones, Scott was experiencing hearing problems. "Sometimes we had to speak up so he could hear his cue, but it didn't seem to be much of a problem," Drury recalled. Everyone displayed patience with the extensive camera set-ups for the final gunfight, which encompassed 150 different shots. Bill Catching said the area was engulfed in a massive forest fire at the time of shooting, which gave Peckinpah twice as many challenges in that he had to avoid capturing the smoke in the camera shots.

Scott and McCrea must have enjoyed sneaking onto the MGM set of *How the West Was Won* (which, in comparison to *Ride the High Country*, was budgeted at $15 million dollars) to shoot their night-time confrontation over the gold. MGM didn't know it, but the tents in the mining camp sequences were made out of ship sails from the company's *Mutiny on the Bounty* production. But MGM was undergoing yet another regime change and the new management wasn't enthused over a minor-league Western starring Joel McCrea and Randolph Scott. Sol Siegel, the previous head of MGM, liked the script and gave it the green light, but by the time Peckinpah was editing it, Siegel was out and Joe Vogel was in. Vogel told Peckinpah he thought the film was the worst he'd ever seen and that he'd prefer not to release it. But it was in the can, MGM needed product, and so the film was released in the summer of 1962 on a double-bill with a Victor Mature mini-epic called *The Tartars*. The final version was nonetheless Peckinpah's final cut, minus about 30 feet of footage of the bordello wedding.

The film never did make much money, though it may have broke even, and as with the Ranown films it did better in Europe than in the United States. It did receive critical acclaim, baffling Vogel and setting Peckinpah's career on course for a while. "Pure gold," *Newsweek* said. *Time* felt the film "has a rare honesty of script, performance and theme — that goodness is not a gift but a quest." *Variety* felt Scott and McCrea were "better than they have ever been," but wondered whether their names would draw mainstream crowds. The film won several foreign film festival awards, including the Grand Prix at Belgium's International Film Festival and the Diosa de Plata (Silver Goddess) for Best Foreign Film at Mexico's International Film Festival.

That it didn't do great box office business didn't disturb McCrea, who wrote Peckinpah late in 1962 to say, "Congratulations! As Dick [Lyons] will tell you, business is poor everywhere on most films. But I keep telling him that the important thing is we made a good one (The cream rises!). Your old friend, Steve Judd."

In an interview years later, McCrea said that one day near the end of filming, Scott approached him and said, "Jo-El, now we've probably done the best picture we've done for a long time, and probably the best we'll ever do. So why don't we both get out while we're lucky?" McCrea wouldn't say yes, and he wouldn't say no, but the truth is, he would come back to do two more pictures, neither of them good enough to make one happy for his return.

But for Scott, there was nothing more to prove. The times were-a-changin', as was the Western, and whether there was room for an aging cowpoke like him in the cinematic landscape of the 1960s really didn't matter. He had ridden the high country enough.

The Last Sunset: 1962–1987

Though Chris Scott's book *Whatever Happened to Randolph Scott?* does not necessarily reveal a lot about Scott's off-screen life, it does give a good sense of what the actor did when he was home. His house was bordered by the third and fourth tee of the Los Angeles Country Club's north course, which was perfect being that Scott loved golfing more than just about anything else (except, perhaps, making money). Scott installed a putting tee in his own backyard and often spent the evenings outdoors practicing his game. In the early 1960s, Scott finally joined the prestigious Los Angeles Country Club, despite their long-term ban on allowing actors into the club. How did Scott get in? The story, still apocryphal but amusing, has it that Scott told them, "I'm no actor, and I have a hundred films to my credit to prove it."

Jon Tuska has said he believes that line, if true, masks an inner pain that Scott suffered regarding the way his acting career was viewed by critics. That's certainly possible, but it's just as likely Scott understood that despite some fine work in some well-known films, his movie career would probably not be remembered by anyone other than Western film fans. More than half of Scott's 100 or so films were Westerns; film critics never took them seriously and still don't. The rest of Scott's film canon, with a handful of exceptions, is made up of routine pictures or prestigious productions in which he played a supporting role (i.e., *Roberta*). In any event, the fact that Scott did indeed join the country club suggests that he figured his acting career was over.

He certainly didn't need the money. He was, according to obituary reports filed after his death in 1987, worth at least $100 million. (Way back in 1965, Mike Connolly wrote in *The Hollywood Reporter* that Scott was worth that much.) So the 1960s and 1970s were dominated by golf, gardening, and maintaining a private business office to tend to his investments.

Scott kept in shape by golfing and swimming nearly every day, and boasted in 1980 that he still had the same waistline he had when he went to Hollywood some 50 years before. Now and then he'd pop up in a trade column or newspaper article. In a February 1966 *Daily News* column, Florabel Muir suggested that the Academy of Motion Pictures Arts and Sciences should award Scott with an Honorary Oscar. "He has won no Academy Award," she wrote. "I don't believe he has ever been nominated. His face and stalwart figure on the screen do not send reviewers thumbing for adjectives. But exhibitors loved him." The Academy didn't bite.

In 1967, Danny Thomas made an abortive attempt to lure Scott out of retirement, asking the 69-year-old actor to play his father in a television special. Scott declined. Whether the actor was offered any film roles during this decade is not known. A.C. Lyles said he did not even consider Scott when casting his 1960s series of Paramount Westerns featuring aging matinee stars like Rory Calhoun, Dale Robertson and Dana Andrews. There were fewer and fewer mainstream Western films being made, and it's unlikely that spaghetti Western producers felt inclined to ring Scott up to ask him to come to Spain to play a continental cowboy.

Occasionally Scott would consent to short telephone interviews, telling *Coronet* magazine in 1974, "I don't like the pictures they make today. I'm glad I'm out of the business." That same year he told some anecdotes about filming *The Spoilers* to Joseph Cassidy of *The National Enquirer*. In 1980 Phil Roura and Tom Poster got Scott on the phone for the news piece, "Randolph Scott: An 83-Year-Old Cowboy Views Our Future," for the *New York Daily News*. "I wish I had more versatility to do other things," Scott told the duo regarding his film career. "But no, I don't miss it [acting]. I have other things to take its place." He also said he planned to vote for Ronald Reagan in the 1980 Presidential election.

Three years later, Bettelou Peterson of *The Philadelphia Inquirer* wrote a small piece in which she quoted Scott as saying, "My retirement is both voluntary and involuntary. One reason is the impact of television and all the movies turning up on it. And frankly, making pictures doesn't interest me any more. The other reason is that the film industry is in a declining state."

Scott and his wife Pat (who continued to field Scott's fan mail) would be seen out in public now and then. Scott stayed friendly with Fred Astaire and Donna Reed into the 1980s; he apparently saw little of Cary Grant, although Chris Scott relates a story of running into Grant, who asked Chris to pass on a greeting to his dad, sometime in the 1970s. (The story of Scott and Grant meeting in dimly lit restaurants and holding hands around this time period, as reported in one Grant biography, seems to be based on third-person accounts.)

The younger Scott noted that his father was a "deeply religious individual" who attended regular services at All Saints Church in Beverly Hills. The Reverend Billy Graham became a close friend of Scott's; he delivered the eulogy at Scott's funeral in 1987, citing Scott as one of the "greatest men" he had ever known.

Scott's health declined in the 1980s. It became harder and harder for him to hear conversations around him, and by 1984 or so he was no longer up to playing golf. Being denied this last personal love depressed the actor; in his final years he was withdrawn and inactive. He died early in March 1987, at 89 years of age. (His widow, Patricia Stillman Scott, died 17 years later in May 2004.) David Hinckley, in a *New York Daily News* piece of the time, wrote of Scott, "With his drawl and willingness to give even low-down yellow-bellied weasels the benefit of the doubt, Scott was actually closer to an American Everyman who didn't fight until he had to."

"God grant me the serenity to accept those things I cannot change, the courage to change those things I can, and the wisdom to know the difference," Randolph Scott believed, according to his son Chris. If Scott's film career had been the result of accepting his fate, then like one of his cowboy characters who rides over the last hill towards the next town after cleaning up a corrupt city or avenging the death of a loved one, Scott left an impressive body of work behind him. "No one, including Wayne, was as believable a Westerner as Scott," Lee Adams and Buck Rainey wrote in the book *Shoot-Em-Ups* (Arlington

House, 1978). Echoing their view, Edward Busombe, editor of *The BFI Companion to the Western*, wrote, "The more Westerns I see, the more I realize that Randolph Scott was the best actor who ever rode a horse."

That would be a fitting epitaph for Scott's tombstone (he was buried in Elmwood Cemetery in Charlotte, North Carolina) but for movie fans, leave it to Adams and Rainey to cap Scott's screen career with this line: "One knew that Scott in a Western was good enough for an enjoyable night at the movies."

Annotated Bibliography

Books

Adams, Lee, and Buck Rainey. *The Shoot-Em-Ups*. New Rochelle, New York: Arlington House, 1978.

Astaire, Fred. *Steps in Time*. New York: Harper & Brothers, 1959.

Boetticher, Budd. *When in Disgrace*. Santa Barbara, California: Neville Publishing, 1989. Surprisingly, Boetticher doesn't have too much to say about the films he made with Scott, though he offers a few anecdotes of note.

Bogdanovich, Peter. *Who the Devil Made It?* New York: Alfred A. Knopf, 1997. Features interviews with film directors Allan Dwan, Howard Hawks, Fritz Lang, Joseph H. Lewis and Leo McCarey, all of whom worked on Scott films.

Brim Crow III, Jefferson. *Randolph Scott: A Film Biography*. Madison, North Carolina: Empire Press, 1987. A good-looking film book written from a fan's perspective, but don't expect detailed analysis or background information on the films or the actor.

Conn, Peter J. *Pearl S. Buck: A Cultural Biography*. Cambridge: Cambridge University Press, 1996.

DeToth, Andre, with Anthony Slide. *DeToth on DeToth*. London: Faber & Faber, 1996.

Dietrich, Marlene. *Marlene*. New York: Grove Press, 1989.

Dowd, Nancy, with David Shepard. *King Vidor: A Directors Guild of America Oral History*. Metuchen, New Jersey: Scarecrow, 1988.

Dunne, Phillip. *Take Two: A Life in Movies and Politics*. New York: McGraw-Hill, 1980.

Ehrenstein, David. *Open Secret: Gay Hollywood 1928–1998*. New York: William Morrow, 1998.

Gruber, Frank. *Zane Grey: A Biography*. New York: World Publishing, 1970.

Hardy, Phil. *The Overlook Film Encyclopedia: The Western*, 2d ed. Woodstock, New York: Overlook Press, 1994.

Harris, Warren G. *Cary Grant: A Touch of Elegance*. Garden City, New York: Doubleday, 1987.

Higham, Charles. *Howard Hughes: The Secret Life*. New York: G.P. Putnam's Sons, 1993.

_____, and Roy Moseley. *Cary Grant: The Lonely Heart*. San Diego, California: Harcourt Brace Jovanovich, 1989.

Kitses, Jim. *Horizons West*. Bloomington: Indiana University Press, 1969.

Kennedy, Burt. *Hollywood Trail Boss*. New York: Boulevard Books, 1997.

Leider, Emily Worth. *Becoming Mae West*. New York: Farrar Straus & Giroux, 1997.

Maltin, Leonard. *Behind the Camera*. New York: Signet Books, 1971. Includes an interview with cinematographer Lucien Ballard, who speaks about *Buchanan Rides Alone*.

McCann, Graham. *Cary Grant: A Class Apart*. New York: Columbia University Press, 1996. Graham makes a persuasive argument that Grant and Scott were *not* lovers.

McGilligan, Patrick. *Interviews with Hollywood Legends*. New York: St. Martin's Press, 2000. Includes a good interview with Joel McCrea, who talks about *Dynamite* and *Ride the High Country*.

Meyer, Gary. *Gary Cooper: An American Hero*. New York: William Morrow, 1988.

227

Miller, Don. *Hollywood Corral*. New York: Big Apple Film Series, Popular Library, 1976. This book has a few paragraphs on Scott's Zane Grey westerns, and it is a great book about "B" westerns.

Nelson, Nancy. *Evenings with Cary Grant: Recollections in His Own Words and by Those Who Knew Him Best*. New York: William Morrow, 1991.

Nott, Robert. *Last of the Cowboy Heroes: The Westerns of Randolph Scott, Joel McCrea, and Audie Murphy*. Jefferson, North Carolina: McFarland, 2000.

Platt, Polly. *Henry Hathaway: A Directors Guild of America Oral History*. Rudy Behlmer, ed. Lanham, Maryland: Scarecrow, 2001.

Quirk, Lawrence J. *Child of Fate: Margaret Sullavan*. New York: St. Martin's Press, 1986.

Ralsten, Esther. *Some Day We'll Laugh*. Metuchen, New Jersey: Scarecrow, 1985.

Rothel, David. *The Great Cowboy Sidekicks*. Metuchen, New Jersey: Scarecrow, 1984.

Sarris, Andrew. *Interviews with Film Directors*. New York: Avon Books, 1967. Includes a lengthy Q&A with director Sam Peckinpah, who discusses *Ride the High Country*.

Scott, Christopher. *Whatever Happened to Randolph Scott?* Madison, North Carolina: Empire Press, 1994. A decent account of Scott's private life from the 1950s on, but often takes the spotlight off of its subject matter.

Scott, Marion duPont. *Montpelier: The Recollection of Marion duPont Scott*. New York: Scribner's, 1976. No help at all, as she doesn't mention her former husband once.

Tuska, Jon. *The Filming of the West*. Garden City, New York: Doubleday, 1976.

Wansell, Geoffrey. *Cary Grant, Dark Angel*. New York: Arcade Publishing, 1996.

Weaver, Tom. *John Carradine: The Films*. Jefferson, North Carolina: McFarland, 1999.

Magazine and Newspaper Articles

Asher, Jerry. Interview with Scott about his marriage to Marion duPont, source unknown, circa 1939.

Creelman, Eileen. "Picture Plays and Players: Randolph Scott Talks of Making a Musical Melodrama, *High, Wide and Handsome*," *New York Sun*, July 28, 1937.

Franchey, John R. Interview with Randolph Scott, source unknown, circa 1942. Scott discusses his World War I service, his approach to film acting, and his personality in this revealing article.

Hoover, Helen. "Popping Questions at Randolph Scott," fan magazine, circa 1943.

Hopper, Hedda. "Randy Scott's Horse Operas Made Him Wealthy and Famous; At Home, Tho, He Never Thinks of Spurs or Chaps," syndicated column, 1952.

Hunt, Julie Lang. "The Story Behind Randolph Scott's Marriage," fan magazine, 1938.

Maddox, Ben. "I Hope It Lasts": Randolph Scott Doesn't Take Hollywood or His Art Too Seriously," *Silver Screen*, November 1935.

Morley, Dickson. "I Won't Be a Hollywood Hero!" *Screenland*, October 1935.

New York Post, August 3, 1937. This article has some great quotes on Scott's marriage and Paramount's Zane Grey series.

"Randolph Scott: Stubborn Cowboy Who Made Millions," *Coronet*, February 1974.

"Randy the Rage," *Silver Screen*, September 1942.

"On Again, Off Again, To Stardom," *New York Herald-Tribune*, August 1, 1937.

Phillips, Malcom. "Stay West, Young Man," *Picturegoer*, July 26, 1941. Probably the best analysis of Scott's film career up to that point.

Ringold, Gene. "Randolph Scott Embodied Everyone's Idea of a Southern Gentleman," *Films in Review*, December 1972.

Solsky, Sydney. "Virginia Gentleman — Tintyped: Randolph Scott," *The New York Post*, August 24, 1952.

Steele, Joseph Henry. "Portrait of an Easy Listener," *Photoplay*, March 1944.

Thirer, Irene. "Randy Scott Graduated from Westerns; Likes 'Em," *The New York Post*, November 6, 1935.

Tribe, Dr. Ivan M. "Brother Randolph Scott: Riding the Trail Alone," *Knight Templar*, August 2003. This article provides an interesting account of Scott's Masonic membership.

Wallace, Inez. "A Vacation to Fame," *New York Herald-Tribune*, March 21, 1937. In this piece Scott talks of his introduction to Hollywood and notes that his grandfather fought in the Civil War.

White, Janet. "Randolph Scott, a Western Hero on the Screen, Is a Southern Gentleman Off, But Strictly the Outdoor Type," *Brooklyn Daily Eagle*, July 26, 1937.

Index

Macready, George 139, 140, 150, 151, 170
The Magnificent Seven (1960) 144
Mahoney, Jock 150, 156
Malone, Dorothy 151, 164, 181
The Maltese Falcon (1941) 92, 135
Maltin, Leonard 171–172, 205
Mamoulian, Rouben 59, 61–62
Man and Superman 9
Man Behind the Gun (1952) 113, 124, 167–169
The Man from Laramie (1955) 3
The Man from the Alamo (1953) 188
Man in the Saddle (1951) 122, 159–162, 177–178
Man of the Forest (1933) 32–33
Man of the West (1958) 3
Mann, Anthony 3, 140, 191
Marin, Edwin L. 64, 121, 122, 125, 126, 135, 140, 152, 154, 159
Marin, Ned 122, 125
Maritza, Sari 12
Marshal, Alan 74
Marshall, Connie 130
Marshall, George 88–89
Martell, Donna 178–179
Martin, Chris-Pin 79
Martin, Dean 124
Martin, Tony 52
Marvin, Lee 20, 165, 166, 170, 171, 191–193, 207, 221
Massey, Raymond 155, 157, 163, 164
Masterson, Bat 130
Matthews, Lester 178
Mattison, Frank 177
Mature, Victor 222
Maynard, Ken 131
Maynard, Kermit 131
Mayo, Virginia 211, 212
McCarey, Leo 88
McCarthy, Joseph 174
McCrea, Joel 2, 3, 15, 17, 18, 64, 81, 123, 160, 181, 186, 217–218, 220–223
McDonald, Grace 113
McGilligan, Patrick 151, 221
McGraw, Charles 172
McLaglen, Andrew 193
McLaglen, Victor 16
Meek, Donald 43
Mercer, Beryl 36
Meredith, Madge 131
Miles, John 133
Miller, Winston 176
Millican, James 157, 174
Mintz, Sam 42

Miracle on 34th Street (1947) 100
Mitchell, Cameron 160
Mitchell, Grant 22
Mitchell, Margaret 50
Mitchell, Steve 188, 189, 193, 194
Mitchell, Thomas 111
Mitchum, Robert 113, 114, 186
Monroe, Marilyn 88, 146
Montgomery, George 101
Moran, Dolores 133, 134
Morgan, Dennis 123
Morris, Chester 50, 136
Morris, Wayne 174
Moscovitch, Maurice 77, 78
The Most Dangerous Game (1932) 45
Move Over, Darling (1963) 88
Murders in the Zoo (1933) 27–28
Murfin, Jane 42
Murphy, Audie 3, 101, 123, 149, 155, 162, 172, 176, 188, 190, 215, 216
Murphy, Ralph 123
Murray, James 17
Mutiny on the Bounty (1962) 222
My Favorite Wife (1940) 86–88, 148

Nader, George 12
Naish, J. Carrol 147, 148, 179–180
The Naked Spur (1953) 3
The Name's Buchanan 203
Neal, Patricia 156
Nedell, Bernard 108, 136
Nellie, the Beautiful Model 9
Nevada (1944) 142
The Nevadan (1950) 151–152
Newman, Paul 182
Nigh, Jane 149
Night Cargo (1938) 19
Night Passage (1957) 101
Nixon, Richard 47
No Name on the Bullet (1959) 176
Norman, Lucille 164

Oakie, Jack 10, 22
Oates, Warren 2
Oberon, Merle 58
O'Brien, George 9, 15
O'Brien, Margaret 39
O'Brien, Pat 101, 109, 110, 142
O'Connor, Donald 42
Of Human Bondage (1934) 43
O'Hara, Maureen 100
O'Keefe, Dennis 27
Olds, Major Robin 145–146
Oliver, Robert 136

Olson, Nancy 146, 148
O'Malley, Pat 98
One Mysterious Night (1944) 188
One Way Passage (1940) 124
O'Neill, Eugene 44
Orry-Kelly, George 12
O'Sullivan, Maureen 198
The Outlaw Josey Wales (1976) 3
The Overlook Film Encyclopedia: The Western 39

Packer, Peter 194
Paget, Debra 215
Panghorn, Franklin 70
Paris Calling (1942) 66, 97–99, 102
Parker, Eddie 102
Parker, Jean 136
Parsons, Louella 146
Partos, Frank 20
Pasadena Playhouse 9, 17
Pate, Michael 183–185, 211, 212
Patrick, Gail 27, 35, 39
Patterson, Elizabeth 49
Payne, John 99–101, 137
Peckinpah, Sam 2, 64, 220–223
The Perils of Pauline (1947) 89
Pershing, General "Black Jack" 8
Phelps, Buster 36
Phillips, Malcolm 65
Picerni, Paul 159, 174, 177
Pichel, Irving 125, 156
Pine, William 136
Pine-Thomas (film unit) 61, 136, 137
Pirate Party on Catalina Island (1936) 50, 171
Pitfall (1947) 122
Pittsburgh (1942) 66, 103, 104–107
The Plainsman (1936) 3, 71
Pomeroy, Alan 102
Powell, William 124
Power, Tyrone 75–76
Powers, Mala 67, 68, 179–180
Preston, Robert 138, 186
Pullman, Bill 18
Pyle, Denver 179, 195

Quigley Poll of Exhibitors 4, 123
Quinlan, David 122
Quinn, Anthony 116
Quirk, Lawrence J. 48

Raft, George 15, 29, 35, 114, 133–135
Rage at Dawn (1955) 67, 68, 179–181